WORKERS' COMPENSATION: FOUNDATIONS FOR REFORM

Edited by Morley Gunderson and Douglas Hyatt

Workers' compensation, begun in the early 1900s to address some of the human costs of the Industrial Revolution, was the first of Canada's social institutions. It aimed to redress social instability by reimbursing workers for their suffering while protecting companies from costly court cases. The need for its regulatory function did not diminish over the course of the century; indeed the need is just as significant today. Nevertheless, making workers' compensation work in present-day Canada is a difficult task.

Today employers feel overburdened and workers believe they are undercompensated. Litigation, which the system intended to avoid, has been increasing. Little-understood environmental illness, lower-back pain, and computer-related injuries are just some of the results of new work environments that make injury assessment a constant source of conflict.

Industrial relations experts Morley Gunderson and Douglas Hyatt have responded to the multifaceted nature of the dilemma by bringing together top authorities from the disciplines of law, economics, sociology, medicine, and epidemiology to grapple with the most pressing issues. These ten essays, along with a comprehensive introduction, explore the new breed of injuries, the impact of workers' compensation on the macro-economy, public versus private provision of compensation, the nature of appeals litigation, and the efficacy of regulatory control and cost incentives in reducing work-related injuries. Policy makers, lawyers, and scholars will find this book an irreplaceable tool for understanding workers' compensation reform in the upcoming century.

MORLEY GUNDERSON is the CIBC Professor of Youth Employment at the University of Toronto, and a professor at the Centre for Industrial Relations and the Department of Economics. He is a research associate of the Institute for Policy Analysis, the Centre for International Studies, the Institute for Human Development, Life Course, and Aging, and an adjunct scientist at the Institute for Work and Health.

DOUGLAS HYATT is an associate professor at the Faculty of Management, the Centre for Industrial Relations, and Scarborough College at the University of Toronto.

D0921082

WORKERS' COMPENSATION

Foundations for Reform

Edited by
Morley Gunderson and Douglas Hyatt

UNIVERSITY OF TORONTO PRESS
Toronto Buffalo London

© University of Toronto Press Incorporated 2000
Toronto Buffalo London
Printed in Canada

ISBN 0-8020-4453-0 (cloth)
ISBN 0-8020-8239-4 (paper)

Printed on acid-free paper

Canadian Cataloguing in Publication Data

Main entry under title:
Workers' compensation : foundations for reform
   ISBN 0-8020-4453-0 (bound)   ISBN 0-8020-8239-4 (pbk.)

   1. Workers' compensation – Canada.   I. Gunderson, Morley,
   1945– . II. Hyatt, Doug.

   HD7103.65.C3W674 2000   368.4'1'00971   C99-932893-X

University of Toronto Press acknowledges the financial assistance to its
publishing program of the Canada Council for the Arts and the Ontario
Arts Council.

University of Toronto Press acknowledges the financial support for its publishing activities of the Government of Canada through the Book Publishing
Industry Development Program (BPIDP).

To our wives, Melanie Brady and Kathryn Shaver,
our parents, Ann and Magnus and Anne and Herb,
and to
Richard Allingham,
a pioneer of workers' compensation research and evaluation in Canada

Contents

Acknowledgments

We are grateful to the many people who provided valuable assistance with all aspects of this volume. In particular, we wish to express our appreciation to Judge Gurmail Singh Gill and Terry Robertson for many spirited and thought-provoking discussions on workers' compensation reform; Terry Sullivan for his support of this project and for facilitating regular meetings with members of the workers' compensation community to review and discuss many of the papers in this volume; anonymous referees for their careful reviews of an earlier version of the manuscript; Virgil Duff, Siobhan McMenemy, Barbara Porter, and John St James from the University of Toronto Press for shepherding us through the editorial process; Patrick Luciani for his encouragement to undertake this project; and the Donner Foundation for financial support.

Contributors

John F. Burton, Jr
Rutgers University

Donald N. Dewees
University of Toronto

Peter Dungan
University of Toronto

John W. Frank
Institute for Work and Health

Morley Gunderson
University of Toronto

Douglas Hyatt
University of Toronto

Boris Kralj
Ontario Medical Association

David K. Law
Emond Harnden

Esther Shainblum
McMillan Binch

Terrence Sullivan
Institute for Work and Health

Terry Thomason
University of Rhode Island

WORKERS' COMPENSATION:
FOUNDATIONS FOR REFORM

1 Foundations for Workers' Compensation Reform: Overview and Summary

MORLEY GUNDERSON and DOUGLAS HYATT

Workers' compensation is one of Canada's oldest social institutions. The modern era of workers' compensation began in the early 1900s, predating by decades other cherished institutions, like public health care, unemployment insurance, and old age pensions, that have come to define the Canadian identity. A product of the industrial revolution, workers' compensation sought to remedy the physical and financial suffering of workers injured in the course of their employment, to provide protection for employers from costly litigation with potentially survival-threatening outcomes, and to achieve an amelioration of societal instability that might result without a coherent approach to addressing these problems.

While these purposes of workers' compensation remain relevant today, there is uncertainty about the continuing ability of the workers' compensation system to serve those purposes. Since workers' compensation is about preventing and compensating injuries and diseases that *arise out of and in the course of employment*, environmental factors that have changed the institution of work have created challenges for the institution of workers' compensation.

A clear symptom of the struggle to adapt workers' compensation to the modern work environment is the reality that, during the 1990s, virtually every province and territory in Canada has formally and publicly scrutinized its workers' compensation system. Two examples are illustrative of the depth of re-examination of the role and delivery of workers' compensation. In 1994 in Ontario, a royal commission was established, though subsequently disbanded upon the election of a new government, with a mandate to enquire into, and make recommendations on, the following:

1 Ways to make clearer the definitions of compensable injuries and diseases, and the process for determining the compensability of new types of ailments
2 The rights of appeal, and the efficiency of the dispute resolution process
3 Creating and enhancing the incentives for employers and workers to prevent accidents and take ownership of the problems arising out of the occurrence of injuries in the workplace
4 Benefit and assessment structures that are equitable and ensure the long-term viability of the system
5 Incentives to encourage and facilitate the return to work
6 Sealing the sources of revenue leakage, such as unregistered employers and experience rating rebates in excess of surcharges.

In 1997, a royal commission on workers' compensation was also established in British Columbia. Its terms of reference were as follows:

- To examine the statutory framework, mandate, structure, organization, governance, and administration of the British Columbia workers' compensation system in order to meet the needs of the province's people for a high-quality public system that is equitable, effective, and efficient in the context of changing workplaces and consistent with the underlying principles of workers' compensation in British Columbia, namely,
  (a) accident prevention,
  (b) no fault compensation,
  (c) collective employer liability,
  (d) industry funding,
  (e) universal coverage, and
  (f) administrative adjudication.
- To examine the process for the development and implementation of health and safety regulations and to provide recommendations for an efficient, timely process; to establish and update these regulations appropriate to changing workplaces and work organization into the twenty-first century; to examine the current statutory framework to ensure that appropriate legislation protects and promotes workplace health and safety, including (a) the need for a new health and safety statute and (b) the consolidation of regulatory jurisdiction.
- To inquire into recurring and current issues pertaining to the oper-

ation and administration of the workers' compensation system and, without limiting the number, nature, and scope of these issues, to include

(a) benefits for fatality claims,
(b) other compensation matters,
(c) rehabilitation and re-employment matters,
(d) assessments,
(e) appeals, and
(f) organizational performance and service.

The tumult and politically charged environment surrounding workers' compensation reform is fuelled by a dearth of information on many of the issues at the core of reform debates. The purpose of this volume is to provide a set of analytical studies that compile existing information and offer new perspectives and, in some instances, new empirical evidence to inform the discourse on workers' compensation reform. The papers that make up this volume highlight the difficult trade-offs that are inevitably involved, and the consequences of alternative actions or inaction.

This volume is not intended to touch upon each of the multitude of topics in workers' compensation. Just lifting such a book would create a health and safety hazard of its own! Instead, this collection of papers is focused on topics that, in our consultations with the workers' compensation community, are among the most vexatious, and for which there is the least information; or which, because of their technical nature, are sometimes the least accessible to non-specialist readers.

The questions that are addressed in this volume include the following:

- What are the major changes associated with the 'new world of work' and what are the implications of these changes for workers' compensation?
- What challenge do the 'non-traditional' injuries and conditions pose for workers compensation?
- Why are the workplace parties questioning the current relevance of the historic compromise, and what are the implications and possibilities of a return to tort?
- What are the macroeconomic effects on such factors as employment, unemployment, inflation, and productivity of workers' compensation and other payroll taxes, and what are the implications if the tax is shifted back to workers themselves?

- What are the equity and efficiency implications of unfunded liabilities for future generations of workers and firms?
- How do the costs of workers' compensation compare between Canada, with its monopoly provision, and the United States, with its mixture of provision through monopolies and private insurance carriers?
- What are the key considerations for privatizing different aspects of workers' compensation in Canada, and what, if anything, could be gained?
- What are the pros and cons of using regulatory mechanisms (e.g., health and safety regulations) compared to financial incentives (e.g., experience rating of firms) to reduce workplace injuries?
- Why has there been an explosion in appeals litigation given that the system was designed to avoid litigation and provide expedited, no-fault insurance?

Because the questions facing workers' compensation are multi-faceted, the contributors to this volume include some of the top authorities from the disciplines of law, economics, sociology, medicine, epidemiology, and industrial relations.

We begin this introductory chapter with a brief description of the workers' compensation system. This is followed by a contextual summary of the contributions to the volume and their major findings. We conclude by outlining some of the broader implications of the findings for workers' compensation reform.

Basic Description of Workers' Compensation

Before the advent of workers' compensation, those suffering work-related injuries could obtain compensation only by suing their employer through the common-law courts. The process was time-consuming and expensive, with employers generally having 'deeper pockets' than their employees. Furthermore, employers were not liable if the accident, even in part, was attributed to negligence on the part of the employee experiencing the accident (the doctrine of 'contributory negligence') or a fellow co-worker (the 'fellow servant doctrine'). Furthermore, the 'doctrine of the assumption of risk' held that workers should be expected to be reasonably aware of occupational risk, and they should reasonably be presumed to have voluntarily assumed that risk by accepting the job and the compensating wage premium that is generally associated with risky work.

In this environment, compensation through the tort liability system was achieved in only about 15 to 30 per cent of the cases that went to court. Obviously, this is only the tip of the iceberg, since the number of cases that went to court would also be severely curtailed by the expense, delay, and modest likelihood of receiving compensation.

The 'historic compromise' of workers' compensation, achieved in North America in the early 1900s, was a response to the shortcomings of the common-law system. Workers' compensation provides expedited, no-fault compensation to workers who suffer work-related injuries and disease, and relief for employers from the vagaries and expense of tort litigation that could threaten the survival of the firm. Three types of indemnity benefits are paid through the system: temporary disability (until the worker fully recovers and returns to work or is transferred to the permanent disability system); permanent disability (for workers who continue to suffer some residual impairment, whether or not they return to work); and fatality benefits in cases where a worker dies from the injury or work-related disease. Temporary disability benefits are typically in the order of 70 per cent of gross earnings to 90 per cent of net earnings, subject to a maximum and a minimum benefit level. Permanent disability benefits typically compensate for lost earnings and in some instances for non-economic losses and foregone retirement savings. In other North American jurisdictions, permanent disability benefits are based on rating schedules, which designate the degree of functional impairment that is associated with particular injuries, and compensation is based on applying that degree of impairment to previous earnings, irrespective of the injured workers' subsequent employment status or earnings history.

Coverage also varies considerably by jurisdiction in terms of both the proportion of the workforce that is covered and the scope of injuries and diseases covered (Hyatt, 1999). Slightly over 80 per cent of the workforce are covered in Canada, ranging from around 70 per cent in Ontario to over 95 per cent in Quebec. Typical exclusions include the self-employed, domestics, outworkers who perform tasks in their home, casual or seasonal workers, small firms, non-profit organizations, and, in some jurisdictions, banks and financial institutions.

Not all injuries and diseases that may be work-related may be recognized by the workers' compensation system, and the scope of what is recognized varies across jurisdictions. For example, compensation for many diseases, chronic stress, and repetitive strain injuries may be restricted or even precluded. These excluded injuries and diseases may represent a growing proportion of potentially workplace-related injuries.

In Canada, workers' compensation is provided through a single monopoly board in each provincial/territorial jurisdiction. This is in marked contrast to the United States, where different states follow different practices, with monopoly boards existing in only six states and the others having different combinations of state and private insurance carriers, or private insurance carriers exclusively.

The Canadian workers' compensation systems are financed by a payroll tax levied on employers, although the ultimate incidence of that tax is subject to debate as detailed in chapters 5 and 6. The tax averages around 3 per cent of covered payroll, and varies considerably by industry, reflecting their different accident experiences. Experience rating of firms is increasingly being introduced. This rating more closely links the workers' compensation tax paid by an individual firm with the firm's claims-cost experience, relative to that of similar firms. A firm with a record of lower than average claims cost would pay a lower rate than a firm in the same industry with a record of higher costs.

Summary and Major Findings

Workers' compensation, since its inception, has been a highly contentious program. At a fundamental level, it is a mechanism that transfers money from capital (employers) to labour. The interests of these parties with respect to the scope and quantum of these transfers is in conflict, so a natural tension is always close to the surface. If party politics enters the picture, such that the parties ally more closely with labour or capital and where the party in power acts in the interests of its central constituent, the workers' compensation system can become a pendulum. Those away from whom the policy pendulum swings during political cycles feel a heightened sense of injustice. In light of these tensions, it is not surprising that workers' compensation has been the subject of more royal commissions in Canada than any other single topic (Chaklader, 1999).

Given the constant state of hand wringing in discussions of workers' compensation, it is reasonable to ask what has precipitated the present crescendo of discontent? We believe that the cumulative evolution of the nature of the work environment is now beginning to overwhelm the patchwork of reforms that have been implemented over time in attempts to maintain the currency of the workers' compensation system. In addition, it has become more difficult to ignore issues that have been lying fallow, but which the evolving environment of work has cultivated into live and urgent crises.

What are these environmental factors that are affecting work and, in turn, workers' compensation? In his chapter entitled 'Workers' Compensation in the New World of Work,' Morley Gunderson analyses the changing nature of work with respect to four main dimensions:

- The nature of the workforce (ageing with increased life-expectancy, increased labour-force participation of women and the dominance of the two-earner family, and increased ethnic and other diversity)
- The nature of the workplace (technological change, industrial restructuring from manufacturing to services, growth of small firms, the birth and death of firms, and downsizing)
- Workplace practices (broader job classifications, flattening of organizational structures, pay for performance, just-in-time delivery, employee involvement, workplace teams, and non-standard employment)
- Workplace institutions (union retrenchment, substitute laws and policies, government restraint, and inter-jurisdictional competition for investment and jobs).

Gunderson highlights the implications of these changes for various dimension of workers' compensation, including accident prevention, vocational rehabilitation, return to work, reasonable accommodation, financing, coverage (especially of non-traditional injuries), attribution of cause, benefit payments, and coordination with other programs. He concludes that virtually all aspects of workers' compensation are being affected by the changing nature of work, and that responding to these changes is crucial to ensure the survival of cherished programs like workers' compensation.

As Gunderson describes, one of the obvious manifestations of the changing nature of work is the emergence of 'non-traditional' injuries and diseases such as repetitive-strain and other musculoskeletal disorders, mental stress, and cardiovascular disease. Challenges arise because of multiple causes, long latency periods, complex interactions, lack of effective diagnostics, and difficulties in measuring exposures uniquely attributable to employment and specific worksites.

This theme is expanded upon in 'Multicausality, Non-Traditional

Injury, and the Future of Workers' Compensation,' by Esther Shain-blum, Terrence Sullivan, and John Frank. Workers' compensation was designed to provide compensation for injuries 'arising out of and in the course of employment.' They argue that making this determination was relatively straightforward in the old world of work, when workers did heavy labour in hazardous conditions and tended to suffer from traditional 'hard' injuries such as broken bones and severed limbs, usually arising from a specific event directly traceable to the work-place. However, the new world of work, with advanced technology and service-sector employment, gives rise to non-traditional injuries and diseases. The authors cite the growing epidemiological literature linking these adverse health outcomes to socio-economic status and general working conditions involving such characteristics as high demands, low job control, high stress (generally resulting from high demands and low control), monotony, and lack of social support. Such job characteristics are emerging as being more important than genetic factors and individual life-style behaviour in influencing health out-comes.

These non-traditional injuries and diseases pose challenges for workers' compensation, especially with respect to attributing the cause as 'arising out of and in the course of employment,' because they often have long latency periods, multiple causes, complex interactions, ambiguous clinical diagnostics, and ineffectual treatments. Shain-blum, Sullivan, and Frank outline the options for dealing with these non-traditional injuries and diseases. Restricting the coverage of non-traditional injuries and diseases on the grounds that it is too difficult to attribute the cause to workplace issues is one option, but that option obviously can mean that some legitimate cases are uncompensated, and costly adjudication and litigation could result. Scientifically trying to apportion the relative contribution of the different causes is another alternative, and this is often done in personal-injury cases in the courts. However, such risk attribution is technically very difficult, and can also lead to costly adjudication and litigation. The third option, which the authors suggest merits serious consideration and which does exist in some countries, involves universal, comprehensive coverage that does not require distinguishing work-related and non-work-related diseases. They argue that this system could facilitate coverage of non-traditional diseases, and reduce duplication, overlap of administration, adjudication, and litigation. Controlling costs, however, may necessi-tate a reduction in benefits in return for the more comprehensive coverage. Clearly, the changing nature of workplace injuries and diseases is necessitating a fundamental reconsideration of the role and form of workers' compensation, and its broader integration into issues of workplace health and well-being.

There may be no better demonstration of the multiple challenges faced by the workers' compensation system than the struggle to come to grips with what has now become the most common ailment among modern workers – low-back pain (LBP). John Frank, in 'Paradoxical Aspects of Low-Back Pain in Workers' Compensation Systems,' documents the 'epidemic' rise of low-back pain in workers' compensation cases. In addition to being the largest single cause of claims, total treatment and rehabilitation costs of LBP are five times those associated with the treatment of a more widely acknowledged epidemic, HIV/AIDS. Frank also argues that the current system of workers' compensation, which was designed more to deal with 'acute injuries' emanating from specific traumatic events or accidents, is ill suited to deal with the growing number of claims for soft-tissue low-back pain. Frank proposes four paradoxical reasons for the inability of workers' compensation to deal with low-back pain: (1) LBP cannot be objectively diagnosed; (2) its underlying causes can seldom be determined, making it difficult to attribute it to work and to a specific work environment; (3) in most cases there is no obvious cure, and in fact physician-induced over-diagnosis and over-treatment are apt to be harmful; (4) for these reasons, there is often a tendency to view LBP claims as unnecessary and even fraudulent, running the risk that the less common but severe cases may be lumped in with the more common mild cases.

Frank also documents the failures of the conventional incentives in workers' compensation to deal with the growing problem of LBP. Physicians have little incentive, or in fact capability, to do anything but legitimize the claim. Employers have little capability of dealing with the problem, even when they bear some of the claims costs through experience rating. This is so because in large firms, claims managers are seldom able to get production managers – with their emphasis on production quotas – to modify work assignments or to accommodate the return to work of workers with LBP. In small firms modified work assignments may be difficult and there is often simply no expertise to deal with return-to-work issues.

Frank suggests that this growing problem requires that workers' compensation systems come to terms with three challenges: (1) to discourage medical over-diagnosis and over-treatment in the very early stages (e.g., up to three weeks after the onset of LBP); (2) to encourage employers to provide immediate modified work to avoid the start of lost time; and (3) to provide rehabilitation interventions in the middle or subacute stages (e.g., between three weeks and three months after onset of LBP) in such forms as supervised exercise, targeted to the worker's specific job demands.

Frank also suggests a number of practical reforms of the system to meet these challenges. Many of these reforms involve providing the appropriate incentives, which are now often non-existent or even perverse. For example, experience rating could penalize firms disproportionately for short-term claims. This would encourage them to offer modified work so as to avoid the commencement of such claims and hence the likelihood that these would evolve into self-fulfilling long-term claims. Rewards could also be provided for the prompt offering of modified work. For small firms, pooling arrangements could be encouraged whereby disability management expertise is made available and where credits are given for firms that offer modified work for employees from other firms. Elements of 'managed care' could be introduced to provide standardized guidelines for medical and other services, and to require justifications for deviating from such norms. Physicians should be encouraged to interact with workplace managers to facilitate modified work and the return to work. This could be made easier by providing them fees for filling out modified work prescriptions or making contacts with insurers or workplace disability managers.

Frank makes clear that reforms are necessary to deal with this growing issue if the workers' compensation system is to continue to provide its functions of prevention, compensation, return to work, and the reduction of occupational injury and disease.

The costs of providing workers' compensation reflect the challenges the system is facing. Thomason and Hyatt (1997) found that between 1961 and 1993, workers' compensation costs in Canada increased by over 600 per cent in *real* terms. Stated differently, the real cost per worker increased by an average of 3.9 per cent per year, which is twice the growth rate of real productivity. Workers' compensation costs doubled from 0.32 to 0.70 per cent of Canada's economic output. It is notable that these real cost increases have occurred in the face of declining total injury and illness rates. In the early 1970s, 12 of every 100 workers made a workers' compensation claim, compared to 6.5 per 100 workers in early 1996. Even compensation claims for lost work time declined from over 5 per 100 workers in the early 1970s to 3.6 by 1996.

Employers argue that these cost increases are harming their ability to compete in the global economy. Further, some evidence (Abbott and Beach, 1997) has raised concerns that payroll taxes like those used to finance workers' compensation may induce employers to hire fewer workers. There is the counter-argument, however, that if the payroll taxes are appropriately assigned to where the injuries occur, they should provide an incentive to deter such injuries and to insure that the costs of the products we consume reflect their true social costs of production, including injury costs. It is better to kill unsafe jobs, where the costs of production do not include injury costs, than to kill people.

Furthermore, the costs of such payroll taxes ultimately may be shifted to employees in the long run in the form of lower wages. This tax shifting to workers, however, can still create strain, since substantial amounts of unemployment and output losses can occur until wages adjust downwards. Furthermore, the ultimate downward wage adjustments can create economic hardship for workers whose real wages have been relatively stagnant since the mid-1970s.

Policy makers have little information on the practical importance of the workers' compensation system to the macroeconomy. Are workers' compensation payroll taxes 'killers of jobs' or merely a tempest in a teapot? In 'The Effect of Workers' Compensation and Other Payroll Taxes on the Macro Economies of Canada and Ontario,' Peter Dungan, uses the FOCUS and FOCUS-Ontario macroeconemetric forecasting models to simulate the impact that changes in workers' compensation payroll taxes in Ontario would have on the Ontario and the Canadian economies. The results for the Canadian economy would be similar to those that would occur for changes in the payroll taxes of any other provincial jurisdiction, adjusted for their relative size.

Will workers' compensation tax increases reduce employment? Dungan's analysis suggests that this is unlikely to be the case in the long run, to the extent that the cost of the payroll tax is ultimately shifted back to labour in the form of lower compensating wages in return for the benefits of the workers' compensation system. However, significant job losses may occur in the short-run transition until the costs are shifted back to labour as wage rigidity leads to reductions in employment and output and hence to increases in unemployment. Furthermore, even in the long run there may be job and output losses if the payroll tax is not shifted completely back to labour, as has been suggested in some studies.

Four illustrative simulations are provided. The first corresponds to the reduction that occurred in 1997 in Ontario, involving a 5 per cent reduction in the workers' compensation payroll tax (e.g., if the payroll tax were 3.00 per cent of payroll it would be reduced to 2.85 per cent). For the Ontario economy, the maximum short-term impact tended to occur after three years, leading to an increase in real GDP of 0.16 of 1 per cent; a reduction in inflation of 0.07 of a per cent; creation of 8000 new jobs and a reduction in the unemployment rate of 0.08 of a per cent (e.g., from 9 to 8.92 per cent); and a wage increase of 0.02 of 1 per cent. The provincial tax revenues that result from these economic improvements offset about one-quarter of the $154 million of initial lost revenues from the payroll tax reduction. For the Canadian economy as a whole the changes are generally in the same direction, albeit somewhat smaller, reflecting the dissipation of the gains across the whole economy. The impacts on employment and output tend to dissipate after about six years, converging towards zero as wages and salaries adjust downwards, reflecting the cost shifting back to labour.

A second simulation matches the 5 per cent reduction in the workers' compensation payroll tax with a reduction in benefits that also occurred in Ontario at that same time. The results are similar to those of the first simulation, in part because the benefit reductions were slightly smaller than the premium reductions, but mainly because the premium reduction directly stimulates the economy by reducing prices. In essence, a reduction in the payroll tax, even if accompanied by a corresponding reduction in benefits, would generally have positive macroeconomic effects.

A third simulation involves a 10 per cent increase in the workers' compensation payroll tax in Ontario, an amount that would be necessary to compensate for the unfunded liabilities of the system. The results are the reverse of those in the first simulation, and of about twice the magnitude. After three years, employment is reduced by about 16,000 jobs and output by about $1 billion. These impacts dissipate to close to zero by eight years as the costs are ultimately shifted to labour in the form of reduced wages.

A fourth simulation assumes that the same revenue as in the 10 per cent payroll tax increase is raised through the Ontario provincial income tax. The short-term negative macroeconomic effects of the income tax are much smaller, in large part because the workers' compensation payroll tax increase directly affects inflation as firms pass on some of the cost increases in higher prices. Furthermore, the immediate increase in labour cost emanating from the payroll tax sets off an immediate reduction in employment and hence of labour income and consumption.

Overall, the analysis suggests that payroll tax increases can lead to substantial short-term adjustment costs in the form of reduced employment and output and increased unemployment, and that these adjustments can last for several years. Furthermore, there is some evidence (albeit a minority) that suggests these adjustments may be permanent. The adverse employment and output effects of the payroll tax may also be larger than those from personal income taxes. Nevertheless, these potential negative effects of payroll taxes must be weighed against other factors, including the fact that they are easy to enforce, they have low administrative costs, and they do not discourage work effort as much as income taxes do.

Given these trade-offs, Dungan suggests four possible policy responses. First, tie the payroll tax to experience rating so that the firm is essentially 'paying' for its accidents and not able to shift the tax, in which case the slow wage adjustments that otherwise lead to reduced employment and output do not occur. Second, tie the payroll tax to specific benefit changes, in which case the perceived benefits makes it easier to immediately shift the tax to labour in the form of compensating wage adjustments without the short-run wage stickiness that otherwise leads to reductions in employment and output. (In the first scenario wage adjustments do not occur, while in the second they occur immediately; in either case the short-run sticky wage adjustments that lead to reduced employment are avoided). Third, change payroll taxes as little as possible, using other revenue sources. Fourth, recognize that labour ultimately bears the burden of the tax and therefore apply it directly to labour in the form of an employee payroll tax, thereby avoiding the shifting of the tax through a short-run sticky wage adjustment that leads to reduced employment and output. While this latter policy response is likely to have the most favourable macroeconomic effect, it is also likely to be a political 'non-starter,' highlighting the difficult trade-off that often exists between good economic policy and political acceptability.

The impact of workers' compensation cost increases has been ameliorated in some Canadian jurisdictions by permitting employers to pay less than the full costs of compensable injuries and illnesses. This can occur through indirect subsidies of some (high cost) industries by other (low cost) industries. That is, some industries pay more, and other less, than the full cost of claims for which they are accountable. In addition, employers as a whole may be charged less than the current and expected future costs of the claims they incur. Unfunded liabilities result when the costs of expected future benefit liabilities arising from existing claims exceed the value of the assets in reserve to meet those liabilities.

When the employers who are accountable for these costs go out of business, the benefit obligations still remain. The burden of paying these 'stranded' benefit liabilities falls on surviving and new firms and their workers. The distribution of this burden has potentially important fairness considerations, both within and across generations of workers and firms.

In 'Unfunded Liabilities under Workers' Compensation,' Morley Gunderson and Douglas Hyatt use intergenerational accounting procedures to provide an additional perspective on the unfunded liability that exists in the Ontario workers' compensation system. In 1996, that unfunded liability was about $10.5 billion or $3362 per worker. Across industries, the unfunded liability per worker ranged from $900 in service jobs and $1000 in government jobs to about $21,000 in mining and $23,000 in construction. They have been increasing over the 1980s, although the growth has ceased in the early 1990s, with small surpluses occurring after 1993 that are slowly reducing the unfunded liability.

Such unfunded liabilities mean that current generations of firms and workers will be subsidized by future generations of firms and workers, with that intergenerational burden being enhanced by other unfunded liabilities associated with pay-as-you go systems, such as the Canada/Quebec Pension Plan (C/QPP), as well as growing medical expenses associated with an ageing population with longer life expectancy. The unfunded liability may discourage the growth of new firms, and it may subsidize more hazardous firms and industries, since the subsidies tend to be greater in those industries with relatively high injury rates.

Although the unfunded liabilities can be reduced only by decreasing expenses or increasing revenues, there are a wide range of policy options whereby this can occur. Expenses can be decreased by reductions in such factors as the incidence and duration of injuries and claims; the magnitude and duration of benefits; vocational rehabilitation expenses; administrative expenses; and the types of injuries for which compensation is provided. Expenses could also be reduced by shifting the cost to other transfer programs like Employment Insurance, C/QPP disability, or social assistance, or to employers in the form of more stringent return-to-work and reasonable-accommodation requirements. Increases in revenues can come mainly from increases in the payroll tax rate or the tax base in the form of expanded coverage. The unfunded liability may also increase the pressure for privatization, so as to reduce administrative costs or to reduce the ability of workers' compensation insurance providers to have unfunded liabilities.

Clearly the unfunded liabilities have important redistributive effects, across both generations and industries. These in turn can affect the growth of new firms as well as the incentive to reduce injuries. As well, the unfunded liabilities will give rise to pressure to reduce expenses and increase revenues, and these policy responses in turn have important implications for the design and delivery of the workers' compensation system.

While the dominant approach to containing workers' compensation costs in the 1990s has been benefit reductions and reduced access to the system (Spieler and Burton, 1998), there are alternatives. There is little disagreement that the best way to reduce costs is to prevent injuries from occurring in the first place. In 'Occupational Health and Safety: Effectiveness of Economic and Regulatory Mechanisms,' Boris Kralj analyses the pros and cons of regulatory mechanisms versus market incentives in workers' compensation and occupational health and safety. The United States tends to follow the regulatory model, emphasizing the enforcement of detailed health and safety regulations. Canada has similar regulations, but some provinces also rely more on the internal responsibility system, where employers and employees take joint responsibility for health and safety issues. Employees are given legal rights, especially pertaining to three basic rights: the right to know or be informed about workplace hazards; the right to refuse unsafe work; and the right to be consulted, largely through joint health and safety committees.

Kralj concludes that the empirical evidence on the impact of health and safety regulations is mixed, generally indicating that the regulations have little or no impact on health and safety outcomes. The limited Canadian evidence tends to find the internal responsibility system to have a positive effect on improving health and safety outcomes. The evidence also tends to find that economic or market incentives, through experience rating of workers' compensation, have a more pronounced effect on improving health and safety at the workplace, since employers have a monetary incentive to reduce accidents and hence their premiums. He argues that market incentives through experience rating are particularly appealing since they simply raise the costs of accidents, leaving it up to employers as to how best to reduce injuries and hence costs.

On the basis of theory and evidence, Kralj suggests that more attention should be paid to the internal responsibility system and to economic incentives embodied in pricing mechanisms, such as experience rating, as approaches to reducing workplace injuries.

A more controversial approach to containing costs, at least in Canada, is to harness the market mechanism of competition among providers of workers' compensation insurance. This would entail breaking the state monopolies through the introduction of private-sector insurance companies. Don Dewees, in 'Private Participation in Workers' Compensation,' examines the pros and cons of various degrees of private-sector participation in workers' compensation, including (1) monopoly public provision (as in all Canadian jurisdictions and six U.S. states); (2) mixed public and private systems, where private carriers are allowed to compete against the public system (as in 18 U.S. states); (3) purely private provision with state regulation of rates; (4) purely private provision with no rate regulation. He emphasizes that different functions of workers' compensation may be more amenable to subcontracting and privatization, including accident and disease prevention, vocational rehabilitation, claims management, return to work, and administering the system.

Dewees also sets out a variety of criteria that have to be considered in evaluating the pros and cons of public versus private provision. Those criteria include prompt response to and disposition of inquiries and claims; involvement of and responsiveness to stakeholders in developing policies and procedures; horizontal equity to ensure that similarly situated workers are treated similarly; control over the accumulation of unfunded liability and the ability to deal with any existing unfunded liabilities; assurance that injured workers will receive their compensation if an insurer should fail; and flexibility and reversibility of policies and decisions so as to respond to an ever-changing workplace and claims environment.

He then assesses the ability of public- and private-sector institutions to meet these criteria, according to various economic theories including agency theory, transactions-cost theories of the firm, and property-rights theories of the firm. These theories generally imply that the private sector is likely to be more efficient than the public sector in both cost and performance, even though trade-offs are involved. Specifically, private-market provision is preferred when the service is easily specified and relatively constant; compliance with contractual terms is easily monitored; there is little possibility for 'chiselling' by contractors; negotiation of the contract is inexpensive; and the inputs are highly differentiated, with few economies of scale and scope but large returns to specialization. In contrast, 'in-firm' public provision is likely to be preferred when services are more difficult to specify or are in a state of continuous evolution and change; compliance with contractual terms becomes hard to monitor; contractors can 'chisel'; and contracts are difficult or expensive to negotiate.

With this framework, Dewees then evaluates three alternative arrangements for delivering workers' compensation that recognize its different functions and the different criteria for evaluating the degree to which public and private systems can perform those functions. The three alternative arrangements are (1) public monopoly provision, but contracting out some of the functions to the private sector; (2) a mixed public and private system, where private insurers are allowed to compete with the public monopolies; and (3) a purely private system.

On the basis of theory and empirical evidence Dewees argues that, as a minimum, if a public monopoly is continued, it should expand its contracting-out of many of its functions to the private sector. This is especially the case with respect to routine support and administrative functions, albeit the potential for cost saving there is small since such costs amount to less than 15 per cent of workers' compensation expenditures. The bulk of expenditures are associated with benefit claims, and here the greatest potential for cost saving would likely come from reducing the proportion of temporary disability claims that become permanent.

In addition, Dewees suggests that study and consideration should be given to moving towards a mixed system, where private carriers are allowed to compete with public monopolies. This would reveal the efficacy of each system, since the most cost-effective system would expand its market share. If the private carriers consistently were the most cost-effective, then eventually the system would become privatized.

Thus, Dewees also rejects the immediate conversion to a purely private system. It would not be necessary to impose such a system, since it would automatically emerge from a mixed system if it proved to be cost-effective and hence garnered market share. On the basis of theory and evidence, Dewees suggests that the features of workers' compensation are such that the usual merits of privatization are not obvious. In such circumstances, a mixed system would enable marginal adjustments towards the optimal balance between public and private delivery of the different functions of workers' compensation.

The United States is fertile ground for examining the cost impacts of competition because, as Dewees has noted, workers' compensation is delivered in purely public, purely private, and mixed systems, depending on the state. In 'The Costs of Workers' Compensation in Ontario and British Columbia,' Terry Thomason and John F. Burton, Jr undertake the daunting task of comparing the costs of workers' compensation in the United States with those in Ontario and British Columbia.

Thomason and Burton first construct uniform cost measures that adjust the premium or assessment rates for a number of factors, including loading factors reflecting insurance-carrier expenses; experience-rating modifications; constant or flat charges of issuing and servicing a policy; premium discounts or retrospective ratings; and adjustments for any dividends to policy holders. The resulting adjusted manual premium rates reflect the percentage of payroll actually expended on workers' compensation by employers. A second cost measure, net costs, is obtained by multiplying this premium rate by average weekly wages, to get a measure of actual total workers' compensation costs.

Aggregate measures of costs are then constructed for forty-five U.S. states and two Canadian jurisdictions (Ontario and BC) over the period 1975 to 1995. The aggregate measures for each jurisdiction in each year were constructed by weighing the adjusted assessment rates for seventy-one common rate groups by the proportion of payroll attributable to each rate group.

These aggregate measures of cost (adjusted manual rates and total net costs) are then used as dependent variables in regression analysis based on 925 observations (45 U.S. jurisdictions, 2 Canadian jurisdictions, over 21 years, with some missing observations owing to data limitations). To isolate the pure cost effect of being in a Canadian as opposed to a U.S. jurisdiction, a wide range of control variables were also utilized. These included injury rates that reflect different compositions of the workforce; wage-loss-benefit generosity; medical-benefit generosity; the proportion of permanent partial-disability claims; union density; and various dimensions of coverage. In other words, the regression procedure is designed to isolate the effect on costs of private, competitive provision as in the United States, versus monopoly, state provision as in Canada, after controlling for cost differences that reflect such factors as the different injury rates, benefit generosity, and coverage.

The results, somewhat surprisingly, suggest that costs are substantially lower in the state-provided monopoly system in Canada compared to the privately provided competitive system in the United States. Relative to the United States, costs were approximately 55 per cent lower in British Columbia (ranging from 47 to 64 per cent in their preferred specification) and approximately 35 per cent lower in Ontario (ranging from 26 to 43 per cent in their preferred specification). A substantial component of the cost difference, however, reflects the fact that the state governments have increasingly allowed firms to self-insure by opting out of the system, in which case the higher-cost firms tend to remain in the system.

Given these and other qualifications raised by the authors, they caution against using their results to conclude that the provision of workers' compensation through state-controlled monopolies is more cost-effective than through private competitive carriers. Nevertheless, their results certainly suggest the more conservative conclusion that private competitive carriers are not necessarily more cost-effective; if anything, the opposite may be true. As they highlight, this controversial conclusion merits more research.

As the system struggles to address non-traditional injuries, and the allocation of the rising costs of workers' compensation has become increasingly consequential for employers, the incidence of disputes between the workers' compensation authority, injured workers, and employers has increased. The appeals structure is the last resort for those who feel that the workers' compensation system has failed them. David Law, in 'Appeals Litigation: Pricing the Workplace Injury,' outlines how workers' compensation historically was established as a quid pro quo whereby workers gave up their right to sue their employer in return for immediate 'no-fault' compensation with a minimum of litigation. He examines the Ontario case to show how the appeals procedure has thwarted this objective and brought about a 'veritable litigation mill.' This state of affairs was fostered by many factors that are common to workers' compensation systems across Canada:

- the creation of an external appeals body and the publication of its decisions, along with the counter expansion of advocates for employers;

- the expansion of experience rating, which created the incentive for employers to appeal cases to reduce their experience-rated premium;
- the creation of the Offices of the Worker and Employer Advisor to provide free information and advocacy and government lobbying potential;
- the use of new technology to speed up the process, which encouraged people to appeal given that the appeal would be handled quickly;
- the provision of an 'older worker supplement' to persons who voluntarily retired under certain conditions that led to appeals;
- the shift to compensating for wage loss, which reduced the monetary incentive to return to work, leading to disputes over whether the worker could be deemed capable of returning to work;
- the associated expansion of requirements for rehabilitation, return to work, and reasonable accommodation;
- the expansion into more contestable claims in areas such as chronic pain;
- and the increased value of claims to employees given declining labour market opportunities.

While these changes usually served other important functions, they tended to increase appeals and the contesting of claims. This growth in litigation flowing from expanding the scope of workers' compensation highlights the inevitable trade-offs involved in such systems. It also highlights the tendency of systems to become litigious when due process is emphasized and when there is a monetary incentive to contest and counter-contest claims. This is so even in the case of workers' compensation, where the 'no-fault' nature of the system was explicitly designed to avoid litigation.

Frustration with the apparent shortcomings of the workers' compensation system to deliver what it promised have led many in the stakeholder communities to call for a return to tort compensation. The privative clause in workers' compensation legislation has strictly limited the rights of workplace parties to sue in the event of a work-related injury or disease. This modern rebuke of workers' compensation raises basic questions. Is workers' compensation something worth saving? Does it have any relevance to workers and employers as we approach the new millennium or is it an anachronism?

In 'Should Work Injury Compensation Continue to Imbibe at the Tort Bar?' Douglas Hyatt and David Law critically examine the merits of tort versus workers' compensation. They argue that, for a number of years, workers' compensation was able to serve its three functions of redress for workers who suffer the consequences of work-related accidents and diseases, protection for employers from destructive litigation, and social stability, to the benefit of employers and workers alike.

Pressures on the workers' compensation system to control costs through benefit reductions and a reluctance to expand the concept of compensable injuries and diseases has shaken workers' commitment to the historic compromise. Expansion of their role from first payer for the system to provider of services such as re-employment and labour-market re-entry initiatives has similarly reduced employers' already shaky commitment to the system.

The authors highlight the fact that the tort and workers' compensation systems seek to address different 'wrongs.' Tort provides for damages, apportions fault, and penalizes those at fault for their negligence, and creates incentives for members of society to avoid tortious conduct. Workers' compensation, as a no-fault system, carries no notion of 'wrong,' and offers instead an administrative approach to addressing the consequences of an 'accident.' The authors conclude that it is far from obvious that tort will provide benefits superior to those under workers' compensation, even if the employer is found to be at fault.

Hyatt and Law see no immediate threat that the courts will significantly weaken the tort bar in workers' compensation, based on a review of recent challenges. Any such initiatives will have to be explicitly enacted by legislatures. They suggest that if legislatures do move in the direction of bending the tort bar, potential areas for incursion include intentional torts, where the injury or illness did not occur by accident but by intentional, wilful misconduct; removing non-physical forms of injury, such as harassment, from the scope of the privative clause; access to the courts if the degree of damage exceeds some threshold; and a two-track system in which pecuniary damages fall under the jurisdiction of workers' compensation and non-pecuniary damages would fall within the purview of the courts.

Concluding Observations

Specific policy options and recommendations are contained in the separate chapters. There are also a number of common threads that run through the papers, and that have implications for workers' compensation policy reform. We conclude this introductory chapter by highlighting some of these observations.

Incentives matter. The parties will respond to the different costs and benefits they face, including those related to accident prevention, return to work, unfunded liabilities, accessing different public and private income-support systems, and litigating claims. The policy challenge is to harness these incentives rather than work against them. It is important to 'get prices right' (e.g., through experience rating) so that the prices of the products we consume reflect the full social costs of producing them, including accident costs. It is also important to create the correct incentives for employers and employees to take adequate precautions against risk and to facilitate the return to work of injured workers. Creating the correct economic incentives will also go a long way to reduce the need for bureaucratic, regulatory procedures that tend to be costly and ineffective.

Litigation fills policy voids. Even though the system of workers' compensation was designed to minimize litigation, it has become more litigious in response to its own complex regulations, inconsistencies in the treatment of similar workers or firms, and the absence of policy that address leading-edge developments in workplace injury and disease. In addition, litigation is fostered by attempts to place the costs of injuries and illnesses more directly on the parties through, for example, more extensive experience rating of employer premiums in the case of employers, or reduced scope of coverage and benefits in the case of injured workers.

Where opportunities arise, cost shifting will occur. Any tightening up or restrictions on one part of the system will create new pressures on other parts of the system as the parties try to offload costs and shift responsibility. Hopefully, this will lead to the costs and responsibility being shifted to the appropriate place, but there is a very real risk of simply 'churning,' with considerable real resources being used up in the process. There is also a risk that governments may try to reduce their own costs by shifting them to the private parties in the form of regulations such as those pertaining to return to work and reasonable accommodation. This action may be merited, but it may also be simply a form of cost shifting. Clearly, coordination is necessary across different parts of the system to ensure that responsibility is appropriately assigned and that costs are not simply shifted.

Unfunded liabilities can be an important form of cost shifting, in this case to future generations of workers and firms. Such burdens may be increasingly difficult to bear given the other intergenerational burdens that we are passing on, raising the risk that the nation's implicit social contract may be abandoned. Unfunded liabilities can also decrease the incentive to reduce risk, and they may discourage the growth of new firms and associated job creation.

Payroll taxes used to finance workers' compensation can also discourage job creation, although the long-run impact of this effect is mitigated by the fact that most of the cost likely is shifted back to labour in the form of lower compensating wages in return for the benefits of the system. This does mean, however, that any excess costs are also born by employees who have already been experiencing stagnant real wages for a considerable period of time. Costs seldom disappear, they simply reappear in subtle forms, unless structural reforms yield real efficiencies in the system.

While the workers' compensation system is in drastic need of reform, privatization – and this is likely to be one of our most contentious conclusions – is not an obvious solution. This may seem at odds with our earlier conclusion that incentives matter, since privatization generally builds on incentives. Nevertheless, comparisons with the more highly privatized U.S. system, and an analysis of the pros and cons of privatization in this area, do not point to privatization as an obvious cure. Certainly, gains may be made by privatizing more aspects of the system, and by having a mixture of public and private provision, but the case for drastic surgery through full privatization does not appear to be there, at least given our current state of knowledge.

The changing workplace and the emergence of new injuries and diseases have shaken the foundations of the workers' compensation system. Our ability to reform the system will determine whether it will survive in the new world of work. We hope that the papers in this volume can help to elucidate some of the policy choices.

REFERENCES

Abbott, M., and C. Beach. 1997. 'The Impact of Employer Payroll Taxes on Employment and Wages: Evidence for Canada, 1970–1993.' In M. Abbott, C. Beach, and R. Chaykowski, eds, *Transition and Structural Change in the North American Labour Market*, 154–234. Kingston: Industrial Relations Centre and John Deutch Institute, Queen's University, distributed by IRC Press.
Chaklader, Anjan. 1999. 'History of Workers' Compensation in B.C.' A report to the Royal Commission on Workers' Compensation in British Columbia.

Hyatt, Douglas E. 1999.'Risk-Shifting in Workers' Compensation.' Unpublished manuscript.
Spieler, Emily A., and John F. Burton, Jr. 1998. 'Compensation for Disabled Workers: Workers' Compensation.' In T. Thomason, J.F. Burton, Jr, and D.E. Hyatt, eds, *New Approaches to Disability in the Workplace*, 205–14. Ithaca: Cornell University Press for the Industrial Relations Research Association.
Thomason, Terry, and Douglas Hyatt. 1997. 'Workers' Compensation Costs in Canada: 1961–1993.' In M. Abbott, C. Beach, and R. Chaykowski, eds, *Transition and Structural Change in the North American Labour Market*, 235–55. Kingston: Industrial Relations Centre and John Deutch Institute, Queen's University, distributed by IRC Press.

2   Workers' Compensation in the New World of Work

MORLEY GUNDERSON

The nature of work is changing dramatically in Canada and throughout the world.[1] Many of our labour policies, however, were established in earlier periods, under conditions that were often vastly different than they are today. Workers' compensation systems in Canada, for example, were first established in 1914 in Ontario, with other provinces generally soon following in step.[2]

But what is the relevance of these policies to the current employment relationship? Would the same policies be instituted today, if we were to start with a clean slate? Are they evolving to meet changing circumstances, or are they mired in history, unable to change because of the vested position of interest groups? If they are outdated, what are the barriers to change? If change does occur, what are the implications for the stakeholders – labour, management, and governments?

In the new global marketplace, organizations must develop a strategic response in order to adapt and survive. This is true of both business organizations and labour organizations. It is increasingly difficult to sustain conventional practices behind the protection of tariffs, closed economies, or high transportation and communication costs. In this 'new world,' governments are being subjected to similar pressure to reconsider their policies and practices. This is so not only because of increased fiscal pressure, but also because business investment and the jobs associated with that investment are now more mobile, and can locate in countries and jurisdictions with less onerous regulations.

This need not mean that all regulation will dissipate as jurisdictions compete for business investment and the jobs associated with that investment. Regulations can obviously serve positive functions even in terms of the productivity and competitiveness of organizations. At its inception, workers' compensation, for example, involved a societal-level trade-off whereby employees were to be provided with 'no-fault' compensation in return for giving up their right to sue their employer. As noted by Hyatt and Law (this volume) and Law (this volume), workers' compensation has provided a more orderly means for compensating workplace injuries than might have been the case under alternative schemes.

While workers' compensation *may* involve elements of efficient regulation, it may also embody inefficiencies that jeopardize its survival in a globalized economy. If cherished institutions are to survive, they must adapt to the new environment. This is as true for government policies as it is for businesses and unions.

The purpose of this paper is to outline the changing background, the environmental factors that are having the most important implications for labour market policies. Their specific implications for workers' compensation are then outlined. The paper concludes with a discussion of the main implications, of the evolving nature of work for public policy.

Environmental Changes

The background environmental changes that are impacting most on labour-market regulation pertain to the changing nature of the work-force, the workplace, workplace practices, and workplace institutions. Each of these are discussed in turn, with illustrations provided of their implications for workers' compensation. In a subsequent section, their implications are recapitulated with respect to a number of workers' compensation policy areas, such as demands on the system, prevention measures, vocational and medical rehabilitation, financing, coverage, and the relationship to complementary and substitute policies.

Changing Nature of the Workforce

AGING WORKFORCE AND INCREASED LIFE EXPECTANCY

The average age of the Canadian workforce is increasing, with the large baby-boom population, born in the period 1946 to 1966, now entering their fifties.[3] In addition, thanks to improvements in health technology as well as healthier lifestyles, men and women are living longer. The life expectancy of women is projected to increase from 78.2

years in 1992 to 86.9 years by 2010. Similarly, male life expectancy, which was 72.1 years in 1992, is expected to increase to 80.3 years by 2010 (Office of Superintendent of Financial Institutions, 1995; Peron and Strohmenger, 1994). This increase in life expectancy, coupled with the aging of the baby-boomers, means that substantially larger portions of the population will be in the older age brackets. The Canadian population aged sixty-five and older as a proportion of the working-age population is expected to *triple* from 13 per cent in 1960 to 39 per cent by 2030 (Organization for Economic Cooperation and Development, 1996, 101).

These simple demographic realities have potentially profound implications for workers' compensation. Work-related injuries and diseases that are more common to older workers will become more prominent, and the composition of claimants will be shifted towards older workers. To the extent that older workers disproportionately have more claims or more costly claims, and may be less likely to return to work following their injury, the total system cost will also increase.

Demographic issues also have important implications for inter-generational equity given the pay-as-you-go nature of the funding system, especially in jurisdictions that have permitted the accumulation of substantial unfunded liabilities (Gunderson and Hyatt, this volume). Claims costs of a large cohort of older workers will be funded by a smaller cohort of younger workers. This financial burden will be exacerbated by other burdens faced by younger generations of workers: health expenditures for the aged; elder-care responsibilities in the home and community; other unfunded liabilities such as those associated with the Canada/Quebec Pension Plan; government budget deficits; and stagnant productivity and real wage growth.

Demographics also have important implications for the range of functions of workers' compensation. Vocational rehabilitation (VR) will be increasingly required to address the special challenges faced by older workers, possibly implying longer rehabilitation times. Return to work may be complicated by the fact that the adjustment is more difficult for an older worker when displaced from a job for whatever reason. Early retirement becomes a more viable option since that option is increasingly taken by the regular workforce. Given the long latency periods of many occupational diseases, the issue of attribution of the cause to workplace issues will also be more prominent. This situation will be exacerbated by the trend to early retirement (since the disease may manifest itself when these people are in retirement) as well as increased life expectancy (since the disease now has a longer time to appear).

INCREASED PARTICIPATION OF WOMEN AND DOMINANCE OF DUAL-EARNER FAMILY

The increased participation of women in the labour force[4] also means that workers' compensation issues will continue to shift towards those associated with women and work. The dominance of the two-earner family[5] may also have potentially important implications. Balancing work and family responsibilities and the 'time crunch' associated with such dual responsibilities can lead to stress-related problems that can be exacerbated by pressures at the workplace.

ETHNIC AND OTHER DIVERSITY

The workforce is becoming increasingly diverse, with most of the new growth in the labour force coming from women and visible minorities.[6] This can give rise to a variety of challenges, including those associated with the dissemination of information if there are language barriers, and ensuring that the different groups know their rights and responsibilities.

Changing Nature of the Workplace

Workplaces are also changing, as is the nature of work itself. Many of these changes emanate from new pressures faced by firms in their product and service markets.

Technological change has been dramatic, especially that associated with computerization and the information economy. The use of computers has given rise to new health and safety risks associated with repetitive-motion activities. Back strain is now as likely to occur from prolonged seating and faulty ergonomics as it is from heavy lifting. While technological change can lead to new diseases, it can also lead to new treatments. It may facilitate the accommodation of injured workers by removing the necessity that work be performed at a traditional workstation or workplace (e.g., telecommuting).

The industrial restructuring from manufacturing to services is changing the nature and composition of claims and claims costs since they tend to be different across sectors.[7] Coverage can also vary by sector, so that changes in the industrial distribution of the workforce have implications for coverage. Manufacturing tended to be associated with clearer and less contested *traditional* physical injuries. Services, in contrast, can be associated with different injuries and diseases,[8] including stress, psychological disorders, repetitive strain, and musculoskeletal injuries. High-end professional and administrative service workers can also experience stress-related problems emanating from long hours and intensity of work, especially as downsizing places increased burdens on those who remain. Low-end services can be associated with stress-related problems resulting from lack of control over the volume and flow of one's work.

The growth of small firms has also been prominent, and net new-job creation is higher in small firms than in large firms,[9] suggesting that the workforce will be increasingly concentrated in small firms. This can have important implications for workers' compensation to the extent that issues such as coverage, experience rating, return to work, reasonable accommodation, and claims vary by firm size. Small firms, for example, are more difficult to experience rate because they generally have sporadic accident experience, such that a single accident can have a large impact on a small firm's claims-cost experience. As well, small firms often do not have the infrastructure to deal with regulatory requirements such as those embodied in health and safety and workers' compensation. For them, simplicity in the regulatory requirements, and assistance in complying with them, can be important components of an effective compliance strategy.

In addition, as the traditional smokestack industries decline and new industries emerge, the burden of financing the unfunded liabilities left by defunct firms will be an important source of contention (Gunderson and Hyatt, this volume). The extent to which such unfunded liabilities could discourage the formation of new firms and associated job creation is a further source of concern, but its practical importance is unknown.

The Canadian labour market has experienced prolonged recessions, especially in the early 1980s and 1990s, with unemployment rising to successively higher plateaus and not returning to previous levels. Recoveries have been characterized as involving 'jobless growth.' Downsizing and the threat of unemployment can give rise to general health problems,[10] which can occur even for those who are fortunate enough to retain their job but who suffer from increased workload and the threat of further downsizing. Health problems can also occur for those who lose their job and are therefore not in the workers' compensation system, and the effects can spill over to family members.[11] When the job losses happen concurrently with lost-time injuries that are compensated with wage-loss benefits and where return to work is now more difficult, workers' compensation may be a substitute for UI (Fortin and Lanoie, 1992).

Changing Workplace Practices

The workplace practices of firms are evolving in step with the changing nature of the workplace and of work itself. Job classifications are becoming broader, so that workers do a wider range of tasks, potentially making it more difficult to identify a unique source of injury. Workers may also be less familiar with the hazards associated with the different components of a job. Vocational rehabilitation can be more demanding, if multi-skilling is required to deal with the broader array of tasks. Alternatively, employers may be required to narrow the range of tasks in order to accommodate the return of injured workers.

The flattening of organizational structures and reduced supervision can also mean less monitoring and enforcement of health and safety practices. Pay-for-performance can lead to more stress-inducing pressure as well as possibly reduced attention to health and safety issues, even though performance criteria could include health and safety performance. Just-in-time delivery pressures may also lead to job-related stress, and the possibility of 'cutting corners' with respect to health and safety precautions.

Greater employee involvement in workplace decisions, and the increased use of teams, provides a new focus for information dissemination as well as for individual and team responsibility for health and safety issues. A new emphasis on quality that is now placed on individual workers (with less oversight by quality-control officers) can be translated into an emphasis on health and safety quality (without external health and safety monitoring). The increased use of teams, however, can also lead to a possible tendency not to report accidents if they are regarded as a negative outcome of team performance. It may also lead to additional pressure and stress on other team members if they are required to 'cover' for the work of the injured worker.[12]

Non-standard employment is also becoming more prominent in such forms as part-time work, subcontracting, limited-term contracts, temporary-help agencies, self-employment, and telecommuting (Krahn, 1995). These employment relationships have in common a reduced attachment to any one employer or worksite. Non-standard jobs give rise to a number of challenges for workers' compensation: determining coverage, disseminating information on rights and responsibilities, attributing the unique source of the injury or disease, assessing reasonable accommodation requirements, and providing workplace-specific health and safety training.

Changing Workplace Institutions

The changing nature of the workforce and the workplace is also giving rise to changes in workplace institutions such as unions, laws, and government policies – all of which have important implications for workers' compensation.

UNION RETRENCHMENT

Unions in Canada have generally been able to maintain their representation in the workforce in spite of rapidly declining union membership in the United States. Historically, union representation in Canada and the United States were fairly similar. In the mid-1960s unionization rates were fairly similar in each country, at approximately 30 per cent of the workforce that could potentially be unionized. Subsequently, unionization rates in the United States declined continuously, to approximately 15 per cent today. In Canada, they have fluctuated somewhat, but have generally been maintained at slightly more than 30 per cent of the potentially eligible workforce (Riddell, 1993).

While unionization rates have generally been maintained in Canada, unions have operated under the threat of the de-unionization that has occurred in the United States and in most developed countries. This has been compounded by the fact that greater international competition and mobility of capital means that the non-union environments can be a greater threat to unions, at least to the extent that unions increase labour costs. Employers now have a more credible threat of relocating to non-union environments, especially when those environments are also often associated with lower labour costs and fewer regulations in general.

In such circumstances, unions have had to develop strategic

responses for their survival. Such responses include organizing in non-conventional areas, entering into joint labour-management cooperative efforts to enhance productivity and competitiveness, and emphasizing new areas such as services to employees that do not necessarily increase labour costs.

Unions can serve an important role in the area of workplace health and safety and workers' compensation. They can be an important vehicle for providing information to their employees and ensuring their rights and responsibilities in these and other areas. Unions can also be a source of 'bottom-up' information, eliciting and articulating employee preferences and possible trade-offs to management. They can protect employees against reprisals by management, and represent employees in claims-adjudication procedures. Just as they can assist in the design and implementation of training programs, they can provide similar assistance with respect to vocational rehabilitation, reasonable accommodation, and return-to-work issues. The collective agreement can formalize practices and policies, and compel the parties to make trade-offs that recognize their common and competing interests. The grievance procedure can be an important ongoing forum for solving disputes over the interpretation of issues in the collective agreement. Unions can play important roles at all levels: at the workplace through health and safety committees; at the industry level through sector councils where they exist; and at the aggregate industry level through political bargaining in the broader political arena.[13]

These functions can be jeopardized if unions decline or become powerless. Their importance extends beyond the unionized sector, since policies and practices in that sector are often emulated in the non-union sector. In essence, unions can act as a check in the non-union sector, just as global competition can act as a check on unions.

Furthermore, global and competitive pressures, including de-unionization elsewhere, compel the remaining unions to shift some focus from traditional bargaining goals such as wages and fringe benefits that increase labour costs, and to focus on providing services to their members that do not increase labour costs. In essence, the very pressures that are challenging unions are also presenting them with an opportunity to strategically refocus their efforts towards practices that are in the mutual interests of both their members and employers. Such services could include those pertaining to education about, and enforcement of, health and safety rights and assisting injured members though the workers' compensation process.

SUBSTITUTE LAWS AND POLICIES

Other laws and policies can have important implications for workers' compensation to the extent that they are complements or substitutes. Policies to promote the health and safety and well-being of workers can be complementary to workers' compensation, since they can reduce the number of workers who have to access that system and the time they spend on workers' compensation. An ounce of prevention may be worth a pound of cure. Vocational rehabilitation programs can facilitate the return to work of injured workers, as can requirements for employers to reasonably accommodate the return to work of injured workers. In the latter vein, however, care must be taken to ensure that the requirements are not designed more to reduce the financial commitments of the workers' compensation system, at the expense of excessive costs being shifted to employers and to injured workers if they prematurely return to work.

Other policies can be a substitute for workers' compensation. In such circumstances, restrictions placed on the use of these substitute policies can lead to a substitution into workers' compensation. Restrictions on unemployment insurance, for example, can lead to a substitution into workers' compensation, especially when the income replacement rate is higher under workers' compensation, at around 90 per cent, compared to unemployment insurance, at around 60 per cent (Fortin and Lanoie, 1992). This substitution could occur because otherwise unemployed workers may try to access other income-support systems if unemployment insurance is denied them or made less liberal, and because employers may try to shift employees to workers' compensation if they feel they are less likely to lose them permanently under that system than under UI.

The substitution, of course, can work both ways. Workers' compensation systems can try to shift claims to the disability component of the Canada Pension Plan if the latter is administered with less stringency. This may become more prominent if the ability to distinguish between work-related injuries and diseases (compensable through workers' compensation) and non-work-related injuries and diseases (compensable through CPP) becomes more blurred. As well, workers' compensation systems may try to shift employees to welfare or to the private disability-insurance system of employers.

These cost-shifting issues will increasingly be prominent as budgets are squeezed and policies are reformed, usually in a fashion to make them more stringent and to save on costs. Cost shifting was less of an issue in earlier times when all programs were expanding. The temptation to cost shift is even greater when a cost can be shifted to different jurisdictions or levels of government. Cost shifting from workers' compensation to CPP, for example, did not appear to occur in Quebec, where that government had responsibility for both workers' compensation and the Quebec Pension Plan. As stated by Robson (1996: 26): 'The explosion of CPP disability benefits appeared to have been caused by efforts to move beneficiaries of provincial disability benefits onto the more generous CPP benefits. Perhaps revealingly, given the lack of comparable jurisdiction-shifting incentives in Quebec, the QPP has experienced no comparable increase in disability benefits.'

GOVERNMENT RESTRAINT

Pressures for government restraint, especially to reduce the deficit, are also exerting a powerful influence on systems like workers' compensation. Deficits can be reduced only by some combination of tax increases or expenditure reductions. Tax increases will be resisted stringently, especially with respect to payroll taxes, which have increased dramatically in recent years (Abbott and Beach, 1997) and are often regarded as 'killers of jobs' since they initially add to labour costs. That leaves expenditure restraint as the only mechanism. Pressure for expenditure restraint and cost containment is occurring at all phases of the system: health and safety measures and accident prevention to reduce the numbers and severity of the cases coming into the system; vocational and medical rehabilitation, and reasonable accommodation requirements, to facilitate the return to work of injured workers; reductions in indexing and in the magnitude of the benefit payouts; and enhanced efforts to reduce abuses of the system and to increase efficiency in the delivery of services. This pressure has also led to increased attention to market incentives through such mechanisms as experience rating (Kralj, this volume) and the possible privatization of functions (Dewees, this volume).

INTER-JURISDICTIONAL COMPETITION

Perhaps the most subtle but potentially important institutional change that is occurring is inter-jurisdictional competition for business investment and the jobs associated with that investment (Gunderson, 1998a).

Such investment is now more mobile for a variety of reasons. With trade liberalization, businesses can now more easily locate their plants in countries or jurisdictions that impose the lowest regulatory costs, and they can export back into the higher-cost countries. Dramatic reductions in communication and transport costs enable multinationals to coordinate their activities on a global basis, shifting their 'flexible factories' to the lowest-cost areas. They are less tied to specific locations at transport or raw-resource nodes. Financial capital is also more mobile and capable of shifting quickly to the new investment opportunities.

In such circumstances, countries and different jurisdictions within countries are under considerable pressure to compete for such investment and the jobs associated therewith. The competition can occur in the form of reducing the regulatory costs associated with such programs as workers' compensation. In the minds of some, this 'open for business' strategy can lead to a 'race to the bottom' or 'harmonization to the lowest common denominator' as jurisdictions compete for investment by lowering their regulatory and legislative standards in response to the threat of plant-relocation decisions. This is a threat that is now more credible in the new global economy.

In the minds of others, this is normal and healthy competition that is forcing governments and the public to pay attention to the cost consequences of their regulations. Regulations that serve a positive function and provide an efficient public infrastructure will not only survive but thrive. This can be the case with workers' compensation, since the alternative may be a more costly tort system for compensating workplace injuries. Regulations that will be under the greatest pressure to dissipate are those that do not save on costs elsewhere in the system, but rather simply protect the 'economic rents' and privileged positions of those who are able to capture the benefits of policies for their own interests.

While this is not the forum to resolve this important debate, the fact remains that such inter-jurisdictional competition will be a more important force in constraining jurisdictions in the policy arena, including workers' compensation. Canadian provinces will increasingly compare themselves with each other and with US and other jurisdictions that could compete for business investment. It will simply be more difficult to be an 'outlier' with respect to having costly regulations that do not serve other positive functions. More attention will also be placed by government policy makers on 'best practices' that are used in other jurisdictions so as to provide benefits in the most cost-effective fashion.

In addition, more attention will be placed on trying to develop co-operative efforts across political jurisdictions to prevent a 'race to the bottom' with respect to policies serving mutually agreed-upon broad social and equity-oriented rationales that could be jeopardized by inter-jurisdictional competition. The challenge here will be to distinguish these efforts from ones that are pure political rent-seeking, which amount to high-cost jurisdictions imposing their regulations on low-cost jurisdictions as a way of mitigating such competition. Clearly, interesting challenges are being imposed on the political arena in this and other areas.

Implications for Workers' Compensation

The previous discussion highlighted a variety of sources of pressure for change on the workers' compensation system, and illustrated the implications for that system. In this section, a variety of functions and characteristics of the workers' compensation system are set out, with the implications for those functions related back to the changes that are occurring in the new world of work. This necessitates overlap with the previous material, but it does highlight how the pressures for change and the resultant changes are related to specific functions and characteristics of the workers' compensation system.

Demands on the System

Overall demands on the workers' compensation system may increase for a variety of reasons, including increased expenditures associated with an ageing and longer-lived workforce, non-traditional injuries associated with the new workplace, and pressures from integrating family responsibilities with labour-market work. Demands on the system, however, may decrease because of the decline of riskier blue-collar work and the possibility of technological change that can prevent injury and mitigate disability.

Whether overall demands on the system increase or decrease, two things are certain: the demands will be *changing* from those associated with the old world of work; and they will be more *complex*. The complexity comes from a number of factors, including the latency periods of diseases and the difficulty of attributing the cause of an injury or disease (Shainblum, Sullivan, and Frank, this volume). Problems of coverage, information dissemination, administration, and enforcement will also be compounded given the growth of small firms and of non-standard employment and workforce diversity.

The changing and more complex demands place a premium on the system to adapt to the new world of work. This is analogous to the pressures for adaptability that are being faced by businesses and unions in order to survive. The premium on adaptability is further enhanced by the need for cost-effective regulation given the increased competition for business investment and the jobs it brings.

Prevention Measures

Prevention of accidents and diseases has always been regarded as a first line of defence in the workers' compensation system. Better to prevent the problem than to deal with its consequences. While prevention has always been important, the changing environment is likely increasing its significance for a number of reasons.

Pressures to contain costs in the system obviously lead to a focus on the prevention of the problem as a potential cost-effective solution that also has humane consequences. The premium placed on preventative measures is also consistent with the general philosophy in the medical delivery system that considerable system cost can be saved by the devotion of resources to prevention.

Preventative measures are also likely to be better received by both employers and employees. In blue-collar and physically arduous jobs, preventative measures were often associated with expensive and inconvenient alterations in the work environment and in clothing and equipment. Prevention was often not part of the work culture. In the more knowledge-based economy of today, prevention often means more minor alterations in the environment, and can be taught as part of the knowledge base that is a prerequisite for the job. Prevention measures are more likely to be positively received by ageing workers who increasingly are having to think of prevention in other aspects of their lives and lifestyles. As well, the general increased emphasis on health and safety in areas such as lifestyle and consumer protection obviously has spillover effects to the area of occupational health and safety and well-being.

In essence, an emphasis on prevention is likely both to become more important and to have a more receptive audience in the new world of work. It can be a win-win situation, being both a cost-saving and health-saving measure.

Vocational and Medical Rehabilitation

After prevention as a first line of defence in the workers' compensation area, a second line of defence is vocational and medical rehabilitation to facilitate the return to work of injured workers. This too can be a win-win situation, since rehabilitation is both health-improving and can save on system cost by enabling injured workers to return to work.

As indicated previously, this important function will be under competing pressures from the changing work environment. VR issues are likely to be different for an ageing workforce, with rehabilitation times being slower. They are also likely to be different for the growing proportion of females in the workforce. The expected benefit period over which VR costs are amortized is also likely to be changing. It is shorter for older workers, who may not be in the labour force much longer, especially if the trend to early retirement continues. Adjustment issues are also likely to be greater for older workers, if the adjustment experience of injured workers is similar to that of workers who are displaced through mass layoffs or plant closings. In essence, for older workers the VR time may be longer, the adjustment more difficult, and the work-related benefit period shorter. This suggests that attention be paid to early retirement as an alternative to VR, just as early retirement is increasingly taken by a growing portion of the general workforce.

By contrast, longer life expectancy works in the other direction, leading to a longer benefit period over which to amortize the non-work-related benefits of medical rehabilitation. While this aspect does not directly enter as a 'benefit' into the workers' compensation accounts (in the sense of leading to a substantially longer work-related benefit period over which to amortize the costs of VR), it certainly is a benefit for society in general.

The appropriate nature of VR is also changing, as is the appropriate type of training for the new world of work. As job changing becomes more prominent, training for a particular job may be less relevant, with more general training becoming more important. Multi-skilling is more suitable for the multi-tasking and broader job classifications of today, as is team-based training. Increased emphasis in the training area is also being placed on the private sector (as opposed to institutional training) as a viable vehicle for the delivery of training; a similar emphasis may be merited for VR.

Financing

Workers' compensation is financed out of a payroll tax levied on employers. As indicated previously, resistance to such taxes is growing as part of the trend towards government restraint. Tax increases can be political suicide for current governments. The resistance to payroll taxes is especially strong because they have increased so rapidly in recent years and they are often regarded as 'killers of jobs.' Payroll taxes are particularly overt and hence can influence plant location and investment decisions. Governments have to be particularly sensitive to the tax-base and job-creation implications of payroll taxes.

The financing issue is also important given the potential financial and generational equity implications that can arise from the unfunded liabilities of workers' compensation, since these liabilities imply that payments from current generations are being used to finance the benefits of earlier generations who are supported by the system. As the baby-boomers become benefit recipients or retire from the taxpaying base, and a smaller population forms the taxpaying base (also paying for the retirement and health-care expenses of their parents), the impending financial implications becomes even more apparent. Placing an additional tax burden on younger workers will likely be intolerable, and jeopardize the inter-generational social contract that is the foundation of such systems. This in turn can mean subtle cost-saving adjustments on the expenditure side in various forms: tightening eligibility requirements; reduced VR; reduced benefits; increased pressure to return to work and for employers to accommodate that return; reduced retroactive liberalizations and indexing; and increased attempts to shift costs to other systems such as the disability component of CPP or the long-term-disability programs of private employers.

Placing an additional tax burden on new generations of firms will also be difficult. There is little rationale to do so given that they were not responsible for the unfunded liabilities of older failing firms. In essence, older failing firms will not be paying for the full social costs of their production if they leave an unfunded tax liability, just as would be the case if they left a toxic waste deposit. Furthermore, placing an additional tax burden on new firms will be particularly difficult given the inter-jurisdictional and international mobility of such firms. This situation is compounded by the fact that new firms tend to be smaller and their survival is often more sensitive to small cost increases.

The financing issue is also complicated by the fact that empirical evidence suggests that in the long run most of the payroll tax is shifted backwards to workers in the form of lower compensating wages in return for the benefits of the programs financed by the payroll taxes.[14] In the short run, this may lead to unemployment until the wages adjust downwards (realistically, increase more slowly) to absorb the payroll tax. This ability to shift the costs backwards to workers is likely to be more prominent in the new work environment for a number of reasons. It is more difficult to shift the tax forward to consumers since global competition means that they can shift their purchases in response to cost increases. Similarly, under global competition firms have less ability to absorb such cost increases, and the greater mobility of capital means that capital can move to escape the tax. This essentially leaves labour as the immobile factor of production that cannot escape the tax. This is especially true of less-skilled labour since it is the least mobile.

The burden of having the tax shifted backwards to less-skilled labour is compounded by the fact that real wages have been relatively stagnant since the mid-1970s, and low-wage labour has been particularly disadvantaged by the increased wage polarization that has occurred.[15] Any decline in union power and increase in non-standard employment is also likely to further disadvantage this group, making it more difficult for them to ultimately absorb the tax increase.

Coverage of Employers and Employees

Under these circumstances, where increasing the tax *rate* becomes more difficult, increased attention obviously will be placed on increasing the tax *base* – that is, the employers and employees who will be taxed for workers' compensation. This is a potentially important policy instrument since it is subject to a degree of policy control. For example, the proportion of workers covered by workers' compensation ranges from about 65 per cent of the workforce in Manitoba and 70 per cent in Ontario to around 90 per cent in British Columbia and 97 per cent in Quebec (Association of Workers' Compensation Boards of Canada, 1997). Exemptions are usually based on the dimension of occupation or of industry or firm size. Common exemptions include professional athletes, casual or seasonal employees, clergy, domestics, farm labourers, independent truckers, teachers, banks and financial institutions, volunteer/non-profit organizations, and small firms.

Extending coverage to pay for the unfunded liabilities is questionable since the previously uncovered sectors were not responsible for those liabilities. This is similar to adding a surcharge for the unfunded liabilities, since that surcharge will also be borne by new firms that had no part in cumulating the liability, and it will not be paid by old firms that go out of business and are not held responsible for discharging those liabilities. In such circumstances, it would seem most appropriate to pay for the liabilities out of general tax revenues, at least for the liabilities of those firms that are no longer in existence. For firms that are still in existence, the surcharge could be prorated in accordance with the extent to which they contributed to those liabilities. This would be in line with the principle of having the parties pay for the full social costs of their production. These coverage issues will loom larger as the birth and death of firms increase, and as organizations in the growing service sector and employees in non-standard jobs become more subject to the coverage issue than are the old conventional firms in manufacturing.

A policy of extending coverage to expand the tax base also has to confront the issue that expanded coverage will also expand the system's expenditures. It is true that the non-covered sectors are often ones where the risks of occupational injuries and disease are likely to be small (e.g., banks and financial institutions). But that augers for their having a low assessment rate to reflect the low costs they impose on the system. If they are taxed for political expediency (e.g., they can afford the tax and are receiving regulatory rents), then that rationale should be judged on its own merits.

The coverage issue, of course, is important in its own right, in addition to its implication for paying for some of the unfunded liability. Any decision to change the coverage rate should deal with the reasons for exemption from the workers' compensation system in the first place. The next question should then be: have those reasons changed given the changing nature of work and the workforce? Firms that are exempt can 'self-insure' by having their own disability programs or by subcontracting for one. This is typically the case in sectors like banking and financial institutions, where accident rates are low and where there is substantial certainty that the organization can discharge its disability obligations. The self-employed also tend to be exempt, in part because of a moral hazard problem: they have a high degree of control over their disability status. If they are on disability, it is difficult to monitor their self-employment income or work activity.

It is not obvious that these reasons for exemption from coverage have changed dramatically in the new world of work to merit extended coverage. If these jobs become more prominent, then it is true that more people will not be covered by the workers' compensation system. But that is not an automatic argument for expanding the coverage. That argument should be made on its own merits in terms of the pros and cons of workers' compensation, as opposed to other systems, when applied to the new jobs. As discussed, that depends on such factors as the ability to self-insure, and the potential to monitor and control potential abuses in the system. Such abuses will increase the costs to all parties, or reduce the extent to which legitimate users have access to the benefits of the system.

Multicausality and Coverage for Non-Traditional Injuries

Similar issues arise with respect to the policy issue of extending coverage for non-traditional workplace illnesses and diseases such as those related to stress, mental illness, repetitive motion and musculoskeletal injuries. The traditional physical injuries of blue-collar jobs and physical labour are often being displaced by these non-traditional injuries, giving rise to a need to rethink the whole notion of work-related illness and disease.

As outlined in Shainblum, Sullivan, and Frank (this volume) there is growing medical evidence linking health outcomes such as cardiovascular and musculoskeletal disease to socio-economic status, psychosocial factors, and general working conditions. Adverse health outcomes are associated with jobs of high demands, low job control, high stress (often resulting from high demands coupled with low control), monotony, and lack of social support. These job characteristics are emerging in importance, relative to genetic factors and individual lifestyle behaviour, in influencing health.

Demand-control tensions are prevalent in all forms of work, including occupations in the emerging information economy. The 'lower-end' occupations, typically associated with job insecurity, lack of job control, and increasing demands as the number of tasks they are required to perform have been bumped up by downsizing, are often used as illustrative examples of health-threatening demands-control imbalance. However, the 'higher end' professional, technical, and administrative occupations are not immune. The time cruch associated with greater numbers of responsibilities falling on a smaller core staff, who are expected to perform their duties with fewer support personnel, is a reality for the modern manager. Downsizing often results in the spreading of the same number of tasks across fewer remaining persons at all levels of the organization.

Furthermore, as our income increases, we likely will be prepared to devote more resources to illnesses and diseases that are not simply physiological in origin. This is enhanced by the mounting medical evidence that problems that are psychological in origin can manifest themselves in physiological problems such as heart disease. The distinction between physiological and psychological becomes blurred.

Many of the non-traditional injuries and diseases, especially those associated with carcinogens, toxins, and new technology, can have long latency periods before the health consequences become apparent. These can become more important issues to the extent that such carcinogens, toxins, and technologies are more prominent in the workplace, and their impacts are compounded by their increased prevalence outside the work environment.

Strong arguments can be made to extend coverage to these growing numbers of non-traditional injuries and diseases, since their consequences can be just as real as those of traditional injuries. Simply because the consequences cannot be as easily or immediately diagnosed as can a broken arm or leg, it does not mean that the consequences are not severe. A continued emphasis on traditional injuries would appear to be not in keeping with the evolution of the nature of work and the workplace, especially as non-physical labour becomes more important relative to physical labour.

This argument, however, must confront the likelihood that it is more difficult to monitor abuses in cases of non-traditional illnesses and diseases that do not have easily observable physical manifestations. The functional capacities of a person who lost a limb are easier to determine than those of a person who suffers from stress-related conditions, even though the latter can be just as disabling. As a society, we do not like to think that we would deny protection simply because it is difficult to measure the need. Nevertheless, we do this in many areas of social policy. Transfer payments to the poor are often made on the basis of observable measures like income and need as evidenced by family size, and not on the basis of whose well-being would be improved more from the transfer. Wage-loss compensation is based on measured wage-loss, not on loss of general well-being that may differ tremendously across individuals.

In such circumstances, the policy is compelled to rely on observable and measurable outcomes for determining compensation. Determining transfers on the basis of non-measured outcomes, even though they can be more important than the measured ones, would open a 'Pandora's Box' that could jeopardize the system. Either costs would grow considerably or benefits would have to be reduced elsewhere. Although we do not like to admit it, 'bean counting' can be an important component of a fair and effective transfer system. On the other hand, it may well be necessary to open this Pandora's Box, if the system we are saving by keeping it closed becomes unable to serve the needs of growing numbers of workers.

We may want to approach the debate as to how far to extend workers' compensation into non-traditional injuries as a Rawlsian thought experiment where we are in an 'original state' without any knowledge of whether we as individuals may have a traditional or non-traditional injury. Both are equally serious in the sense of reducing our well-being. However, the non-traditional injury is more difficult to verify and monitor. As such, it has the potential to be more subject to abuse. Such abuse would either raise the cost of the system or reduce benefits that are available for the traditional injuries. Clearly, in such a system it is possible for society to 'vote' not to have extensive coverage for the non-traditional injuries, or to limit that coverage to those cases that can more easily be monitored. It may be preferable to take a chance on not having workers' compensation protection for non-traditional injuries rather than to be taxed more extensively to have them covered under workers' compensation. This is not because such injuries are 'frills' or 'not real' or simply 'in the minds of the injured' (they were assumed to be equally serious in this example), but rather because they are difficult and costly to monitor.

This does not mean that such injuries should not be covered. It simply means that in the coverage decision it is legitimate to consider the cost and difficulties of monitoring non-traditional injuries.

Attribution Issues

Workers' compensation is designed to compensate for work-related injuries. Obviously, this approach gives rise to problems of attributing the cause to the workplace. In the case of traditional physical injuries, attribution is made easier by the fact that the injuries were often associated with a specific event – an accident at work. In the case of non-traditional injuries, the attribution issue is obviously more difficult. Stress and repetitive strain injuries can obviously arise from work, the home, commuting from home to work, and from complex interactions from multiple sources. The same attribution problems can arise from toxins, carcinogens, and substances in the workplace and general environment, especially when long latency periods are involved.

These attribution issues are likely to increase in the new work environment for a number of reasons. Non-traditional injuries are becoming more prominent, especially because of the shift from blue-collar to white-collar work. Other contributing factors can include pressures from team production, broader job classifications, pay for performance, downsizing and unemployment, increased workloads owing to downsizing, and reduced union protection. Diseases with long latency periods are more likely to come to fruition in an aging workforce with longer life expectancy. Furthermore, they may not show up until the person has retired from employment. The rise of the two-earner family can lead to stress-related problems associated with managing work and household responsibilities. The increased use of toxins and carcinogens in both the work and general environment can create complex health-related interactions, again with long latency periods. Downsizing and the threat of unemployment can give rise to health-related problems both for those who lose their jobs and for those who retain their jobs, especially where workloads are increased to cover the work of those who have left. The attribution problem can also be exacerbated by greater turnover of employees as they shift among different employers. It can also be enhanced by non-standard employment, multiple job holding, temporary help, and subcontracting among different employers.

Clearly, the attribution issue is becoming more important. This implies difficult policy decisions with respect to the options for dealing with the attribution problem (Shainblum, Sullivan, and Frank, this volume). Increased efforts may have to be devoted to determining the relative contribution of the different sources of injury, although this is technically difficult and can lead to costly adjudication. Alternatively, given the difficulties of such determination, increased attention may have to be paid to the possibility of universal, comprehensive coverage (sometimes termed '24-hour coverage') that does not make a distinction between work-related and non-work-related injuries and diseases. This can reduce duplication and adjudication over attribution; however, it may require careful monitoring to prevent abuses, and it may necessitate a trade-off of reduced benefits for expanded coverage to control costs. Whatever the pros and cons of that system, it becomes potentially more relevant in the new world of work with its non-traditional injuries, multicausality, long latency periods, monitoring difficulties, and attribution problems. Increased emphasis may also be merited on more general policies pertaining to workplace well-being that are integrated with general health and lifestyle issues. Examples include health clubs and employee well-being programs at the place of employment.

If the attribution problem cannot be solved, and comprehensive, universal coverage with a greater emphasis on workplace well-being turns out to be infeasible, then the default option may be to simply accept that workers' compensation may not be able to deal with all problems that *theoretically* merit compensation, but for which the *practical* implementation problems are too difficult to master, at least under the current state of knowledge.

Substitute and Complementary Programs

The integration of workers' compensation with other substitute and complementary programs will also take on increased importance in the new world of work. As indicated previously, as these other programs such as UI are restricted, there may be an increased use of workers' compensation as a means of providing income support. Conversely, if workers' compensation becomes more restricted, there may be a substitution into other programs such as the disability component of CPP, general welfare, or private disability insurance.

Other programs and policies can be complementary to many functions of workers' compensation. A full-employment economy can reduce the fraudulent use of workers' compensation to maintain income. It can also facilitate the return to work of injured workers, as can reasonable accommodation requirements. Control of the unfunded liabilities under other pay-as-you-go systems such as CPP will reduce the need to deal with unfunded liabilities under workers' compensation. Improved health and safety measures and an emphasis on workplace well-being can be a preventative substitute for workers' compensation.

Considering these substitute and complementary policies is important for a variety of reasons. Many of these policies are under review and being made more stringent, thus increasing the likelihood that workers' compensation will be used to fill any vacuum. The same applies, of course, to restrictions on workers' compensation, which can lead to pressures for substitution into other programs like CPP disability or private disability programs or for more extensive accommodation requirements on employers. Increased inter-jurisdictional competition can lead to greater efficiency in regulations, but it can also lead to a 'race to the bottom' that only cooperation can overcome. Furthermore, real resources are used up as administrators respond to incentives to shift costs to other programs or levels of government. Such resources might be better spent compensating workers or providing benefits elsewhere in the system.

Concluding Observations

Table 2.1 summarizes the different pressures that are affecting the workers' compensation system, and illustrates some implications for various workers' compensation issues. Table 2.2 summarizes the range of functions of workers' compensation and highlights how those functions are being affected by the changing nature of work. Virtually all aspects of the system are being affected.

The demands on the system are changing rapidly and becoming more complex. Preventative measures are not only becoming more important, but they are also being accepted by a more receptive audience. Both the benefits and costs of vocational and medical rehabilitation are being affected, especially by the aging workforce. As well, the requirements of the changing work environment are for training that is more general, multi-skilled, team-based, and possibly provided through the private sector. Financing the system is under pressure from increased resistance to payroll taxes, concerns over the unfunded liabilities, and the negative ramifications of the costs being shifted back to workers who are under the burden of stagnant real wages and growing wage inequality.

Temptations clearly exist to expand the coverage of employers and employees, especially to help finance the unfunded liabilities. This raises issues of the fairness of such a 'tax grab' as well as the possibility of coverage expansion being a false economy if it expands the number of non-traditional injuries that are covered. The coverage issue should be decided on its own merits, that is, on the basis of whether the rationales for exclusion are relevant to the new world of work.

TABLE 2.1
Pressures for change and implications for workers' compensation

Source of pressure for change	Illustrative implications for workers' compensation (WC)
Nature of workforce	
Aging workforce and increased life expectancy	• Composition of claims towards older workers • Increase in claims costs • Financial burden of unfunded liability on future generations • VR geared to older workers • Return to work adjustments more difficult • Integration issues with CPP and other age-related programs • Latency periods more of an issue
Increased labour-force participation of women; dominance of two-earner family	• Stress issues related to balancing work and family
Ethnic and other diversity	• Information problems associated with language
Nature of workplace	
Technological change	• Non-traditional disease and injuries • New cures and opportunities for reasonable accommodation
Industrial restructuring from manufacturing to services	• Coverage issues • Changing nature of injuries and diseases
Growth of small firms	• Coverage issues • Information and monitoring problems and difficulties with return to work and reasonable accommodation
Birth and death of firms	• Unfunded liabilities of old firms transferred to new firms
Downsizing	• Stress from threat or reality of layoffs • Increased workload on remaining employees
Workplace practices	
Broader job classifications	• Problem of attributing source of injury • Unfamiliarity with range of hazards • VR more demanding if multi-skilling required
Flattening of organizational structures	• Reduced supervision re H&S issues
Pay for performance	• Enhanced stress and reduced attention to H&S, although these can be incorporated into performance requirements

TABLE 2.1 – concluded
Pressures for change and implications for workers' compensation

Source of pressure for change	Illustrative implications for workers' compensation (WC)
Just-in-time delivery	• Job stress and cutting corners on safety
Employee involvement	• Focus for information and responsibility and potential to integrate H&S into quality emphasis
Workplace teams	• Potential focus for information dissemination • Possible tendency to not report injuries • Pressure on team if covering for injured worker
Non-standard employment	• Enhances problems of coverage, attributing source of injury, disseminating information, assigning accommodation requirements
Workplace institutions Union retrenchment	• Jeopardizing union role in information, protection against reprisals, representing employees, VR, reasonable accommodation, and return to work • May lead to unions focusing on service issues in area
Substitute laws and policies	• Restrictions on other policies like UI can induce reallocation to WC • Pressure also to reallocate off WC and onto other programs like CPP and private disability insurance
Government restraint	• Resistance to increased payroll taxes • Pressure for expenditure restraint through accident prevention, VR, reasonable accommodation, benefit restraint, and system efficiency
Inter-jurisdictional competition for investment and jobs	• More attention to the cost consequences of WC and to the practices in other jurisdictions • Pressure for harmonization and for cost-effective delivery • Pressure for cooperation

Pressure also exists for extended coverage of non-traditional injuries that are increasing dramatically in the new world of work. Such injuries are often characterized by long latency periods, multiple causes, complex interactions, and difficulties in measuring and attributing their cause. The attribution problem is becoming more difficult given the increase in non-traditional injuries, as well as other changes such as team production, broader job classifications, pay for performance, downsizing, non-standard employment, job turnover, and pressures

TABLE 2.2
Function of WC and implications of pressure for change

Function of WC	Implication of pressure for change
Demands on the system	• Increase demands from ageing workforce and non-traditional injuries • Reduced demands from decline of riskier blue-collar work • Changing and more complex demands associated with latency periods, multicausality, attribution problems, non-traditional injuries as well as small firms, non-standard employment, diversity, and jurisdictional competition
Preventative measures	• Premium on prevention as both cost-saving and health-saving • Greater receptivity for prevention in medical community and among knowledge-based industries and ageing workforce
Vocational and medical rehabilitation	• Shorter benefit period and higher VR and other costs for ageing workforce • New workplace may require different VR that is more general, multi-skilling, team-based, and applied through the private sector
Financing	• Increased resistance to payroll taxes • Unfunded liabilities burden on future generations and new firms, possibly jeopardizing the implicit social contract and leading to future subtle benefit reductions • Cost-shifting back to workers more likely, but creates difficulties given stagnant real wages and greater wage inequality
Coverage of employers and employees	• Temptation to extend coverage to pay for unfunded liability confronts issues of fairness and possible new expenditures • Unclear that rationales for exemptions have changed in new world of work; coverage issue should be made on own merits
Coverage for non-traditional injuries	• Non-traditional injuries increasing in new world of work • Often characterized by long latency periods, multiple causes, complex interactions, and difficulties in 'measuring' • Legitimate need to cover must confront difficulties of monitoring and attribution that are similarly faced in other transfer programs and that often lead to reduced coverage
Attribution problems	• Greater difficulty in attributing source of injury for non-traditional injuries with their long latency periods, multiple causes, complex interactions, and difficulties in 'measuring'

TABLE 2.2 – concluded
Function of WC and implications of pressure for change

Function of WC	Implication of pressure for change
	• Difficulties exacerbated by team production, broader job classifications, pay for performance, downsizing, non-standard employment, job turnover, and pressures from two-earner families.
	• Policy implications include more attention to the attribution issue, to 24-hour coverage, and to the possibility that attribution problems make coverage impractical in certain areas
Substitute and complementary programs	• Greater pressure to substitute into other programs given program cutbacks and inter-jurisdictional competition
	• Pressure both ways (e.g., UI into WC; WC into CPP or private disability)
	• Greater emphasis also on complementary policies such as full employment, reasonable accommodation under human rights, controlling unfunded liabilities under other pay-as-you-go systems like CPP, and workplace well-being in general

from two-earner families. The attribution problem suggests that more attention must be paid to the possibility of 24-hour coverage, which does not require attributing the cause to specific events at the workplace. It also suggests, in the opposite direction, that the practical problems of attribution and monitoring may make it impractical to cover many non-traditional injuries. Such practical problems constrain other social policies where it is theoretically appropriate but impractical to provide compensation.

More policy attention must also be paid to the relationship between workers' compensation and other substitute and complementary programs. The changing pressures are creating incentives both ways, for example, to substitute from UI to WC, and to substitute from WC to CPP disability or private disability coverage. The burden on workers' compensation could also be reduced by complementary policies such as full employment, reasonable accommodation under human rights, control of unfunded liabilities under other pay-as-you-go systems such as CPP, and attention to workplace well-being issues in general.

Clearly, there are a wide range of important and controversial policy issues that have to be dealt with in this area. Virtually all aspects of workers' compensation are being affected by the changing nature of work in all of its dimensions – the workforce, the workplace, workplace practices, and workplace institutions. Responding to these changes is crucial to ensure the survival of cherished programs like workers' compensation.

NOTES

1 See Appelbaum and Batt (1994), Betcherman, McMullen, Leckie, and Caron (1994), and Gunderson and Riddell (1996).
2 For more detail see Hyatt (1995), Chaykowski and Thomason (1995), Shainblum, Sullivan, and Frank (this volume), and Thomason, Vaillancourt, Bogyo, and Stritch (1995).
3 The implications of this aging population for public expenditures and economic dependency are discussed in Foot (1989).
4 The labour-force participation rate of women increased from 29 per cent in 1961 to 60 per cent in 1991, approaching the 70 per cent participation rate of men in 1991. As such, women made up about 45 per cent of the workforce in 1991 (Gunderson, 1996b).
5 Dual-earner families increased from 33 per cent of husband-wife families in 1967 to 60 per cent in 1994, while the proportion of families where the husband was the sole earner went from 58 per cent to 18 per cent over that same period (Statistics Canada, 1994).
6 Johnston and Packer (1987) and Taylor (1995a, 1995b).
7 Gunderson and Hyatt (1998), for example, indicate that the industrial restructuring that is forecasted to occur in British Columbia between the years 2000 and 2005 should lead to system cost savings of around 20 per cent, since the restructuring will be from industries with high injuries and assessment rates to ones of lower injuries and assessment rates.
8 For a detailed discussion of these conditions and their implications for the future of workers' compensation, see Shainblum, Sullivan, and Frank (this volume).
9 Annual net job creation in the early 1990s was 3.3 per cent in firms of zero to 19 employees, declining steadily as firm size increases, and being almost zero in large firms of 500 and more employees (Picot, Baldwin, and Dupuy, 1994).
10 Catalano (1991), D'Arcy (1986), D'Arcy and Sidduque (1985), Grayson (1989), Jin, Shaw, and Svoboda (1995), Shainblum, Sullivan, and Frank (this volume).

11 Pauler and Lewko (1984).

12 A *Wall Street Journal* article (20 May 1998: A1, A6) described the problems that were arising with work teams at the Levi Strauss plants in the United States, indicating that 'Team Members could be merciless to injured colleagues ... Co-workers called them 'fakers' and heckled them.'

13 For an excellent review of the role of unions and collective bargaining in supporting health and safety, see Schurman, Weil, Landsbergis, and Isreal (1998).

14 For reviews of this evidence see Dahlby (1993), DiMateo and Shannon (1995), Dungan (this volume), and Kesselman (1996). Gunderson and Hyatt (1996) provide similar evidence for the costs of reasonable-accommodation requirements for injured workers who return to work to an employer other than the employer where the accident occurred.

15 Beach (1995) and Morissett, Myles, and Picot (1995).

REFERENCES

Abbott, M., and C. Beach. 1997. 'The Impact of Employer Payroll Taxes on Employment and Wages: Evidence for Canada, 1970–1993.' In M. Abbott, C. Beach, and R. Chaykowski, eds, *Transition and Structure Change in the North American Labour Market*, 154–204. Kingston: IRC Press.

Applebaum, E., and R. Batt. 1994. *The New American Workplace*. Ithaca: ILR Press.

Association of Workers' Compensation Boards of Canada. 1997. *Workers' Compensation Industry Classification, Assessment Rates and Experience Rating Programs in Canada*. Edmonton.

Beach, C. 1995. *Are We Becoming Two Societies?: Income Polarization and the Middle Class in Canada*. Toronto: C.D. Howe Institute.

Betcherman, G., K. McMullen, N. Leckie, and C. Caron. 1994. *The Canadian Workplace in Transition*. Kingston: IRC Press.

Catalono, R. 1991. 'The Health Effects of Economic Insecurity.' *American Journal of Public Health* 81(9): 1148–52.

Chaykowski, R., and T. Thomason. 1995. 'Canadian Workers' Compensation: Institutions and Economics.' In T. Thomason and R. Chaykowski, eds, *Research in Canadian Workers' Compensation*, 1–42. Kingston: IRC Press.

Dahlby, B. 1993. 'Payroll Taxes.' In A. Maslove, ed., *Business Taxation in Ontario*, Toronto: University of Toronto Press.

D'Arcy, C. 1986. 'Unemployment and Health.' *Canadian Journal of Public Health* 77: 124–31.

D'Arcy, C., and C.M. Sidduque. 1985. 'Unemployment and Health: An Analysis of the Canadian Health Survey.' *International Journal of Health Services* 15(4): 609–35.

DiMatteo, L., and M. Shannon. 1995. 'Payroll Taxation in Canada: An Overview.' *Canadian Business Economics* 3(4): 5–22.

Foot, D. 1989. 'Public Expenditures, Population Aging and Economic Dependency in Canada, 1923–2021.' *Population Research and Policy Review* 8: 97–117.

Fortin, B., and P. Lanoie. 1992. 'Substitution between Unemployment Insurance and Workers' Compensation.' *Journal of Public Economics* 49: 287–312.

Grayson, J.P. 1985. 'The Closure of a Factory and Its Impact on Health.' *International Journal of Health Services* 15(1): 69–93.

Grayson, J.P. 1989. 'Reported Illness from the CGE Closure.' *Canadian Journal of Public Health* 80(1): 16–19.

Gunderson, M. 1998a. 'Harmonization of Labour Policies under Free Trade.' *Relations Industrielles / Industrial Relations* 53(1): 24–54.

– 1998b. *Women in the Canadian Labour Market*. Toronto: Nelson.

Gunderson, M., and D. Hyatt. 1996. 'Do Injured Workers Pay for Reasonable Accommodation?' *Industrial and Labor Relations Review* 50: 92–104.

– 1998. 'Workforce and Workplace Changes: Implications for Injuries and Compensation.' Report to the BC Royal Commission on Workers' Compensation. Vancouver.

Gunderson, M., and C. Riddell. 1996. 'The Changing Nature of Work: Implications for Public Policy.' Ottawa: Institute for Research on Public Policy.

Hyatt, D. 1995. 'Workers' Compensation in Canada: An Overview.' Vol. 5 of *Unfolding Change: Workers' Compensation in Canada*. Toronto: Liberty International Canada.

Jin, R., C. Shaw, and T. Svoboda. 1995. 'The Impact of Unemployment on Health: A Review of the Evidence.' *Canadian Medical Association Journal* 153: 529–40.

Johnston, W., and A. Packer. 1987. *Workforce 2000: Work and Workers for the Twenty-First Century*. Indianapolis: Hudson Institute.

Kesselman, J. 1996. 'Payroll Taxes and the Financing of Social Security.' *Canadian Public Policy* 22: 162–79.

Krahn, H. 1995. 'Non-standard Work on the Rise.' *Perspectives on Labour and Income* 7 (Winter): 35–42.

Morissette, R., J. Myles, and G. Picot. 1995. 'Earnings Polarization in Canada, 1969–1991.' In K. Banting and C. Beach, eds, *Labour Market Polarization and Social Policy Reform*, 23–50. Kingston: Queen's University School of Policy Studies.

Office of Superintendent of Financial Institutions. 1995. *Canada Pension Plan Fifteenth Actuarial Report*. Ottawa: Supply and Services.

Organization for Economic Cooperation and Development. 1996. *Aging in OECD Countries*. Paris: OECD.

Pauler, K., and J. Lewko. 1984. 'Children's Worries and Exposure to Unemployment.' *Canada's Mental Health* (September): 14–18.

Peron, Y., and C. Strohmenger. 1994. *Demographic and Health Indicator*. Ottawa: Statistics Canada Catalogue 82-543.

Picot, G., J. Baldwin, and R. Dupuy. 1994. 'Have Small Firms Created a Disproportionate Share of New Jobs in Canada?: A Reassessment of the Facts.' Ottawa: Statistics Canada, Analytical Studies Branch.

Riddell, C. 1993. 'Unionization in Canada and the United States.' In D. Card and R. Freeman, eds, *Small Differences That Matter: Labor Markets and Income Maintenance in Canada and the United States*, 109–48. Chicago: University of Chicago Press.

Robson, W. 1996. 'Putting Some Gold in the Golden Years: Fixing the Canada Pension Plan.' *C.D. Howe Institute Commentary* 76: 1–28.

Schurman, S., D. Weil, P. Landsbergis, and B. Israel. 1998. 'The Role of Unions and Collective Bargaining in Preventing Work-Related Disability.' In T. Thomason, J.F. Burton Jr, and D. Hyatt, eds, *New Approaches to Disability in the Workplace*, 121–45. Ithaca: Cornell University Press.

Statistics Canada. 1994. *Characteristics of Dual Earner Families*. Ottawa: Statistics Canada Catalogue 13-215.

Taylor, C. 1995a. *Dimensions of Diversity in Canadian Business: Building a Business Case for Ethnocultural Diversity*. Ottawa: Conference Board.

– 1995b. 'Building a Business Case for Diversity.' *Canadian Business Review* 22: 12–15.

Thomason, T., F. Vaillancourt, T. Bogyo, and A. Stritch. 1995. *Chronic Stress: Workers' Compensation in the 1990s*. Toronto: C.D. Howe Institute.

3 Multicausality, Non-traditional Injury, and the Future of Workers' Compensation

ESTHER SHAINBLUM, TERRENCE SULLIVAN, and JOHN W. FRANK[1]

Systems of workers' compensation are intended to compensate victims of all workplace injuries without regard to fault. Under most workers' compensation legislation, an injury or disease must be caused by the employee's work if it is to be compensable. However, the seemingly simple question of factual causation is becoming increasingly problematic in view of what we are learning about disease. We are beginning to understand that disease is multifactorial, emanating from a multitude of possible causes, including work. Recent evidence demonstrates that the working environment exerts a powerful influence on health and that a broad range of diseases – even those not traditionally attributed to work – have a work-related component. Existing mechanisms for determining entitlement to workers' compensation may no longer be sustainable in light of the growing scientific evidence showing that multiple factors contribute to disease, and given the rise of 'non-traditional' diseases and injuries with a work-related attribution.

The manner in which the multicausal nature of disease is commonly expressed is to assess the additional risk imposed upon, for example, pneumoconiosis or mesothelioma, by smoking behaviour. This type of analysis recognizes the different factors both in and outside of the workplace associated with disease. In contrast, a number of modern studies suggest that the structure and nature of work, including job strain, appear to have pervasive effects on health and ill health, and that a number of prevalent conditions can be shown to have some work-related attribution.

It is not our intention in this paper to explore the many social, political, and discursive factors that underpin and influence the meaning and history of occupational disease. Others have told this story well

(Dembe, 1995). Rather, this paper deals more narrowly with the question of whether current public policy arrangements for determining entitlement to workers' compensation are sustainable, given that a range of diseases can now be shown to have a work-related component. We examine in particular back pain and heart disease, two common conditions that have clear risk attributable to work.

Origins of Workers' Compensation

Today's workers' compensation systems are the embodiment of a historic bargain struck between workers and their employers. In exchange for receiving guaranteed no-fault benefits whenever they suffer a work-related injury, workers have relinquished the right to sue their employers for damages for the harms they suffer. In return for being spared costly, uncertain, and time-consuming litigation, employers have agreed to forego the opportunity to attempt to avoid payment of compensation.

This trade-off, or 'social contract,' between workers and employers evolved in direct response to the 'paradox of ever-increasing industrial injuries and ever-decreasing judicial remedies for them' (Larson, 1952: 223) that were the hallmark of the industrial revolution. Historically, injured workers possessed only one potential remedy for injuries suffered at work – an action in tort against their employer (Tarpley and Jagmin, 1982: 188). Employers, by contrast, have always been relatively well equipped in terms of both means and legal defences. Employers could also invoke an 'unholy trinity of defences' (Tarpley and Jagmin, 189) that easily allowed them to evade liability for harm to workers at common law and under early employers' liability legislation in Canada, the United Kingdom and the United States. Employers could assert that a worker had been injured through his or her own negligence (contributory negligence) or through the negligence of a fellow worker (the fellow servant rule) – thus defeating any negligence on the part of the employer itself – or the employer could argue that the worker had voluntarily assumed the risks of employment and was thus barred from redress (Tarpley and Jagmin, 197–201; Larson, 1952: 226–8). This arrangement seems to have been constructed upon considerations of expediency and laissez-faire economic thought (Larson, 223). One author notes, 'One need not be a keen student of nineteenth century English history to sense that the servant did not bargain at arms' length with his master; that there was a dearth of jobs and a surfeit of labor; and that the hazards and risks of railroad, mine and factory were not fully disclosed to the servant by the master' (Tarpley and Jagmin, 191–2).

Judicial opinion nevertheless continued to weigh in favour of employers, even in the face of the 'industrial slaughter' (Tarpley and Jagmin, 198) that was taking place at the time. Workers were left remediless in the vast majority of cases (Larson, 224–5).

Ultimately, public opinion was galvanized against the injustice of the pre-compensation situation and workers' compensation legislation, as we currently understand it, was enacted. Germany was the first jurisdiction to enact workers' compensation legislation in 1884, followed by England thirteen years later (Larson, 229). In 1914, Ontario passed its first such legislation (R.S.O. 1914, c. 146) and all Canadian provinces had enacted workers' compensation legislation by 1950 (Ison, 1989: 1). Workers' compensation laws went into place in the American states between 1920 and 1949 (Tarpley and Jagmin, 202).

Modern workers' compensation legislation arose in response to the failure of negligence law to deal with the human toll taken by the industrial revolution. By compensating victims of all workplace injuries without regard to fault, workers' compensation ensures that victims of work-related harm are no longer left remediless, and that 'the cost of the product bears the blood of the working man' (Tarpley and Jagmin, 196, citing Lloyd George). These are the philosophical foundations underlying workers' compensation legislation.

Workers' compensation usually includes both ameliorative expenditures – that is, disability benefits – and corrective expenditures – that is, promoting rehabilitation, restoring earning capacity, and getting people back to work (Aarts and de Jong, 1996). In Canada, as in many other countries, the workers' compensation system takes the form of social insurance. Coverage is generally compulsory and the system is financed, at least in the initial instance, by employer contributions – based on the type of business each employer operates – that are gathered into a common accident fund (Gilbert et al., 1995; Ison, 1989). In this way, the costs of industrial injuries are shifted in part to consumers in the form of higher product prices (Larson, 1952: 206; Tarpley and Jagmin, 1982: 196), and they may also be shifted back to workers in the form of lower wages in return for the benefit of workers' compensation protection. With respect to the ten Canadian jurisdictions for which figures are available, approximately 84 per cent of the labour force is covered by workers' compensation (Association of Workers' Compen-

sation Boards of Canada, 1996).[2] The remainder of labour force participants must either forego coverage or are required to turn to private
insurance.

Causation in Workers' Compensation

Workers' compensation systems share the key requirement that the
injury suffered by the employee must be work-related if the worker is
to be compensated. Workers' compensation is a cause-based system of
compensation – one in which payment of benefits depends on the
cause of the injury (Ison, 1994: 3). In Ontario, this limitation is summed
up by the legislative requirement, similar to those in other jurisdictions, that a worker must suffer a 'personal injury by accident arising
out of and in the course of employment' in order to be entitled to benefits (R.S.O. 1990, c. W. 11, s. 4(1); Gilbert et al., 1995: 13). Thus, in order
for an injury or disease to be compensable under a system of workers'
compensation, it must have arisen 'out of and in the course of employment.' This coverage formula imports issues of factual causation into
workers' compensation regimes in an analogous manner to the investigation of causation carried out in common-law personal-injury actions
(Joseph, 1983: 283). The 'out of and in the course of employment' concept may have been intended to move compensation issues away from
tort law concepts such as proximate cause, which tended to limit
employer's liability, in favour of a formula perhaps less tied to the old
tort system (Vinson, 1996: 756–61).

One author has distilled the rather vague requirement expressed by
'arising out of and in the course of' into a single question – 'Was there a
work-connected injury?' (Larson, 1952: 208). This deceptively simple
formulation, however, is based upon the assumption that a direct
causal relationship between work and injury will always be perceptible. As we shall see, this is not always the case.

Furthermore, the 'arising out of' question may conflate questions of
what actually happened with who ought to pay for it, hiding a question of policy behind a veneer of fact (Vinson, 1996: 739–46).

In cases of acute physical injury resulting from the workplace, the
causal connection between work and harm is quite likely to be readily
apparent. If a hand has been mangled by machinery, a worker has
fallen from a scaffold or been burned by a welder, or a foreign object
has entered an eye, the causal connection is quite clear. In such cases
involving objective, finite, physical trauma or acute pathophysiology,

occurring at a specific place and at a definite moment in time, with unequivocal onset and rapidly resulting in an immediate impact on the worker, there is little room for debate as to causation. These events establish the prima facie case that the injury arose 'out of employment' – that is, the nature or character of the employment was the origin or cause of the injury (Gilbert et al., 1995: 17) – and that it arose 'in the course of employment' – that is, the time, place, and circumstances of the injury were at least reasonably incidental to the employment (Gilbert et al., 18; Sullivan, 1980: 1387).

Given the rapid process of industrialization under way at the time when most workers' compensation legislation was passed, as well as the nature of the work then being carried out in the factories, mills, and mines, policy makers were probably preoccupied with the most prevalent hazards of the day. The drafters of such legislation likely had in mind extending coverage to bona fide victims of the new technology of the machine age (Vinson, 1996: 756–7). Workers' compensation systems were initially conceived primarily in terms of compensating workers for acute injuries sustained in the workplace, and so the requirement of a causal link between the work and the injury did not pose much of a problem.

Similarly, with respect to the coverage of disease, it was originally contemplated that workers' compensation should not turn into a general sick-pay scheme and that coverage should be restricted to diseases that were specific to industry and did not normally result from other causes (Ison, 1989: 39).

This historical assumption, that we can always make these sorts of etiological classifications, stands in stark contrast to the reality that it is not always possible to determine that a particular condition has resulted from an identifiable event or originated exclusively in the workplace. Moreover, a caused-based system like workers' compensation runs into difficulty when it encounters multicausality. As Ison states: 'In particular, it is notoriously difficult to establish etiology in most cases of permanent disablement from disease, in bad back cases, or in many others involving sprains, strains, heart attacks or strokes, and in some cases of dental damage' (1994: 4–5).

The historical concept of causation that underlies workers' compensation legislation originated in a world where workers performed heavy labour in hazardous conditions, and tended to suffer from 'hard' injuries such as lacerations, broken bones, or severed limbs. While such injuries have not entirely disappeared, the workplace and the nature of work itself have undergone transformations. Technology has replaced hard labour, service industries now employ more people than does the manufacturing sector, new methods of organization and production have altered workers' traditional roles, and there has been a transition from premature death arising from infectious disease to longer life and chronic disabling conditions. Both firms and workers feel the pressures of competitive trade. The changing workplace is reflected in the growing prevalence of soft-tissue and repetitive-motion injuries among workers, diseases of unknown or imprecise etiology, long latency periods, and insidious onset,[3] as well as mental illness and stress.

Yet, despite the transition from the unequivocal conditions of the old world of work to those associated with the new competitive order for which workers tend to be compensated today, and despite our growing understanding of the pervasive role played by occupation and socio-economic status in the causation of disease, workers' compensation systems continue to view causation in the traditional linear sense.

The next portion of this paper will address the issue of socio-economic status and occupational position and their important role in disease causation.

Socio-economic Status and Health

There is, as noted above, a great deal of evidence to suggest a powerful connection between health and the social and physical environment. In particular, the correlation between social status and health is well established. Higher-status individuals live longer and healthier lives than lower-status people. This pattern, which begins at birth and yields lifelong effects on health and well-being, indicates that a series of life events and conditions has a cumulative effect on health, well-being, and mortality (Hertzman, 1994).

For instance, low status at birth can lead to lack of readiness for schooling, which in turn may lead to behavioural problems and low achievement at school, low levels of well-being in adulthood, and work in high-strain (high demand / low control) jobs, resulting in absenteeism and health problems and, eventually, in early death (Hertzman, 1994). Higher-status children seem to be at least partially protected from the long-term consequences of negative exposures such as birth stresses (Hertzman, Frank, and Evans, 1994)[4] and environmental lead (Hertzman, 1994).

Literate people experience lower levels of dementia and mental decline in later life than do illiterate or less-educated people, indicating that there are critical periods of brain development that, if capitalized on, will enhance development and provide a lifetime protective effect (Hertzman, 1994).

There is also a strong association between birth weight and weight gain in the first year of life and the risk of death from heart disease later in life (Hertzman, 1994). Low birth weight, particularly in males, has also been shown to be associated with overcrowding and adverse conditions in childhood and with lower social-class status in adulthood (Power and Bartley, 1996). Therefore, birth weight seems to be a marker for subsequent socio-economic circumstances, which will continue to differ, depending on birth weight, well into later life (ibid.).

Height in adult life, which reflects levels of nutrition in the growing years, including the fetal period, is inversely associated with risk of chronic disease and mortality, indicating that early life environment has strong health consequences in adult life (Frank and Mustard, 1994; Marmot, Smith, et al., 1991). Stress in infancy and childhood can reduce physical growth as well as affecting stress responses and social functioning, with consequential effects on health, occupational mobility, and emotional well-being (Wilkinson, 1996). Thus, taller people tend to be healthier as well as more upwardly mobile, reflecting not a genetic advantage, but rather, the effect of environmental influences in early childhood (ibid.).

Tobacco addiction, with its lifetime health consequences, also typically commences in childhood (Evans and Stoddart, 1994), indicating that powerful influences exerted early in life can affect adult lifestyle and behaviour, often with significant health effects. Therefore, social status is a powerful determinant of an individual's lifetime health expectations.

In adulthood, social class is a good predictor of mortality in industrialized nations. Different countries with different primary causes of death all show an inverse association between social class and mortality (Marmot, Kogevinas, and Elston, 1987) and between social class and health outcomes across a range of conditions studied (Kaplan, 1996). All-cause mortality and morbidity rates decrease as one moves up the socio-economic scale. This inverse relationship does not appear to be a factor of less-healthy individuals sliding down the socio-economic ladder (the reverse-causality argument), it extends to a broad range of conditions including heart disease, arthritis, back problems, cancer, and others (Anderson and Armstead, 1995); and it does not appear to be simply associated with 'unhealthy lifestyles.'

The latter view, which tends to place responsibility on individuals for their own illnesses, is not supported by the evidence, which shows that, even after controlling for lifestyle risk factors such as smoking, weight, and blood-pressure and cholesterol levels, the social gradient in heart-disease deaths persists to the detriment of people working in lower-status occupational groups. Only a small fraction of the persisting gradient can be explained by known risk factors associated with lifestyle (Wilkinson, 1996; Rose and Marmot, 1981). In fact, occupational status is a greater risk predictor of dying from heart disease than any of the conventional lifestyle risk factors (Rose and Marmot, 1981). In other words, higher status people live longer and are healthier through their lives than lower-status people.

Differences in access to health care do not account for this difference in health outcomes, as the gradient persists in countries that have universal health coverage (Anderson and Armstead, 1995).

Various life circumstances closely tied to socio-economic status have a profound impact on individuals' health expectations. Residence in a poverty area in the United States and Canada has been found to be independently associated with an elevated risk of death, after controlling for other individual risk factors (Kaplan, 1996; Premier's Council on Health Strategy, 1991).[5] This association may be attributable to any number of factors, including environmental exposures (Anderson and Armstead, 1995), the strain of living in an area of high demand – having to deal with daily challenges such as crime (Kaplan, 1996), grinding work, and financial and other problems. Residential choices are clearly more limited for people lower down the socio-economic ladder (Anderson and Armstead, 1995).

Work insecurity and periods of unemployment among young men have also been found to be associated with increased self-reporting of poorer general health – elevated numbers reporting their health as 'poor' or 'fair,' rather than 'good' or 'excellent' (Bartley, Montgomery, et al., 1996) – which, in turn, has been found to be a powerful predictor of mortality (ibid.).

Furthermore, even though the principal causes of death have changed over time and general life expectancy has improved since the beginning of the century, class inequality in mortality has not been reduced in the latter half of the century (Marmot, Kogevinas, and Elston, 1987). Moreover, this inequality does not merely affect extremes of rich and poor, with the worst health effects being clustered at the lowest end of the scale (Marmot, Smith, et al., 1991). Rather, these class differences in health status are manifested at all levels of the social hierarchy, so that mortality in each class is lower than in the classes above, but higher than in those below.

The pattern of an increase in morbidity and mortality with each drop in social class is most clearly illustrated by the Whitehall studies of thousands of British civil servants. The first Whitehall study, commenced in 1967 and followed up over a ten-year period, showed that office workers in the highest employment category had about one-third of the mortality of office workers in the lowest category (Marmot, Smith, et al., 1991). In Whitehall II, conducted twenty years later, these socio-economic differences in health status persisted, and the same clear inverse relationship between social class – as assessed by employment grade – and absenteeism, due to sickness from a wide range of diseases, was demonstrated (ibid.).[6] With each slip down the employment grade, the higher the morbidity rates.

In general, Whitehall II showed that office workers in lower-status jobs had a higher prevalence of ischemic heart disease (Marmot, Smith, et al., 1991). There was a difference between employment grades in the prevalence of chronic bronchitis, with nearly twice as many in the lowest grade suffering from chronic cough as in the highest (ibid.).

In addition, behavioural and biological risk factors also seemed to follow a similar pattern in relation to occupational position. The study showed a strong inverse relationship between smoking and job status, with a higher prevalence of smoking among women than men in most job categories. Obesity in men was more prevalent in lower-status jobs, and physical exercise was less prevalent. Consumption of a healthier diet was more common in higher-status jobs (Marmot, Smith, et al., 1991). However, once again, separating out the risk factors associated with 'unhealthy lifestyle,' by controlling for smoking and obesity for example, only minimally reduces the risk differences between occupational levels (Wilkinson, 1996; Rose and Marmot, 1981). The persistence of these differences in health status between occupational levels, even after controlling for lifestyle factors, implies that a broader set of factors are at play here, going beyond simple considerations of personal choice, and that these broader factors act to mediate occupational differences in health.

A strong inverse relationship between job status and rates of absence for sickness, which is used as a measure of ill health (North et al., 1993), was also documented in the Whitehall studies, with higher absence rates in employees of lower status. This may be attributable, at least in part, to self-perceived health status, which tended to be worse in the lower employment grades and is also a predictor of mortality (North et al., 1993). An association has also been found between job status and concentrations of plasma fibrinogen, a possible risk factor for cardiovascular disease. Fibrinogen concentration was found to be higher among men in lower employment grades, and it has been suggested that this is one reason for social class differences in mortality from heart disease (Markowe, Marmot, et al., 1985).

In a finding that confirmed the link between employment category and socio-economic status, lower-status employees were less likely to have had higher education, and were more likely to have had fathers who worked in manual occupations, to live in rented accommodations, and to have no access to a car (Marmot, Smith, et al., 1991).

Other studies have also demonstrated similarly strong links between social position and health. The Alameda County study revealed that those with inadequate family incomes had elevated risk of death compared to those with very adequate incomes (Marmot, Kogevinas, and Elston, 1987).

Decreasing socio-economic status has also been shown to be linked to increased smoking, reduced activity levels, and decreased knowledge about health (Anderson and Armstead, 1995). Clearly, behaviour is partly determined by the social environment in which people operate, and there seem to be powerful social forces at work that condition certain risk behaviours among certain socio-economic classes. Since this phenomenon appears to indicate that a whole range of socio-political conditions play an intrinsic role in behaviour, it means that, as one author states, 'to change behaviour it may be necessary to change more than behaviour' (Wilkinson, 1996), that is, the very structure of society and jobs may have to change.

Yet, as noted above, behavioural risk factors appear to be only minimally responsible for the social gradient in morbidity and mortality. As discussed, even after controlling for known risk factors, a major social gradient in heart-disease deaths persists. Further, there is also a clear social gradient for diseases that do not have known behavioural risk factors (Wilkinson, 1996). The persistence of class differentials in death and illness rates *regardless of* risk factors shows clearly that simplistic explanations for socio-economic differences in health status will not suffice. These class differentials may, in fact, be inextricably linked to aspects of the socio-economic environment itself (ibid.), such as job strain, which will be discussed in greater detail below.

Clearly, people at the lowest end of the social scale – people with the least education, doing the least desirable jobs for the lowest pay and living in the worst neighbourhoods – have worse health and die earlier than their higher-status counterparts. Yet, poverty is not the only answer to the question of why there is such a strong connection between social class and mortality. As noted by Robert Evans, all of the civil servants followed by the Whitehall studies were office workers, facing low physical risk and not living in conditions of severe deprivation or poverty (Evans, 1994). Yet, the gradient in mortality between employment classes persists across this population. As Evans states: '[T]here is *something* that powerfully influences health and that is correlated with hierarchy per se. It operates, not on some underprivileged minority of "them" over on the margin of society, to be spurned or cherished depending upon one's ideological affiliation, but on all of us. And its effects are *large*' (Evans, 1994, Introduction).

Nor can this phenomenon be attributed solely to inherited characteristics. British social classes tend to be heterogeneous (Rose and Marmot, 1981) and examination of blood groups among social classes has produced no evidence of systematic genetic differences between them (Wilkinson, 1996). In addition, the distribution of many diseases among the social classes reversed itself during this century, indicating that genetics does not play a major role in class differentials in health status (ibid.). For example, heart disease – which used to be characterized as a disease of the affluent in developed countries – has now become more prevalent among the less-affluent classes within industrialized nations. It would seem that genetic factors can hardly be held responsible for this about-face in the incidence of heart disease among social classes. As one author notes: 'Very few people are doomed by their genetic make-up to live in disease or to die prematurely. Most of us have the potential to be healthy and live a long life, given the most beneficial combination of circumstances. Social, economic and health policies could help provide such circumstances, as we can see from the evidence from the most privileged groups of the world population today' (Vagero, 1995).

Class differences in health status persist across a wide range of diseases, and the diseases with the steepest gradients differ from one country to another (Wilkinson, 1996). Genetic explanations for a phenomenon that persists across such a broad range of diseases seem implausible.

It has also been shown that the distribution of income among classes has an effect on mortality and health expectations. In countries where income is more equitably distributed among the social classes, that is, where there is less of a discrepancy between the worst-off and best-off classes, there is overall longer life expectancy (Anderson and Armstead, 1995; Hertzman, Frank, and Evans, 1994), and countries with a more egalitarian distribution of wealth tend to have better general health than those with larger income differences between rich and poor (Wilkinson, 1996). Since, as we shall see below, the Canadian labour market has been increasingly characterized by high unemployment levels and by the growing stagnation, polarization, and inequality of wages for the last twenty years or so (Betcherman, 1996; Gunderson, this volume), the link between income dispersion and health is likely to become increasingly problematic as inequities in distribution worsen. Conversely, by taking steps to address inequities in income dispersion, policy makers may be able to counter-act these negative health impacts and to have a positive effect on the health of the population (Sullivan, 1998). Clearly, the relationship between social class and disease is a complex one, and complete explanations remain elusive.

In writing about problems of disease causation, Sylvia Noble Tesh struggles with fundamental questions about how disease-prevention policies often conceal hidden assumptions and beliefs about disease causality. Tesh points out that the theory one chooses to explain disease causation will have implications for disease prevention. Scientific theories of disease causation – focusing on identifying germs, oncogenic viruses, and other biological processes (one is tempted to add biomechanical processes) – allow policy makers to restrict health to the technical rather than the social realm. In this way, disease is viewed as a personal problem, leaving social pathways out of the equation (Noble Tesh, 1988). As Tesh states, this approach to disease, 'allows policy makers justifiably to ignore people's complicated interaction with their social and physical environments, for it means that the *real* cause of disease, the fundamental cause, is tangible, identifiable, and individual' (ibid.).

Similarly, personal-responsibility views of health allow policy makers to blame individuals for their ill health – they get sick because they smoke, drink, or make poor dietary choices – and prevention efforts become focused on behaviour modification, rather than on modifying the social conditions that gave rise to these behaviours, or on the need for social change (Noble Tesh, 1988). Many employers' workplace health efforts are focused on changing individual behaviour, with a view to reducing employee health costs as much as possible. Yet, as we have already seen, the social gradient in disease and mortality persists even after controlling for known individual-level risk factors. Thus, these workplace health programs do not succeed in improving health outcomes to any large extent, while the emphasis on individual behaviours permits workers to be blamed for, rather than supported through, their health problems.

At the same time, most of these programs totally fail to address the larger issues of the organization of work and the workplace job structures that contribute to ill health and that might, if ameliorated, actually lead to improvements in employee health as well as to reductions in health-care costs (Polanyi, Frank, et al., forthcoming).

Tesh's hidden-argument thesis raises interesting echoes of the 'unholy trinity of defences' that used to permit employers to evade liability for the harms that they caused to workers. Just as employers used to be able to slough off their own legal responsibility for an injury if a worker was even slightly negligent, today workers' compensation systems may be seen as evading responsibility for disease causation by attributing liability to factors outside of the workplace. Since causation is ascribed to elements such as micro-organisms or individual lifestyle choices, the suggestion seems to be that this external contribution negates or outweighs any contribution, no matter how large, on the part of the workplace, the job structure, or the workers' occupational status. The modern version of this unholy-trinity argument seems to be that if workers indulge in unhealthy lifestyles, then they have brought ill health upon themselves and should not seek to claim compensation from employers. This view ignores the very large role played by occupational position and job factors in disease causation.

The hidden reason behind the reincarnation of the unholy trinity is not so hidden – the idea that the structure of the workplace itself contributes to disease would, if accepted, impose tremendous potential liabilities upon employers. Thus, society searches for genetic predispositions and viral, bacterial, and environmental agents that cause disease, and focuses health-promotion efforts on individual lifestyle choices, which employers prefer to perceive as the cause of ill health rather than tackling the larger, and more daunting, issues of the organization of work.

Work and Health

We have seen that social class is inversely associated with mortality and ill health, and that those at the bottom of the ladder are generally the most severely afflicted. There are few simple answers as to why social status has this effect on health – whether social position is the cause in itself, or simply associated with some underlying factors yet to be identified.

It is clear, however, that work is a key determinant of social status, because it has a direct impact upon an individual's income level, living conditions, opportunities, and general well-being, and upon his or her chances for personal growth and development, self-esteem, and social approval (Marmot and Feeney, 1996). Individuals acquire much of their social and psychological experience at work, and spend a great deal of their time in the physical environment of the workplace (ibid.). Work is also a key indicator of an individual's social status and recognition as indicated by the Whitehall II study. Job status is linked to a range of social-hierarchy factors such as level of education, housing tenure, and car ownership (Marmot, Smith, et al., 1991).

As noted earlier in this paper, workers in the first half of this century tended to be preoccupied with reducing the physical demands and dangers they faced at work (Karasek and Theorell, 1990). Thus, the risk of immediate physical hazards, the physical burdens of work, and the problems of day-to-day survival tended to obscure issues of the social and psychological aspects of the work environment. As the technological innovations of the last fifty years have alleviated many of the physical hazards and backbreaking labour conditions that had confronted workers in previous centuries (ibid.) – replacing hard labour with machinery – these social and psychological considerations have risen in prominence. In addition, the traditional social structures of the work environment have changed. With the advent of technology, the artisans and tradesmen who used to control their own skills and work processes are gradually being replaced by less-skilled labourers, performing specific, limited tasks (ibid.). Service industries are replacing manufacturing as the main employers (ibid.). Physical demands are being replaced by psychological pressures and demands. Where labour has been organized into limited-skill tasks, this has led to restricted power for workers as managers are called upon to coordinate all this specialized activity (ibid.).

Most recently, other forces have been reshaping the nature of work.

Since the 1970s, the Canadian labour market has undergone a major restructuring, characterized by high unemployment levels, the proliferation of non-standard employment such as part-time and short-term work, wage stagnation, polarization and inequality of wages, and growing job insecurity (Betcherman, 1996; Gunderson, this volume). Increasing globalization of international trade and investment has contributed to this job shift by exerting downward pressure on wages and encouraging corporate managers to emphasize the advantages of a small, flexible, mobile, and inexpensive job force (Betcherman, 1996). This corporate philosophy has translated into downsizing and 're-engineering,' focusing on core business competencies, a small core of regular employees, the adoption of non-standard work arrangements such as temporary and part-time work and contracting out, as well as 'just-in-time' methods of production and cycle-time analysis – all of this contributing to pervasive job insecurity and uncertainty on the part of workers. There is now growing evidence about the importance of the social and psychological aspects of work to the health of workers.

We will now consider two very common conditions, both of which can be shown to be associated with work, and both of which affect a huge proportion of the workforce.

Cardiovascular Disease

In their research on work and illness, Karasek and Theorell have shown, using a two-factor demand/control model, that the organizational characteristics of jobs are a significant risk factor for coronary heart disease. Workers who face high psychological demands, on the one hand, and who have low decision latitude and little control over job demands or how they use their skills, on the other hand, are at elevated risk for cardiovascular disease (Karasek and Theorell, 1990). More workers are now employed in psychologically demanding work than in jobs involving heavy lifting or dirty work (ibid.), and hazards such as loss of control, great psychological demands, and social isolation seem to have gained pre-eminence over dangers associated with the physical aspects of work. Workplace social support has been added to the two-factor model as a third major characteristic affecting psychological strain outcomes (Schnall, Landsbergis, et al., 1994).

The hypothesis that high-strain jobs, characterized by a high-demand/low control work environment, lead to adverse psychological and physiological consequences has been supported in a number of industrialized countries, across occupational and gender boundaries (Karasek and Theorell, 1990). A correlation between job strain and cardiovascular disease has been found in a variety of studies among men and women (Schnall, Lansbergis, et al., 1994), and among both blue- and white-collar workers (Hammar, Alfredsson, and Theorell, 1994). Higher risk of heart disease owing to job strain was found among older women, suggesting that age might reflect greater cumulative exposure to job strain or indicating that exposure has a latency effect, with greater impact felt several years after exposure (Schnall, Landsbergis, et al., 1994). Blue-collar men and men with low education in Sweden showed a stronger association between job strain and heart disease than did higher-status groups, as did women in clerical jobs in the United States (ibid.). A strong association between low-status jobs and high blood pressure was also found in Sweden (ibid.).

The highest risk for heart disease for men in both blue- and white-collar occupations has been found to be associated with hectic work, combined with few possibilities to learn new things and low influence on the planning of work and working hours (Hammar, Alfredsson, and Theorell, 1994). Jobs classified as high on monotony and low on the opportunity to learn new things have been associated with higher risks of mortality from heart disease (Marmot and Feeney, 1996). Studies have confirmed that, in particular, professional drivers, cooks and waiters, police, and salvage employees are at increased risk of heart disease (ibid.).

A number of studies have also examined the impact of workplace social support and social isolation on the development of heart disease. Social support seemed to reduce job-strain mortality risk in a study of retired men in Sweden (Falk, Hanson, et al., 1992), a study of factory workers in Sweden (Schnall, Landsbergis, et al., 1994), and in a Swedish national study (Johnson and Hall, 1988). In the Whitehall II study, it was found that married and cohabiting men and women had lower rates of short spells of absence from work than others, although social isolation seemed to be associated with lower rates of long spells of sickness absence, perhaps owing to the lack of social contact outside work (Rael, Stansfeld, et al., 1995). Increasing levels of skill and variety, job control, and job support were found to be related to greater well-being and satisfaction and to less psychiatric disorder in both male and female civil servants (Stansfeld, North, et al., 1995). In general, social support seems to buffer the negative effects of job strain (Falk, Hanson, et al., 1992).[7]

Karasek and Theorell postulate that the job-strain phenomenon is induced when environmental factors bring about a biological state of arousal – stress – that, owing to constraints in the work environment, becomes psychological strain – the result of high demands combined with low control over environmental circumstances (Karasek and Theorell, 1990). As workers' stress cannot be discharged by being translated into action and, in fact, may last for hours, the unused energy is transformed into residual strain, with severe consequences for the affected worker (ibid.). It is their view that this phenomenon occurs in a great number of jobs and affects a wide variety of workers, ranging from assembly-line workers to waitresses, garment workers, and white-collar workers (ibid.). On the basis of these studies, workers labouring under conditions such as heavy deadline and/or quota pressures, bureaucratic rules, rigidly limited behaviour, lack of control over their work, no ability to let off steam, and social isolation would seem to be at increased risk of cardiovascular disease.

In other words, in view of the widespread support found for Karasek and Theorell's job-strain model, a large number of workers in the modern world are at risk of developing heart disease as a result of their job environment. Further, the association between job strain and heart disease appears to be intensified for workers at the lower end of the socio-economic scale, who tend to have the least control over their work.

Recently, it has been shown that shift work is also associated with increased risk of coronary heart disease. In one study of nurses, it was found that rotating shift work was associated with higher risk of heart disease, and that the risk increased after six or more years (Kawachi, Colditz, et al., 1995). Other studies have indicated that shift work is associated with increased prevalence of coronary risk factors, including smoking, higher blood pressure, and increased cholesterol levels (ibid.). The occupation of firefighter, typically a shift-work profession, has also been recognized as a risk factor for heart disease (Industrial Disease Standards Panel, 1994). As a multitude of workers do shift work, including medical personnel, firefighters, police officers, bakers, cleaners, taxi drivers, and, nowadays, grocery store and pharmacy clerks, the health implications are potentially serious (Marmot and Feeney, 1996).[8]

Similarly, the notion that jobs characterized by high effort coupled with low rewards can have adverse health impacts might be seen as applying with particular vehemence to workers at the bottom of the socio-economic ladder, who tend to do the heaviest jobs for the lowest pay – that is, who expend disproportionately high effort compared to the reward they receive. Siegrist has recently shown that high-effort/ low-reward jobs, as perceived by workers, carry a three- to seven-fold elevated risk for having cardiovascular risk factors (hypertension / serum lipid elevations) (Siegrist, 1996).

Musculoskeletal Pain

Back pain is a pervasive disorder, affecting some 80 per cent of adults at some time in their lives (Deyo, Cherkin, et al., 1991). In the United States, it is the second most common reason for work absenteeism, the third leading cause of total work disability, and the leading cause of activity limitation among young adults (Deyo and Diehl, 1988; Frank, Brooker, et al., 1995).

In Ontario, about 7.8 per cent of working-age adults report long-term back pain (Liira, Shannon, et al., 1995). About 66 per cent of people experiencing a bout of back pain will have a recurrence within one year, and 5 to 10 per cent will develop chronic pain (Linton, 1990).

Back pain, which primarily affects people during their working years, leads to enormous health expenditures, a tremendous amount of human suffering, dysfunction, and disability, and, because of lost working days, has a profound cost impact on business. In 1981, the province of Quebec alone paid out approximately $173 million in medical costs and disability payments owing to back pain (Frank et al., 1996). Worse, the rate of disability due to low-back pain is increasing at a tremendous rate, making this a very prevalent and hugely expensive condition within industrialized nations (Frymoyer and Cats-Baril, 1987; Bongers et al., 1993). Yet, only a small minority of back-pain sufferers accounts for the majority of costs incurred (Deyo, Cherkin, et al., 1991).

The tendency in workers' compensation issues, as noted earlier, is to seek discrete, precipitating events for personal injuries in order to establish causation. Yet, etiology in back-pain cases remains unclear; in many cases, there is no specific diagnosis, no constellation of reliable physical signs (i.e., objective evidence of injury) and, up until recently, little consensus on appropriate care (see Liira, Shannon, et al., 1995, and Linton, 1990). Back pain falls somewhere along the continuum between an accident, an injury, and a disease.

Further, occupational back pain is often insidious in onset and progressive in nature (Hadler, 1978). In such cases, the absence of a specific causal event and the emphasis placed by adjudicators on 'objective' physical evidence of disease often stands in the way of compensation, particularly with respect to soft-tissue injuries. As in the case of cardiovascular disease, however, it is plain that back pain and other musculoskeletal diseases are multifactorial in origin (Bongers et al., 1993), and therefore the search for a specific, precipitating event may be fruitless in the majority of cases.

Many studies have concentrated on the physical and ergonomic aspects of the relationship between back pain and work. Some occupations, such as nursing, truck driving, and materials-handling jobs, have been linked with the risk of low-back disability (Frymoyer and Cats-Baril, 1987). There is evidence that ergonomic risk factors for low-back pain associated with work include prolonged bending and twisting, heavy physical work such as lifting, motor-vehicle driving, and exposure to vibration (Walsh et al., 1989; Bongers et al., 1993; Frank et al., 1996). Low-back injury also seems to be more common when the physical demands of the job do not match the worker's physical capabilities (Frymoyer and Cats-Baril, 1987; Messing et al., 1995).[9]

Studies have also noted that there is a greater likelihood of disability resulting from back pain when there is less possibility of a lighter job during recovery and when the worker perceives that the job is too heavy (Frymoyer and Cats-Baril, 1987). Indeed, the provision of light and alternative duties to workers stricken with back pain is critical in preventing chronicity and long-term disability.

In addition to ergonomic factors and features of the physical work environment, individual factors such as age, sex, muscle strength, fitness, and previous incidence of back pain have also been linked to disability due to back pain.[10] Psychological traits such as hypochondria, hysteria, somatization, and low self-esteem have been linked to back pain as well.[11] However, there seems to be some question as to whether these indicators of neuroticism cause or result from disability that is due to low-back pain.[12] Self-assessed health and subjective complaints and reports of non-back pain have also been found to be associated with disability due to low-back pain (Astrand and Isaacsson, 1988; Frymoyer and Cats-Baril, 1987). As noted earlier, self-assessed health, which is linked to socio-economic status, is a powerful predictor of health outcomes and mortality.

Educational level is conversely related to disability from low-back pain and other musculoskeletal diseases.[13] Among men, income is also correlated with absenteeism due to back pain (Deyo and Tsui-Wu, 1987).

Obviously, men with lower levels of education, working in low-paying jobs, are less likely to have safer sedentary occupations, and are more likely to do heavy work that places a great deal of stress on the back (Deyo and Tsui-Wu, 1987; Deyo and Diehl, 1988). Most people working in manual occupations probably do so owing to a lack of educational and other opportunities that would have allowed them to select more desirable, better paying, and safer occupations.

It has been suggested that educational level may influence the 'attractiveness' of a person's work and therefore their motivation to return to it, and that people with higher levels of education are better able to understand and adjust to various health risks (Deyo and Tsui-Wu, 1987; Deyo and Diehl, 1988). Greater educational attainment has also been linked to access to safer jobs, less likelihood of future unemployment, and less incidence of smoking, which has been identified as a risk factor for low-back pain (Deyo and Diehl, 1988). Others have suggested that education may reflect a whole host of other attributes such as intrinsic abilities, income, access to care, personal responsibility for health, and problem-solving experience (ibid.).

It is overly simplistic, however, to suggest that people with low levels of education suffer from back pain simply because they work in manual occupations. As we have seen, lower social position is linked to lower educational levels, lower job status, increased risk factors and, ultimately, to poor health and mortality from a wide range of diseases. People at the bottom of the social ladder tend to have worse health and to die earlier than their higher-status counterparts. It follows that low status would also be associated with musculoskeletal problems.

One possibility – as noted in the discussion concerning cardiovascular disease – is that the stress generated by high-demand/low-control jobs may affect an individual's ability to cope not only with the emotional pressures but also with the physical and mechanical loads of the workplace (Bongers et al., 1993). It is possible that the same forces that intensify the association between job strain and heart disease for those at the bottom of the ladder also act to intensify the association between job strain and musculoskeletal diseases such as low-back pain.

Workplace features such as monotonous work, time pressure, perceived high workload, and little control over one's job have been linked with musculoskeletal conditions such as back pain and other musculoskeletal injuries (Bongers et al., 1993). Dissatisfaction with job status, performance of repetitive, monotonous tasks, and self-reported fatigue at the end of the day have also been associated with greater disability and absenteeism due to back pain (Frymoyer and Cats-Baril, 1987). Monotony seems to be a particular risk factor for neck pain (Linton, 1990).

Studies have also indicated that workers with low-back pain are less satisfied with their work than are workers without back pain (Linton, 1990). A study of female secretaries demonstrated that a poor psychosocial work environment – in that case expressed in terms of work content, social support, job demands, and position in the office hierarchy – was consistently related to neck and shoulder pain (Linton and Kamwendo, 1989).

In fact, workers in a poor psychosocial work environment were found to have double the risk of experiencing pain problems requiring a health-care visit than they had the previous year, with both the oldest and youngest workers having the most difficulty in tolerating the poor environment (Linton, 1990).

As in the case of cardiovascular disease, the psychosocial workplace factors – including job strain, monotonous, repetitive work, poor work content, time pressure, perceived high workload, and low control over one's work – are very important in the development of musculoskeletal pain (Linton and Kamwendo, 1989).

Implications of the Link between Work and Health

These compelling associations between work and health conditions such as heart disease and back pain have significant implications for workers' compensation systems.

Heart disease is the major cause of death in industrialized countries, yet there have been relatively few workers' compensation claims for heart disease. When workers' compensation claims are made for heart accidents, the relationship with work is often not identified as causal but only temporal (Juge and Phillips, 1982: 23) – that is, a heart attack happened to take place at work rather than at home eight hours later. This assessment seems to be based upon a linear (accident) view of causation, in which a preceding, precipitating event – usually physical exertion or emotional stress – must be identified. If no specific, preferably proximate, event can be pinpointed, the fact that a heart attack took place at work may be seen as a mere coincidence, although it is still likely to be compensated (Sullivan, 1980: 1367; Ison, 1989: 38).[14]

The logical extension of this view is that the heart attack itself is merely a reflection of the aging process, bad habits, or an underlying disability, that it likely would have happened eventually regardless of work, and that it therefore cannot really be attributed to work per se (Juge and Phillips, 1982: 25; Sullivan, 1980: 1380). This linear view of causation ignores the multifactorial evidence about the relationship between job strain and cardiovascular disease, as well as the larger association between job, socio-economic status, and increased ill health in general. This approach also has the effect of eliminating the vast majority of workers with such diseases from the pool of eligible claimants – an apparently inequitable result in view of the philosophical underpinnings of workers' compensation.

The view of causation that our workers' compensation systems have chosen to adopt seems to exclude consideration of any larger issues about the organization of work that are associated with increased risk and that are modifiable – social isolation at work, monotony, lack of control over work and working hours, and heavy deadline pressure. All of these are linked to incidence of disease and could be modified in order to prevent future illness. However, such prevention efforts would require a profound change in our view of injury causation and our approach to work organization.

The more we learn about the various causes of and risk factors for a given disease, the harder it is to assess the relative importance of each. For instance, if the elimination of a particular risk factor from the population would prevent the occurrence of a disease, then its 'population attributable risk' (PAR) is 100 per cent (Brooker, Frank, et al., 1997). The problem is that there might be several such factors for any given disease, and therefore the sum of PARs of causal factors for that disease will often exceed 100 per cent – a fact known to epidemiologists but often not to their audiences (ibid.).

Such a result does not assist us in estimating the relative contribution of each cause. In other words, we know that there is a link between work and musculoskeletal disease. We also know that disease is multifactorial, and that work is not the only causal factor. If there are multiple causes for diseases, only some of which can be related to work, adjudication of workers' compensation claims becomes increasingly arbitrary, in that adjudicators do not know the relative importance of the respective factors involved in bringing about a disease or condition.

Thus, the 'arising out of' formula of causation becomes little more than an exercise in line-drawing. Moreover, this approach seems to hearken back to the days of the 'unholy trinity of defences' discussed earlier, if workers' compensation systems are able to evade responsibility for conditions caused by work simply because other causal factors have also been involved.

Expanding the Categories of Disability

In addition to the changing nature of work and growing evidence on the multicausal nature of disease, a further challenge to the sustainability of our workers' compensation system is presented by the slow enlargement of the categories of conditions considered to be disabling.

In part, this phenomenon may be attributed to our society's infatuation with medical technology and medical categories, the medicalization of life in industrial society, its tendency to attach labels such as 'patient' or 'disabled' to individuals within it, and the consequent reduction of the autonomy of persons so labelled (Illich, 1975).

As well, pressures to expand the categories of the disabled are constantly exerted by a multiplicity of players. These include individual applicants, who define and see themselves as disabled; physicians, who diagnose disability and who are trained to treat, not to act as gatekeepers; the courts and the legal system, which determine disability; and the various interest and advocacy groups that may inadvertently induce people to think of themselves as disabled and, by lobbying for expanded rights and privileges, cause various maladies, such as repetitive motion injuries and mental-health and stress-related conditions, for example, to be recognized as 'disabilities' (Stone, 1984). Business-cycle factors, including recessions and periods of high unemployment, will also tend to expand the categories of disability as more people will apply for benefits in tough economic times, and the system – at various levels – will be more likely to let them through (ibid.).

Defining large numbers of people as disabled may also disguise labour surpluses and high rates of unemployment in difficult economic times. Shifting certain individuals from the workforce into a category that has a legitimate claim to assistance – such as the disabled – preserves the work ethic, and thus public notions of 'worthiness' versus 'unworthiness,' and masks decreasing labour-force participation in a society in which the prevalent ideology dictates that everybody should work, even though there is not work enough for all (Stone, 1984).

As we have seen, the Canadian labour market, like that of many other OECD nations, is increasingly characterized by high unemployment levels, part-time and short-term work, and growing job insecurity. It is arguable that the present predicament confronting workers' compensation systems may simply reflect the fact that economic conditions have changed, that rates of unemployment are high, and that society is reducing the pressure placed on the work-based system by shifting labour surplus into the disabled system.

Combined with the changing nature of work and improvements in our scientific understanding about the role that work plays in the causation of disease, the slow growth of categories of disablement is placing increasing pressure upon workers' compensation systems. The attempts in several Canadian jurisdictions in the last couple of years to limit the compensability of chronic pain arising from musculoskeletal injury and 'stress' are an acknowledgment of this pressure.

The Crisis in Workers' Compensation: Where Do We Go from Here?

Systems of workers' compensation are intended to compensate victims of all workplace injuries without regard to fault, and to ensure that 'the price of a product bears the blood of the working man,' or woman. Yet, for an injury or disease to be compensable under a system of workers' compensation, it must be found to have arisen out of and in the course of employment. This question of factual causation is becoming increasingly problematic in the light of what we now know about the complexity of factors involved in the causation of disease.

There is a distinction between medical or scientific causation and legal causation sufficient to establish entitlement under a system of workers' compensation. Even where causation may be scientifically established, legal and moral judgments will still determine which system will be designated to compensate a disability (Ison, 1994: 5).

In North America, we relegate a great many sufferers – those whose conditions have not been attributed to work – to their private long-term disability plans or, if they have none, to the health-care and welfare systems at large, which will provide some, but not all, of the coverage that an injured worker would receive from workers' compensation, and out of the public purse at that.

Yet, it is apparent that the 'arising out of' formulation in workers' compensation provides adjudicators with sufficient leeway to narrow or broaden coverage as they see fit, in keeping with whatever underlying policy objectives may have been identified (Vinson, 1996: 730–3). As one author writing in the American context notes: 'Most arising-out-of opinions lean on boilerplate language about the sufficiency of evidence, which is generally used in cases where the historical facts are uncontested and the only evidence in sight is arguments for and against coverage' (ibid.: 732).

Concepts of causation 'recycled' from the world of negligence law have slipped into the workers' compensation process (Vinson, 1996: 759) and are helping to obscure the choices that we are making about how to distribute the cost of work-related harms. It is suggested that these implicit policy choices should now be made explicit.

Millions of people in the industrialized world are, at this time, suffering from various conditions that have some causal relationship to their work, but that are currently deemed to be non-attributable to work. Excluding such individuals from the pool of eligible claimants under workers' compensation seems to fly in the face of the philosophical principles underlying these systems – that workers should be compensated, without regard to fault, for the harms they sustain owing to work, and that the price of a product must reflect the toll taken on their bodies by its production.

Current arrangements for attributing responsibility for disease to the workers' compensation system become even more problematic when we take into account issues of latency and length of exposure, progressive conditions, and problems of intergenerational equity. If, over the course of their working life, individuals have worked for a number of different employers or industries or been exposed to a number of different contaminants or adverse work conditions, their cumulative occupational and exposure history will make it very difficult to attribute a disease to any specific source or employer (Ison, 1994: 8).

As well, given business-cycle changes and the simple passage of time, it is possible that, with respect to any disease characterized by a lengthy latency period, the worker's original employer/s may no longer exist at the moment when the symptoms of the disease are finally made manifest, leaving responsibility for payment of compensation in the hands of industries and employers that may have had nothing to do with bringing about the condition in question. Adjudication of workers' compensation claims becomes little more than a set of capricious judgment processes when much work-related disease cannot be traced to a specific employer or origin, and when adjudication assumes various relationships and responsibilities among institutions that may no longer be valid, or that may no longer exist.

While many of these issues have already been faced for relatively rare cases of occupational cancer, they would tax current adjudication systems to the limit if compensation claims for coronary heart disease, the main killer in mid-life, were to be processed in a similar manner (Sullivan and Frank, 1999). Recognizing the legitimacy of a multitude of such claims under workers' compensation would have tremendous economic consequences and could threaten the sustainability of the system as a whole, particularly in light of the concerns that we already have about affordability.

Even if the workers' compensation system were ultimately held responsible only for the small fraction of each person's diseases that can be attributed to their work, it simply could not pay for all of the costs that would thus be generated. Such an approach would likely result in diminished coverage for all workers or, worse, in the collapse of the entire system.

The frightening scope of this potential entitlement to workers' compensation benefits seems to be preventing us from looking clearly at the reality of the situation that now confronts our workers' compensation systems. Yet, political and economic pressure not to expand the scope of coverage under workers' compensation should not be a barrier to a rethinking of the current arrangements for attributing responsibility for workplace harms.

Policy Options

Once we accept the proposition that existing arrangements for attributing responsibility for disease to the workers' compensation system are neither scientifically justified nor financially sustainable, where do we go from here? Three main options suggest themselves at this time, all of which have strengths as well as shortcomings.

First, we can foreclose the entire issue of attribution of responsibility for disease by imposing narrow constraints upon workers' compensation and by limiting entitlement to cases of unequivocal, acute injury and to diseases that are limited to industry, that is, that do not normally result from other causes. Stringent limits on entitlement to workers' compensation would obviously have a cost-saving effect at the outset, as the range of conditions eligible for compensation would be narrowed significantly.

These limits might be imposed by attempting to set higher legislative or regulatory thresholds and higher attribution requirements for the acceptance of disease causation and injury attribution. Such a system would restrict the discretion of administrators in terms of the benefits and coverage provided, and might enhance the protections granted to those employees remaining within the parameters of the system.

This sort of strategy – the logical extension of current practices and policies aimed at limiting coverage and benefits – may be seen as an outgrowth of a school of thought that views workers' compensation as public insurance, governed by fiscal, administrative, and actuarial considerations, rather than as a social-contract model between workers and employers, with overarching legal, moral, and philosophical obligations on both sides. This approach would certainly result in short-term financial gains to the system.

However, this approach would also have a down-side, in financial terms, as it may also signal the return of tort litigation for those conditions outside the narrow scope of the coverage provided. The original rationale for the social contract between workers and employers regarding the compensation of harms to workers was to provide workers with guaranteed no-fault benefits on a timely basis, *in exchange* for relinquishing their common-law right to sue for damages. If certain conditions are then placed unequivocally outside of the scope of this bargain, denying no-fault benefits to affected workers, it would be inequitable to continue to tie the hands of afflicted workers by prohibiting them from resorting to tort litigation to obtain compensation.

A significant alteration of the terms of the original bargain between workers and employers might lift the ban on litigation (see Hyatt and Law, this volume). Tort litigation is very time-consuming and costly (Ison, 1994: 123). This approach may have the counter-intuitive result of driving up the costs of adjudicating workplace harms, and thus might not be either the most cost-efficient or efficacious choice.

If exclusions from coverage become too massive or too random to predict or handle, they may risk violating section 15 of the Canadian Charter of Rights and Freedoms, which prohibits discrimination on the basis of, *inter alia*, mental or physical disability (part I of the *Constitution Act* 1982, enacted by the *Canada Act 1982* (U.K.) c. 11). A blatantly discriminatory approach might also run counter to the intent and spirit of remedial legislation, which is meant to be given a fair, large and liberal construction, so that it can achieve the purposes for which it is intended (*Interpretation Act*, R.S.O. 1990, c. I.11, s. 10).

Of course, the purposes and intent of the legislation can also be revised in light of these considerations to make clear its limited coverage intentions, as was recently done in Ontario.

The second policy approach would be to choose to reduce or eliminate the distinction between work-related and non-work-related diseases – which may be losing its coherence – and to accept a broad social responsibility for illness and disability, regardless of causation. This type of universal or comprehensive compensation strategy – derived from a view of workers' compensation as a social contract between workers and employers complete with ethical and philosophical underpinnings – would entail creating a broad system of disability compensation to deal not only with medical costs but with all wage loss due to disability, and to rationalize the existing uncoordinated patchwork of systems (Ison, 1994).

Such a comprehensive system would have the advantage of a coherent design that promotes societal health objectives and equitable distribution of costs, and eliminates duplication and overlap of administrative, adjudicative, and social-insurance functions (Ison, 1994). A comprehensive disability system would also solve the problem of deciding which system ought to compensate a disability, thus preventing disease cases from falling through the cracks (ibid.).

Although they are quite distinct, the Netherlands, Sweden, the United Kingdom, and Germany, among others, provide some version of comprehensive social-insurance programs to cover employees against the risk of wage loss owing to temporary or permanent disability, whether or not it is work-related and whether or not the disabled persons are labour-force participants (Mashaw et al., 1996).

While Holland and Sweden have run into trouble by failing to control their disability benefit programs and by inadvertently providing disincentives to rehabilitation and to return to the labour force, there is tremendous discretion within comprehensive disability plans, as demonstrated by the great variation among these European systems (Aarts and de Jong, 1996). The German system, which has arguably performed better than other Western European systems in terms of getting people back to work, has tended to focus entitlement narrowly and to compel return-to-work efforts among the social partners.

We need not assume that comprehensive disability insurance requires taking a cookie-cutter, fiscally irresponsible approach to compensation. Rather than simply throwing open the doors to bottomless wage-replacement benefits, we can choose instead to emphasize, and to provide economic incentives for, recovery of loss of earning capacity, rehabilitation, retraining, and redeployment, with a view to returning all workers to maximal employability. The trade-off in universal systems is reduced benefit levels in return for an expanded scope of coverage.

A universal approach in Canada would require the exertion of great political will and cooperation among all levels of government and among fragmented stakeholder groups. For this reason, this approach is not likely to be politically feasible in the near future.

These two diametrically opposed options might best be framed in terms of the outgrowth or extension of two contradictory views of workers' compensation. In the first case, the system is viewed as an insurance model, which naturally leads to resolving the crisis in workers' compensation by means of particularistic moves to de-insure the most expensive or problematic conditions.

The second, social-contract view of the system leads to a more comprehensive approach to disability issues, and thus to a trade-off between benefits and coverage, in which diminished benefit levels are accepted in order to retain a broad overall scope of coverage. Neither of these models addresses both of the key factors at issue in this paper – that is, that workers' compensation systems are about to confront the simultaneous challenge of dealing with the multicausal nature of a host of disease conditions while, at the same time, grappling with the recognition that many diseases and conditions not previously attributed to work have a clear work-related component.

There is a third possible approach to workers' compensation, one that might be able to reconcile the multicausal nature of disease with the idea that workers should be compensated for non-traditional, yet work-related, injuries and diseases. In this approach, which might be called the apportionment model, benefits and entitlements would be awarded to workers in accordance with the proportion of their disease or injury that can be attributed to their work. In this way, injured workers suffering from diseases or injuries that are multicausal or indeterminate in etiology would not be totally excluded from workers' compensation if their injury cannot be attributed completely or directly to their work. Conversely, the workers' compensation systems would not be forced to bear the entire cost of compensating workers whose conditions might be partly or greatly attributable to causes outside of work.

This model, advanced in the writings of Muir (1993, 1998) promises the elegant solution of a science-based attribution model of adjudication, and would replace capricious judgment processes with rational, justifiable, and ethical decisions as to entitlement that would build public confidence in adjudication around workers' compensation benefits.

However, as in the previous approaches, there are several flaws in this particular option. First, it presumes that good science exists to explain the etiology of a host of disease conditions. This view does not take into account those conditions for which good science may not exist, leaving us with the presumption of no attribution because a condition in question may not have been adequately or carefully studied, if studied at all.

Second, this model again raises the spectre of the unholy trinity of defences that used to operate to the detriment of workers. As is the case with respect to much tort litigation, individual lifestyle factors will, of necessity, be factored into any adjudication of what proportion of an injury or disease is attributable to a particular individual's work. This suggests that workers' lifestyles, choices, and behaviours might be subjected to the same sort of scrutiny currently reserved for nominees to the U.S. Supreme Court.

Although this model is in theory elegant, as we noted earlier, there are technical problems with the precision of risk-attribution estimates. Risk attribution is limited by the statistical models and the presumptions that are made about risk, and thus should not be perceived as a completely accurate or objective standard.

Indeed, in the one recent English judgment we identified, Justice Turner did apportion disease attribution and the awards considering exposure (coal dust) and off-the-job (smoking) for several individual coal miners (British Coal Respiratory Disease Litigation [BCRDL, 1998]). In this precedent-setting and complex judgment Justice Turner noted, '[A]pportionment cannot be satisfactorily achieved by a reliance on numbers whether they be of exposure to dust from day to day, year to year, or over the whole period of employment ... [T]hese considerations must ineluctably impose on the court the solution sometimes praised, sometimes vilified and most often not fully understood that the solution is to be found as an answer to a "jury question"' (BCRDL, 1998, S122: 37).

Conclusion

Systems of workers' compensation are confronted by two separate, yet related phenomena. On the one hand, we are beginning to understand that disease is multifactorial, emanating from a multitude of possible causes, including work. On the other hand, scientific evidence is accumulating that demonstrates that the working environment exerts a powerful influence on health and that a broad range of diseases – even those not previously attributed to work – have a work-related component. We know, therefore, that work is not the only cause of disease. Yet, even if only a small fraction of work-related diseases were attributed to the workplace, workers' compensation systems simply could not pay for it. It is clear that current methods for determining entitlement to workers' compensation are not sustainable in light of the convergence of these two developments.

Moreover, in the 'new' world of work – so different from the world that existed at the time when workers' compensation legislation was originally developed – we are witnessing the growing frequency among workers of claims for chronic conditions and diseases of multifactorial etiology, characterized by long latency periods, insidious onset, and gradual progression. Among them are musculoskeletal conditions and heart disease, as discussed here. These conditions present difficult problems of causation under workers' compensation legislation, and the inequitable outcomes that result cannot be easily justified in light of the original ethical and philosophical underpinnings of the system.

In the long run, existing models of workers' compensation will have to change. The current change appears to be in the direction of narrow constraint on coverage. Alternatives include an acceptance of broader disability coverage without regard to causation or, down the road, moving towards the technical determination of proportional compensation. Regardless of the path ultimately chosen, what is crucial at this time is for policy makers and stakeholders alike to recognize that changing realities have brought about a transformation in workers' compensation and that some fundamental rethinking is required.

NOTES

1 An earlier version of this paper was presented at the 3rd International Congress on Medico Legal Issues in Work Related Injury, Munich, April 1997.

Thanks are due to Prof. Allard Dembe, Dr Bob Elgie, two anonymous reviewers, and the editors for comments on an earlier draft of this paper and to Vincy Perri for able help with the manuscript. Errors or omissions remain our responsibility.

2 As confirmed by the Association of Workers' Compensation Boards of Canada, 6 December 1996. The jurisdictions for which figures are available are as follows: Alberta, British Columbia, Manitoba, New Brunswick, New-foundland, Northwest Territories, Ontario, Quebec, Saskatchewan, and the Yukon.

3 For example, in 1994, 190,557 claims for sprains and strains were accepted by workers' compensation boards and commissions across Canada. In the same year, only 23,457 fracture claims were accepted. See Statistics Canada 1995.

4 The Kauai Longitudinal Study of infants born in Hawaii indicates that children who undergo severe or moderate birth stress will show little or no disadvantage in development if raised in stable or high economic status households, but children in poor households will suffer quite serious con-sequences of birth stress. See Evans 1994 and Hertzman, Frank, and Evans 1994.

5 See Kaplan 1996: 509–10 and Premier's Council on Health Strategy, 1991: 1, citing an Ontario study that showed that a baby born in a poor neighbour-hood in 1986 was twice as likely to die in infancy as a baby born in a wealthy neighbourhood, that the life expectancy of a poor urban man is, on average 5.3 years less than that of a rich man, and that of a poor woman is 1.8 years shorter than that of a rich woman.

6 Despite the passage of twenty years, there was no difference in the preva-lence of ischemic heart disease in various employment categories. See Marmot, Smith, et al. 1991.

7 It should be noted, however, that, as married women are usually responsi-ble for most of the work to be done in the home, they often experience the double burden of housework and paid work. While some studies have shown that social support from spouses is important in mitigating these psychosocial stresses, it also appears that the combination of excess demand resulting from the need to perform home-based tasks, plus the low control experienced by many women at the job site, may produce a lethal level of psychosocial strain in such women, leading to increased risk of heart disease and other negative health effects. See Ostry and Hertzman 1996.

8 Another two-factor explanation for the effects of the psychosocial work environment on health has been postulated by Siegrist, who deals with

effort/reward imbalances. Focusing on three types of rewards – money, esteem, and status and job security – Siegrist has suggested that jobs in which high effort combines with low rewards produce sustained stress leading to increased risk of cardiovascular disease. See Marmot and Feeney 1996: 238–9.

9 Frymoyer and Cats-Baril, 1987: 91. We also know that women's occupational health problems tend to be minimized or unrecognized, and that women's 'natural' tasks, such as lifting children in day-care centres, carrying heavy trays in restaurants, or loading bags of groceries in the check-out line are often not seen as being equivalent to the materials-handling jobs held by men, even though the total weight handled in a day may be similar. See K. Messing et al. 1995.

10 Bongers, de Winter, et al. 1993: 297, Deyo and Diehl, 1988: 1559, 1562; Ryden et al. 1989; and Liira, Shannon, et al. 1995.

11 E. Viikari-Juntura, 1991; 1056–7; Frymoyer and Cats-Baril, 1987: 92–5; N.E. Astrand and S.O. Isaacsson, 1988.

12 Frymoyer and Cats-Baril, 1987: 95 and Bongers, de Winter, et al., 1993: 302, who note that neuroticism did not predict disability due to back pain.

13 Deyo and Tsui-Wu, 1987; Viikari-Juntura et al., 1991; Astrand (1987).

14 R. Sullivan (1980: 1367) refers to the American situation. Although, see Ison 1989, who states that, if a heart attack occurred in the course of employment, it is presumed to have arisen out of the employment unless the contrary is shown. He goes on to state, 'Yet there has been an ongoing reluctance to read the Act to mean what it says, and a burden has often been placed upon the worker to prove employment causation.'

REFERENCES

Aarts, L.J.M., and P.R. de Jong. 1996. 'European Experiences with Disability Policy.' In J.L. Mashaw, et al., eds, *Disability, Work and Cash Benefits*. Kalamazoo, Mich.: Upjohn Institute for Employment Research.

Anderson, N., and C. Armstead. 1995. 'Toward Understanding the Association of Socioeconomic Status and Health: A New Challenge for the Biopsychosocial Approach.' *Psychosomatic Medicine* 57: 213.

Astrand, N.E. 1987. 'Medical, Psychological and Social Factors Associated with Back Abnormalities and Self Reported Back Pain: A Cross-Sectional Study of Male Employees in a Swedish Pulp and Paper Industry.' *British Journal of Industrial Medicine* 44: 335.

Astrand, N.E., and S.O. Isaacsson. 1988. 'Back Pain, Back Abnormalities, and

Competing Medical, Psychological and Social Factors as Predictors of Sick Leave, Early Retirement, Unemployment, Labour Turnover and Mortality: A 22 Year Follow Up of Male Employees in a Swedish Pulp and Paper Company.' *British Journal of Industrial Medicine* 45: 393.

Bartley, M., S. Montgomery, D. Cook, and M. Wadsworth. 1996. 'Health and Work Insecurity in Young Men.' In David Blane, Eric Brunner, and Richard Wilkinson, eds, *Health and Social Organization: Towards a Health Policy for the Twenty-First Century*, 255–60. London and New York: Routledge.

Betcherman, G. 1996. 'Globalization, Labour Markets and Public Policy.' In Robert Boyer and Daniel Drache, eds, *States against Markets: The Limits of Globalization*, 250. London: Routledge.

Bongers, P., C. de Winter, et al. 1993. 'Psychosocial Factors at Work and Musculoskeletal Disease.' *Scandinavian Journal of Work Environment and Health* 19: 297.

British Coal Respiratory Disease Litigation. 1998. Mr Justice Turner. (www.open.gov.uk/courts/court/qb_bcrdl.htm)

Brooker, A-S., J. Frank, et al. 1997. 'The Population Attributable Risk as an Index for Determining Public Health Priorities.' Institute for Work & Health manuscript.

Canada. 1982. *Constitution Act*, 1982, Part I, enacted by the *Canada Act 1982* (U.K.) c. 11.

Dembe, A. 1995. *Occupation and Disease: How Social Factors Affect the Conception of Work-Related Disorders.* New Haven: Yale University Press.

Deyo, R., D. Cherkin, et al. 1991. 'Cost, Controversy, Crisis: Low Back Pain and the Health of the Public.' *Annual Review Public Health* 12: 141.

Deyo, R., and A. Diehl. 1988. 'Psychosocial Predictors of Disability in Patients with Low Back Pain.' *Journal of Rheumatology* 15: 1557.

Deyo, R., and Y-J Tsui-Wu. 1987. 'Functional Disability Due to Back Pain: A Population-Based Study Indicating the Importance of Socio-Economic Factors.' *Arthritis and Rheumatism* 30: 1252.

Evans, R.G. 1994. 'Introduction.' In Robert G. Evans, Morris L. Barer, and Theodore R. Marmor, eds, *Why Are Some People Healthy and Others Not? The Determinants of Health of Populations.* New York: Aldine de Gruyter, 1994.

Evans, R.G., and G.L. Stoddart. 1994. 'Producing Health, Consuming Health Care.' In Evans, Barer, and Marmor, eds, *Why Are Some People Healthy and Others Not?*

Falk, A., B. Hanson, et al. 1992. 'Job Strain and Mortality in Elderly Men: Social Network, Support and Influence as Buffers.' *American Journal of Public Health* 82: 1136.

Frank, J., et al. 1996. 'Disability Resulting from Occupational Low Back Pain,

Part I: What Do We Know about Primary Prevention?' *Spine* (24): 2908–17; Part II: What Do We Know about Secondary Prevention?' ibid.: 2918–29.

Frank, J., A-S. Brooker, et al. 1995. *Disability Due to Occupational Low Back Pain: What Do We Know about Its Prevention?* Toronto: Institute for Work & Health.

Frank, J., and J.F. Mustard. 1994. 'The Determinants of Health from a Historical Perspective.' *Daedalus* 123: 1.

Frymoyer, J., and W.C. Cats-Baril. 1987. 'Predictors of Low Back Pain Disability.' *Clinical Orthopaedics and Related Research* 221: 89.

Gilbert, D.G., J. Mastoras, and L.A. Liversidge. 1995. *A Guide to Workers' Compensation in Ontario*. Ontario: Canada Law Book.

Hadler, N. 1978. 'Legal Ramifications of the Medical Definition of Back Disease.' *Annals of Internal Medicine* 89: 994.

Hammar, N., L. Alfredsson, and T. Theorell. 1994. 'Job Characteristics and the Incidence of Myocardial Infarction.' *International Journal of Epidemiology* 23: 277.

Hertzman, C. 1994. 'The Lifelong Impact of Childhood Experiences.' *Daedalus* 123: 167.

Hertzman, C., J. Frank, and R.G. Evans. 1994. 'Heterogeneities in Health Status.' In Robert G. Evans, Morris L. Barer, and Theodore R. Marmor, eds, *Why Are Some People Healthy and Others Not? The Determinants of Health of Populations*. New York: Aldine de Gruyter.

Illich, I. 1975. *Medical Nemesis: The Expropriation of Health*. London: Calder & Boyars.

Industrial Disease Standards Panel. 1994. *Report to the Workers' Compensation Board on Cardiovascular Disease and Cancer among Firefighters*. Toronto: Industrial Disease Standards Panel, IDSP Report no. 13, September.

Ison, T.G. 1989. *Workers' Compensation in Canada*. 2nd ed. Toronto: Butterworths.

– 1994. *Compensation Systems for Injury and Disease: The Policy Choices*. Toronto: Butterworths.

Johnson, J.V., and E.M. Hall. 1988. 'Job Strain, Work Place Social Support and Cardiovascular Disease: A Cross-Sectional Study of the Swedish Working Population.' *American Journal of Public Health* 78: 1336.

Joseph, L. 1983. 'The Causation Issue in Workers' Compensation Mental Disability Cases: An Analysis, Solutions, and a Perspective.' *Vanderbilt Law Review* 36: 264.

Juge, D.P., and J.H Phillips. 1982. 'A New Standard for Cardiovascular Claims in Workers' Compensation.' *Louisiana Law Review* 43: 23.

Kaplan, G. 1996. 'People and Places: Contrasting Perspectives on the Association between Social Class and Health.' *International Journal of Health Services* 26: 507.

Karasek, R., and T. Theorell. 1990. *Healthy Work: Stress, Productivity, and the Reconstruction of Working Life.* New York: Basic Books.

Kawachi, I., G. Colditz, et al. 1995. 'Prospective Study of Shift Work and Risk of Coronary Heart Disease in Women.' *Circulation* 92: 3178.

Larson, A. 1952. 'The Nature and Origins of Workmen's Compensation.' *Cornell Law Quarterly* 37: 206.

Liira, J.P., H.S. Shannon, et al. 1995. *Long Term Back Problems and Physical Work Exposures in the 1990 Ontario Health Survey.* Toronto: Institute for Work & Health.

Linton, S.J. 1990. 'Risk Factors for Neck and Back Pain in a Working Population In Sweden.' *Work & Stress* 4: 996.

Linton, S.J., and K. Kamwendo. 1989. 'Risk Factors in the Psychosocial Work Environment for Neck and Shoulder Pain in Secretaries.' *Journal of Occupational Health* 31: 609.

Markowe, H.L., M.G. Marmot, et al. 1985. 'Fibrinogen: A Possible Link between Social Class and Coronary Heart Disease.' *British Medical Journal* 291: 312.

Marmot, M., and A. Feeney. 1996. 'Work and Health: Implications for Individuals and Society.' In David Blane, Eric Brunner, and Richard Wilkinson, eds, *Health and Social Organization: Towards a Health Policy for the Twenty-First Century.* London and New York: Routledge.

Marmot, M.G., K. Kogevinas, and M.A. Elston. 1987. 'Social/Economic Status and Disease.' *Annual Review of Public Health* 8: 111.

Marmot, M.G., D.S. Smith, et al. 1991. 'Health Inequalities among British Civil Servants: The Whitehall II Study.' *Lancet* 337: 1387.

Mashaw, J.L., V. Reno, R.V. Burkhauser, and M. Berkowitz, eds. 1996. *Disability, Work and Cash Benefits.* Kalamazoo, Mich.: Upjohn Institute for Employment Research.

Messing, K., et al. 1995. 'Introduction.' In Karen Messing, et al., eds, *Invisible: Issues in Women's Occupational Health.* Charlottetown: Gynergy Books.

Muir, D. 1993. 'Compensating Occupational Diseases: A Medical and Legal Dilemma.' *Canadian Medical Association Journal* 148(11): 1903–5.

– 1998. 'Occupational Dust Exposure and Chronic Obstructive Pulminary Disease.' *Applied Occupational and Environmental Hygiene* 13(8): 606–7.

Noble Tesh, S. 1988. *Hidden Arguments: Political Ideology and Disease Prevention Policy.* New Jersey: Rutgers University Press.

North, F., et al. 1993. 'Explaining Socioeconomic Differences in Sickness Absence: The Whitehall II Study.' *British Medical Journal* 306: 361.

Ostry, A., and C. Hertzman. 1996. 'The Relative Importance of Work and Home in Producing Job Strain.' Unpublished manuscript, Dept. of Health Care & Epidemiology, University of British Columbia, August.

Polanyi, M., J. Frank, et al. Forthcoming. *Promoting the Determinants of Good Health in the Workplace*. In B. Poland, L. Green, and I. Rootman, eds, *Settings for Health Promotion*. New York: Sage.

Power, C., and M. Bartley. 1996. 'Transmission of Social and Biological Risk across the Life Course.' In David Blane, Eric Brunner, and Richard Wilkinson, eds, *Health and Social Organization: Towards a Health Policy for the Twenty-First Century*. London and New York: Routledge.

Premier's Council on Health Strategy. 1991. *Nurturing Health: A Framework on the Determinants of Health*. Toronto: Sessional Paper no. 143, 1st Session, 35th Parliament.

Rael, E., S. Stansfeld, et al. 1995. 'Sickness Absence in the Whitehall II Study, London: The Role of Social Support and Material Problems.' *Journal of Epidemiology and Community Health* 49: 1.

Rose, G., and M.G. Marmot. 1981. 'Social Class and Coronary Heart Disease.' *British Heart Journal* 45: 13.

R.S.O. 1914, c. 146.

R.S.O. 1990, c. W.11, s. 4(1).

Ryden, L.A., et al. 1989. 'Occupational Low-Back Injury in a Hospital Employee Population.' *Spine* 14: 315.

Schnall, P., P. Lansbergis, et al. 1994. 'Job Strain and Cardiovascular Disease.' *Annual Review of Public Health* 15: 381.

Siegrist, J. 1996. 'Adverse Health Effects of High-Effort/Low-Reward Conditions.' *Journal of Occupational Health Psychology* 1996: 127.

Stansfeld, S., F.M. North, et al. 1995. 'Work Characteristics and Psychiatric Disorder in Civil Servants in London.' *Journal of Epidemiology and Community Health* 49: 48.

Statistics Canada, Labour Division. 1995. 'Work Injuries 1992–1994.' Ottawa: Statistics Canada.

Stone, D.A. 1984. *The Disabled State*. Philadelphia: Temple University Press.

Sullivan, R.T. 1980. 'Heart Injuries under Workers' Compensation: Medical and Legal Considerations.' *Suffolk University Law Review* 14: 1387.

Sullivan, T. 1998. 'Health Care Expenditures and Social Spending.' In National Forum on Health, *Canada Health Action: Building on the Legacy*, vol. 4: *Health Care Systems in Canada and Elsewhere*. Ste-Foy, Quebec: Editions Multimondes.

Sullivan, T., and J. Frank. 1999. 'Restating Disability or Disabling the State: Four Challenges.' In T. Sullivan, ed., *Injury and the New World of Work*. Vancouver: University of British Columbia Press.

Tarpley, C.A., and K.E. Jagmin. 1982. 'Workers' Compensation: Third Party Actions against Employers under Comparative Causation.' *Journal of Air Law and Commerce* 47: 187.

Vagero, D. 1995. 'Health Inequalities as Policy Issues – Reflections on Ethics, Policy and Public Health.' *Sociology of Health & Illness* 17: 1.

Viikari-Juntura, E., et al. 1991. 'A Life-Long Prospective Study on the Role of Psychosocial Factors in Neck-Shoulder and Low-Back Pain.' *Spine* 16: 1057.

Vinson, K. 1996. 'Disentangling Law and Fact: Echoes of Proximate Cause in the Workers' Compensation Coverage Formula.' *Alabama Law Review* 47: 722.

Walsh, K., et al. 1989. 'Occupational Causes of Low Back Pain.' *Scandinavian Journal of Work, Environment and Health* 15: 58.

Wilkinson, R.G. 1996. *Unhealthy Societies: The Afflictions of Inequality.* New York: Routledge.

4 Paradoxical Aspects of Low-Back Pain in Workers' Compensation Systems

JOHN W. FRANK

Among the many substantial successes of modern workers' compensation legislation, no one counts the control of disability from low-back pain (LBP). This condition has become rampant within workers' compensation systems, eluding control by legislators and program managers and by their incentives aimed at claimants, employers, and health-care providers. Low-back pain is by far the largest single cause of workers' compensation payments in most jurisdictions, often accounting for nearly half of all pay-outs and typically a third or more of claims. The treatment and rehabilitation costs in 1988 in the United States exceeded $17.9 billion, more than five times the concurrent cost of HIV/AIDS-related health care (Deyo, Cherkin, et al., 1991). A noted Swedish orthopaedic surgeon and back-pain researcher, Alf Nachemson, sees a pernicious combination of workers' compensation incentives and modern societies' high rates of LBP as demonstrating 'the end of the welfare state.' In his own country and in a number of others there is grave concern over the growing epidemic of LBP claims, and particularly chronic-disability awards for them. This concern has led to much hand-wringing and occasionally Draconian measures to deal with the problem, such as drastic cuts in benefit levels, and attempts to adjudicate more strictly those cases that are due and not due to work (Aarts and de Jong, 1996).

Another paper in this volume (Shainblum, Sullivan, and Frank) takes a close look at the intertwined challenges of causation and adjudication for LBP, and for other inherently multifactorial conditions, such as repetitive-strain injuries, that currently make up most claims in workers' compensation systems. In the present paper, we tackle the equally important question of why current workers' compensation systems appear doomed to failure in attempting to reduce disability from this problem. We posit that this failure occurs because of several paradoxical medical/epidemiological and cultural features of this most common cause of chronic disability before mid-life in the industrialized world (Liira et al., 1996; Badley, Rasooly, and Webster, 1994). We will also briefly outline how a properly designed disability-insurance system could, according to current scientific evidence, minimize disability and especially compensated lost time from work in LBP cases, and propose how, in the interim, current workers' compensation arrangements might at least be modestly reformed to deal with the problem.

Basic Epidemiology of Low-Back Pain

The study of the determinants and prevention of health problems is the research domain of epidemiologists, who have focused their attention on disabling LBP only fairly recently (Waddell, 1991; Nachemson, 1992; Frymoyer and Cats-Baril, 1991; Deyo, 1991; Anderson, 1981; Deyo, Cherkin, et al., 1991). There are a number of particular challenges in understanding why so many cases of disabling back pain occur in modern workplaces (Frank, Pulcins, et al., 1995) and why a consistent proportion of workers' compensation claims for this condition – about 7 to 10 per cent – go on to chronicity, after which their prognosis for ever returning to work appears dismal (Frank, Brooker, et al., 1996; Frank, Kerr, et al., 1996a). The present paper addresses the specific features of LBP that make it very unlikely to yield to standard workers' compensation system processes and strategies for reducing work-related disability.

To appreciate how several interrelated factors contribute to this phenomenon, some of the rather unusual medical features of LBP are highlighted here:

- In over 90 per cent of working-age cases of LBP, there are no 'objective' clinical, laboratory, or imaging tests either to confirm the actual presence of a specific pathological lesion, or to indicate its underlying cause (including its 'work-relatedness') (see chapter 3).

Experienced clinicians can only sometimes find clear evidence, on physical examination of acute LBP cases, of actual physical injury to the structures of the low back, such as palpable bony tenderness or muscle spasm. Likewise, only in a small minority of acute cases is there clear evidence of 'functional overlay' – that is, major psychological involvement, for example, as indicated by 'symptom exaggeration' (Matheson, 1988; Hayes et al., 1993; Waddell et al., 1984). Moreover, these relatively specific symptoms and signs are not consistently detected by different observers (Deyo, Rainville, and Kent, 1992). Thus, the diagnosis that doctors officially supply to workers' compensation systems in most such cases is based almost entirely on *listening to the story* given by the patient during history-taking, combined with a few very non-specific signs of painful and perhaps restricted motion on physical examination. These rather vague clinical findings constitute the evidentiary base for disability-claims adjudication in the vast majority of LBP cases in early to mid-life. Having thus eliminated in a basic history and physical exam the more serious (but very rare) causes of LBP in this age group – spinal fracture, cancer, or infection – physicians pronounce the preponderance of cases to be due to 'soft tissue (i.e., muscle, ligament, tendon) strain or sprain,' a diagnosis of exclusion (Agency for Health Care Policy and Research, 1994). The strain/sprain is in fact hypothetical, in that such lesions are not visible on even the most sophisticated CAT or MRI scans now available, nor can they be detected on any known blood, urine, or other laboratory tests. In short, many traditional diagnostic labels applied to this ubiquitous syndrome (LBP, lumbago, paraspinous muscle strain, and a host of others) merely indicate the physician's ignorance of the specific cause, and the absence of a demonstrably more serious diagnosis (Haldeman, 1990; Nachemson, 1983, 1992).

- Not only is it therefore difficult for quasi-legal systems of compensation to establish unequivocally whether a LBP claimant truly has a 'medically certifiable' cause of LBP – it is just as challenging to assess the severity of a given case, and thereby judge its probable prognosis and, in turn, decide on its appropriate management.

In most medical conditions capable of frequently causing permanent disability (up to 10 per cent of cases of compensable LBP), a combination of specific symptoms, physical signs, and laboratory findings generally provides a good indication of clinical severity, and thereby guides management. However, LBP is not assigned, in routine clinical care, any standardized or objective severity rating. (It is ironic and revealing that the workers' compensation literature in fact rather circularly refers to lost-time claim duration *per se* as 'severity.') Indeed, LBP is now generally viewed by expert clinical researchers to be amenable to calibrated measurement by only one type of severity measure: patient-reported pain, disability, and diminished quality-of-life, as recorded on standardized questionnaires (Roland and Morris, 1983; Von Korff et al., 1992; Beaton, Bombardier, and Hogg-Johnson, 1996). Recent research has shown that these subjective measures are impressively repeatable and can predict prognosis as well any 'objective' clinical findings in the vast majority of ordinary LBP cases (S. Hogg-Johnson, Institute for Work and Health, Toronto, personal communication, 1999). Such patient-based severity measures obviously challenge a central tenet of the inherently somewhat adversarial workers' compensation claims adjudication process: the patient's own view of the problem is suspected of bias, supposedly owing to his/her incentive to exaggerate in order to be paid maximal wage-loss benefits. Yet thousands of workers' compensation and disability insurance employees around the world are paid to 'adjudicate' such claims on the basis of 'objective' medical reports, despite the fact that these reports consist largely of doctor-transcribed accounts of pain as related by claimants in the doctor's office, generally accompanied by no 'objective' physical findings.

This is not to say that the LBP claims that are made in workers' compensation systems are frequently bogus. Indeed, the prevailing opinion is that only a tiny fraction of claims do not stand up to intense scrutiny when fraud-investigation techniques are applied. Rather, it is all the more remarkable that more employees in firms covered by such a 'free entry' disability-insurance system do *not* make LBP claims. This is especially so given that LBP is the commonest cause of disability in adult life below age forty-five, even in general-population surveys that include persons with no paid employment, self-employment, or private-insurer disability coverage, as well as those with workers' compensation coverage (Liira et al., 1996). As discussed below, this reluctance to make a claim may be at least partly due to the perception that there is an unpleasant bureaucratic process associated with filing a workers' compensation claim for LBP and other less-visible injuries, including repetitive-strain injuries (Reid, Ewan, and Lowy, 1991).

- Many if not most cases of ordinary LBP do not fit the usual picture of acute injury, which is the assumption underlying standard workers' compensation system procedures and policies.

Further compounding the assessment challenges of LBP in workers' compensation systems is a particularly troublesome aspect of its multi-factorial causation (see chapter 3). Many cases – perhaps the majority (once one controls for the tendency to selectively report back pain as an injury in settings where claimants believe that only acute traumatic cases occurring at work will be fully compensated) – cannot be traced to a particular traumatic event, such as a lift, slip, or fall. This raises the question of whether such cases are a form of slowly developing cumulative trauma disorder – that is, a gradual-onset repetitive-strain injury, like those in the upper limbs and neck now being reported in epidemic proportions throughout the Western world, and which are more akin to a disease than an injury. There is some theoretical rationale for such a view. For example, some biomechanists hypothesize that mechanically important tissues in the back may become frailer over time, owing to repeated micro-trauma, some of it possibly not painful until the late stages (Norman et al., 1997). Current scientific knowledge is, however, simply incapable of helping the clinician accurately to tell the difference between acute and chronic injury in a given patient. Indeed, in middle-aged and older patients, there is considerable difficulty distinguishing injury from specific disease – particularly degenerative joint disease, otherwise known as osteoarthritis. While physicians are trained to believe that ordinary spinal X-ray changes are specific to this condition, studies have shown that there is no correlation between LBP symptoms and the presence of the common radiological signs of osteoarthritis, at least in working-age populations (Boden et al., 1990). As a result, it is perhaps not surprising that much of the usual medical management of LBP cases, which is based on the implicit view that an acute soft-tissue injury has occurred, may be inappropriate (Frymoyer, 1993; Deyo, 1993; Wright, 1945; Deyo, Cherkin, et al., 1991).

- An extraordinarily wide variety of treatments are in use for LBP, many of which have never been demonstrated in well-designed studies to be efficacious, and some of which have been clearly shown to be useless – or worse, iatrogenic contributors to increased disability; yet many third-party payers continue to pay for them.

A recent exhaustive review, by the U.S. Agency for Health Care Policy Research, summarizing over 10,000 published scientific articles on the management of LBP, found only 360 of these to be of sufficiently high quality to be actually useful in the formulation of new empirically based guidelines for care (Agency for Health Care Policy and Research, 1994). Treatments as widely used as transcutaneous electrical nerve stimulation (TENS), traction, and the needling of specific acupuncture points were found to be no better than a placebo in methodologically sound studies. Many other commonly used treatments were so poorly evaluated in the literature that the panel felt no conclusion could be drawn as to their relative benefits. In short, the treatment and rehabilitation industry for LBP is replete with unproven procedures, tests, and treatments. Moreover, there is increasing evidence that a number of interventions in widespread use, particularly in the early phase of LBP, can actually increase the patient's period of disability – that is, lost time from work in the workers' compensation context. For example, early referral to intensive physiotherapy services, instruction in exercises to do at home, or physician prescription of even as little as two days of bed rest have recently all been shown to have this sort of iatrogenic disabling effect (Frank, Brooker, et al., 1996; Frank, Sinclair, et al., 1998; Malmivaara et al., 1995; Sinclair et al., 1997).

Indeed, current evidence-based clinical practice guidelines for the management of uncomplicated LBP suggest that the optimal medical management of acute cases involves nothing more than conducting a basic history and physical exam to rule out 'red flags' that are indicative of possible underlying serious disease (rare in working-age populations, as already noted), advising on the use of over-the-counter analgesics, patient education and reassurance about the usually benign natural history of the condition, and minimal, if any, activity restrictions (Waddell, 1993; Agency for Health Care Policy and Research, 1994). Furthermore, a new high-quality cohort study of various health-care providers' impact on the natural history of LBP suggests that patients' choice of specialists versus chiropractors as primary caregivers leads to no improvement in outcome after some months, but a large extra cost compared to capitated family-physician care (Carey et al., 1995).

Yet any casual examination of what is actually being clinically done to LBP claimants in workers' compensation systems quickly reveals that these results of recent research are not yet being put to use. Furthermore, there is not even a process in place in most workers' compensation systems to eventually bring such ongoing research insights to bear on actual claims management – that is, to limit payment for any form of health-care intervention scientifically demonstrated to be useless or worse. There are many reasons, of course, for this slowness of uptake in the evidence-based management of LBP cases (Liberty International Canada, Frank, et al., 1995; Frank, Sinclair, et al., 1998). A good part of the problem is the enormous variability in natural history across LBP cases, leading in turn to a tendency for physicians to inadvertently over-investigate and over-treat all acute cases, 90 per cent of whom will recover promptly without any treatment in primary-care settings (Hrudey, 1991).

Meanwhile, cases of prolonged disability, people still off work after one or more months of lost time, are often neglected by primary-care providers and insurers alike because of inadequate prompts to ensure aggressive follow-up as incipient chronic pain syndrome is developing (Frank, Sinclair, et al., 1998; Frank, Brooker, et al., 1996). Contributing to the perhaps understandable reluctance of caregivers to intervene decisively in such prolonged cases is the increasingly negative interaction that frequently develops between patient and provider after some weeks of unremitting LBP symptoms. The patient begins to suspect treatment failure and become discouraged, while the provider may feel defensive and frustrated, or even frankly suspicious of malingering, as the pain goes on but no medical cause can be found (Niemeyer, 1991; Feuerstein and Thebarge, 1991; Tarasuk and Eakin, 1994, 1995; Borkan et al., 1995).

- LBP sufferers perceive others' views of them as very negative, since such views appear to involve implications of illegitimacy – either overt malingering, theatrical over-reaction, or ulterior subconscious motives of secondary gain.

This is particularly true as recovery fails to occur when initially expected – 'The doctor can't find anything' – and those around the victim compare his/her prolonged course with their own personal experience of what has usually been rather mild and short-lived LBP (simply because that is the epidemiologically predominant form). Thus it is perhaps not surprising that new studies of factors predicting chronicity of LBP compensation claims suggest that this negativity in social relationships also affects the LBP claimant's workplace relations, interfering with his/her capacity to negotiate a return to work.

There is a widespread view, at least in North American society, that chronic workers' compensation cases of LBP are not primarily due to physical medical problems, but rather are fundamentally psychological and/or involve ulterior-motive factors (Tarasuk and Eakin, 1994,

1995). This misstatement of the very real mind-body problem that occurs in chronic pain (Fordyce, 1994; Waddell, 1987; Frank, Sinclair, et al., 1998; Haldeman, 1990; Frank, Brooker, et al., 1996) arises in part because there is so much variation in the natural history of LBP, and yet it is such a universal human experience. Thus, most middle-aged adults have had it and recovered from it, and most have probably not had to take extended periods off work – particularly if their jobs were not physically demanding and/or allowed some discretionary avoidance of painful tasks such as lifting or bending. Indeed, most people's experience of LBP is sufficiently benign that they have great difficulty understanding why prolonged periods of disability occur in others. This situation is not helped at all by the inability of current medical science to pinpoint exactly where the problem lies, or why recovery is sometimes delayed. In combination, these factors contribute to an atmosphere of suspicion around chronic cases. Receipt of compensation payments is often viewed as the main reason that recovery has not occurred, acting as a perverse incentive to prolong the disability (Hadler, 1989b, 1996a, 1996b; Frank, Pulcins, et al., 1995; Nachemson, 1992). This atmosphere adversely affects relations between the sufferer and his/her entire social environment: caregivers, family, friends, insurer, and the workplace (Deyo and Diehl, 1988; Tarasuk and Eakin, 1994, 1995; Borkan et al., 1995; Reid, Ewan, and Lowy, 1991).

The development of such negative social relationships between LBP compensation claimants and their workplaces has been shown to make a huge difference to the probability of chronicity, as measured by claim duration. In a cohort of some 1560 workers' compensation claimants with LBP and other soft-tissue injuries (i.e., strains and sprains), all those who were still off work after four weeks of lost time were interviewed and then followed up for one year. Workers' perceptions of vulnerability at baseline, such as feeling that filing their compensation claim could affect their job security or that their supervisor had reacted negatively to their filing the claim, interacted strongly with failure of their pain to improve recently (before four weeks of lost time) and the perceived absence of workplace offers of modified work to increase the remaining median time on benefits by seven-fold – from 20 days to 140 days. In other words, claimants not doing well after one month of lost time had their subsequent chances of returning to work adversely affected by perceived negative messages from the workplace (Hogg-Johnson et al., 1998).

Critical here is the failure of the workplace to promptly offer appropriately modified work – perhaps the best established remedy for shortening lost time and speeding recovery in such situations (Crook, 1994; Loisel et al., 1997; Frank, Sinclair, et al., 1998; Frank, Brooker, et al., 1996). In sum, failure to return to work promptly in LBP compensation cases may be largely preventable, if only one could address deepset psychological and cultural reasons for failure of the interested parties to successfully complete the social transaction that lies at the heart of return to work.

Why Current Workers' Compensation Systems Are Not Adequate

Despite the many factors, outlined above, that interfere with the prompt recovery and return to work of LBP cases, surely one could expect the strong economic incentives inherent in modern workers' compensation systems to hold sway and facilitate successful reintegration of the affected worker in the workplace. After all, most such systems now include at least some element of experience rating, so that firms failing to achieve early return to work pay a steep price, in upwards-adjusted future premiums. Unfortunately, in many large workplaces this causal chain of incentives and consequences is broken up by fragmented organizational responsibilities for workers' compensation claims management. In these employment settings, no central figure both sees the whole picture and at the same time has enough authority to overcome a set of complex conflicting perspectives inside the organization. In small firms, on the other hand, there is often no one with appropriate training actually charged with the responsibility for solving these return-to-work problems, or there is just no obvious modified work available.

In large firms, there is often a separation of *responsibility* for managing disability (typically assigned to occupational health services and/or human resources) and the actual *authority* to offer modified work. The latter is often in the hands of front-line production managers, whose primary goal is generally to maintain production to meet quotas, with strong disincentives to take back less-than-able-bodied workers until they are fully recovered from LBP. For example, there is frequently no common cost centre for both lost-time workers' compensation payments, on behalf of the firm as a whole, and the profitability of the actual production units from which modified work offers must come. Thus, no financial incentive is created for frontline managers to disrupt their smooth production processes by offering modified work, since someone else is paying the bill. Furthermore, in settings in which a collective agreement is in place, the authority to offer modified work is often subrogated to the seniority provisions of the agreement, so that modified, lighter duties may be very hard to obtain for injured workers with low seniority. Thus, a conflicting set of goals and responsibilities can stymie firm-wide efforts to *offer* appropriately modified work in a timely fashion – which should ideally occur on the first day of reported pain in mild cases, and certainly within a week even in more severe cases (Frank, Sinclair, et al., 1998; Frank, Brooker, et al., 1996).

To be fair, there can also be union impediments to offering modified work to injured workers, such as rigid seniority rules that reserve lighter jobs for older workers, informally or formally. This is especially likely to occur in settings with older workforces where there is a genuine concern that many able-bodied union members cannot continue to keep up the pace on the job that they once did.

Further complicating matters, in both large and small firm settings, is the tendency for the claimant's personal physician to unwittingly take on an unhelpful iatrogenic role. The physician often writes repeated sick notes in response to his/her patient's understandable anxiety, or outright negativity, about returning to work. In most North American workers' compensation systems, there is no alternative to relying on the claimant's personal physician for the early stages of disability management, partly because of the established rights of injured workers to utilize their own caregiver, and partly owing to the enormous volume of LBP and other soft-tissue injury claims. This claims volume defies active management by third-party payers until the passage of time itself has greatly reduced the number of claimants still off work and thereby needing attention. The rate of claimants currently returning to work is so rapid in the first month or so after lost time begins that only an astonishingly cost-effective and easily implemented third-party-payer intervention in this period can be expected to pay off. Fundamentally, it makes more sense for the large employer or insurer just to wait until the short-lived claims get back to work on their own, and then concentrate on the much smaller number of longer-duration claims that are inherently at the greatest risk of chronicity, simply by virtue of their not having gone back to work early (Frank, Sinclair, et al., 1998; Frank, Brooker, et al., 1996).

This initially laissez-faire disability-management strategy might at first glance be considered compatible with current practice guidelines for the optimal medical care of LBP, referred to above, which discourage aggressive medical management of cases in the first few weeks. However, it does nothing to encourage the *workplace* to do what is essential, by reacting positively and promptly to injury, and by offering modified duties. Nor does it address the existing medical care system's tendency towards iatrogenic over-management of the early mild LBP cases, many of whom could be returning to work even earlier than they do. In short, if workers' compensation systems are to take advantage of current scientific knowledge on how chronic disability due to LBP can be prevented, they need to simultaneously tackle three key challenges: (1) to better motivate firms to quickly and routinely offer modified work as soon as lost time is about to start; (2) to discourage medical over-diagnosis and over-treatment in the first weeks of acute LBP; and (3) to ensure that intensive work-oriented rehabilitation interventions are initiated in the subacute stage, when they are urgently needed. A good example of the latter sort of effective subacute intervention is graded, supervised exercise programs, targeted to the worker's specific job demands. These have been shown in high-quality studies to substantially reverse incipient chronic pain syndrome in workers still off with LBP after a few months of lost time. It is these subacute cases, of three weeks' to three months' duration, that require urgent coordination action before irreversible pain-driven behavioural patterns set in (Philips, Grant, and Berkowitz, 1991; Waddell et al., 1993; Troup and Slade, 1985; Cutler et al., 1994; Fordyce, 1994; Loisel et al., 1997; Frank, Sinclair, et al., 1998; Frank, Brooker, et al., 1996).

Some Suggestions for Change

While there is likely no simple solution to the complex, multifactorial origins of the modern epidemic of LBP occupational disability described above, there are some windows of opportunity worthy of close scrutiny by workers' compensation systems.

Improving Initial Workplace Responses to Complaints of LBP

Firms are currently penalized for encouraging early employee reporting of LBP symptoms by higher workers' compensation premiums, which can sometimes currently be based just as much, or more, on claim rates as on durations. There should be no financial penalty for encouraging employees to report mild LBP and acting promptly to offer those cases modified duties until they heal. There is an unfortunate sense in which most legislation in this field views all new compensation claims as the same – whether they are for traumatic death at work or a crush injury (for both of which the original workers' compensation model was intended and still has merit) or for LBP or repetitive-strain injury (where, by contrast, the challenge is to recognize the problem early and modify the job right away, while providing for high-quality but conservative medical care for the claimant). Penalizing firms for welcoming workers' early complaints of evolving soft-tissue injury symptoms, and dealing with them effectively, makes no sense.

There may be a need to change workers' compensation legislation so as to recognize that many such cases are very difficult if not impossible to prevent in the first place on the basis of current knowledge (although newer ergonomic studies are more promising in this regard: Frank, Kerr, et al., 1996). In short, financial penalties in workers' compensation systems need to be levied against firms that *don't* welcome early formal complaints of such symptoms or take action on them. One way to do this is to specifically reward firms for offering modified work promptly. If current experience-rating systems have any other fault in this regard, it is perhaps that they do not weigh heavily enough the costs associated with more than a few days of lost time (depending on the clinical severity of the case), so as to flag for firms this all-important time-window of opportunity to quickly offer modified work. Perhaps these critical early days of lost time should be billed back to firms with a 'modifiability index' surcharge, increasing weekly to double or triple the value of the actual wage-loss payments accrued to date – to reflect the true opportunity costs of continued inaction. Otherwise there is natural tendency to ignore these cases until the costs climb higher, as chronicity of disability develops, but (unfortunately) reversibility declines (Frank, Brooker, et al., 1996).

While these sorts of economic incentives may be sufficient to improve the performance of large firms in responding to such symptoms in their workforces, they are unlikely to achieve the same success in small firms. Too often there is, as noted above, either no adequately trained (and arm's-length) employee assigned to deal with the problem, or modified duties are simply impossible to find. In such situations, small firms need to pool both their disability management activities and their scarce supply of available modified work. This pooling can be greatly facilitated by large workers' compensation insurers acting as 'bankers' for local (e.g., city/county) *rate groups* of companies. As bankers, the insurers would give credits against future premiums to firms who collectively offer modified work to the employees of other firms in their group unable to do so – while at the same time leaving some margin to act as a financial incentive to all firms to really make an accommodation effort.

A variant of such a scheme has been quite successful in Oregon state, albeit at a later stage in the course of disabled workers' recoveries. This Preferred Worker Program certifies employees with permanent disabilities to be eligible for employment anywhere in the state, subsidized by the Workers' Compensation Division of the Oregon Department of Consumer and Business Services. Such subsidies include three years of premium exemption, full claim cost reimbursement to the new employer for any new claim in the same period, a generous 50 per cent wage subsidy for the first six months of the new job, assistance with job modification, and re-employment/retraining expenses relief for both firm and worker. While this program is obviously so generous as a whole that it is probably only cost-effective for permanently disabled workers, the same principles could be applied much earlier in the course of disability development – for example, before the start of the chronic phase at three months of lost-time, but after intensive work-conditioning interventions to improve the medical condition of workers with low-back pain who may have an employer too small (or rigid) to accommodate them.

One notes that the skills of trained disability-management professionals could also be afforded by local rate groups of small firms, for the first time, and these professionals could build a detailed knowledge of the local labour market for specific kinds of modified work, and thus effectively manage a wide variety of workers' compensation claims, not just those for LBP, throughout the firms' community.

Improving the Quality of Primary and Secondary Health Care and Rehabilitation

Efforts to meet this challenge have included a wide variety of specific strategies, ranging from 'carrot to stick' in terms of their philosophy of interaction with health professionals. The benign educational approach has been extensively evaluated in the context of attempting to change other aspects of physician behaviour (Lomas and Haynes,

1988; Lomas et al., 1989; Lomas, 1993; Davis et al., 1992). While some modest success has been reported, these approaches to improving the quality of care provided in a community tend to be resource-intensive (e.g., they involve the identification, winning-over, and intensive briefing of local influentials, or the assignment of an academic detailer to each caregiver) if they are to have much of an impact on professionals behaviour. More attractive to insurers and compensation boards are various economically oriented strategies pioneered in managed care, generally in the United States. These include detailed computerized surveillance of claim file bills for medical and other services, with prompt feedback to each provider regarding any substantial departure from established (and hopefully scientifically evidence-based) guidelines for the care of the condition in question. Initially this feedback tends to be a polite reminder, while later feedback to continued noncompliers often takes the form of 'Your bill for ... will not be paid unless ...' While some health-care providers may take umbrage at this style of managed care, it is already so ensconced in the United States for a wide range of conditions, in many settings, that its increased use in workers' compensation systems is virtually inevitable. There are even a few published reports of greatly reduced care costs and improved rehabilitation outcomes for LBP using this approach (Wiesel, Boden, and Feffer, 1994). Indeed, early indications of this approach are even being seen in Canada, where there has been no tradition of such interventions in the universal system of government-funded health-care services. As a transitional measure, one also sees Canadian compensation boards in a few provinces beginning to embed evidence-based guidelines in routine compensation reporting forms that physicians must submit to back up a worker's claim. In this strategy, it is hoped that filling out the forms, and being guided by them towards rational care, will occur without necessarily raising providers' hackles regarding professional prerogatives.

Whatever specific modus operandi is chosen for upgrading health-care providers' attention to optimizing recovery and achieving early return to work, there is a special challenge in simultaneously attempting to reduce the tests and treatments used in the early acute phase of LBP – up to three weeks after onset – while achieving a much more aggressive utilization of intensive rehabilitation in the subacute phase, from three weeks to three months after symptom onset (Frank, Sinclair, et al., 1998; Frank, Brooker, et al., 1996). Thus, a key implementation issue is the strategic separation of these two messages. In fact, the former message must be effectively transmitted to all health professionals seeing LBP cases in primary care, since the potential for iatrogenic over-management begins right at the first visit to the provider, often well before the compensating authority is even aware of the claim. The frequent neglect of subacute cases, on the other hand, can be rectified by prompt insurer feedback to the provider, at the three-to-four-week point, for claimants still off work and on benefits. Indeed, some would argue that the risks of chronic disability have become so great in these subacute cases that the third-party payer is justified in absolutely requiring, as a condition of further benefits payments, a rigorous, standardized, multidisciplinary independent assessment and treatment plan on all subacute cases. Certainly leaving the claimant in usual care, until some months of lost time have elapsed, represents both neglectful and unethical treatment of the claimant, and unsound disability management. For we now know how to turn many such cases around at the subacute stage, and get them back to both recovery and work.

Improving the Interactions between Health-Care Providers and the Workplace

There is another major cause of unnecessary disability in occupational LBP – dysfunctional interaction between the workplace and the primary care provider of the affected worker. In a nutshell, many jurisdictions have either legally sanctioned or informally respected the rights of the worker to attend his/her own personal physician upon suspicion of a work-related health problem. This safeguard is understandable in the many North American workplaces where no organized occupational health services exist (or, the impartiality of those that exist is doubted by workers and unions). However, the ordinary primary-care physician cannot be expected to have detailed knowledge of modified work options at his/her patients' workplaces – or even of the physical demands of their patients' usual jobs. Furthermore, there is rarely any provision in the medical reimbursement system to pay the physician to take part in a conference call, or to contact the workplace directly to discuss modified work. Indeed, although a number of recent official statements by several Canadian medical associations suggest that optimal practice should include such physician–workplace communication, it is unlikely to be widely done under the current fee-for-service schedules in Canada. Some physicians even seem to feel it may be ethically questionable to initiate workplace contact, despite their associations' reassurances to the contrary. In the end, these failures of communication too often lead the physician to either prescribe excessive periods off work or, fearing that overexertion at work or employer insensitivity to the injured worker may cause a recurrence, keep sending vague notes recommending light duties back with his/her occupational LBP patients for far longer than is needed.

To remedy this situation, one can immediately think of simple communications devices, such as forms sent by the workplace with the injured worker on his/her first visit to the physician/chiropractor/ physiotherapist of choice detailing the specific modified work options available, and asking the health professional to choose the one most suitable for that worker at that point in recovery. While many firms are using these sorts of forms, and they are some help in improving the degree to which appropriately modified work is utilized, they may be insufficient when busy health-care providers have little incentive to fill them in thoughtfully. More promising are specific economic incentives, such as fees paid for filling out modified work prescriptions or for engaging in conference calls with the insurer and workplace disability managers, to ensure that appropriately modified work is actually available and offered. But, in many jurisdictions, it is unclear who should pay for this work, which is long associated with occupational health care, presumably paid for at the workplace. Yet the vast majority of Canadian workplaces have no access to even occupational nurses, let alone occupational physicians (unlike the situation in much of Europe, where such access tends to be legally required and these specialties are much better developed). If the costs saved as a result of instituting high-quality disability-management programs, involving on-site occupational health services, truly defray the annual workers' compensation bill of firms, then it would seem reasonable for the firms to pay. In practice, however, it is likely that any initiative to implement such payments for essential occupational health services uniformly across firms, which is the most sensible and cost-effective approach, would have to come from large third-party payers, such as state or provincial workers' compensation boards.

Conclusion

Workers' compensation systems throughout the world are facing a slow epidemic of disability due to low-back pain (LBP), the largest single cause of claims and pay-outs. This chapter has reviewed current clinical and epidemiological knowledge concerning the causes, natural history, and treatment of this condition, in the context of workers' compensation systems. It is argued that a number of extraordinary paradoxes apply to LBP in this setting that render the usual economic incentives and disincentives inherent in workers' compensation systems relatively incapable of reducing disability. Specifically, the following features of LBP have been shown to require a different kind of compensation system from that originally developed for acute trauma: (1) LBP cannot generally be objectively diagnosed, with accuracy, as to either its specific mode of development or its severity; (2) the underlying causes of any given case are not amenable to specification by any objective tests or investigations – and even the time and place of occurrence are often unknown, owing to frequent lags between relevant exposures and the experience of pain, and the ubiquitous development of LBP without any specific provocation or accident; (3) the current therapeutic arsenal of medicine against LBP is rather ineffective in the vast majority of cases, and indeed many mild cases appear to suffer iatrogenic (doctor-caused) extensions of disability through over-diagnosis and over-treatment; (4) there is a widespread cultural tendency to suspect persons making LBP workers' compensation claims of symptom exaggeration and secondary gain – partly because the doctor can't find anything, and partly because the natural history of LBP is so variable that the majority of mild sufferers can't easily empathize with the less common, severely affected cases. Each of these paradoxical aspects of LBP has been discussed and analysed here with respect to its effects on the traditional manner of handling LBP claims by workers' compensation systems. Finally, some practical suggestions have been made for system redesign that might overcome the problems described.

To conclude, there are a number of paradoxical features of LBP that make controlling the current global epidemic of LBP disability a difficult challenge. However, in workers' compensation settings, there appear to be reasonable policy and program options, some of them only beginning to be tried, for tackling this problem. Some of these solutions will require the redesign of current disability-insurance systems so as to take advantage of recent insights gained from exciting new research in this field. What remains now for these changes to take place is for the will to be made manifest.

REFERENCES

Aarts, L.J.M., and P.R. de Jong. 1996. 'European Experience with Disability.' In J. Mashaw, ed., *Disability, Work and Cash Benefits*. Kalamazoo, Mich.: W.E. Upjohn Institute.

Agency for Health Care Policy and Research. 1994. *Clinical Practice Guideline Number 14: Acute Low Back Problems in Adults*. Rockville, Md.: U.S. Department of Health and Human Services.

Anderson, J.A.D. 1981. 'Low Back Pain – Cause and Prevention of Long-Term Handicap (A Critical Review).' *International Rehabilitation Medicine* 3(2): 89–93.

Badley, E.M., I. Rasooly, and G.K. Webster. 1994. 'Relative Importance of Musculoskeletal Disorders as a Cause of Chronic Health Problems, Disability, and Health Care Utilization: Findings from the 1990 Ontario Health Survey.' *Journal of Rheumatology* 21(3): 505–14.

Beaton, D.E., C. Bombardier, and S.A. Hogg-Johnson. 1996. 'Measuring Health in Injured Workers: A Cross-Sectional Comparison of Five Generic Health Status Instruments in Workers with Musculoskeletal Injuries.' *American Journal of Industrial Medicine* 29: 618–31.

Boden, S.D., D.O. Davis, T.S. Dina, N.J. Patronas, and S.W. Wiesel. 1990. 'Abnormal Magnetic-Resonance Scans of the Lumbar Spine in Asymptomatic Subjects: A Prospective Investigation.' *Journal of Bone and Joint Surgery, American volume* 72A(3): 403–8.

Borkan, J., S. Reis, D. Hermoni, and A. Biderman. 1995. 'Talking about the Pain: A Patient-Centered Study of Low Back Pain in Primary Care.' *Social Science and Medicine* 40: 977–88.

Carey, T.S., J. Garrett, A. Jackman, C. McLaughlin, J. Fryer, D.R. Smucker, and North Carolina Back Pain Project. 1995. 'The Outcomes and Costs of Care for Acute Low Back Pain among Patients Seen by Primary Care Practitioners, Chiropractors, and Orthopedic Surgeons.' *New England Journal of Medicine* 333: 913–17.

Crook, J.M. 1994. 'A Longitudinal Epidemiological Study of Injured Workers: Prognostic Indicators of Work Disability.' Mimeo, University of Toronto.

Cutler, R.B., D.A. Fishbain, H.L. Rosomoff, E. Abdel-Moty, T.M. Khalil, and R.S. Rosomoff. 1994. 'Does Nonsurgical Pain Center Treatment of Chronic Pain Return Patients to Work? A Review and Meta-Analysis of the Literature.' *Spine* 19(6): 643–52.

Davis, D.A., M.A. Thomson, A.D. Oxman, and R.B. Haynes. 1992. 'Evidence for the Effectiveness of CME: A Review of 50 Randomized Controlled Trials.' *Journal of the American Medical Association* 268(9): 1111–17.

Deyo, R.A. 1991. 'Low-Back-Pain.' *Advances in Pain Research and Therapy* 18: 291–303.

– 1993. 'Practice Variations, Treatment Fads, Rising Disability: Do We Need a New Clinical Research Paradigm?' *Spine* 18(15): 2153–62.

Deyo, R.A., D. Cherkin, D. Conrad, and E. Volinn. 1991. 'Cost, Controversy, Crisis: Low Back Pain and the Health of the Public.' *Annual Review of Public Health* 12: 141–56.

Deyo, R.A., and A.K. Diehl 1988. 'Psychosocial Predictors of Disability in Patients with Low Back Pain.' *Journal of Rheumatology* 15(10): 1557–64.

Deyo, R.A., J. Rainville, and D.L. Kent. 1992. 'What Can the History and Physical Examination Tell Us about Low Back Pain?' *Journal of the American Medical Association* 268(6): 760–5.

Feuerstein, M., and R.W. Thebarge 1991. 'Perceptions of Disability and Occupational Stress as Discriminators of Work Disability in Patients with Chronic Pain.' *Journal of Occupational Rehabilitation* 1: 135–95.

Fordyce, W.E. 1994. *Back Pain in the Workplace. Report of the Task Force on Pain in the Workplace.* Seattle: International Association for the Study of Pain.

Frank, J.W., A. Brooker, S. DeMaio, M.S. Kerr, A. Maetzel, H.S. Shannon, T.S. Sullivan, R.W. Norman, and R. Wells. 1996. 'Disability Resulting from Occupational Low Back Pain, Part II: What Do We Know about Secondary Prevention? A Review of the Scientific Evidence on Prevention after Disability Begins.' *Spine* 21: 2918–29.

Frank, J.W., M.S. Kerr, A. Brooker, S. DeMaio, A. Maetzel, H.S. Shannon, T.S. Sullivan, R.W. Norman, and R. Wells. 1996. 'Disability Resulting from Occupational Low Back Pain, Part I: What Do We Know about Primary Prevention? A Review of the Scientific Evidence on Prevention before Disability Begins.' *Spine* 21: 2908–17.

Frank, J.W., I.R. Pulcins, M.S. Kerr, H.S. Shannon, and S. Stansfeld. 1995. 'Occupational Back Pain – An Unhelpful Polemic.' *Scandinavian Journal of Work, Environment and Health* 21: 3–14.

Frank, J., S. Sinclair, S. Hogg-Johnson, H. Shannon, C. Bombardier, D. Beaton, and D. Cole. 1998. 'Preventing Disability from Low Back Pain: New Evidence Gives New Hope – If We Can Just Get All of the Players Onside.' *Canadian Medical Association Journal* 158(12):1625–31.

Frymoyer, J.W. 1993. 'An International Challenge to the Diagnosis and Treatment of Disorders of the Lumbar Spine.' *Spine* 18(15): 2147–52.

Frymoyer, J.W., and W.L. Cats-Baril. 1991. 'An Overview of the Incidence and Costs of Low Back Pain.' *Orthopedic Clinics of North America* 22(2): 263–71.

Hadler, N.M. 1989. 'Disabling Backache in France, Switzerland, and the

Netherlands: Contrasting Sociopolitical Constraints on Clinical Judgment.'
Journal of Occupational Medicine 31(10): 823–31.

– 1996a. 'Regional Back Pain: Predicament at Home, Nemesis at Work.' *Journal of Occupational and Environmental Medicine* 38: 973–8.

– 1996b. 'Disability Determination and Social Conscience.' *Arthritis Care and Research* 9:163–9.

Haldeman, S. 1990. 'Failure of the Pathology Model to Predict Back Pain.' *Spine* 15(7): 718–24.

Hayes, B., C.A.E. Solyom, P.C. Wing, and J. Berkowitz. 1993. 'Use of Psychometric Measures and Nonorganic Signs Testing in Detecting Nomogenic Disorders in Low Back Pain Patients.' *Spine* 18(10): 1254–62.

Hogg-Johnson, S.H., D.C. Cole, and Early Claimant Cohort Modeling Group. 1998. 'Early Prognostic Factors in for Duration on Benefits among Workers with Compensated Occupational Soft Tissue Injuries.' Working paper no. 64. Toronto: Institute for Work and Health.

Hrudey, W.P. 1991. 'Overdiagnosis and Overtreatment of Low Back Pain: Long-Term Effects.' *Journal of Occupational Rehabilitation* 1(4): 303–12.

Liberty International Canada, J. Frank, A. Brooker, S. DeMaio, M. Kerr, A. Maetzel, H. Shannon, T. Sullivan, R. Norman, and R. Wells. 1995. 'Unfolding Change Workers' Compensation in Canada: A Review by the Institute of Work and Health of Current Knowledge about the Prevention of Disability Due to Low Back Pain.' Liberty International Canada.

Liira, J.P., H.S. Shannon, L.W. Chambers, and T.A. Haines. 1996. 'Long-Term Back Problems and Physical Work Exposures in the 1990 Ontario Health Survey.' *American Journal of Public Health* 86: 382–7.

Loisel, P., P. Durand, L. Abenhaim, R. Simard, J. Turcotte, and J.M. Esdaile. 1997. 'A Population-Based Randomized Trial on Back Pain Management.' *Spine* 22: 2911–18.

Lomas, J. 1993. *Teaching Old (and Not So Old) Docs New Tricks: Effective Ways to Implement Research Findings.* Hamilton: McMaster University.

Lomas, J., G.M. Anderson, K. Domnick-Pierre, E. Vayda, M.W. Enkin, and W.J. Hannah. 1989. 'Do Practice Guidelines Guide Practice? The Effect of a Consensus Statement on the Practice of Physicians. *New England Journal of Medicine* 321(19): 1306–11.

Lomas, J., and R.B. Haynes. 1988. 'A Taxonomy and Critical Review of Tested Strategies for the Application of Clinical Practice Recommendations: From "Official" to "Individual" Clinical Policy.' *American Journal of Preventive Medicine* 4 (Suppl.): 77–94.

Malmivaara, A., U. Hakkinen, T. Aro, M. Heinrichs, L. Koskenniemi, E. Kuosma, S. Lappi, R. Paloheimo, C. Servo, and V. Vaaranen. 1995. 'The Treat-

ment of Acute Low Back Pain – Bed Rest, Exercises, or Ordinary Activity?'
New England Journal of Medicine 332(6): 351–5.

Matheson, L.N. 1988. 'Symptom Magnification Syndrome.' In S.J. Isserhagen,
ed., *Work Injury: Management and Prevention*. New York: Aspen Publishing.

Nachemson, A.L. 1983. 'Work for All: For Those with Low Back Pain as Well.'
Clinical Orthopaedics and Related Research 179: 77–85.

– 1992. 'Newest Knowledge of Low Back Pain – a Critical Look.' *Clinical
Orthopaedics and Related Research* 279: 8–20.

Niemeyer, L.O. 1991. 'Social Labeling, Stereotyping, and Observer Bias in
Workers' Compensation: The Impact of Provider-Patient Interaction on Outcome.' *Journal of Occupational Rehabilitation* 1(4): 251–69.

Norman, R., R.Wells, P. Neumann, J. Frank, H. Shannon, and M. Kerr. 1997. 'A
Comparison of Peak vs. Cumulative Physical Work Exposure Risk Factors
for the Reporting of Low Back Pain in the Automotive Industry.' Unpublished manuscript.

Philips, H.C., L. Grant, and J. Berkowitz. 1991. 'The Prevention of Chronic Pain
and Disability: A Preliminary Investigation.' *Behaviour, Research and Therapy*
29(5): 443–50.

Reid, J., C. Ewan, and E. Lowy. 1991. 'Pilgrimage of Pain: The Illness Experiences of Women with Repetition Strain Injury and the Search for Credibility.'
Social Science and Medicine 32(5): 601–12.

Roland, M., and R. Morris. 1983. 'A Study of the Natural History of Back Pain –
Part I: Development of a Reliable and Sensitive Measure of Disability in
Low-Back Pain.' *Spine* 8(2): 141–4.

Sinclair, S.J., S.A. Hogg-Johnson, M.V. Mondloch, and S.A. Shields. 1997. 'The
Effectiveness of an Early Active Intervention Program for Workers with Soft
Tissue Injuries: The Early Claimant Cohort Study.' *Spine* 22: 2919–31.

Tarasuk, V., and J.M. Eakin. 1994. 'Back Problems Are for Life: Perceived Vulnerability and Its Implications for Chronic Disability.' *Journal of Occupational
Rehabilitation* 4(1): 55–64.

– 1995. 'The Problem of Legitimacy in the Experience of Work-Related Back
Injury.' *Qualitative Health Research* 5: 204–21.

Troup, J.D.G., and P.D. Slade. 1985. 'Fear Avoidance and Chronic Musculoskeletal Pain.' *Stress Medicine* 1: 217–20.

Von Korff, M., J. Ormel, F.J. Keefe, and S.F. Dworkin. 1992. 'Grading the Severity of Chronic Pain.' *Pain* 50(2): 133–49.

Waddell, G. 1987. 'A New Clinical Model for the Treatment of Low-Back Pain.'
Spine 12(7): 632–44.

– 1991. 'Low Back Disability: A Syndrome of Western Civilization.' *Neurosur-
gery Clinics of North America* 2: 719–38.

– 1993. 'Simple Low Back Pain: Rest or Active Exercise?' *Annals of the Rheumatic Diseases* 52: 317–19.

Waddell, G., C.J. Main, E.W. Morris, M. DiPaola, and I.C.M. Gray. 1984. 'Chronic Low-Back Pain, Psychologic Distress, and Illness Behaviour.' *Spine* 9(2): 209–13.

Waddell, G., M. Newton, I. Henderson, D. Somerville, and C.J. Main. 1993. 'A Fear-Avoidance Beliefs Questionnaire (FABQ) and the Role of Fear-Avoidance Beliefs in Chronic Low Back Pain and Disability.' *Pain* 52: 157–68.

Wiesel, S.W., S.D. Boden, and H.L. Feffer. 1994. 'A Quality-Based Protocol for Management of Musculoskeletal Injuries: A Ten-Year Prospective Outcome Study.' *Clinical Orthopaedics and Related Research* 301: 164–76.

Wright, I.S. 1945. 'The Neurovascular Syndrome Produced by Hyperabduction of the Arms.' *American Heart Journal* 29: 1–19.

5 The Effect of Workers' Compensation and Other Payroll Taxes on the Macro Economies of Canada and Ontario

PETER DUNGAN[1]

This study examines the impact of changes in workers' compensation (WC) premiums, and in payroll taxes more generally, on the aggregate economies of Canada and Ontario. Such a change occurred, for example, with the 1996 Ontario Workers' Compensation Board premium-rate (and benefit) decreases, and could occur if there were to be significant across-the-board increases in WC premiums to offset the unfunded liabilities typical of most provincial plans, or to fund new forms of work-related injuries (see Gunderson, this volume, chapters 2 and 6). There have also been recent and relatively large changes in premium rates for Employment Insurance (EI) and the Canada and Québec Pension Plans and more changes are scheduled for future years.

This study investigates the impact of changes in payroll taxes with the aid of computer simulation models of the Canadian and Ontario economies – specifically, the FOCUS and FOCUS-Ontario macroeconometric models built and maintained at the Institute for Policy Analysis of the University of Toronto. Using these tools permits us to take account of the simultaneous interaction of a range of macroeconomic factors and policies and of their interaction over time. We can also investigate the special properties of a payroll tax change by experimenting with alternative tax changes in an identical framework and comparing the results.

Three major sections follow. The first reviews briefly the current state of knowledge on the subject, identifying the major points of agreement and controversy. The second section describes the two macroeconometric models used for the study, concentrating on those features especially relevant for the analysis of payroll taxes. The third section describes the simulation experiments in detail and presents the results.

The Macroeconomic Impacts of Payroll Taxes: A Review of the Issues

There is an ample literature on the impact of payroll taxes. The private sector in Canada in the mid-1990s has put forth a variety of arguments and studies to show the negative effects of payroll taxes on the economy, and their sentiments have been echoed, in word if not deed, by numerous politicians. One of the most careful and most cited of such studies is by Finlayson and McEwan (1996) for the Business Council of British Columbia. They argue that payroll taxes have serious adverse effects on the macroeconomy both in the short and long term and that a significant part of the blame for the poor performance of the Canadian economy since 1990 can be attributed to high and rising payroll taxes.

Kesselman (1996) and Di Matteo and Shannon (1995) provide excellent reviews of the more even-handed academic literature.[2] In what follows, key items of agreement and controversy in the literature on the impact of payroll taxes are summarized as responses to three questions:

1 What is the short-run and long-run incidence and impact of the payroll tax, and how does the transition from short-run to long-run take place?
2 What is the longer-run efficiency and general economic impact of the payroll tax, especially relative to alternative taxes?
3 Are there particular features of Workers' Compensation or other payroll taxes that can alter the general effects identified?

As we examine each question we shall be especially concerned to identify features that either do or do not appear in the macroeconometric models used for the empirical analysis.

The Short-Run and Long-Run Incidence and Impact of the Payroll Tax

There appears to be general agreement in the literature that the *short-run* incidence of a payroll tax falls largely on the employer. The *long-*

run or final incidence depends on the relative wage elasticity of labour supply and labour demand, with most studies concluding that the final incidence is shifted almost fully to employees. As noted by Kesselman (1996: 171–2), this is consistent with the general finding in empirical studies of the labour market that there is little or no elasticity of labour supply with respect to the 'take-home' real wage. That is, reductions in the demand for labour, engendered by a payroll tax increase, ultimately lead to wage reductions because labour supply is not reduced in response to the tax. This is part of the more general economic proposition that tax increases are ultimately shifted to the relatively more immobile factor of production that cannot escape the tax increase. In the case of payroll taxes for programs like workers' compensation, there are also associated benefits to labour (the insurance benefit) so that the reduction in real wages also reflects 'payment' for those benefits. Recently, however, some contrary evidence on long-run impacts and incidence has been forthcoming; this will be reviewed below.

Given that the immediate short-run incidence of a payroll tax change falls on employers, but that all or most of the eventual long-run incidence falls on employees, how does this long-term shifting of incidence take place? The literature is not very specific, but three interrelated mechanisms can be conjectured. Each will be presented in the context of an unanticipated increase in payroll taxes, but each would work analogously (if not always symmetrically in size) for a decrease.

MECHANISMS FOR SHIFTING INCIDENCE

First, the shift in incidence may simply occur in the next round of formal or informal wage bargaining, if it is not too distant from the date of the payroll tax change and if both sides understand the pressures at work (for example, if the employer can make credible forecasts of layoffs or closures if the wages it must pay, inclusive of payroll tax, are not reduced). Second, employers in general may shift an increase in payroll taxes into prices and then resist any changes in nominal wages that might result. A general rise in the price level resulting from a payroll tax increase being passed through to prices will lower *real* wages and shift the tax incidence. Of course, for this mechanism not to 'cost jobs,' it must be the case that the monetary authorities permit the temporary increase in the inflation rate necessary to reduce real wages, and that labour accept the reduction in real wages in subsequent bargaining rounds. However, it is likely that labour, unless widely convinced that the payroll tax increase confers some direct benefit across all workers (e.g., as might be the case with a properly formulated increase in payroll taxes for pensions), may resist a direct wage reduction or a real wage reduction through additional inflation. In this case the third mechanism comes into effect: labour is laid off because at the current real wage (inclusive of payroll taxes) it is 'too expensive.' Excess or 'involuntary' unemployment then results. In time, in the standard Phillips Curve formulation, this increase in unemployment above the 'full-employment' unemployment rate will put downward pressure on real wages in successive wage bargaining rounds until, eventually, the after-payroll-tax real wage to employers falls to earlier levels (and the take-home real wage of workers falls). The incidence of the tax will then have been fully passed onto workers and earlier levels of employment (or full employment) will again occur.

IMPORTANCE OF LABOUR-SUPPLY ELASTICITY

If the supply of labour is completely inelastic with respect to the real wage, as was assumed above, then there will be no long-run change in the level of employment from a change in payroll taxes – although there quite likely will be a short-term change. Once the Phillips Curve mechanism has worked, the full-employment unemployment rate will re-emerge, which, with a given labour force, will yield the original employment level. If, however, labour supply (e.g., labour-force participation) is sensitive to the real wage, then a rise in payroll taxes that eventually reduces real wages will also reduce labour supply. The original full-employment unemployment rate will again re-emerge, but when applied to a smaller labour force the result will be lower long-run employment (and output). The incidence of the tax will be 'shared': employees will earn a lower real wage than before but a higher real wage than if they had to absorb the tax fully; employers will be paying, after payroll taxes, a higher real wage than previously, but to a smaller number of workers. Strictly speaking, even in this case then there is no permanent change in 'involuntary' unemployment; the reduction in employment comes from the voluntary withdrawal of some individuals from the labour market at the offered real wage.

If labour supply is not completely inelastic with respect to the real wage, then it is the combination of labour-supply and labour-demand elasticities that will determine any long-term employment impacts of payroll taxes and the shifting of incidence. Di Matteo and Shannon (1995: 19) give a table of impacts for alternative elasticity measures. For example, if labour-supply and labour-demand elasticities each have absolute values of 0.15 (in my opinion, high for supply and low for demand) then the long-run incidence is evenly split and a 1 per cent rise in the marginal payroll tax rate (roughly a 10 per cent increase in payroll taxes collected) decreases employment in the long run by 0.08 per cent, or about 10,500 (based on 1997 employment of about 14 million). Still following their table, if the supply elasticity is .15 (i.e., still relatively high) but demand elasticity is $-.3$, then labour takes 2/3 of the incidence of the tax, but the employment reduction is 0.1 per cent, or about 14,000 for 1997.

In the macroeconometric models used in the present study, we have not found that labour-force participation depends on the real wage at all (i.e., our labour-supply measure is perfectly inelastic). We therefore know in advance that the model results will show a zero *long-run* impact of a payroll tax change on employment; the incidence of the tax will be shifted fully to labour in the form of real wage reductions (in our model through price increases and wage decreases). In the short run, however, unemployment results until real wages fall sufficiently to restore employment. The models, therefore, shed important light on the workings of the adjustment mechanisms and on the costs and speed of adjustment.

THE THREE ADJUSTMENT MECHANISMS IN PRACTICE

In practice, the three mechanisms for adjusting to a payroll tax change will be difficult to disentangle. In the macroeconometric models used for the present study, the first mechanism is effectively not present: we have found no evidence that wage bargaining in any way 'automatically' passes through payroll tax changes to changes in money wages and hence real wages (although it is still possible to conjecture particular policy changes that might, at least partially, make this occur). The second and third mechanisms are both at work: firms attempt to pass through at least some of a payroll tax increase onto prices, thereby reducing real wages, but employees resist a real-wage reduction and consequently some temporary increase in unemployment occurs, ultimately putting downward pressure on real wages until the original level of employment is restored. How big this increase is, and how long 'temporary' is, are what the present study attempts to show, as the literature for Canada offers very little direct measurement of the short-term or medium-term impacts of payroll taxes on employment and wages.

WHY DO PAYROLL TAX CHANGES INDUCE SHORT-TERM EMPLOYMENT CHANGES?

Given that, under most analyses, it seems clear that the bulk of payroll tax incidence will eventually be borne by workers, it might be asked why workers in general will endure what could be a serious spell of involuntary unemployment in the transition resulting from an increase in general payroll taxation. The reasons are those behind sluggish labour-market adjustment in general: for example, it may appear equally irrational (if less unusual) that labour in general endures a spell of involuntary unemployment rather than cutting real wages in the face of a negative demand shock to the economy. First, the institutional arrangements of periodic formal or informal wage bargaining and the resulting overlapping contracts partly explain a slow response to an unanticipated payroll tax increase. Second, for most workers, resisting the pass-through of a payroll tax increase on one's employer makes individual economic sense: the probability is small that most workers – experienced, with seniority, in relatively profitable industries – will lose their jobs if real wages are 'generally' too high. To accept a lower real wage immediately in the face of a general payroll tax increase is to forego, for most workers, some real income that would otherwise be earned as one stayed employed over the subsequent few years. In the unionized sector particularly, the median union voter may be relatively immune from the threat of unemployment. In fact, the adverse employment consequences may fall mainly on 'outsiders' in the form of reduced new job creation. Third, short-term periods of unemployment are supported by unemployment insurance, while wage reductions obviously are not supported in this way. Fourth, employees may feel that employers are 'bluffing' about their inability to absorb payroll tax increases, in which case employees may compel employers to absorb them through employment reductions (which are also costly to employers) rather than wage reductions (where the costs fall solely on employees). Only gradually, under the pressure of higher unemployment in the general economy and lower profitability within each industry, will wage bargains eventually be struck that shift the incidence of the tax. (A climate in which real wages can be eroded by at least some moderate inflation may also be important to the transition, an argument put forward by Fortin, 1996.)[3]

To help clarify the points above, consider the short-term effects of a payroll tax levied on *workers* rather than employers. (Both Employment Insurance and the Canada and Quebec Pension Plans are, of course, funded by payroll taxes on workers and employers. Conceptually, workers' compensation could be collected from workers [as an insurance premium] rather than from employers.) In this case, the tax is applied exactly where most or all of the eventual incidence will occur. As with any tax increase, there will probably be an effect on the economy through a reduction of purchasing power and aggregate demand, but there will be no 'extra' short-term transition costs of unemployment associated with having to transfer the tax incidence from firms to employees. First, because of slow and periodic wage re-contracting, under a payroll tax increase levied on workers there will be no impact on wage costs of most firms for quite some time. When individual bargaining sessions begin after the payroll tax on employees has been increased, it will be in a situation where most firms (including direct and indirect competitors) are *not* paying the payroll tax increase; therefore, to try to force the tax back onto one's own employer risks making that employer uncompetitive and significantly raises the probability of unemployment, especially relative to the situation in which the payroll tax increase is levied on firms and *all* firms start off at a competitive disadvantage. In this situation, with the long-run incidence in a sense established in the short run, there is likely to be much less short-term labour-market disruption and far less need of the Phillips Curve mechanism of increased unemployment to 'force' the long-run incidence. In essence, imposing the tax directly on where it will ultimately reside can avoid the real resource costs (in this case, of unemployment) associated with it being shifted to its ultimate payer. Interestingly, this suggests that labour could be made better off by directly paying the payroll tax (that it will ultimately pay in any case), at least to the extent that the costs of unemployment falling on a few are greater than the cost of a small real wage reduction spread over the larger workforce (Vaillancourt, 1995). Of course, this flies in the face of the widely held myth, happily encouraged by politicians, that it is employers who 'really' pay payroll taxes.

Long-Run Employment Impacts of Payroll Taxes

All this said, there is still some evidence that payroll taxes have long-term impacts on employment and output. Since we know that the macro-econometric models used for this study will yield no such result (as labour supply is completely wage-inelastic), it is important to review briefly the alternative evidence.

A series of mostly recent studies give some indication of a permanent effect of payroll taxes on employment. Finlayson and McEwan (1996), in putting forward the anti-payroll-tax side of the debate, cite studies by Coe (1990) for the IMF and Poloz (1994) at the Bank of Canada that attribute part of the increase in the Canadian unemployment rate since the 1960s to an increase in payroll taxation. The correlation in time is undeniable, but does not necessarily indicate causality. Coe simply regresses the unemployment rate against a series of possible explanatory terms, including the level of payroll taxation, and finds the latter significant. Poloz (1994: 10–12) reviews other studies at the Bank of Canada and again finds that they show a contemporaneous correlation. However, Poloz is much more cautious in his conclusions, especially for the long term. First, he notes that the Unemployment Insurance system, because it is required to balance its accounts with only a brief lag, has been historically required to raise UI premiums in times of high unemployment, thereby contributing to a correlation of payroll taxes and unemployment.[4] Second, he recognizes that the work he is reviewing does not establish a permanent link between higher payroll taxes and higher unemployment, the long-term impact depending on the degree of pass-through of the tax and the speed of adjustment.

Di Matteo and Shannon (1995) take a different approach and estimate real-wage and employment equations, following an earlier specification by Bean, Layard, and Nickell (1986). Solving through their equations for the long run, they find that a 1 per cent increase in the payroll tax rate (roughly a 10 per cent increase in the level of payroll taxation) would lead to a decline in employment of about 0.32 per cent (or roughly 44,000 jobs using 1996 as a base). Put another way, if the Di Matteo and Shannon estimate of long-run employment loss from payroll taxes is true, then all payroll taxes in 1996 (at a total payroll tax rate of about 10 per cent) cost the economy 438,000 jobs. With unchanged participation, this would have meant an unemployment rate of 6.8 per cent in 1996, instead of the 9.7 per cent actually observed.

However, using results Di Matteo and Shannon provide, it is possible to calculate that their implicit long-run labour supply elasticity is 0.71 – in my opinion a rather extreme value. Many estimates place the upper value at around 0.25 (Gunderson and Riddell, 1993: 178) and, as noted, the value obtained in estimating our macroeconometric models is effectively zero.

Wilton and Prescott (1993), using income and sales taxes as well as payroll taxes, and analysing data on private-sector collective-bargaining agreements, found that 'employers have *not* been able to shift increases in payroll taxes for UI, CPP/QPP and WC onto workers in the form of lower wages' (p. 35). If there has been no pass-through of payroll taxes to wages, then there will definitely have been a long-run impact on employment, unless labour demand is completely wage inelastic.

Abbott and Beach (1996), making use of a new data set on annual employment and payroll taxes by province described in Lin, Picot, and Beach (1996), found large effects of payroll taxes on employment and wages. Their careful analysis and use of new data (and the work of Wilton and Prescott) indicate that the debate is still very much ongoing. Abbott and Beach themselves, however, are very tentative in their conclusion: 'We emphasize ... that our estimates of the employment and wage effects of employer payroll taxes are surprisingly large, and are sufficiently at odds with some of the existing literature that we regard them as very provisional and tentative' (54).

A final observation also helps to put the long-run impact of payroll taxation on employment into perspective: the fact is that, whatever variations one makes in measurement, the relative level of payroll taxation in Canada is significantly lower than in the United States (or in the rest of the Group of Seven, for that matter). Yet the Canadian unemployment rate at the beginning of 1997 is over four percentage points above the U.S. unemployment rate and has generally exceeded the U.S. unemployment rate since the late 1970s (Card and Riddell, 1993). If the *level* of payroll taxation had significant permanent effects on unemployment there would have to be huge offsetting causes for the unemployment difference between Canada and the United States.

Longer-Run Arguments in Favour of a Payroll Tax

The virtual certainty of short-term employment and output loss from an increase in payroll taxes, and at least the possibility of permanent loss, alone would constitute a strong argument against further increases in taxes of this type. However, there are a number of features of payroll taxes apart from their impact on employment and output that cause at least some analysts to view favourably potential increases in this form of taxation, at least in preference to increases in other taxes. Kesselman (1996) argues this point rather strongly and, noting that Canadian payroll taxation is lower as a share of GDP than for most other OECD countries, suggests that Canada may have special opportunities to increase this form of taxation, while reducing other taxes on which the country relies perhaps too heavily. What are the arguments in favour of payroll taxation?

First, payroll taxation, because it rises proportionally with earnings, is one of the few forms of taxation from which social insurance – where benefits also rise with earnings or income – can justifiably be financed. As Kesselman points out, using general taxation to fund any social insurance program where payments rise with past earnings or income is politically unthinkable. Of course, a social insurance system could with some ingenuity be operated through the income tax system, just as Registered Retirement Savings Plans (RRSPs) or Canada Pension Contributions for the self-employed are now operated. Moreover, this first argument for payroll taxes does not require that they necessarily be levied even partially on the employer.

A second argument for payroll taxation is that, as a tax on labour but not on capital income, it is closer to a true 'consumption' tax than is an income tax, and so results in less distortion (has greater 'dynamic efficiency') in the allocation of income between savings and consumption. That is, by effectively taxing only consumption it does not unduly discourage saving and encourage current consumption. Indeed, Kesselman (1996: 165) goes so far as to suggest that the very long-run incidence of a major shift from income to payroll taxes would be on capital, not labour, since the tax shift would increase savings and capital formation and eventually lower the rate of return on capital. He does, however, note that this principle is less likely to apply (or will apply more slowly) to a small, open economy like Canada's.

There are, of course, counter-arguments to the assertion that payroll taxes should be increased relative to income taxes for the purpose of encouraging savings: the present Canadian income tax is in part a consumption tax; income from capital is partially sheltered through a number of features such as RRSPs, dividend tax credits, and some capital-gains exemptions. Moreover, capital sheltering could clearly be enhanced through the present income tax system, for example, by reinstating a limited interest-income deduction.

The third argument put forward in favour of payroll taxes, especially, over income taxes is that they have greater 'static efficiency,' generating less economic loss and distortion through misallocation of economic resources and discouragement of labour supply. Measurement is difficult here, as Kesselman (1996: 164) notes, but evidence for the United States with general-equilibrium models indicates superior efficiency for payroll taxes relative to income taxes, and this is most definitely the finding for Canada in a recent study by Dahlby (1993). Compounded with efficiency issues is the question of costs of tax administration and compliance: again, the simple payroll tax, administered by and through employers, is generally considered to be less costly to administer and to generate greater compliance than the income tax. Of course, while the last factor may be very important for the overall structure of taxation, it is likely to be much less important for marginal changes in the taxes collected by the two systems once both are in operation.

To sum up, the literature suggests that payroll taxes in several respects may be superior to other forms of taxation on efficiency (both dynamic and static) and administrative grounds – aside from any impacts on employment, output, and wages owing to the 'incidence' question. Unfortunately, as will be seen, the models used for this paper do not for the most part incorporate these efficiency and administrative issues. On the other hand, as noted, to the extent that these issues exist they are likely to be much more important for major shifts in the tax system than for the relatively small changes in tax rates that we will be simulating.

Features Particular to Workers' Compensation

The factors discussed so far are most applicable to broad and general payroll taxes. The literature suggests that there are indeed important deviations from the general results in cases where payroll taxes are highly linked to benefits, and most particularly when payroll taxes are 'experience-rated' – especially by firm, which is a small but increasing feature of Canadian workers' compensation (see Kralj, this volume).

Vaillancourt and Marceau (1990) found in a study of Québec industries that while EI and QPP payroll taxes were largely 'passed through' to wage reductions, on the whole Workers' Compensation premiums were not. Rightly, firms view WC payments as offsetting another cost – that of liability for worker injuries. The addition of WC payments, but reduction in any implicit or explicit insurance against liability to workers, would largely balance (except for possible administrative savings) and would not reduce the demand for labour. With no reduction in the demand for labour there is no temporary or permanent employment effect and no shifting of the incidence of the tax onto workers in the form of lower real wages.[5]

Of course, the result might be very different for particular *changes* that might be made in WC premiums. If premiums were to be increased with no immediate benefit to the firm, then the result would likely be an impact on employment, output, and wages more typical of general payroll taxes. This situation could apply, for example, in the case of WC premium increases to address unfunded liabilities (see Gunderson and Hyatt, this volume).

In the United States, state unemployment insurance systems typically operate on some sort of firm-specific experience rating: a firm whose workers use UI more often pays a higher premium. Evidence indicates (Kesselman, 1996: 169 and Anderson and Meyer, 1995) that in this system there is much less pass-through of premium changes into real wages and less general impact on employment and output. Nonetheless, as noted by Anderson and Meyer (1995), there can still be considerable inter-firm and inter-sector labour reallocation. Firms with poor experience ratings, for example, cannot usually raise their prices without becoming uncompetitive or somehow convincing workers to accept lower than the 'going' wage; consequently they often go out of business. Workers in the firm then find employment in a more efficient firm in the same sector or in a more productive sector. While there is less empirical evidence on the point, the experience rating of different industrial sectors in the Canadian WC system could have at least a partial effect in limiting economy-wide impacts on output and employment. This is another reason why Vaillancourt and Marceau (1990) find such different impacts for WC and other payroll taxes.

In summary, benefits linkages and any firm-specific features of a WC or other payroll tax change have the potential of altering impacts on the macroeconomy significantly. The macroeconometric models we use below are, by their aggregate nature, unable to deal with such specific tax changes, and the payroll tax experiments we conduct are for more broad-based rate changes. These simulations are still very relevant, however, for situations in which WC payroll taxes are changed across all industries – for example, to fund unfunded liabilities, or as a 'catch-up' to finance new forms of injuries already notionally included by workers in their estimation of WC benefits (such as lower-back injuries, as described by Frank, this volume, and those emerging from the 'new world of work,' as discussed in Gunderson, this volume).

The FOCUS and FOCUS-Ontario Macroeconometric Models

This section describes the FOCUS and FOCUS-Ontario macroeconometric models used to conduct the analysis of the impacts of payroll tax changes. The models attempt to incorporate what we know about the various key interactions of the macroeconomy, both at one point in time and as the economy moves forward through the years. With their aid it is possible to account not just for the direct impact of payroll taxes on employment or GDP, but also for further indirect (and possibly offsetting) impacts through, for example, adjustments of wages and prices and movements in the exchange rate and interest rates.

FOCUS and FOCUS-Ontario were built at the Institute for Policy Analysis of the University of Toronto, and are maintained there under the Policy and Economic Analysis Program. FOCUS was first built in 1976 and FOCUS-Ontario in 1984, but each model has undergone continuous revision since. The models have been applied to a wide variety of fiscal and monetary policy issues, including analyses of the causes of the last recession (Wilson, Dungan, and Murphy, 1994), the impacts of the Canada-U.S. Free-Trade Agreement (Dungan, Harris, and Wilson, 1991), the GST and its alternatives (Dungan, Mintz, and Wilson, 1990), and potential harmonization of the Ontario sales tax with the GST (Dungan, 1994).

FOCUS is a medium-scale quarterly macroeconometric model of the Canadian economy consisting of 300-plus behavioural equations and identities and somewhat over 600 variables in total. The model has been developed in the tradition of the Keynesian-classical synthesis; that is, markets (especially the labour market) can fail to clear for extended periods of time and most expectations are not 'rational' in the sense of being formed with full knowledge of the model and of the present (and future) values of all exogenous variables.[6] Some care has been taken in developing the model's structural equations to ensure that they embody desirable long-run properties as well as plausible short-run dynamics.

As is of course appropriate, FOCUS is an open-economy model with endogenous (and sensitive) international trade and capital flows. The exchange rate is also fully endogenous, but it is not determined by a regression equation of its own; rather it is a market-clearing price used to 'balance' the balance of payments. Any shock to trade or to capital flows (short or long) can and usually will have an effect on the exchange rate. However, our estimation work for FOCUS does not yield a 'perfect capital mobility,' Mundell-Fleming world in which our interest rate is determined solely by foreign rates. Although capital flows in FOCUS are quite sensitive to interest-rate changes, international trade is also sensitive to domestic demand and to prices, and it is the interaction of both these elements that determines the path of the exchange rate.

Moreover, the 'supply-side' of the model is fully developed and quite powerful in affecting simulation results in the long run, through effects on labour-force participation and, especially, through changes in the capital stock. The wage equation (an 'expectations-augmented Phillips Curve') will tend to push the economy to full employment (although the model's estimated lags and coefficients suggest the process is a protracted one). To the extent that changes in payroll tax rates affect investment, they will have a cumulative effect on the capital stock and on aggregate supply.

Finally, while short-run models often can ignore stock effects, FOCUS tracks both government and foreign debt stocks, which in turn have important feedback effects on interest payments and hence on government deficits and domestic income. These cumulative effects become important in the longer term in some of the simulations below.

A full description of the FOCUS and FOCUS-Ontario models is available in the models' documentation (Dungan and Jump, 1995, and Dungan, 1995). However, there are several equations in the models that bear especially on the subject of the sensitivity of the economy to payroll tax changes. Each is now examined in greater detail. In most cases, the equation used in the FOCUS-Ontario model is very similar to that of the aggregate model. Differences will be noted as they arise.

Private-Sector Employment

In both FOCUS and FOCUS-Ontario, private-sector employment is determined by an equation with three principal terms: output to be produced (defined as real private-sector domestic product at factor cost), after-tax wage costs relative to producer prices, and the capital stock. The after-tax real-wage cost is defined as the average annual wage per employee in the private sector plus the employers' share of Employment Insurance (EI) and Canada/Quebec Pension Plan (CPP) premiums, plus Workers' Compensation (WC) premiums.[7] The equation generates a superior fit when the payroll tax terms are included with the average wage. The output and wage terms enter the equation with distributed and declining lags. The long-run elasticity of demand for labour with respect to output is estimated to be 0.99 (and obviously not statistically different from 1.0) and the total lag is two years. The long-run elasticity of demand for labour with respect to the real after-tax wage term is −.46, and the total lag is six quarters. The capital stock enters without a lag and has an elasticity of 0.12. Given the estimated coefficients and the structure of the equation, it is not surprising that the models show a strong short-term response to payroll tax changes.

Private-Sector Wages

The private-sector wage equation is an expectations-augmented Phillips Curve with an explicit (and exogenous) full-employment unemployment rate. The equation determines the rate of change of nominal wages (defined as annual average wages and salaries per employee) based on four major terms: (1) private-sector labour productivity, (2) past CPI inflation, (3) expected future CPI inflation, and (4) the ratio of the actual to the full-employment unemployment rate. The first term is specified as a five-year moving average, and the coefficient is one; there is thus full pass-through of productivity changes to wages, but only with a long lag. Past CPI inflation enters as a distributed lag, with the sum of the coefficients over six quarters at about 0.69. Expected future inflation is specified as the fitted values of a reduced-form equation for inflation expectations, based on such items as current inflation and changes in the money supply and the exchange rate. The coefficient on this term is approximately 0.34; thus, the combined effect of lagged and expected inflation on nominal wages is just over 1.0. Any permanent and anticipated change in inflation will be reflected in nominal wages. Finally, the ratio of the actual to the full-employment inflation rate has the expected negative sign. The higher is the actual unemployment rate above the full-employment rate, the lower will be nominal wage inflation. The equation is therefore of the form that any deviation from the full-employment unemployment rate will change the rate of wage inflation. In the absence of a continued series of shocks, the wage level will gradually adjust so as to attain full employment.

A slight variation occurs in this equation in the Ontario model. Here, the relevant consumer price term for both past and expected inflation is a simple average of the Ontario and the national CPIs. This reflects the fact that the national CPI is often the more visible indicator of inflation and is often written into even local contracts as the cost-of-living escalator.[8] This specification for the Ontario wage equation, to the extent it is realistic, will mitigate Ontario nominal wage responses to price shocks specific to Ontario.

Private-Sector Output Price

In both models, the price of aggregate private-sector output (the price of output at 'factor cost') is specified as primarily a mark-up over unit labour costs, with some lags in the response to cost changes. Unit labour costs include the employer portion of all payroll taxes. Also present, but of much smaller effect, is a term representing the interest carrying-costs of inventories.

Labour Supply

Labour-force source populations in the models are exogenous. The labour force is determined from the source populations and endogenous equations for participation rates. The FOCUS national model distinguishes six age-sex categories: males and females 15–24, 25–54, and 55+. The FOCUS-Ontario model only distinguishes male and female participation owing to data limitations. The participation-rate equations include some or all of: the employment/population ratio (to capture the 'discouraged worker' effect); relative cohort size; and the size of unemployment insurance premiums relative to the private-sector wages. Real wages themselves, before or after tax, were not found to be significant in any of the equations.

Consumption and Savings

The consumption functions of the model are based on the Permanent Income Hypothesis: consumption depends primarily on a smoothed path of personal disposable income. For durables, consumption also depends on existing stocks. A number of other terms also appear, the most important of which for our purposes is the gap between the actual and full-employment unemployment rate. At a given level of 'permanent income,' consumption of a given type will be lower if the unemployment rate is higher. That is, despite the smoothing of shocks through permanent income, cyclical swings in the economy carry through directly to consumption, as conveyed through changes in unemployment.

There are no terms in the equation relating consumption out of income (and therefore saving) to tax measures such as Registered Retirement Savings Plans (RRSPs), or to the relative proportions of income versus payroll and consumption taxation. Some attempts to include items of this type have failed to establish statistical significance. However – and this is a problem with all 'omitted' causal paths in the model – it is generally not possible in the construction of models like FOCUS and FOCUS-Ontario to check exhaustively for the presence of all possible causal paths in developing each model equation. Omission of a factor from a FOCUS equation – for example, because of statistical insignificance – when that factor is identified as potentially important in the literature, I take as evidence that the effect is neither dominant nor huge. However, without more intensive research it must be conceded that some effect is possible and that the model fails to capture it.

It should also be noted that the consumption equations do not take into account the observation of Hyatt and Law (this volume) that consumption may be higher owing to the presence of social insurance schemes that mitigate the need for precautionary savings. While this effect could be substantial when considering the introduction or elimination of entire social insurance programs, it is likely to be less important for relatively small changes in contribution rates to such schemes, which is what we are simulating in the present paper.

Non-Residential Investment

Investment in FOCUS and FOCUS-Ontario is determined by a modified Jorgensonian approach. Briefly, investment depends on anticipated, after-tax returns to capital compared to after-tax borrowing costs (or the opportunity cost of funds). Anticipated returns are further adjusted for depreciation and for tax effects of depreciation and write-offs. Finally, these adjusted anticipated returns are proxied by the most recent two years of actual tax-adjusted corporate cash flow relative to the size of the existing capital stock. As a result of this specification, investment will be affected somewhat by a change in payroll taxes; until the payroll tax change has been passed through to employees, firms' cash flow will be altered by a change in payroll taxes, and therefore so will the proxy for expected future returns.

It might be argued that this specification will overestimate the impact of payroll taxes on investment, since the effect on corporate returns will actually be only temporary. Offsetting this argument are three counter-arguments: first, that firms themselves may not correctly understand that the incidence of payroll taxes falls eventually on employees (otherwise there would not be the loud objections to payroll taxes that the business community is currently putting forward); second, that even the temporary impact of payroll taxes affects the present discounted value of total future returns (especially if the implicit discount rate is relatively high); and third, that at least some investment is financed out of cash flow and retained earnings – a factor I feel is not yet properly accounted for in the current investment equations.

A final note is appropriate with respect to the investment equations in the FOCUS-Ontario model: the Ontario investment equations respond, as do the national equations, to returns to capital and to borrowing costs. There are no terms in the equation that describe the specific tax regimes of Ontario versus the other provinces – such elements being both difficult to quantify and to insert in investment relationships. Therefore, a change in payroll taxes in Ontario can be expected to have some special effect on Ontario investment through its impact on profitability, but not specifically from the tax regime appearing in the investment equation. We may thus underestimate somewhat the inter-provincial impacts of changing the payroll tax rate in Ontario only.

Corporate Profits and Their Disposition: Income Shares

Following from the discussion of investment above, it is important to understand the allocation of major income shares in the model. The way macroeconomic data are prepared, total expenditure is necessarily equal to total income. This condition is imposed in the models by making one category of income a residual – roughly, total expenditure less the sum of all other income components. The residual category in ·FOCUS and FOCUS-Ontario is corporate profits. Thus, under, say, an increase in payroll taxes (or the employer share of payroll taxes), there will be an automatic and immediate reduction in corporate profits. However, this impact will begin almost at once to be offset as firms raise prices in response to the increase in after-tax unit labour costs, and then as increased unemployment begins to reduce real wages. Still, as noted above, during the period when corporate profits are depressed (firms are paying at least part of the tax), there will be a negative effect on investment.

The Ontario Model: Interprovincial Trade

The FOCUS-Ontario model includes a relatively simple relationship to describe shifts in interprovincial trade between Ontario and the rest of Canada based on relative production costs. Unfortunately, we do not have a very precise estimate of the relevant elasticities – in large part because the time-series data on interprovincial trade are very poor. For purposes of these simulations we have imposed an elasticity of approximately 0.6 on both interprovincial imports and exports with respect to after-tax labour costs. That is, if a payroll tax raises Ontario labour costs by 1 per cent relative to the rest of Canada, exports from Ontario to the rest of Canada will fall by 0.6 per cent and imports rise by 0.6 per cent. This impact probably should occur with a distributed lag, but unfortunately there is no way of estimating the lag impact; it is therefore imposed from the beginning of the experiment at the full elasticity, thereby probably overestimating slightly the impact on the Ontario economy in the early periods of the experiment.

Key Features of the Models Relating to Payroll Taxes

Having reviewed the basic nature of the models and several key equation specifications, we can now summarize those features of the payroll-tax literature that are present in the models (and to what degree) and those that are absent.

The employment and wage equations will yield the result that the short-term incidence of a payroll-tax change is on the employer. Under, for example, a payroll tax increase, wage costs to the firm will immediately rise and corporate profits will fall. Investment demand will begin to decline with lower profitability. However, with a small lag, firms will begin to economize on the more-expensive labour and will also begin to pass through the higher unit labour costs to prices, likely reducing aggregate demand. The fall in aggregate demand will further reduce employment. As employment falls, the unemployment rate will rise almost in proportion (although some of the unemployed become 'discouraged' as the unemployment rate rises). The rising unemployment rate reduces real-wage demands (although nominal wages may rise somewhat in response to the tax pass-through to prices).

Real wages will continue to fall over time as long as the tax increase is causing unemployment. Eventually, real wages decline sufficiently to absorb the full amount of the payroll tax increase; the entire long-run incidence is borne by labour because labour-supply is insensitive to the real wage. Output prices and corporate profits return to their levels before the tax change, and so does investment, but the disturbance may persist for a long time in the capital stock. The switch to proportionally higher payroll taxation (and lower income taxation) does *not* generate an increase in savings in the model because this feature is absent from the equations describing consumption and the distribution of corporate income. There will be no improvement in tax-collection efficiency or unearthing of a portion of the underground economy owing to the shift in relative tax shares, again because these features are absent from the model.

What then do the macroeconometric models tell us that the more general literature does not? Primarily, they put specific values on the qualitative statements about directions of impacts and lengths of lags above. They give us some indication of the amount of unemployment needed to shift the tax incidence from firms to workers, and the length of the adjustment process. That the models do not include some of the longer-term features that argue in favour of proportionally higher payroll taxes in the literature is at least partial evidence that their effect may not be large. To the extent that the models are mis-specified by omitting these longer-term effects, their measurement of the short-term adjustment costs of changes in payroll taxes at least lets us know how large the longer-term benefits would have to be to offset the short-term transition costs.

The Model Experiments: Impacts of Payroll and Income-Tax Changes

We attempt to quantify the impact of payroll taxes on the macroeconomy with four simulation experiments. While each experiment is roughly founded on issues relating to workers' compensation in Ontario, the national results obtained from FOCUS are fully applicable to similar changes in any other province, or a combination of provinces. Moreover, the model impacts may be considered roughly 'linear.' That is, if one wished to estimate the impacts of a policy change, say, three times larger or half as large as those presented here, the responses reported could be multiplied by 3 or 0.5. The simulation results therefore apply more widely than to specific policy changes for Ontario.

The simulations are conducted using base-case forecasts of the Canadian and Ontario economies for 1997–2006 that were prepared recently by the Policy and Economic Analysis Program (Dungan, Murphy, and Wilson, 1997; Murphy and Dungan, 1996). Details of the base cases are generally unimportant since we are concerned solely with the impact of *changes* in payroll-tax policy variables. Most relevant is the fact that the base cases see considerable underemployment in the Canadian and Ontario economies through at least the year 2000; thereafter the two economies are relatively close to full employment. The payroll-tax changes are therefore imposed initially in a situation of less-than-full employment, where some slack exists to produce for additional demand. The short-term results (1997–2001) would generally show less output change and more price response if the base cases were signifi-cantly closer to full employment.

Before proceeding with the model simulations, assumptions have to be made as to the response of the monetary authorities to the policy changes that will be imposed. The announced policy target of the Bank of Canada is the rate of inflation in the CPI – as opposed, for example, to the rate of growth of the money supply or the level of the interest rate, both of which targets it has used in the past. However, it is recog-nized that the CPI target cannot necessarily be met exactly in each quarter or each year without introducing excessive volatility in either monetary policy itself or the response of the real side of the economy. It turns out in the FOCUS model that using the exchange rate as an inter-mediate target for monetary policy in simulations of the type we are doing keeps the price level from changing significantly from base-case in the longer term (the inflation targets are maintained), but avoids any short-term volatility of response. More specifically, we assume that monetary policy targets the Canada-U.S. exchange rate of the base case, adjusting interest rates up or down as needed to yield zero excess demand for foreign exchange (i.e., no change in the overall balance of payments) at the base-case exchange rate. The interest-rate changes required to neutralize exchange-rate impacts in the simulations are generally very small.

Simulation 1: A 5 Per Cent Workers' Compensation Rate Cut in Ontario

Starting 1 January 1997, WC premium rates have been cut an average of 5 per cent in Ontario. Based on 1995 premium collections of about $2.7 billion (the most recent data available) and using more recent data and our own forecasts for growth since 1995 in average payrolls, we estimate the 1997 revenue reduction to be about $140 million. The dollar amount of the revenue reduction grows thereafter with the size of nominal payrolls, reaching approximately $220 million by 2006.

In the first simulation we estimate the macroeconomic impact of this rate cut. The simulation results for both Canada and Ontario are summarized in table 5.1. The simulations have been run for ten years (and, in one case, for 20) to capture not only the shorter-term impacts, but also to indicate impacts in the longer term.

The figures shown in the tables for this and subsequent experiments are all in the form of changes from the base case. Unless otherwise indicated, the changes are in the form of percentage impacts relative to the base. Thus, in table 5.1, real GDP in Canada in 1998 is estimated to be 0.06 per cent higher than would otherwise be the case as a result of the Ontario WC premium cut. Impacts on other variables are reported in the form of changes in various levels (e.g., millions of dollars or percentage points). Thus in 1998 for Canada, real GDP (measured in 1996 dollars) is estimated to be $485 million higher as a result of the WCB premium cut, and the unemployment rate is estimated to be about 0.03 percentage points lower (e.g., 8.97 per cent instead of 9.00 per cent).

The initial reduction in WC premiums accrues to firms. The WC premium reduction is an across-the-board change, involving no alteration in the relative experience rating of firms. Moreover, the premium-rate reduction involves no compensating increase in other expenses to firms (there is no increase in their liability for workplace injury, for example). Therefore, competitive pressures induce them to reduce prices somewhat, increase hiring, and expand production. In both Canada and Ontario the effect is largest in the third year of the simulation, with GDP up 0.06 per cent above base in Canada and 0.16 per cent above base in Ontario. These increases amount to just over $500 million 1996 dollars in Canada and slightly more in Ontario ($574 million). As can be seen, the improved after-tax wage competitiveness in Ontario yields a higher GDP impact in Ontario than in Canada as a whole (and therefore a slight negative GDP impact in the rest of Canada).

Naturally, there is also a favourable short-term impact on employment. As can be seen from table 5.1, employment is increased by about 2600 in Ontario (slightly less in Canada) in the first year of the simulation, with the maximum impact coming in the fourth year, at almost 8500 additional person-years.[9]

In the short term there is also a very small reduction in the price

TABLE 5.1
Impacts of 5% premium rate reduction in Ontario ($141 million in 1997)*

	1997	1998	1999	2000	2001	2002	2003	2004	2005	2006
Impacts for Canada										
Real GDP (change in $ 96 Mill)	208	485	543	469	217	−94	−315	−368	−253	−35
Real GDP	0.025	0.056	0.061	0.051	0.023	−0.010	−0.031	−0.035	−0.024	−0.003
Consumption	0.017	0.057	0.093	0.105	0.088	0.048	0.000	−0.034	−0.041	−0.022
Investment	0.022	0.052	0.047	0.036	−0.001	−0.037	−0.045	−0.032	−0.012	0.006
Exports	0.007	0.020	0.023	0.018	0.007	−0.007	−0.018	−0.022	−0.018	−0.010
Imports	−0.016	0.000	0.035	0.057	0.062	0.046	0.018	−0.009	−0.024	−0.024
Consumer Price Index (CPI)	−0.025	−0.045	−0.043	−0.028	−0.002	0.024	0.040	0.040	0.029	0.012
Unemployment rate (change in % pts)	−0.009	−0.026	−0.035	−0.033	−0.020	0.000	0.015	0.022	0.018	0.007
Employment	0.013	0.037	0.052	0.051	0.033	0.006	−0.017	−0.028	−0.025	−0.011
Employment (change in '000)	1.784	5.370	7.608	7.628	5.097	0.976	−2.661	−4.485	−4.033	−1.812
Interest rate (90-day) (change in % pts)	−0.014	−0.009	0.007	0.018	0.027	0.024	0.012	−0.001	−0.009	−0.010
Wages and salaries per employee	−0.014	−0.017	−0.006	0.016	0.046	0.068	0.072	0.062	0.045	0.029
Productivity change (GDP/employee)	0.012	0.018	0.008	−0.001	−0.011	−0.016	−0.014	−0.007	0.002	0.008
Capital stock	0.000	0.000	0.002	0.006	0.009	0.009	0.008	0.006	0.004	0.003
Federal surplus(+)/deficit(−) (change in $Mill)	28	106	108	91	31	−40	−82	−89	−63	−14
Prov'l surplus(+)/deficit(−) (change in $Mill)	−130	−115	−116	−135	−187	−253	−310	−346	−356	−349
Workers' Comp. premiums (change in $Mill)	−143	−148	−154	−161	−169	−178	−187	−196	−206	−214
Wages and salaries paid (change in $Mill)	0	78	181	276	340	327	249	157	94	90

TABLE 5.1 – concluded
Impacts of 5% premium rate reduction in Ontario ($141 million in 1997)*

	1997	1998	1999	2000	2001	2002	2003	2004	2005	2006
Impacts for Ontario										
Real GDP (change in $ 96 Mill)	271	497	574	521	304	24	−207	−321	−257	−29
Real GDP	0.080	0.142	0.157	0.138	0.078	0.006	−0.050	−0.075	−0.058	−0.006
Consumption	0.051	0.134	0.232	0.270	0.233	0.135	0.004	−0.107	−0.145	−0.096
Investment	0.072	0.155	0.133	0.099	0.015	−0.064	−0.082	−0.057	−0.011	0.044
Exports	0.026	0.037	0.044	0.038	0.025	0.007	−0.006	−0.010	−0.005	0.006
Imports	−0.024	0.000	0.053	0.088	0.097	0.073	0.028	−0.015	−0.040	−0.039
Consumer Price Index	−0.054	−0.079	−0.065	−0.032	0.020	0.068	0.096	0.098	0.080	0.058
Unemployment rate (change in % pts)	−0.030	−0.059	−0.083	−0.084	−0.062	−0.025	0.011	0.033	0.031	0.009
Employment	0.048	0.099	0.140	0.145	0.109	0.048	−0.013	−0.052	−0.053	−0.018
Employment (change in '000)	2.618	5.490	7.985	8.454	6.499	2.913	−0.776	−3.241	−3.361	−1.156
Wages and salaries per employee	−0.009	−0.004	0.016	0.058	0.114	0.154	0.165	0.153	0.128	0.108
Productivity change (GDP/employee)	0.032	0.043	0.017	−0.007	−0.031	−0.042	−0.037	−0.023	−0.006	0.011
Capital stock	0.001	0.005	0.013	0.024	0.033	0.037	0.036	0.033	0.030	0.028
Prov'l Surplus(+)/deficit(−) (change in $Mill)	−136	−124	−107	−107	−131	−175	−231	−285	−317	−317
Workers' Comp. premiums (change in $Mill)	−142	−148	−154	−163	−172	−181	−192	−202	−212	−222
Wages and salaries paid (change in $Mill)	63	147	258	352	405	382	299	206	164	220

*Impacts are percentage changes unless otherwise noted.

level. However, under the assumed monetary response, the Bank of Canada has taken advantage of the incipient lower prices (stemming from lower unit labour costs) to ease monetary policy slightly – as can been in the small reduction in nominal interest rates.

The positive impact on GDP extends through consumption, investment, and exports. The increase in investment, owing to higher returns to capital, leads gradually to some expansion of the capital stock – an effect that persists through the ten years of the simulation horizon.

Finally, it should be noted that the provincial government achieves some significant tax recapture – at least in the short run. By the third and fourth year of the simulations, the increase in the provincial deficit, at $107 million, is considerably less than the $150–60 million in foregone WCB premiums.

In the longer run, of course, the short-term positive impacts of the WCB premium reduction do not persist. The increase in employment leads, with a lag, to increases in real wages and to a readjustment of employment. The positive GDP effect diminishes and, because of the interaction of the various long lags in the employment, wages, and expenditure equations, there is by the sixth or seventh year of the simulation an 'overshoot' into a negative GDP impact. The negative GDP impact is naturally coupled with a negative impact on employment that then serves to reduce real wage demands and stimulate employment again. What results is a damped series of fluctuations in GDP (and employment) that gradually converge back to base-case levels. This is most clearly seen in figure 5.1, which shows the impact on real GDP (in $ 96 millions) when the simulation is carried forward twenty years. The damped oscillations and convergence to a zero impact in GDP are apparent.

Part of the longer-term convergence to the base case is the passing of the incidence of the payroll tax cut to labour. Observe that the impact of the simulation on wages and salaries rises through the first five to six years of the simulation, overshooting the cut in WC premiums but gradually converging on the level of the cut. The payroll tax cut does lead to a longer-run increase in disposable income and in consumption.

There is also a longer-run permanent impact on the provincial government deficit. While the shorter-term economic stimulus leads to considerable tax recapture for several years, eventually, as real GDP returns to base levels and as the additional deficits (or reduced surpluses) from past years accumulate into higher debt and debt-service

FIGURE 5.1 Sim 1: Impact on real GDP – Canada (long horizon)

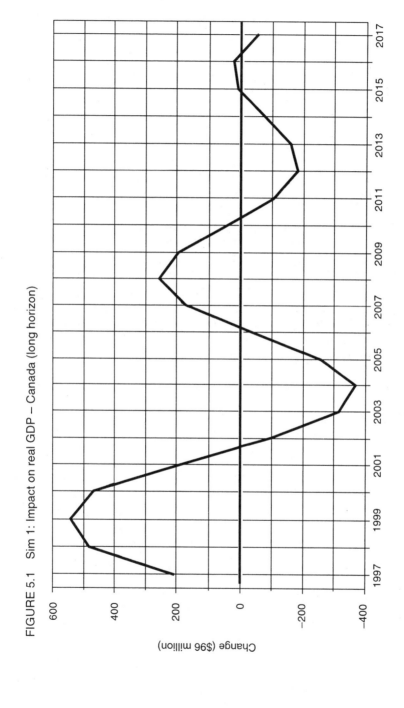

payments, the provincial deficit begins to worsen continually. After our ten-year horizon, the deficit continues to widen and eventually crowds out investment, leading to gradual declines in the capital stock and in productivity.

Simulation 2: A 5 Per Cent Workers' Compensation Rate Cut in Ontario Combined with Benefit Cuts

The first simulation represents only a part of the WC reforms initiated in Ontario in 1997. The second part of the reforms was a 5 per cent reduction in WC benefits for new claims. It has been estimated that the net effect of this benefit reduction will be a 3.5 cut in benefits beginning in 1997, and rising to approximately 4.5 per cent of what benefits would otherwise have been by 2020. Based on 1995 benefit payments of about $2.4 billion (the most recent data available) and using more recent data and our own forecasts for growth since 1995 in average payrolls, we estimate the 1997 benefit reductions to be about $89 million. The dollar amount of the benefit reduction grows thereafter with the size of nominal payrolls and as the benefit cuts expand from 3.5 per cent to 4.5 per cent (because benefit payments initiated before the reduction gradually drop out of the system). By 2006, the benefits reduction is just under $160 million.

The benefits reduction has been modelled as a simple cut in transfer payments to persons. Following a recent study by Hyatt (1996) that showed minimal labour-force participation response to WC benefit changes, we make no adjustment to labour-force participation in response to the benefit cuts.

Results for the simulation are summarized in table 5.2. The GDP impacts for Simulations 1 and 2 are compared in figure 5.2.

A quick comparison of tables 5.1 and 5.2 and an examination of figure 5.2 will show that the benefit cuts make generally very little difference in macroeconomic impacts when added to the WC premium cuts of Simulation 1. There are two main reasons for this: The first is that the benefit cuts are smaller than the premium rate cuts in dollar magnitude. The second and much more important reason is that the premium cuts have a much higher short-term macroeconomic impact, dollar for dollar, than do the changes in benefits (transfers to persons). This is because the reduction in benefits simply reduces disposable income and so works through the usual multiplier mechanisms. The premium reduction, by contrast, not only removes more 'tax' dollars

FIGURE 5.2 Sim 1 vs. Sim 2: Impact in employment (1: Premium cut; 2: Plus benefit cut)

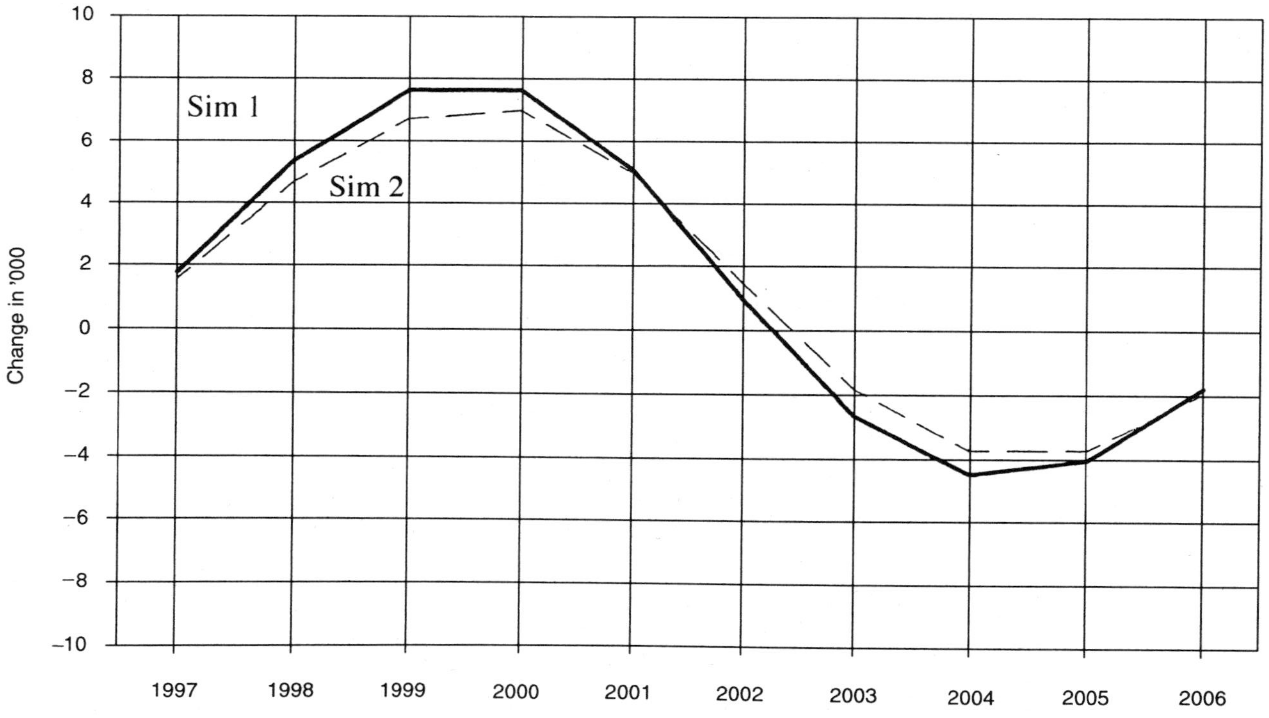

TABLE 5.2
Impacts of 5% premium rate reduction in Ontario ($141 million in 1997), plus benefit cuts starting at 3.5% ($89 million in 1997)*

	1997	1998	1999	2000	2001	2002	2003	2004	2005	2006
Impacts for Canada										
Real GDP (change in $ 96 Mill)	173	417	483	443	234	−37	−244	−316	−241	−54
Real GDP	0.021	0.048	0.054	0.048	0.024	−0.004	−0.024	−0.030	−0.023	−0.005
Consumption	0.008	0.037	0.067	0.082	0.072	0.040	−0.002	−0.034	−0.044	−0.031
Investment	0.020	0.048	0.048	0.041	0.006	−0.028	−0.034	−0.023	−0.008	0.010
Exports	0.007	0.020	0.024	0.021	0.012	−0.001	−0.011	−0.015	−0.013	−0.007
Imports	−0.019	−0.011	0.019	0.040	0.048	0.036	0.014	−0.009	−0.024	−0.026
Consumer Price Index (CPI)	−0.025	−0.046	−0.046	−0.035	−0.013	0.011	0.027	0.030	0.022	0.007
Unemployment rate (change in % pts)	−0.008	−0.022	−0.031	−0.030	−0.020	−0.003	0.011	0.019	0.017	0.008
Employment	0.011	0.033	0.046	0.047	0.033	0.009	−0.012	−0.023	−0.023	−0.012
Employment (change in '000)	1.566	4.675	6.710	6.974	4.980	1.465	−1.835	−3.729	−3.722	−1.973
Interest rate (90-day) (change in % pts)	−0.014	−0.012	0.001	0.013	0.023	0.021	0.011	0.000	−0.008	−0.011
Wages and salaries per employee	−0.014	−0.020	−0.013	0.005	0.032	0.053	0.060	0.054	0.040	0.025
Productivity change (GDP/employee)	0.009	0.015	0.008	0.001	−0.008	−0.013	−0.012	−0.007	0.001	0.007
Capital stock	0.000	0.000	0.001	0.005	0.009	0.010	0.009	0.008	0.007	0.007
Federal surplus(+)/deficit(−) (change in $Mill)	6	78	78	59	2	−61	−100	−115	−101	−61
Prov'l surplus(+)/deficit(−) (change in $Mill)	−56	−38	−32	−36	−69	−113	−151	−174	−173	−152
Workers' Comp. premiums (change in $Mill)	−143	−149	−155	−162	−170	−178	−187	−197	−206	−215
Wages and salaries paid (change in $Mill)	−8	49	130	214	277	276	217	140	77	65

TABLE 5.2 – concluded

Impacts of 5% premium rate reduction in Ontario ($141 million in 1997), plus benefit cuts starting at 3.5% ($89 million in 1997)*

	1997	1998	1999	2000	2001	2002	2003	2004	2005	2006
Impacts for Ontario										
Real GDP (change in $96 Mill)	241	422	488	455	282	46	−169	−297	−265	−108
Real GDP	0.072	0.120	0.134	0.120	0.072	0.011	−0.040	−0.069	−0.060	−0.024
Consumption	0.031	0.078	0.158	0.199	0.182	0.107	−0.006	−0.107	−0.147	−0.124
Investment	0.066	0.141	0.122	0.090	0.010	−0.062	−0.079	−0.064	−0.033	0.010
Exports	0.026	0.037	0.047	0.043	0.032	0.016	0.004	−0.002	0.002	0.010
Imports	−0.029	−0.017	0.029	0.063	0.075	0.057	0.022	−0.015	−0.039	−0.043
Consumer Price Index	−0.054	−0.082	−0.074	−0.049	−0.006	0.036	0.062	0.064	0.048	0.024
Unemployment rate (change in % pts)	−0.029	−0.051	−0.069	−0.071	−0.054	−0.023	0.009	0.032	0.035	0.019
Employment	0.046	0.085	0.117	0.121	0.095	0.045	−0.010	−0.050	−0.058	−0.034
Employment (change in '000)	2.492	4.721	6.653	7.089	5.662	2.727	−0.602	−3.151	−3.691	−2.210
Wages and salaries per employee	−0.010	−0.010	0.002	0.035	0.081	0.118	0.130	0.121	0.095	0.071
Productivity change (GDP/employee)	0.026	0.035	0.017	−0.001	−0.023	−0.034	−0.031	−0.019	−0.002	0.010
Capital stock	0.001	0.004	0.010	0.018	0.025	0.028	0.026	0.023	0.019	0.015
Prov'l surplus(+)/deficit(−) (change in $Mill)	−57	−47	−26	−13	−20	−45	−82	−120	−140	−139
Workers' Comp. premiums (change in $Mill)	−142	−148	−155	−163	−172	−182	−192	−203	−213	−223
Wages and salaries paid (change in $Mill)	58	115	196	271	322	308	234	139	79	84

*Impacts are percentage changes unless otherwise noted.

from the system, but also directly impacts prices (through the process of unit-labour-cost mark-up), making the inflation-fighting task of the Bank of Canada easier, and offers a direct (if temporary) incentive for additional employment. These two additional factors significantly outweigh the standard multiplier of the transfers cut.

In the longer run, of course, Simulation 2 converges back to the base case just as does Simulation 1. Since the initial total impact is not as large (owing to the offsetting benefit cut), the resulting overshoot in the other direction is not as large either and the oscillations back towards the base case are smaller. One significant difference between the two simulations is in the path of provincial deficits. The deficit impact is still negative (since the premium cut is larger than the benefits cut), but much smaller than under the premium cut alone. The worsening of the government balance still grows over time (as the economy returns to base case and as the debt and debt interest accumulate), but the rate of growth in the deficit impact is of course much smaller.

Simulation 3: A 10 Per Cent Workers' Compensation Rate Increase in Ontario

While the FOCUS and FOCUS-Ontario models are largely linear around a particular experiment and the effects of an increase in payroll taxes could be determined by reversing signs on the simulations above, it is nonetheless more convenient to conduct the experiments of a payroll tax increase directly. One study of the Ontario WCB (Mercer, 1996) has suggested that WC premiums need to rise on the order of 10 per cent in order to compensate for the unfunded liabilities accumulated by the WCB in Ontario in past years. In Simulation 3, accordingly, we raise WC premiums by 10 per cent. This simulation is effectively twice that of Simulation 1 in absolute size and the opposite in sign. Since, conceptually, the purpose of the rate increase is to fund past errors in the plan and not to enrich future benefits (although it does make payment of those benefits more likely), there is no reason for either firms or employees to voluntarily and immediately reduce either profits or real wages to accommodate the premium increase. Therefore, we again undergo a period of adjustment in which the incidence of the premium increase passes from employers to employees via the deviations in the unemployment rate from base levels.

A 10 per cent increase in Ontario WC premiums is estimated to collect an additional $280 million in 1997, with the increased collections rising to about $440 million after ten years. Again, while the long-run impact of this payroll tax increase is very small, the short-run cost is considerable. As can be seen in table 5.3, after three years the premium rate increase costs just over 1 billion 1996 dollars to the Canadian and Ontario economies, and employment is reduced by just over 16,000 person-years. Consumption and investment are both hit and the capital stock falls. While the impact is large, it is temporary: by the eighth and ninth year of the experiment the impact on employment is actually a modest positive, as the economy oscillates back from the negative impact in the short run. Moreover, the policy is effective in raising funds: the provincial balance shows a sustained improvement and, in later years, is further improved by reduced debt interest charges as the effect of cumulative improvements in the balance results in lower debt. In the long run, wages and salaries are gradually reduced roughly in line with the increase in WC premiums.

We conclude this simulation by comparing the employment impacts obtained with results from Di Matteo and Shannon (1995) and Abbott and Beach (1996), both of which found permanent effects of payroll taxes on employment. The comparison is only approximate, since the other studies present their results for somewhat different changes in payroll taxes and for different base years. The comparison is detailed in table 5.4. Note that the 10 per cent increase in WC premiums for Ontario turns out to be about a 2.3 per cent increase in total payroll taxes in Ontario and a 1 per cent increase in payroll taxation for Canada.

Table 5.4 shows that the long-term impacts on employment estimated by Di Matteo and Shannon are just over one-quarter the size of the maximum short-term impacts generated by FOCUS. For the Abbott and Beach study (with their highly qualified results), the 'low' estimate of permanent employment impact is just under half the maximum short-term impact from FOCUS, while the 'high' estimate of permanent impact is very high indeed, at almost twice the FOCUS maximum short-term impact.

Simulation 4: Ontario Provincial Personal Income Tax Increase
Equivalent to a 10 Per Cent Workers' Compensation Rate Increase

To provide a comparison of the short-term costs of a payroll tax increase in relation to other tax increases, one further experiment is conducted. This experiment raises, *ex ante*, the same amount of reve-

TABLE 5.3
Impacts of 10% premium rate increase in Ontario ($282 million in 1997)*

	1997	1998	1999	2000	2001	2002	2003	2004	2005	2006
Impacts for Canada										
Real GDP (change in $ 96 Mill)	−411	−971	−1091	−945	−446	174	616	724	504	73
Real GDP	−0.050	−0.113	−0.122	−0.102	−0.047	0.018	0.061	0.070	0.047	0.007
Consumption	−0.034	−0.113	−0.185	−0.209	−0.177	−0.097	−0.002	0.066	0.080	0.044
Investment	−0.043	−0.104	−0.097	−0.074	0.000	0.073	0.088	0.063	0.025	−0.011
Exports	−0.014	−0.040	−0.046	−0.037	−0.014	0.014	0.036	0.043	0.035	0.019
Imports	0.031	0.002	−0.069	−0.113	−0.123	−0.091	−0.036	0.017	0.048	0.048
Consumer Price Index (CPI)	0.050	0.091	0.086	0.058	0.007	−0.046	−0.078	−0.080	−0.057	−0.024
Unemployment rate (change in % pts)	0.018	0.051	0.070	0.067	0.040	0.002	−0.030	−0.043	−0.037	−0.015
Employment	−0.026	−0.075	−0.104	−0.102	−0.068	−0.014	0.033	0.055	0.049	0.023
Employment (change in '000)	−3.577	−10.723	−15.279	−15.342	−10.327	−2.152	5.136	8.780	7.969	3.703
Interest rate (90-day) (change in % pts)	0.028	0.019	−0.013	−0.035	−0.053	−0.047	−0.024	0.001	0.017	0.020
Wages and salaries per employee	0.027	0.035	0.014	−0.031	−0.091	−0.134	−0.143	−0.124	−0.090	−0.058
Productivity change (GDP/employee)	−0.023	−0.036	−0.017	0.001	0.021	0.031	0.027	0.014	−0.003	−0.016
Capital stock	0.000	−0.001	−0.004	−0.011	−0.018	−0.019	−0.016	−0.012	−0.009	−0.007
Federal surplus(+)/deficit(−) (change in $Mill)	−53	−213	−219	−183	−64	77	161	178	129	32
Prov'l surplus(+)/deficit(−) (change in $Mill)	262	229	232	269	373	502	616	690	711	699
Workers' Comp. premiums (change in $Mill)	286	297	308	322	337	355	373	392	411	429
Wages and salaries paid (change in $Mill)	0	−154	−359	−547	−675	−653	−499	−318	−192	−179

TABLE 5.3 – concluded
Impacts of 10% premium rate increase in Ontario ($282 million in 1997)*

	1997	1998	1999	2000	2001	2002	2003	2004	2005	2006
Impacts for Ontario										
Real GDP (change in $ 96 Mill)	−555	−997	−1150	−1047	−621	−62	402	603	328	−137
Real GDP	−0.165	−0.284	−0.316	−0.277	−0.158	−0.015	0.096	0.140	0.074	−0.030
Consumption	−0.109	−0.266	−0.461	−0.540	−0.469	−0.274	−0.013	0.196	0.212	0.112
Investment	−0.145	−0.315	−0.274	−0.200	−0.030	0.128	0.164	0.115	0.005	−0.122
Exports	−0.052	−0.073	−0.089	−0.077	−0.050	−0.015	0.012	0.021	0.013	−0.001
Imports	0.048	0.002	−0.106	−0.176	−0.193	−0.144	−0.058	0.028	0.077	0.079
Consumer Price Index	0.108	0.159	0.131	0.068	−0.033	−0.128	−0.184	−0.188	−0.152	−0.112
Unemployment rate (change in % pts)	0.062	0.119	0.167	0.169	0.125	0.050	−0.021	−0.064	−0.051	−0.005
Employment	−0.100	−0.198	−0.281	−0.290	−0.220	−0.098	0.023	0.100	0.085	0.013
Employment (change in '000)	−5.441	−11.038	−16.023	−16.940	−13.121	−5.939	1.431	6.311	5.467	0.821
Wages and salaries per employee	0.018	0.008	−0.030	−0.111	−0.219	−0.299	−0.322	−0.299	−0.259	−0.237
Productivity change (GDP/employee)	−0.065	−0.086	−0.035	0.013	0.062	0.083	0.073	0.040	−0.011	−0.043
Capital stock	−0.002	−0.011	−0.028	−0.049	−0.067	−0.075	−0.073	−0.066	−0.061	−0.062
Prov'l surplus(+)/deficit(−) (change in $Mill)	268	248	215	214	262	350	461	563	598	592
Workers' Comp. premiums (change in $Mill)	284	295	308	325	342	362	383	405	425	444
Wages and salaries paid (change in $Mill)	−134	−296	−514	−695	−797	−752	−587	−411	−386	−528

*Impacts are percentage changes unless otherwise noted.

TABLE 5.4
Employment impacts in Canada of an increase in payroll
tax of 1% for Canada or 2.3% for Ontario (corresponding to
a 10% increase in WC premiums for Ontario)

	'000	% of base
FOCUS – maximum short-term	−15.3	−0.10
– long-term	0	0
Di Matteo and Shannon	−4.4	−0.03
Abbott and Beach – low	−7.1	−0.05
– high	−28.1	−0.20

nue as the payroll tax increase in Simulation 3 above, but through an increase in the Ontario provincial income tax (PIT). The results of this experiment are presented in table 5.5. Impacts on national employment from Simulations 3 and 4 are compared in figure 5.3.

The short-term damage associated with raising the same *ex ante* revenue is much less with the PIT compared with WC premiums: the maximum loss in GDP in Ontario is just under 300 million 1996 dollars (as compared to over $1 billion for the WC premium) and the maximum loss of person-years in employment is under 5000 (vs. over 16,000 for the WC premium increase). In addition, raising revenues through the PIT does less damage to the capital stock – indeed, the capital stock is higher after ten years under the PIT increase, as improvement in the government balance has left room for private-sector net investment. In contrast, under the WC premium increase the damage to investment caused by the initial hit on corporate incomes is not repaired after ten years. The improvements in the provincial budget under the PIT and WC increases are roughly equivalent.

Why is the PIT increase apparently such a less-damaging method of raising revenue, when both the PIT and WC premium increase reduce personal disposable income by the same *ex ante* amount and initiate a 'multiplier' reduction in output, employment, and income, and so on? The WC premium increase also raises inflation temporarily (as firms attempt to pass on the increase in unit labour costs), requiring the Bank of Canada under current money rules to tighten monetary policy somewhat, amplifying the multiplier reduction in output and employment. In addition, the sudden rise in the real after-tax wage paid by firms sets off an immediate employment reduction; this further reduces labour income and, through the consumption functions,

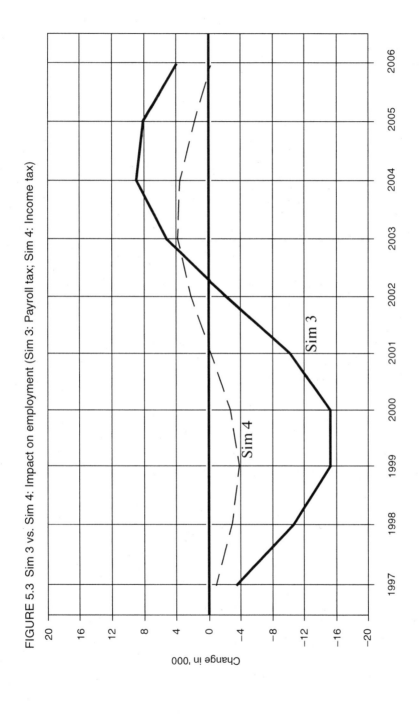

FIGURE 5.3 Sim 3 vs. Sim 4: Impact on employment (Sim 3: Payroll tax; Sim 4: Income tax)

TABLE 5.5
Impacts of Ontario provincial personal income tax increase equivalent to a 10% premium rate increase in Ontario ($282 million in 1997)*

	1997	1998	1999	2000	2001	2002	2003	2004	2005	2006
Impacts for Canada										
Real GDP (change in $ 96 Mill)	-149	-296	-262	-111	79	254	324	241	72	-73
Real GDP	-0.018	-0.034	-0.029	-0.012	-0.008	0.026	0.032	0.023	0.007	-0.007
Consumption	-0.037	-0.089	-0.112	-0.100	-0.067	-0.030	-0.003	0.007	-0.004	-0.027
Investment	-0.010	-0.015	0.005	0.024	0.032	0.042	0.050	0.039	0.021	0.017
Exports	0.000	0.001	0.005	0.012	0.021	0.027	0.029	0.025	0.018	0.011
Imports	-0.014	-0.046	-0.069	-0.070	-0.057	-0.038	-0.013	0.006	0.008	-0.002
Consumer Price Index (CPI)	0.000	-0.003	-0.014	-0.030	-0.045	-0.055	-0.053	-0.042	-0.027	-0.016
Unemployment rate (change in % pts)	0.004	0.014	0.017	0.011	-0.001	-0.012	-0.018	-0.015	-0.006	0.004
Employment	-0.007	-0.021	-0.027	-0.019	-0.003	0.014	0.023	0.021	0.010	-0.003
Employment (change in '000)	-0.914	-2.979	-3.943	-2.799	-0.388	2.122	3.655	3.361	1.555	-0.572
Interest rate (90-day) (change in % pts)	-0.003	-0.015	-0.024	-0.022	-0.018	-0.013	-0.005	0.003	0.004	-0.003
Wages and salaries per employee	-0.003	-0.010	-0.015	-0.017	-0.015	-0.008	0.003	0.009	0.010	0.006
Productivity change (GDP/employee)	-0.011	-0.013	-0.002	0.007	0.011	0.012	0.008	0.002	-0.003	-0.003
Capital stock	0.000	-0.002	-0.003	-0.002	0.001	0.003	0.006	0.010	0.014	0.017
Federal surplus(+)/deficit(−) (change in $Mill)	-30	-49	-47	-45	-22	17	38	17	-22	-51
Prov'l surplus(+)/deficit(−) (change in $Mill)	263	256	276	321	385	456	511	543	562	586
Workers' Comp. premiums (change in $Mill)	0	-2	-3	-3	-4	-3	-2	-1	-1	-1
Wages and salaries paid (change in $Mill)	-31	-122	-215	-263	-262	-210	-199	-51	-38	-69

TABLE 5.5 – concluded
Impacts of Ontario provincial personal income tax increase equivalent to a 10% premium rate increase in Ontario ($282 million in 1997)*

	1997	1998	1999	2000	2001	2002	2003	2004	2005	2006
Impacts for Ontario										
Real GDP (change in $ 96 Mill)*	−114	−279	−296	−189	3	177	232	167	32	−97
Real GDP	−0.034	−0.079	−0.081	−0.050	0.001	0.044	0.056	0.039	0.007	−0.022
Consumption	−0.083	−0.228	−0.305	−0.285	−0.194	−0.095	−0.023	0.013	−0.004	−0.057
Investment	−0.016	−0.020	0.014	0.043	0.059	0.079	0.082	0.048	0.008	−0.001
Exports	0.001	0.002	0.008	0.019	0.031	0.038	0.038	0.033	0.024	0.014
Imports	−0.021	−0.070	−0.106	−0.109	−0.090	−0.059	−0.020	0.009	0.013	−0.003
Consumer Price Index	−0.001	−0.011	−0.033	−0.061	−0.089	−0.107	−0.107	−0.093	−0.076	−0.068
Unemployment rate (change in % pts)	0.004	0.029	0.048	0.043	0.018	−0.009	−0.023	−0.024	−0.011	0.008
Employment	−0.007	−0.047	−0.081	−0.076	−0.034	0.012	0.037	0.040	0.021	−0.011
Employment (change in '000)	−0.387	−2.598	−4.624	−4.418	−2.058	0.724	2.272	2.519	1.317	−0.713
Wages and salaries per employee	−0.004	−0.013	−0.020	−0.023	−0.022	−0.009	0.007	0.013	0.011	0.006
Productivity change (GDP/employee)	−0.027	−0.033	0.000	0.026	0.035	0.032	0.019	−0.001	−0.013	−0.011
Capital stock	0.000	−0.002	−0.003	−0.002	0.001	0.003	0.007	0.011	0.015	0.018
Prov'l surplus(+)/deficit(−) (change in $Mill)	270	253	257	292	350	413	469	515	546	566
Workers' Comp. premiums (change in $Mill)	0	−1	−2	−2	−2	−2	−1	−1	−2	−2
Wages and salaries paid (change in $Mill)	−14	−112	−220	−274	−256	−196	−125	−80	−100	−172

*Impacts are percentage changes unless otherwise noted.

causes an additional reduction in consumption over and above that caused by lower incomes. The result is a still greater amplification of the multiplier decrease in output and employment under the WC premium increase compared to a PIT increase.

The model results clearly show PIT increases being superior to payroll tax increases on the basis of short-term economic damage caused. Nonetheless, arguments from the literature in favour of payroll over income taxes in the long run should be kept in mind. Briefly, income taxes in the long run may distort the savings/consumption decision, leading to lower savings, lower investment, and lower long-term growth. In addition, income taxes may be less economically efficient, distorting allocation and especially work effort and again reducing long-term growth. Finally, income taxes may be administratively more costly, both for governments and the private sector. None of these longer-term factors in favour of payroll over income taxation is present in the model. Still, the model results indicate that these long-term factors need to be relatively large (or the discount rate relatively low) if they are to outweigh the much-higher costs of payroll tax increases in the shorter term. Again, simply for relatively modest changes in rates, rather than wholesale changes in tax systems, their effects are small. But the results clearly show that, in terms of mitigating shorter-term economic damage, it would be wiser to fund the unfunded liabilities of WC systems through the PIT rather than by an across-the-board increase in WC premiums. This approach may also be fairer, since using the WC premium to fund unfunded liabilities places all the burden on only a segment of the population (namely, those currently working and covered by WC, and generally only up to an income cap) rather than on the full tax-paying population under at least some tax progressivity (as will be the case with using the PIT).

Conclusion

Payroll taxes (on employers) are an important component of Canadian taxation, and one closely tied to social benefit systems like Workers' Compensation, Employment Insurance, and public pensions. Moreover, at least some analysts in public finance find that payroll taxes, especially in comparison to pure income or capital taxes, are more economically efficient and have higher compliance and lower administrative cost. The conundrum facing policy makers is that *changing* payroll taxes may involve significant disruptions to output, employment, and real wages. Some recent research indicates that these impacts may be permanent. More mainstream or traditional analysis indicates no permanent impact, but recognizes that short-term adjustments could be significant because most or all of the incidence of the payroll tax is passed from employers to employees. Past research also recognizes that there may be some cases – when benefits to firms are tightly linked to payroll taxes or when payroll taxes are experience-rated by individual firm, or perhaps by industry – where the tax incidence is not transferred from firms to employees and where, consequently, short-term adjustment costs are much lower. These cases can sometimes be relevant to workers' compensation, but do not apply in the case of across-the-board premium changes not linked to changes in direct benefits to firms – e.g., to cover unfunded liabilities or new forms of injury already taken as included by workers.

The macroeconometric model results presented in this paper attempt to measure the short-term disruption from changes in payroll taxes, even though they find no long-term impact. It is found that the short term disruptions are indeed large, compared to changes in income taxes or benefits payments, and that the short term is not particularly short, lasting for several years.

Payroll taxes (compared at least to income taxes) thus appear to have potential positive attributes in terms of economic efficiency, compliance, and administration costs, but negative macroeconomic effects in terms of employment and output in the short run and possibly in the long run. How is this conundrum to be addressed? There are at least three possible responses.

The first is to tie employer payroll taxes wherever possible to experience rating (preferably by firm) and specific benefits. As we have seen, this either keeps the tax incidence in the firm or makes much easier the transfer of incidence to workers (as there is a perceived benefit). In either case, under a payroll tax increase there is little impact on inflation and little need for a period of excess unemployment to force incidence from firms to workers. Adjustments of WC premiums among individual firms, or perhaps industries, should therefore have relatively little macroeconomic impact – although they will likely shift the level of economic activity *among* firms or industries.

The second response is simply to change payroll taxes as little as possible, using changes in deficits/surpluses or more general taxation instead. Under this principle, for example, cyclical ups and downs in the Employment Insurance balance would not be addressed by changing employment insurance premiums (which has in the past turned out to be cyclically destabilizing), but by letting the government deficit or surplus change or by adjusting income taxes. In the same way, the unfunded liabilities of the Ontario or other provincial workers' compensation systems, or of the Canada Pension Plan, could be financed out of general revenues and not from increases in payroll taxes (since, given what the taxes are to be used for, it is impossible to experience-rate them or to tie them to future benefits).

The third response is the simplest but the most unlikely: in all cases where experience rating is not possible and where payroll tax changes cannot be tightly linked to benefits to firms, recognize the ultimate incidence of the tax change and apply it directly to *employee* payroll taxes only. This solution removes the short-term disruption to the economy needed to shift the incidence of payroll taxes to employees. Unfortunately, it also flies in the face of the widely held myth that firms actually 'pay' payroll taxes, and is therefore probably a political 'non-starter.'

NOTES

1 The author is indebted to Doug Hyatt and Morley Gunderson for initiating this research and for much helpful advice as the study progressed. Two anonymous referees also provided useful suggestions. Any remaining errors or oversights, however, are the author's own.
2 An additional, more empirical, review can be found in Marchildon, Sargent, and Ruggeri, 1996.
3 The case of a payroll tax decrease is not so clear and may indicate a possible asymmetry of impacts that, unfortunately, the macro-econometric models will not capture. With a payroll tax decrease it might be asked why existing workers do not immediately press for a rise in their real wages – again, as we know that the long-run incidence of the cut will be on employees. Self-interest argues for more rapid pass-through in this case, but periodic and uncoordinated wage bargaining will still slow the process.
4 Dungan and Murphy (1995) use the FOCUS model to demonstrate how this necessity under the law has made the Employment Insurance system in the past almost useless as an 'automatic stabilizer' in the economy in all but the very short run.
5 This result occurs only because firms already faced legal liability for worker injuries and real wages reflected that fact.

6 There are, however, some mechanisms in FOCUS for explicitly recognizing expectations and for permitting them to change relatively quickly in light of changes in, for example, money supply or the exchange rate.

7 The FOCUS-Ontario model also includes the Ontario Employers' Health Tax.

8 In fact, until about five years ago there was technically no 'Ontario' CPI produced by Statistics Canada, but only a series of individual city CPIs.

9 There are relatively few other empirical studies with which these results can be compared. A recent study released by the Employers' Council on Workers' Compensation (ECWC) (1996) and conducted by Data Resources Inc. found that a $582 million WC premium cut in Ontario would create 33,000 jobs. The ratio of maximum person-hours generated per million dollars of premium cut (33,000/582 = 56.7) is quite close to the simulation results obtained from FOCUS and FOCUS-Ontario (8454/141 = 60.0). However, the ECWC results were 'accelerated' such that the 33,000 was achieved in the second year of the rate reduction, ostensibly because the reforms would be announced and well perceived in advance and would consequently be acted upon quickly by firms, an assumption the present author finds questionable. Moreover, the ECWC study does not examine the impacts in later years as the labour market adjusts and real wages respond to the increased employment.

REFERENCES

Abbott, Michael, and Charles Beach. 1996. 'The Impact of Employer Payroll Taxes on Employment and Wages: Evidence for Canada, 1970–1993.' Mimeo (October), Queen's University, Kingston.

Anderson, Patricia M., and Bruce D. Meyer. 1995. 'The Incidence of a Firm-Varying Payroll Tax: The Case of Unemployment Insurance.' Working paper 5201, National Bureau of Economic Research, Cambridge, Mass.

Bean, C., R. Layard, and S. Nickell. 1986. 'The Rise in Unemployment: A Multi-Country Study.' *Economica* 53: S1–22.

Card, D., and C. Riddell. 1993. 'Comparative Analysis of Unemployment in Canada and the United States.' In D. Card and R. Freeman, eds, *Small Differences That Matter: Labour Markets and Income Maintenance in Canada and the United States*, 149–90. Chicago: University of Chicago Press.

Coe, David. 1990. 'Structural Determinants of the Natural Rate of Unemployment in Canada.' *IMF Staff Papers* 37: 94–115.

Dahlby, Bev. 1992. 'Taxation and Social Insurance.' In R.M. Bird and J. Mintz, eds, *Taxation to 2000 and Beyond*, 110–56. Canadian Tax Paper no. 93. Toronto: Canadian Tax Foundation.

– 1993. 'Payroll Taxes.' In A. Maslove, ed., *Business Taxation in Ontario*, chapter 3. Toronto: University of Toronto Press.

Di Matteo, Livio, and Michael Shannon. 1995. 'Payroll Taxation in Canada: An Overview.' *Canadian Business Economics*, Summer: 5–22.

Dungan, Peter. 1994. 'The Macroeconomic Impacts of Harmonizing the Ontario Retail Sales Tax with the Federal GST: Simulations with the Focus-Ontario Model.' In A. Maslove, ed., *Issues in the Taxation of Individuals*, 155–71. Toronto: University of Toronto Press.

– 1995. *FOCUS-Ontario: Quarterly Forecasting and User Simulation Model of the Ontario Economy: Version 94A*. Institute for Policy Analysis, University of Toronto.

Dungan, Peter, Richard Harris, and Thomas Wilson. 1991. 'The Canada-U.S. Free Trade Agreement – A Symposium.' *Journal of Policy Modeling* 13(3) (Fall): 417–58.

Dungan, Peter, and Gregory Jump. 1995. *FOCUS: Quarterly Forecasting and User Simulation Model of the Canadian Economy: Version 94A*. Institute for Policy Analysis, University of Toronto.

Dungan, Peter, Jack M. Mintz, and Thomas Wilson. 1990. 'Alternatives to the Goods and Services Tax.' *Canadian Tax Journal* 38(3): 644–65.

Dungan, Peter, and Steve Murphy. 1995. *The UI System as an Automatic Stabilizer in Canada*, Unemployment Insurance Program Evaluation Report. Ottawa: Human Resources Development Canada.

Dungan, Peter, Steve Murphy, and Thomas Wilson. 1997. 'National Projection Through 2020.' Policy and Economic Analysis Program Policy Study 97-1, Institute for Policy Analysis, University of Toronto.

Employers' Council on Workers' Compensation. 1996. 'Workers' Compensation Reform Will Create 33,000 New Jobs, Study Finds.' Press release and attachments, 9 May 1996.

Finlayson, Jock, and Tim McEwan. 1996. 'Why Too Few Jobs? Payroll Taxes, Government Regulation and Employment Growth in the 1990s.' Business Council of British Columbia Research Paper, Vancouver, October.

Fortin, Pierre. 1996. 'Presidential Address: The Great Canadian Slump.' *Canadian Journal of Economics* 29(4): 761 87.

Gunderson, M., and C. Riddell. 1993. *Labour Market Economics in Canada*, 3rd ed. Toronto: McGraw-Hill.

Hyatt, Douglas E. 1996. 'Work Disincentives of Workers' Compensation Permanent Partial Disability Benefits: Evidence for Canada.' *Canadian Journal of Economics* 29(2): 289–308.

Keil, M.W., and J.S.V. Symons. 1990. 'An Analysis of Canadian Unemploy-
    ment.' *Canadian Public Policy / Analyse de Politiques* 16(1): 1–16.
Kesselman, Jonathan R. 1996. 'Payroll Taxes in the Financing of Social Security.'
    Canadian Public Policy / Analyse de Politiques 22(2): 162–79.
Lin, Zhengxi, Garnett Picot, and Charles Beach. 1996. 'What Has Happened to
    Payroll Taxes in Canada over the Last Three Decades.' *Canadian Tax Journal*
    44(4): 1052–77.
Marchildon, Lori, Timothy C. Sargent, and Joe Ruggeri. 1996. 'An Economic
    Analysis of Payroll Taxes.' Mimeo (March). Ottawa: Economic Studies and
    Policy Analysis Division, Department of Finance.
Mercer, William M. 1996. 'Appendix A: Report of William M. Mercer.' In *New
    Directions for Workers' Compensation Reform*. Report of the Honourable Cam
    Jackson, Minister without Portfolio Responsible for Workers' Compensation
    Reform, Queen's Park, Toronto.
Murphy, Steve, and Peter Dungan. 1996. 'Ontario Short-Term Forecast.' Policy
    and Economic Analysis Program Policy memo 96-7. Institute for Policy
    Analysis, University of Toronto.
Organization for Economic Co-operation and Development. 1994. *The OECD
    Jobs Study: Evidence and Explanations, Part II, The Adjustment Potential of the
    Labour Market*. Paris: OECD.
– 1995. *The OECD Jobs Study: Taxation, Employment and Unemployment*. Paris:
    OECD.
Poloz, S. 1994. 'The Causes of Unemployment in Canada: A Review of the Evi-
    dence.' Working paper 94-11. Ottawa: Bank of Canada.
Stokes, Ernie. 1995. *Canada's Unemployment Insurance Program as an Economic
    Stabilizer*. Unemployment Insurance Program Evaluation Report. Ottawa:
    Human Resources Development Canada.
Vaillancourt, F. 1995. 'The Financing and Pricing of WCBs in Canada: Existing
    Arrangements, Possible Changes.' In *Chronic Stress: Workers' Compensation in
    the 1990s*, 69–91. Toronto: C.D. Howe Institute.
Vaillancourt, F., and N. Marceau. 1990. 'Do General and Firm-Specific
    Employer Payroll Taxes Have the Same Incidence? Theory and Evidence.'
    Economics Letters 34: 175–81.
Wilson, Thomas A., Peter Dungan, and Steve Murphy. 1994. 'Sources of the
    Recession in Canada.' *Canadian Business Economics* 2(2): 3–15.
Wilton, D., and D. Prescott. 1993. 'The Effects of Tax Increases on Labour
    Costs.' Government and Competitiveness Project, Discussion paper 93-29.
    School of Policy Studies, Queen's University, Kingston.

6 Unfunded Liabilities under Workers' Compensation

MORLEY GUNDERSON and DOUGLAS HYATT

Unfunded liabilities arise under workers' compensation when the expected future benefit obligations exceed the value of the assets committed to meet those liabilities. Much is at stake when substantial unfunded liabilities accumulate at workers' compensation boards. Addressing these liabilities requires some combination of reducing benefit payments to current and future injured workers, reducing administration costs, shifting costs to parties or other income maintenance programs outside the workers' compensation system, or increasing workers' compensation payroll taxes.

Further, unfunded liabilities can have important redistributive consequences, both intergenerationally (i.e., between existing and new firms and their employees) and across different firms and industries. Doing nothing about unfunded liabilities implies the current generation's acceptance of a tacit policy of passing the cost burden of work injuries to future generations of workers and firms in the hope that they will unquestioningly assume these accrued liabilities.

The purpose of this chapter is to systematically analyse the cost and policy implications of workers' compensation unfunded liabilities. Myriad associated policy implications are first outlined, to highlight the importance of the topic and to provide a motivation for issues that we subsequently address. The meaning and dimensions of unfunded liabilities are outlined in more detail and their magnitudes illustrated. A particular focus of this chapter is on an intergenerational consideration of unfunded liabilities. These are described, and placed in the context of other transfers that have intergenerational consequences. An illustrative simulation is provided of the degree of cost-shifting under the Ontario system.[1] Implications of the redistribution of workers' compensation costs are discussed for both employees and firms, as are alternative options for dealing with the unfunded liabilities. The chapter concludes with summary remarks.

Associated Policy Issues

A wide range of policy issues are associated with the cost burden of unfunded liabilities as well as with the likely policy responses to that liability and how it will ultimately be 'paid.' As shall be outlined in more detail subsequently, unfunded liabilities have important redistributional effects, both across firms and industries at a given point in time and across generations of firms and individuals over time. This redistribution also gives rise to important efficiency implications, since the cost shifting associated with the unfunded liabilities means that some parties are not paying the full cost associated with their injuries and diseases. This, in turn, means that they have less of a monetary incentive to reduce such injuries and diseases, and that there may be a deterrence to the growth of new firms and the associated job creation because they would bear the expense of discharging the unfunded liability.

Reflecting the different components of the expenses and revenues of the workers' compensation system, there is a wide range of policy responses that may be used to reduce the unfunded liabilities, and each of these responses has different implications. Pay-outs or expenses, for example, can involve many components: workers' compensation benefits to workers who are permanently, temporarily, or fatally injured; medical and vocational rehabilitation expenses; and administrative expenses associated with operating the system, including the adjudication of claims. Revenues can also have different components: payroll taxes on employers and employees; general tax revenues; and earnings from fund investments or perhaps even liquidating assets. Revenues can be raised by increasing the tax *rates* or by increasing the tax *base* (i.e., the groups who pay the tax). Increasing the tax base could be accomplished, for example, by extending coverage to those currently not covered by workers' compensation.[2]

Both the pay-out and revenue aspects also have an inter-temporal component in that different 'generations' can be involved: the *current recipients* of payments, whose employers paid into the system in the past; the *current workers*, whose employers are paying into the system and who may draw from it if injured or disabled; *current uncovered workers*, who are not currently covered by workers' compensation but who may be brought into the system in the future; and *future genera-tions*, not yet working or not yet born, whose employers can be expected to pay into the system and who may draw from it. Similar intergenerational considerations apply to firms: failed firms may have accrued liabilities that they will not pay; current firms may be accruing liabilities or paying off the liabilities of previous firms; new firms may acquire such unfunded liabilities. This intergenerational aspect is par-ticularly relevant since the system is partially 'pay-as-you-go,' with pay-outs to current recipients coming largely from taxes on current firms and workers, and with future pay-outs to current workers *expected* to come from taxes on future generations – with expected being the operative word.

Each of these generations also has different degrees of 'claims' on the system. Current recipients of benefits have a quasi-legal claim in that those who are permanently injured or disabled have a promised amount based on their award, although some workers may be in a stage where that promised amount is still being determined. As well, there may be some discretion in the extent of medical and vocational rehabilitation expenses that will be incurred, or on whether adjust-ments will be retroactive, or on how the compensation is indexed to compensate for inflation. For those who are temporarily injured there may be more immediate adjustments that could be made to the pay-outs. Current workers, whose employers are paying into the system and largely supporting the current recipients, have an expectation of benefits that may be based on those being received by current recipi-ents, but this expectation is complicated by the changing nature of occupational injuries and diseases, and by the fact that the pay-outs will largely come from taxes on future generations. As discussed sub-sequently, the willingness and ability of future generations to 'honour' this historical commitment implied in pay-as-you-go systems may be severely jeopardized by other debt burdens we pass on as well as by other expenditures associated with an aging population.

The payments associated with workers' compensation claims can also be altered by 'shifting' the obligations of those claims. For exam-ple, legal requirements for employers to accommodate the return to work of injured workers can be regarded as a form of shifting some of the cost of workers' compensation, since return to work reduces the need for such compensation. Occupational health and safety regula-tions and policies like experience rating can have similar effects to the extent that they reduce accidents and disabilities and hence reduce pressures on the compensation system itself.

Costs can also be shifted to other transfer programs. Reductions in workers' compensation pay-outs, for example, may put more pressure on other systems like unemployment insurance, or the disability component of the Canada/Quebec Pension Plan, or on social assistance itself. The unfunded liability may increase pressure to achieve administrative efficiencies, for example, through privatization. However, Dewees (this volume) suggests that the actual cost savings from additional administrative efficiencies are likely to be modest. Privatization may also be regarded as a mechanism to reduce the unfunded liability, since there are likely to be more restrictions on the extent of underfunding under privatized systems.

In essence, while unfunded liabilities of workers' compensation can be eliminated only by reducing the pay-outs or increasing the revenues, the wide range of dimensions associated with these simple two sides of the balance sheet highlight that a large number of policy options are available for dealing with the unfunded liability (as summarized in table 6.1). The unfunded liability can be reduced, for example, by reductions in benefits or increases in taxes. But they could also be passed to future generations by continuing the current pay-outs and tax levels that are giving rise to unfunded liabilities, although that raises the issue of whether future generations will 'honour' such 'commitments,' which were made on their behalf but when they were not 'at the table.' The unfunded liability could also be lessened by more subtle ways of reducing pressure on the workers' compensation system, such as through stronger requirements on employers to accommodate the return to work of injured workers, or by shifting claimants to other transfer systems. Privatization may also be used to reduce administrative costs and possibly even to restrict the practice of unfunded liabilities.

Understanding the extent of the unfunded liability and the burden it may put on different groups and generations is therefore important in order to determine the pressure that will be placed on different parts of the workers' compensation system and the tax-transfer system in general. It may also be important to understand the responses that may be engendered by these groups, especially future generations. Unfunded liabilities under workers' compensation clearly give rise to a wide range of policy issues.

TABLE 6.1
Dimensions of options for dealing with unfunded liabilities under workers' compensation

Expenses (pay-outs)	Revenues
Reduce direct expenses and increase revenues	
Workers' compensation payments	Payroll tax rates on employers and
Vocational rehabilitation expenses	employees
Administrative expenses	Payroll tax base
No compensation for certain injuries	Fund investments and earnings
(e.g., repetitive strain, stress)	Liquidate assets
Expense- and revenue-shifting options	
Duty to accommodate return to work of	General tax revenues
injured workers	Differential higher tax on public sector
Occupational health and safety regulations	to effectively convert liability into
to reduce claims	public debt
Other transfer systems (UI, CPP/QPP,	
social assistance)	

Intergenerational expense- and revenue-shifting options

- Current recipients of benefits
- Current workers covered by workers' compensation
- Current workers not covered by workers' compensation
- Future generations

Privatization options

- To reduce administrative costs
- To reduce ability to have unfunded liabilities

Meaning and Magnitude of Unfunded Liabilities

Unfunded liabilities in workers' compensation systems arise in large part because insufficient reserve funds are set aside to cover the future expenses associated with workers who are permanently disabled (partial or total disability). Long-term permanent disability payments are by far the largest expense associated with workers' compensation, accounting for approximately 60 per cent of expenses.[3] The expenses are mainly for cash benefit pay-outs, but they also include such factors as ongoing medical and vocational rehabilitation as well as administrative expenses. Since they are projected expenses into the future, they are based on actuarial calculations involving such factors as mortality and the expected severity and duration of injuries. They can also be affected by retroactive adjustments and legislative changes on such factors as indexing of benefits. These expected future expenses constitute liabilities of the system.

The system is financed by a payroll tax levied on employers. Some of the current assessment is used to pay for the current expenses and some is placed in a fund and invested to pay for the future liabilities. Future liabilities, associated with those accidents that occur today, are therefore to be paid out of these invested funds, and hence they depend in part on the return on those funds.

An unfunded liability occurs if the reserve funds set aside are insufficient to cover the present value of projected expenses. In a given year, there is an addition to the unfunded liability if the new commitments that come on stream associated with the injuries of that year are greater than the revenues that come on stream from the assessments and the fund investments. Over time, this can lead to an accumulation of unfunded liabilities. The accumulated unfunded liabilities represent the funds that would have to come from other sources to discharge the liabilities if the system were to wind down its operations today (assuming, of course, that the obligations would be honoured).

Table 6.2 illustrates the magnitudes of these unfunded liabilities, and their sources, for the workers' compensation system in the province of Ontario in 1996. The total unfunded liabilities accumulated by 1996 were $10.5 billion; that is, if the system were to wind down as of 1996, $10.5 billion would have to come from other sources to pay for the expected future liabilities of the system. On a per capita basis, this amounts to $3362 per worker who is covered by the workers' compensation system (there being 3.11 million covered workers in 1996 in Ontario). That is, if the system were to wind down today, approximately $3362 per assessed worker would have to come from outside the system to pay the unfunded liability.

During the year 1996, approximately $2.4 billion in workers' compensation indemnity benefits were paid, and a further $468 million of administrative and other expenses were incurred. A charge of $50 million was incurred as a result of actuarial adjustments or legislative changes in benefits. The net effect of these was $2.9 billion in expenses.

The total revenues of $3.3 billion came mainly from payroll tax assessments ($2.6 billion) with an additional $711 million from returns on the fund investments.

Since revenues exceeded expenses in 1996, the unfunded liability

TABLE 6.2
Sources of unfunded liability, Ontario Workers' Compensation Board, 1996 ($ millions)

Expenses or pay-outs		
Indemnity benefits paid	2371	
Net increase (decrease) in benefit liability	50	
Administrative and other expenses	468	
Total expenses		2889
Revenues		
Payroll tax assessments	2610	
Return from funds investments	711	
Total revenues		3321
Unfunded liabilities		
Accrued in 1995 (i.e., expenses – revenues)		−432
Total accumulated unfunded liability by 1996		10,460
Per covered worker unfunded liability accrued in 1996 ($)		−139
Per covered worker unfunded liability accumulated by 1996 ($)		3,362
Ratio assets to expected future benefit liability		42.9

Source: Ontario Workers' Compensation Board, *Annual Report*, 1996
Note: The net increase (decrease) in benefit liabilities reflects such factors as actuarial adjustments or legislative changes to benefits in that year.

was reduced by $432 million. However, this was less than 5 per cent of the accumulated unfunded liability at that time. As figure 6.1 illustrates, since 1981 the unfunded liability has increased each year, with surpluses to reduce the unfunded liability having occurred since 1994.

As illustrated in figure 6.2, the unfunded liability grew each year[4] until 1994 because of the deficiencies (bottom panel of the diagram) created from the fact that revenues were insufficient to cover contemporaneous costs. In some years, like 1985, the differences were dramatic. In that year inflation indexing was instituted and made retroactive so as to enrich previous benefit commitments, giving rise to more than a doubling of the unfunded liabilities in one year. Expenses appear to have peaked in the early 1990s and thereafter have come down. Revenues have generally been stable since 1989. This combination of falling expenses and stable revenues has given rise to a steady reduction in unfunded liabilities accruing since 1991, with surpluses applied to the unfunded liability since 1994. In essence, by the 1990s,

FIGURE 6.1 Total unfunded liabilities, Ontario Workers' Compensation, 1981–96

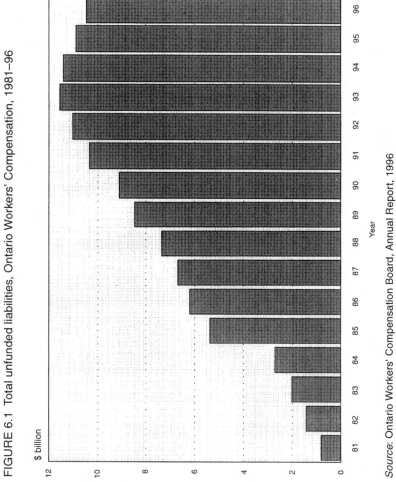

Source: Ontario Workers' Compensation Board, Annual Report, 1996

FIGURE 6.2 Revenues and expenses, Ontario Workers' Compensation, 1981–96

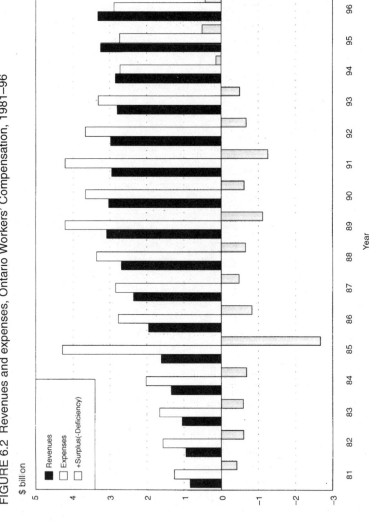

$ billion

Revenues
Expenses
+Surplus(-Deficiency)

Year

Source: Ontario Workers' Compensation Board, Annual Report, 1996

the tide seems to have been turned in terms of curbing the growth, and even reversing the direction, of the unfunded liability, but the existing magnitude of the liability remains an important issue.

As indicated in table 6.3, the unfunded liabilities vary dramatically by industry, largely reflecting the fact that the payroll tax assessments are generally insufficient to 'pay for' the liabilities that are created by the injuries incurred in each industry. Over one-third of the unfunded liabilities arise from the manufacturing sector; however, that largely reflects the fact that almost one-third of covered employment is in that sector. Another one-third of the total unfunded liability is attributed to the construction industry, in spite of the fact that it only employs about 4 per cent of the workforce that is covered by workers' compensation. The per capita unfunded liability in construction averages over $23,000; the per capita unfunded liability is almost as large in mining, and considerably above average in forest products. The per capita unfunded liability is slightly above average in transportation and storage, manufacturing, and in other primary metals. By contrast, it is considerably lower than average in retail and wholesale trade, and especially in government and other services.

The cumulative effect of these different factors shows up in the funding ratios of column 3 in table 6.4. In construction, for example, assets only account for 16 per cent of the benefit liabilities that are committed, while in government they account for almost 60 per cent of the liabilities. In other words if the board were to wind down its operations and liquidate its assets (which are mainly its investment funds), it could only cover 16 per cent of its outstanding liabilities in construction. Even in the government sector it could cover less than 60 per cent of its liabilities.

Table 6.5 (p. 174) highlights the different components of the assessment rates across the different industries. Approximately 60 per cent of the assessments go to cover new claims, slightly over 10 per cent to cover administrative and other related expenses, and about 4 per cent to cover legal obligations like benefit or actuarial adjustments that occur in that year. Notably, almost one-third is a surtax imposed to cover the unfunded liabilities that have accumulated over time. This surtax is clearly related to the magnitude of the unfunded liability, being highest in construction and mining, and lowest in government and other services.

Clearly, there has been considerable inter-temporal and inter-industry variation in the unfunded liabilities of workers' compensation. The liabilities have grown over time, and they tend to be greatest

TABLE 6.3
Workers' compensation unfunded liabilities by industry, Ontario, 1996

| Industry | Unfunded liability ($ million) | | Employment | Per covered worker liability | Unfunded ($) |
	Accumulated (1)	Change 1996 (2)	(3)	Accumulated (4)	Change 1995 (5)
Forest products	486.0	−21.5	43,173	11,257	−50
Mining & related	524.5	31.6	24,894	21,069	−127
Other primary	140.7	−4.0	37,173	3,785	−108
Manufacturing	3,646.0	−281.8	956,474	3,812	−294.6
Transport & storage	532.4	−65.2	114,805	4,637	−568
Retail & wholesale	1,019.6	−52.6	695,755	1,465	−76
Construction	3,042.5	83.9	130,788	23,263	64
Government	549.1	−25.1	538,608	1,019	−46
Other services	519.7	−33.3	569,260	913	−58
Total	10,460.5	−431.2	3,110,930	3,362	−139

Sources: Unfunded liability figures from Ontario Workers' Compensation Board, *Statistical Supplement to the 1996 Annual Report*. The unfunded liability changes in 1996 are the surpluses in that year that reduce the unfunded liability (if negative) or deficiencies that increase the liabilities (if positive).

Employment figures are for 1996, from Ontario Workers' Compensation Board, *Assessment Rate Manual*, 1997. The employment figures refer to full-time equivalents assessed for the payroll tax. Columns (4) and (5) are calculated by dividing columns (1) and (2) respectively by the employee figures of column (3).

TABLE 6.4

Injury rates, assessment rates, and funding ratios by industry, Ontario workers' compensation, 1995

Industry	Lost-time injury rate (1)	Assessment rate (2)	Funding ratio (3)
Forest products	2.91	4.56	37.6
Mining & related	2.32	6.92	51.7
Other primary	4.50	5.23	52.4
Manufacturing	3.48	3.40	47.4
Transport & storage	5.99	6.49	56.0
Retail & wholesale	2.43	2.20	44.1
Construction	3.88	8.44	15.6
Government	2.09	1.32	58.8
Other services	2.21	1.94	48.8
Total	2.88	3.00	42.9

Sources: Lost-time injury rates for 1994 from the *Assessment Rate Manual*, 1997. Assessment rates for 1996 from the *Assessment Rate Manual*, 1995. Funding rates for 1996 (ratio of assets to future benefit liabilities) from Ontario Workers' Compensation Board, *Statistical Supplement to the 1996 Annual Report*.

in industries like construction and mining, where the rate of new claims is the highest. Yet it appears that checks are being put in place. Surpluses of revenues over expenses have turned the deficiencies into surpluses in the last few years, and these are reducing the accumulated unfunded liabilities. Furthermore, industries with high per capita unfunded liabilities are being subject to higher assessment rates, including a higher surtax to help discharge the unfunded liabilities. These changes are part of the 'revenue strategy' that has been put in place by the Ontario board to address the unfunded liability issue. Our simulations suggest that these changes have 'turned the tide.' Yet the unfunded liability remains substantial and it exists across all industries.

Redistributive Aspects of Unfunded Liabilities

The immediate winding-down of the workers' compensation system is not a likely scenario, although it could be if extensive privatization were to occur, since the unfunded liability would have to be dealt with.

TABLE 6.5
Assessment rate components, Ontario workers' compensation, 1996 (cost per $100 of assessable payroll)

Industry	Overall rate (1)	New claims (2)	Administrative (3)	Legal obligations (4)	Unfunded liability charge (5)
Forest products	4.56	2.57	0.49	0.15	1.35
Mining & related	6.92	3.86	0.68	0.33	2.05
Other primary	5.23	2.91	0.72	0.05	1.55
Manufacturing	3.40	1.89	0.38	0.13	1.01
Transport & storage	6.49	3.71	0.78	0.08	1.92
Retail & wholesale	2.20	1.22	0.23	0.10	0.65
Construction	8.44	4.79	0.93	0.23	2.50
Government	1.32	0.75	0.11	0.09	0.38
Other services	1.94	1.07	0.20	0.94	0.56
All industries	3.01	1.68	0.32	0.12	0.89

Above the component columns (2)-(5): **Components**

Source: Ontario Workers' Compensation Board, *Assessment Rate Manual*, 1996.
Notes: (1) The overall rate of column (1) is the sum of the different expense components as indicated in the other columns, and is the rate that would discharge these expense obligations. It differs slightly from the rate that was the actual rate charged in 1996, because the actual rate included a transition adjustment designed to phase in the expense adjustment over a two-year period.
    (2) Administrative expenses of column (3) include charges for safety associations and special training programs.
    (3) Legal obligations of column (4) reflects the costs of legislated changes that are applied in that year, including benefits adjustments, indexation, or actuarial adjustments.
    (4) The unfunded liability charge of column (5) is the surtax imposed to eliminate the unfunded liability, over a period of 20 to 25 years.

Even if it does not have to be dealt with immediately, the unfunded liability does represent costs that are not assigned to the employers in whose workplaces the accident occurred. The costs are redistributed to other firms at a given point in time as well as intergenerationally over time. The redistribution at a given point in time occurs because different firms and industries have different injury rates, and their payroll-tax assessment rates may not equal their expected claims costs; hence, they contribute in different magnitudes (positive and negative) to the unfunded liabilities. The intergenerational redistribution over time occurs for similar reasons. That is, existing firms may have unfunded liabilities that they pass on to new generations of firms. As indicated previously, special surtax assessments have been assigned to both existing and new firms to reduce the unfunded liability. To the extent that the surtax is insufficient for existing firms to discharge their liabilities, and to the extent that new firms face a surtax for unfunded liability to which they did not contribute, then there will be a redistribution or subsidy from new firms to existing firms.

The implied redistributions are important for policy purposes since they have both equity and efficiency implications. The equity or distributional implications are obvious: some firms are paying for the costs of injuries incurred in other firms, and, conversely, some firms are not paying for the full costs of the injuries suffered by their workers. The efficiency implications are more subtle. If firms do not pay for the full cost of their injuries, then they likely will under-invest in health and safety. The price of their products will not reflect the costs of injuries incurred in producing those products, and hence consumers will consume 'too much' of the products that have health and safety risks associated with their production, therefore exposing workers to 'too much' risk.

The inter-temporal redistribution that occurs as the current generation of firms pass unfunded liabilities on to future generations of firms has similar equity and efficiency implications. New firms will be paying for liabilities to which they did not contribute. This in turn can deter the growth of new firms, and sustain the existence of inefficient firms that otherwise may go out of business except for the fact that they are not 'paying for' the costs of injuries they create. Even if there were some merit in slowing the decline of inefficient firms (perhaps to 'buy time' for labour readjustment), it is unlikely to be desirable to do it 'through the back door' by having their survival depend upon not paying for the costs of their injuries. Such an industrial policy of sustaining declining firms should be debated on its own merits. This debate would be informed by having estimates of the intergenerational transfers that are involved with the unfunded liabilities of workers' compensation.

The equity and efficiency implications are further complicated by the fact that while the payroll tax for workers' compensation is initially imposed on employers, they ultimately shift it forward to consumers or backwards to investors and workers. In a world of increased globalization and competitive product markets, the tax cannot easily be shifted forward to consumers since they have viable alternatives in international markets – their purchases are sensitive to any price increases induced by cost increases, including payroll taxes. Similarly, in a world of global capital markets, the tax cannot easily be shifted backwards to investors since they can easily invest elsewhere. That leaves labour as the relatively immobile factor of production that cannot easily 'escape' the tax by moving elsewhere. In the long run, the tax can easily be shifted back to workers in the form of lower wages in return for the workers' compensation benefits.[5] Since it may take considerable time for wages to adjust downwards, short-run transitional unemployment would result associated with the rigid wages (Dungan, this volume). Given the high unemployment and stagnant real wages that have characterized the Canadian labour market since the mid-1970s, such an adjustment poses an additional burden on labour.

The redistributions from unfunded liabilities can also distort savings and investment decisions. Organizations that can pass costs to future generations of firms (or workers) will tend to save less, since they will not need reserves for their future liabilities. This in turn can dampen the investment that can foster growth. Current generations of families that pass unfunded liabilities off on to future generations may try to bequest more of their private wealth to offset the reduction of public wealth, but evidence suggests that this private offset does not occur (Altonji, Hayashi, and Kotlikoff, 1992).

The ultimate impact of the distributional burden of transferring unfunded liabilities to future generations depends in part on the assets that are associated with those liabilities and that are also transferred. When the costing of these assets is straightforward, then they can be directly deducted to arrive at net liabilities. This is the case, for example, with the assets of workers' compensation boards, which include funds that are invested and even physical assets like buildings. If operations were wound down, these could be liquidated to reduce any net liabilities that are passed on. In cases where the unfunded liabilities are used to finance public-sector infrastructure or even environmental protection, the unfunded liabilities can be regarded as investments in the future, and hence may offset at least part of the cost of the unfunded liability. In the case of workers' compensation, however, the financing tends to be for the benefit of the current generation of workers, with the spillovers to future generations mainly in the form of the unfunded liability.

Clearly, the unfunded liabilities under workers' compensation have redistributive effects, both over time and across industries and firms. These in turn have equity or distributional implications with respect to paying the cost of workers' compensation, as well as efficiency impli-

TABLE 6.6
Population aged 65 and over as % of total population and working-age population, Canada,
1960–2030

Year	As % of total population	As % of working-age population 15–64
1960	7.6	13.0
1990	11.3	16.7
2000	12.3	18.2
2010	13.8	20.4
2020	18.2	28.4
2030	23.1	39.1

Source: Organization for Economic Co-operation
and Development, Aging in OECD Countries
(Paris: OECD, 1996), 101–2.

cations with respect to the incentives that are created, especially to curb occupational injuries and diseases.

Intergenerational Aspects of Other Transfers

The intergenerational transfers of unfunded liabilities of workers' compensation to future generations of firms and workers are coming on top of other intergenerational burdens that are being placed on future generations. This is the case, for example, with respect to the Canada/Quebec Pension Plan. Current generations of workers are paying for the retirement pensions of previous generations who are not retired, and future generations will be paying for the pension obligations of current workers, when they retire.

Such pay-go systems work fine when there is stable population growth and productivity (and hence earnings) growth. However, productivity and earnings growth in Canada have been stagnant since the mid-1970s. Of greater consequence, the large baby-boom population born in the late 1940s will soon be reaching normal retirement age and drawing pensions. Their increasing life expectancy also means that they will be drawing on that pension for a longer period. This will be occurring at the very time that the taxpaying base population is dwindling in size. As illustrated in table 6.6, in 1960 the proportion of the population aged 65 and over was only 7.6 per cent of the total popula-

tion and 13 per cent of the working-age (usually taxpaying) population. By the year 2030, the older population aged 65 and above is
expected to be 23.1 per cent of the total population and 39.1 per cent of
the working-age population.[6] Even if there were no unfunded liability,
the tax burden of the working-age population would be extensive
because they are few in numbers and the retired population is large in
numbers. Adding an unfunded liability simply compounds the burden. The problem is worsened by the fact that the aging (and increasingly long-lived) population will give rise to other age-dependent
public expenditures, namely health care – another pay-go system. As
well, as pointed out by Oreopoulos and Kotlikoff (1996), future generations will be inheriting a huge burden of servicing the national debt if
current social programs and tax-transfer structures continue.

In essence, the burden on future taxpayers of the intergenerational
transfers associated with the unfunded liabilities of workers' compensation are coming on top of additional burdens associated with other
pay-go systems, especially CPP/QPP and health care. For the current
taxpaying base, this has been sustainable, since there is a large base
paying for a small group at the apex of the age triangle. In the near
future, that triangle will be inverted, with a large group in the top age
groups that draws benefits, and only a small base that pays taxes. Even
without unfunded liabilities being passed on, this would not likely be
sustainable. With unfunded liabilities, it becomes even less sustainable.

This simple picture highlights the generic policy options: increase
the tax rates for the few at the bottom; increase the tax base by expanding the numbers at the bottom; reduce expenditures for the large numbers of the aged population. Increasing the tax *rates* for the children of
the baby-boom population is likely to be resisted strongly, especially
because of the slow growth of their real income, and the fact that such
an increase would be for expenditures they 'inherited,' and to which
they did not explicitly agree. Furthermore, increasing tax rates can
affect job creation and work incentives in a fashion that would reduce
tax revenues.

In the workers' compensation area, the tax base could be expanded
by increasing the coverage from its current level of around 70 per cent
in Ontario. Groups not covered currently include domestics, professional athletes, casual or seasonal workers, farm workers, independent
truckers, teachers, clergy, volunteers, and workers in small firms, non-
profit organizations, banks, and financial establishments. Expanding
this base, however, will give rise to another set of issues. Some are not

covered because it would be difficult to attribute an injury to their regular work environment. Expanding coverage in those areas would expand not only the revenue base, but also expenditures, including administrative expenditures associated with determining the source of an injury. Furthermore, if their assessment includes a surtax to reduce the unfunded liability, there is the issue of why such newly covered groups should have to finance past unfunded liabilities for which they are not responsible. The coverage of many of these new groups will also increase the pressure to allow claims in areas like stress that are not conventionally covered by workers' compensation. Again, the short-run revenue gains may be offset by long-run expenditure increases.

If expanding the tax rate or the tax base is not viable, then the pressure will exist to reduce expenditures on the aged population. This is more likely to be allowed by the tax-paying base population, if they feel that the retired population did not adequately 'fund' their own subsequent expenditures, especially because they knew of the issues – an aging population is not an unanticipated event. In essence, the viability of pay-go systems depends upon the willingness and ability of future generations to sustain the commitments. This willingness may be sorely tested if they are burdened with multiple unfunded liabilities that were anticipated and could have been acted upon.[7]

The expenditure reductions can be indirect. For example, they can come in the form of reduced indexation to benefit pay-outs in the case of pensions or workers' compensation benefits. Clawbacks can be instituted for those who continue to earn income, and raising the age of normal retirement could be used to reduce pay-outs. Banning mandatory retirement could facilitate continued employment and reduced pension withdrawals depending upon the actuarial adjustments that would be made. In the health care area, expenditure reductions can occur in the form of 'deinstitutionalization' and more family-based elder care.

Such expenditure restraints are not necessarily undesirable. They have to be judged on their own merits. They tend not to be emphasized, however, as a likely response to the inevitable balancing act that is forthcoming. The implicit assumption tends to be that the current expenditure patterns will prevail as part of an intergenerational social contract. The fragile nature of this contract, however, has to be recognized, especially with respect to the intergenerational burden of unfunded liabilities under workers' compensation.

Intergenerational Accounting Applied to Workers' Compensation

The intergenerational transfers involved in workers' compensation can be illustrated through calculations based on the Ontario system. The procedure we use is intergenerational accounting adapted to the special circumstances of workers' compensation.[8] Essentially, the procedure involves calculating the present value of future payroll taxes that new firms can expect to pay for their own obligations as well as for the unfunded liabilities of existing firms. The steps are as follows:

1 Calculate the future payroll-tax assessment liability that new firms can expect to pay for the future benefit indemnities for their injured workers.
2 Add to this the future tax assessments of existing firms less their future indemnity benefits (this is the gross unfunded liability of existing firms).
3 Subtract the net assets passed on from existing firms (this gives the net unfunded liability of existing firms).

This procedure yields the net tax assessment that new firms can expect to pay for their own benefit indemnities as well as for the net unfunded liability of existing firms.

Assessment and benefit estimates involve present-value calculations and hence assumptions about discount rates, time periods over which the unfunded liability is to be eliminated, changes in payroll tax rates and payrolls, and the effect of the 'birth' of new firms and 'death' of existing firms in the industry. Since our analysis is meant to be illustrative rather than a precise actuarial calculation of the tax burden of the unfunded liability, we utilize the aggregate nine industries that were previously used to describe the unfunded liability, injury rates, assessment rates, and the components of the unfunded liability.[9]

Illustrative Simulation Results

Table 6.7 illustrates the intergenerational and inter-industry transfers inherent in the Ontario workers' compensation program. In the left panel, the first column gives the unfunded liability (when it is negative, which is generally the case) that is being passed on by existing firms. This situation occurs because the present value of their expected payroll tax assessments plus assets is less than their expected pay-outs

TABLE 6.7

Unfunded liabilities(−) or surplus(+) by industry, existing and new firms, Ontario workers' compensation, 1997

Industry	$ million			As % of payroll		
	Existing firms	New firms	All firms	Existing firms	New firms	All firms
Forest products	−213.6	60.6	−152.8	−1.35	1.73	−0.79
Mining & related	−256.5	143.7	−112.8	−2.23	2.33	−0.64
Other primary	34.4	93.9	128.3	−0.40	2.04	−0.97
Manufacturing	−464.3	1428.5	964.2	−0.15	1.01	0.21
Transport & storage	138.5	377.9	516.5	0.40	1.92	0.94
Retail & wholesale	−233.2	852.5	1085.7	−0.14	0.75	0.39
Construction	−1808.0	731.5	−1076.5	−3.71	2.53	−1.39
Government	129.2	313.9	443.1	0.08	0.44	0.20
Other services	104.4	609.7	714.1	0.08	0.49	0.28

Source: Calculations by authors, as outlined in text.

to their injured workers, those pay-outs reflecting current commitments to those already injured and future commitments for future injuries. The second column gives the same figures for new firms that will be coming on stream, and that therefore have not contributed to the unfunded liability. The figures are all positive, illustrating that they will pay more in tax assessments than the value of benefits received by their injured workers. The intergenerational transfer from new to existing firms occurs because the new firms all pay more into the system than they benefit from in the pay-outs to their workers, while the existing firms generally pay less into the system than they benefit from in pay-outs to their workers.

The third column of the left panel illustrates the unfunded liability (if negative) or surplus payment (if positive) associated with both existing and new firms in each industry. The inter-industry transfers are illustrated by the fact that some of the entries in the third row are negative (and hence contribute to the total unfunded liability) while others are positive (and hence contribute a surplus that reduces the unfunded liability). Industries with a positive entry effectively cross-subsidize those with a negative entry.

The right panel puts the figures in perspective by expressing them as a percentage of payroll. The average payroll tax assessment rate is about 3 per cent of payroll (i.e., $3.00 per $100 of payroll as given in table 6.4); hence, an unfunded liability of 3 per cent of payroll would be equivalent to a year of payroll tax.

Figures for the forest-products industry illustrate that existing firms in that industry are passing on an unfunded liability of $213 million (1.35 per cent of payroll), since their expected pay-outs exceed their tax assessments. New firms, in contrast, are contributing a surplus of $60.6 million (1.73 per cent of payroll), since their tax assessments exceed their expected pay-outs. Clearly, there is an intergenerational transfer from new firms to existing firms in that industry. The magnitude of that transfer is a little over 3 per cent of payroll (since the existing firms 'drain' 1.35 per cent of payroll, while the new firms 'contribute' 1.73 per cent of payroll). The contribution of new firms does not, however, fully compensate for the unfunded liability of existing firms, so that the forest-products industry as a whole adds an unfunded liability equivalent to 0.79 per cent of its payroll to the system as a whole.

The largest relative magnitude of the intergenerational transfer within an industry (as measured by the difference between the liability of existing firms and the surplus from new firms, both as a percentage of payroll) is in construction, followed by mining and forest products. The smallest intergenerational transfer within an industry is in government followed by other services.

With respect to the redistributive effects across industries, the cross-subsidies go to construction (1.39 per cent of payroll), forest products (0.79 per cent), and mining (0.64 per cent). The transfers come from all other industries.

Clearly there are substantial redistributive transfers associated with the funding of workers' compensation. Those transfers are both intergenerational (from new to existing firms) and across different industries. Thus, new firms are subsidizing the workers' compensation costs of existing firms. As well, construction, other primary and the forest-products industries are being cross-subsidized by all other industries.

Summary Comments

Workers' compensation systems can give rise to unfunded liabilities that have redistributive effects both intergenerationally over time, and across different firms and industries at a point in time. The many approaches to discharging these liabilities each have important efficiency and equity consequences. Logical extensions of our analysis reveal a number of reasons why unfunded liabilities cannot be treated as benign by policy makers.

Particular industry groups can generate unfunded liabilities, even if the workers' compensation system as a whole is fully funded. In Ontario, as we illustrated, relatively high-accident-risk industries (construction, other primary industries, and forest products) enjoy cross-subsidies of their workers' compensation costs by other industries. If, as is argued in some circles, employers will respond to high injury costs through reducing injury risks (see Kralj, this volume), then cross-subsidies that artificially lower the costs of workplace injuries to high-risk employers result in more injuries than would have occurred in the absence of the subsidies.

Through the mechanism of transferring costs from past and present to future generations of firms, emerging industries are forced to assume the burden of costs that are unrelated to the production of their goods and services. This mechanism places these firms at a disadvantage in comparison with otherwise similar firms that operate in unfunded liability-free jurisdictions.

Both the cross-subsidies and the intergenerational transfer of costs represent perverse industrial policy from the perspectives of both reducing injuries and their costs and enhancing growth opportunities for emerging industries and firms. In other words, they encourage the growth of more hazardous firms and industries, and discourage the growth of new firms.

One of the more interesting implications of our cost-transfer analysis is that government employers will be a net contributor towards eliminating Ontario's workers' compensation unfunded liability. This means that, indirectly, the burden of erasing the unfunded liability is being passed to taxpayers. On its face, this appears to be a subsidy by government to industry located in Ontario and could be the fodder for a dispute between Ontario and the United States under the North America Free Trade Agreement (as could the workers' compensation unfunded liabilities more generally).

NOTES

1 Vaillancourt (1995: 73) indicates that Ontario tends to account for about 70 per cent of the unfunded liabilities in Canada.
2 Coverage rates vary considerably, highlighting the potential importance of

extending coverage as a policy response. Currently about 70 per cent of the workforce in Ontario is covered by workers' compensation, while coverage is virtually universal in Quebec.

3 The Workers' Compensation Board of Ontario annual report for 1996 gives the following percentage distribution of benefit expenses in 1996: long-term (permanent disability) 56.6; rehabilitation expenses 16.5; health care 11.5; short-term disability 9.3; and survivor benefits 6.1. Some of the unfunded liability is also attributable to fatal injuries, since compensation can include some future liabilities such as pensions and vocational training for the surviving spouse.

4 Vaillancourt (1995: 73) indicates that the total unfunded liabilities across all Canadian boards increased consistently from 1980 to 1992 (the last year of his data) with Ontario accounting for the bulk of those liabilities.

5 In a review of the evidence of the ultimate incidence of payroll taxes, Dahlby (1993) concludes that approximately 80 per cent is shifted back to labour in the long run.

6 More detailed calculations of the burden on the taxpaying population associated with the aging of the population in Canada are given in Foot, 1989.

7 This issue is also discussed with respect to the Canada/Quebec Pension Plan in Gunderson, Hyatt, and Pesando, 1996.

8 Details of this procedure are outlined in Gunderson and Hyatt, 1998. The intergenerational accounting approach was originally developed in Auerbach, Gokhale, and Kotlikoff, 1991 and Kotlikoff, 1992. The procedure and its applications is reviewed in Auerbach, Gokhale, and Kotlikoff, 1994, and applied to the national debt in Canada in Oreopoulos and Kotlikoff, 1996.

9 A discount rate of 5 per cent was assumed, as is common in this literature. A period of 25 years is assumed for eliminating the unfunded liability. This broadly corresponds to the time period often used in workers' compensation policy discussion of the issue, and it corresponds to the period used for calculating the unfunded liability surtax in Ontario. The different industry benefit pay-out rates were based on WCB data. Payroll tax assessment rates are based on the rates for new claims costs plus the unfunded liability surcharge for each industry as given in table 6.5. Payrolls are assumed to grow in each industry at the same rate that they grew over the period 1980 to 1995 (based on CANSIM data for Ontario), except for the government sector, where payroll growth was set at zero to reflect current trends. The effect of the death of firms was approximated by assuming that the payroll of existing firms diminishes at a rate of 4.6 per cent per year. The effect of the birth of new firms was approximated by assuming that their payroll grew each year by an amount that would maintain the industry payroll growth rate in light of

the attrition of payroll of the older firms. If the overall industry payroll rate was growing, this would mean that the effect of the birth of new firms was greater than the effect of the death of some old firms. In essence, the overall industry payroll growth rate would capture the overall effect of the birth and death of firms, with the assumptions regarding the separate impact of births and deaths being used to do the calculations for existing and new firms. These assumptions are outlined in more detail in Gunderson and Hyatt 1998.

REFERENCES

Altonji, J., F. Hayashi, and L. Kotlikoff. 1992. 'Is the Extended Family Altruistically Linked?' *American Economic Review* 82: 1177–98.
Auerbach, A., J. Gokhale, and L. Kotlikoff. 1991. 'Generational Accounts: A Meaningful Alternative to Deficit Accounting.' In D. Bradford, ed., *Tax Policy and the Economy*, 55–110. Cambridge: National Bureau of Economic Research.
– 1994. 'Generational Accounting: A Meaningful Way to Evaluate Fiscal Policy.' *Journal of Economic Perspectives* 8: 73–93.
Dahlby, B. 1993. 'Taxation and Social Insurance.' In R. Bird and J. Mintz, eds, *Taxation to 2000 and Beyond*, 110–56. Toronto: Canadian Tax Foundation.
Foot, D. 1989. 'Public Expenditures, Population Aging and Economic Dependency in Canada, 1921–2021.' *Population Research and Policy Review* 8: 97–117.
Gunderson, M., and D. Hyatt. 1998. 'Inter-generational Considerations of Workers' Compensation Unfunded Liabilities.' In M. Corak, ed., *Government Finances and Generational Equity*, 21–38. Ottawa: Statistics Canada and Human Resources Development Canada.
Gunderson, M., D. Hyatt, and J. Pesando. 1996. 'Public Pension Plans in the United States and Canada.' W.E. Upjohn Institute Conference on Employee Benefit, Labor Costs, and Labour Markets in Canada and the United States.
Kotlikoff, L. 1992. *Generational Accounting: Knowing Who Pays, and When, For What We Spend*. New York: Free Press.
Ontario Workers' Compensation Board. 1995. *Assessment Rate Manual*. Toronto: Ontario Workers' Compensation Board.
– 1996. *Statistical Supplement to the 1996 Annual Report*. Toronto: Ontario Workers' Compensation Board.
Ontario Workplace Safety & Insurance Board. 1997. *Assessment Rate Manual*. Toronto: Ontario Workplace Safety & Insurance Board.
Oreopoulos, P., and L. Kotlikoff. 1996. 'Restoring Generational Balance in

Canada.' *Choices: Public Finance.* Montreal: Institute for Research on Public Policy.

Organization for Economic Co-operation and Development. 1996. *Aging in OECD Countries.* Paris: OECD.

Vaillancourt, F. 1995. 'The Financing and Pricing of WCBs in Canada: Existing Arrangements, Possible Changes.' In T. Thomason, V. Vaillancourt, T. Bogyo, and A. Stritch, eds, *Chronic Stress: Workers' Compensation in the 1990s,* 66–91. Toronto: C.D. Howe Institute.

7 Occupational Health and Safety: Effectiveness of Economic and Regulatory Mechanisms

BORIS KRALJ[1]

Government regulation is a fact of life in the modern labour market, and workplace health and safety is no exception. Workers' compensation and occupational health and safety laws and other legislation all seem to be aimed at enhancing the level of safety and at compensating victims in the workplace. Some economists have objected to the lack of faith these programs reveal in the ability of the market mechanism itself to provide safety. A number of well-known arguments have been put forward to justify government intervention in workers' compensation. These include moral hazard, adverse selection, the free-rider problem, and information asymmetries.[2] The goal of government intervention is to ameliorate these potential market failures by protecting workers against work-related risks and by inducing employers to invest more resources in safety.

The existence of informational asymmetries between workers and employers may provide the most convincing argument for government intervention with respect to safety regulations and workers' compensation legislation. If one of the parties is misinformed concerning the risks of injury, that party will incorrectly calculate the marginal benefits of investment in safety and will, as a result, devote either too few or too many resources to safety. Workers are likely not to be well informed about the safety levels prevailing at different firms. In fact, workers are assumed to be systematically misinformed in that they generally understate the actual hazards they face every day at work. In addition, since employers are better informed than their employees concerning the technology of workplace accidents and safety equipment, if the workers were to be liable for their own injuries, they would under-invest in safety. Since market outcomes will be inefficient in these cases, various policy options, including workers' compensation and enforcement of safety standards, can bring about improvements.

Government intervention in occupational health and safety has increased steadily over the past twenty-five years or so. In Canada, provincial governments play a dual role in the area of occupational health and safety policy. They attempt to promote workplace safety through variations in workers' compensation insurance pricing, both at the more aggregate or rate-group level as well as at the micro or individual-firm level through experience rating. In addition, they set numerous safety regulations or standards that are enforced by a system of inspections and fines. In the United States, safety regulation is the responsibility of the Occupational Safety and Health Administration (OSHA), created in 1970 to promote workplace safety. The purpose of this chapter is to provide the reader with a summary of the empirical evidence available to date on the effectiveness of these two approaches on occupational health and safety within the North American context. Within Canada, much of the policy innovation and empirical evaluation of health and safety initiatives has been conducted in Ontario and Quebec. As such, these two provinces provide the major focus of the chapter when describing the Canadian experience.

The chapter proceeds as follows. In the next section, I review the U.S. and Canadian experience with the regulatory approach to occupational health and safety. This includes a discussion of the Internal Responsibility System that is the foundation of Ontario's approach to health and safety. The third section outlines the economic-incentive approach to workplace safety. A description of the experience-rating mechanism is provided along with summaries of the literature on its effects on injury frequency, disability-claim duration, and other outcomes.

Regulatory Approach to Workplace Health and Safety

Generally, North American governments have set numerous safety standards with which firms must comply. In the United States, the vast majority of these standards are imposed on firms and stipulate either equipment specifications or performance, while some of the standards focus on worker conduct. Inspections, prosecutions, and fines are used to enforce the safety standards and penalize firms who fail to comply. While Canadian jurisdictions pursued a similar strategy in the 1970s, however, they also implemented a number of safety-enhancing measures not present in the United States. These measures include the right to refuse unsafe work, the formation of joint labour-management worksite safety committees, mandatory prevention programs, the right to protective reassignment, and the right to know about health risks in the workplace through such mechanisms as the Workplace Hazardous Materials Information System (WHMIS). In general, most analysts would agree that the Canadian approach expresses more confidence in the worker's ability to participate in solving occupational safety concerns.

Despite the passage of the Occupational Safety and Health Act in 1970, injury rates in the United States have not generally declined. In a review of the topic Smith (1992: 558) writes: 'After two decades of discussion, research, tightened regulation, and resource reallocation directed toward workplace safety and health, it is profoundly disturbing that injury rates appear to have been unaffected.'

As outlined in the next section, various U.S. studies have applied regression analysis to aggregate data at the industry level and found that OSHA regulation has had little or no impact on workplace safety. Excellent reviews are provided in Smith (1992), Curington (1988b), and Viscusi (1986). In Canada, studies by Lanoie (1992a, 1992b), and by Cousineau, Girard, and Lanoie (1995) on the Commission de la Santé et Sécurité du Travail (CSST) have arrived at similar conclusions with respect to Canadian occupational health and safety laws.

U.S. Experience with Regulatory Mechanisms

Mendeloff (1979), using data from California, and Curington (1986), using data from New York, examined pre- and post-OSHA manufacturing injury rates in an attempt to gauge the overall effect of OSHA standards. Both of these investigations focused their analysis on specific injury types that were believed to be preventable through safety regulation. Specifically, these include 'caught in or between' injuries, 'struck by' injuries, eye injuries, and injuries involving electrical contact. Curington found that the injury frequency rates of specific injury types in New York State were lower following the implementation of OSHA. Mendeloff also found a lower injury rate for specific injury types following OSHA, but estimated that fewer than 20 per cent of all injuries were avoidable or preventable by compliance with OSHA standards. These studies provided more positive evidence regarding

OSHA effectiveness than did other studies that employed aggregate industry-level data.

The most convincing empirical studies of the impact of OSHA have concentrated on the effects of inspections. Generally, these studies present only weak evidence of positive impacts of inspections on injury rates. However, many analysts would offer two reasons to expect limited impacts on injury rates from compliance with set standards. First, the standard-setting process tends to be complex and cumbersome, whereas workplaces tend to be diverse and much more dynamic; therefore, it is unlikely that standards can be kept current, especially in the face of changing work practices and advancing technology. Second, limited effects of compliance with standards can be expected given that some injuries are caused by 'random' events. Therefore, it is unclear whether standards applying to permanent, physical hazards in the workplace should have significant effects on injury rates.

Although inspections matter, historically OSHA has opted for engineering-based design standards, which are often prohibitively expensive, especially in relation to the number of lives saved. Potential losses to employers not in compliance with OSHA standards are the product of the probability that the plant will be inspected, the size of the fine, and the number of violations the inspector is likely to find. If the per-worker costs of compliance exceed this potential loss, employers driven exclusively by the cost-minimization motive will not comply, holding other factors constant.

Viscusi (1986) analysed injury rates while controlling for inspection probability and expected fines, industry, year, and non-OSHA variables that could have resulted in changes in the injury rate. He used pooled time-series and cross-section industry-level data for the 1973–83 period. He found no significant effects of OSHA inspections on injury rates. Further, he found no evidence that increasing expected penalties would result in lower injury rates.

Bartel and Thomas (1985) estimated a simultaneous equation model that included equations for inspections, inspection penalties, and the lost workday injury rate. They pooled industry-level data covering the period 1974–78. Their results revealed that a greater incidence of inspections resulted in increased OSHA compliance, but this increased compliance had only a small effect on reducing injury rates. Overall, Bartel and Thomas conclude that the linkage between compliance and injury rates is weak, but that statements claiming OSHA achieved no improvement in injury rates would probably be incorrect.[3]

Some studies have been able to employ plant-level longitudinal data to compare changes in the injury rates of firms inspected early in a given year with those of firms inspected late in the year. The early inspection should have had an effect on the injury rate for the year, while the late inspection should not significantly affect the year's injury rate. The 'early' group is used as the treatment group and the 'late' group is used as a comparison group. This early-late methodology was first applied by Smith (1979) and subsequently it has been replicated by Ruser and Smith (1991) and McCaffrey (1983). This approach has been used to analyse the effects of inspections in 1973, 1974, 1976, 1977, and 1980–85. Overall, these early-late studies provide little or no evidence of a significant and persistent OSHA inspection effect on injury rates.

Gray and Scholz (1993) analysed data from large U.S. manufacturing plants over the seven-year period spanning 1979–85. This longitudinal, plant-level data set allowed them to measure the total number of inspections and the number of these inspections that resulted in OSHA penalties being imposed. Unlike most other studies, the Gray and Scholz study compared individual employers, avoiding the problems that arise from aggregating data on injuries and penalties at the industry level. They also tested and corrected their estimates for potential biases that can arise with longitudinal data, including endogeneity of inspections.[4] Findings by Gray and Scholz provide evidence that inspections with penalties resulted in reductions in lost-workday injury rates. They estimate that a plant that is inspected and penalized in any given year will record a 22 per cent reduction in lost-workday injuries in the following three-year period.

Kniesner and Leeth (1995) develop a computable general equilibrium model of the labour market in order to numerically simulate the interactions between employers and workers as affected by government regulation intended to improve occupational health and safety. This unique application of this methodology concludes that OSHA had only a small effect on improving workplace safety, with large effects only at extreme levels of enforcement.

Using longitudinal data on 250 establishments from the custom woodworking industry for the period 1972–91, Weil (1996) analysed the determinants of establishment-level compliance with specific OSHA standards. Logit modelling of plant compliance revealed that the probability of compliance increases appreciably with OSHA inspections. This finding of a strong link between OSHA enforcement and compliance bolsters earlier findings of Bartel and Thomas (1985) and Gray and Scholz (1993).

Canadian Experience with the Regulatory Mechanism

Lanoie (1992a) utilized both pooled time-series and cross-sectional industry-level data from Quebec for the period 1982–87 to evaluate the effectiveness of policies adopted by the CSST (the Quebec board responsible for regulating health and safety) on improving workplace health and safety. In a major improvement upon previous studies of the impact of safety regulations, Lanoie considers all of the most important aspects of government intervention in workplace safety (i.e., inspections, fines, safety committees, right of refusal, and workers' compensation experience rating) rather than just focusing on one aspect. His results show that, at best, policies adopted by the CSST led to a minor reduction in injury frequency. Specifically, the rate of inspections was the only safety-enforcing measure to be statistically significantly associated with a reduction in lost-time injury frequency. Lanoie (1992a: 657) states: 'Although disturbing, this result is in line with American econometric studies (based on aggregate data) that found little or no impact of OSHA regulation on workplace safety. Furthermore, it suggests that the innovative prevention policies adopted by the CSST (right of refusal, compulsory prevention programs) were no more effective in influencing the risk of accident than more traditional measures.'

Cousineau, Girard, and Lanoie (1995) employ direct measures of the intensity of regulation adopted by the CCST to estimate specific injury-rate equations. Four different specific injury rates were used as the dependent variable: 'caught in or between' injuries; 'struck by or striking against' injuries; 'falls or slips' injuries; and the overall rate of all injuries. Their econometric study used annual pooled time-series and cross-sectional data collected for twenty-three industries for the period 1982 to 1984 inclusive. Unlike earlier U.S. studies of the impact of occupational safety regulation (i.e., Mendeloff, 1979, and Curington, 1986, on specific injury rates), Cousineau, Girard, and Lanoie utilized direct measures of the intensity of regulation, such as inspection rates, fines, and prosecutions. In addition, they examined the determinants of *changes* in injury rates to avoid making spurious inferences resulting from simultaneity biases. Such biases may be generated because more injuries in a given industry could lead to heightened intervention by the regulating government agency. Other than for the Gray and Scholz (1993) study, this issue had been neglected in previous research.

Overall the empirical results presented by Cousineau, Girard, and Lanoie are consistent with the U.S. literature showing that regulation has a greater impact on the rates of particular types of injuries than on the overall injury rate. They concluded that the rate of *fines* imposed after an infraction significantly reduced total injury rates, with this effect being even greater for specific injuries. While *prosecutions* significantly reduced 'caught in or between' injury rates, *inspections* had the opposite effect. This unexpected latter result is most likely due to simultaneity bias in their regressions; that is, higher injuries may have led to more inspections. They conclude: 'Overall, the findings confirm those of the American literature showing that the impact of safety regulation is larger on specific injury types than on the global injury rate. These specific injuries represent only half of all injuries, and policy makers may have to rely on other policy instruments, such as financial incentives for employees, to substantially improve safety in the workplace' (p. 51).

The Internal Responsibility System

The workplace internal responsibility system (IRS) is the foundation of Ontario's approach to health and safety. With the internal responsibility system, workers obtain some legal rights to participate in local health and safety decision making. While these rights vary across jurisdictions, they almost always include rights to know, to be consulted, and to refuse unsafe work. In Ontario, the IRS and the associated joint health and safety committees (JHSCs) were introduced in 1978. Workers received a statutory right to refuse unsafe work, a right to accompany and be consulted by the inspector, and protection against retaliation, while the government was empowered to order the establishment of JHSCs and/or appoint worker safety representatives in certain workplaces. In 1978, Ontario enacted the Occupational Health and Safety Act (Bill 70), which overhauled the province's health and safety system, including the participatory rights of workers. The act made JHSCs mandatory in most workplaces with more than twenty employees.

The IRS model contemplates more active enforcement of local health and safety policies. JHSCs with equal representation from workers and employers are the central mechanism through which workers can participate in the IRS. This means that employers and employees, who are

closest to and most familiar with workplace conditions and requirements, are responsible for controlling hazards in their workplaces and
proactively promoting workplace health and safety. Inspection-related
field visits are initiated by Ministry of Labour (MoL) inspectors to
monitor compliance with the legislation and promote the IRS at workplaces. Investigative field visits are made by the MoL in response to a
reported event such as a fatal accident, critical injury, occupational illness or disease, reprisal, complaint, work refusal, or dispute. Consultations and promotional meetings take place between the MoL staff and
workplace parties from one or several workplaces to promote the IRS
and explain the requirements of legislation, policies, and procedures.
The Ministry of Labour's goal in the area of occupational health and
safety is to foster a healthy and safe working environment through
compliance with the Occupational Health and Safety Act and to
encourage employers and workers to cooperatively identify and control health and safety hazards.

Table 7.1 provides a summary of Ontario Ministry of Labour health
and safety field visit and enforcement activity. There has been a dramatic decline (i.e., 57 per cent) in inspection-related field visits
between 1988/89 and 1995/96. An even larger decline occurred in
orders issued. The number of stop-work orders issued has fallen from
over 5000 in 1988/89 to about 2000 in 1995/96. The cause of these
declines is unknown, perhaps reflecting changes in enforcement policy,
ministry staff reductions, more intensive and hence time-consuming
inspections, or safer workplaces.

Ontario's commitment to the IRS model was further reflected in the
introduction of the Workplace Hazardous Materials Information System (WHMIS) in 1987 and the passage of Bill 208 in 1990. WHMIS was
designed to ensure that information about hazardous materials in the
workplace flowed from the manufacturer or supplier to the end-user
and the worker. It also required that workers be trained in the use of
hazardous materials to which they were exposed. Bill 208 brought
mandated JHSCs to most of the sectors not covered in the 1978 act. It
also imposed certain procedural requirements such as compelling
written response from employers to recommendations made by the
JHSC. In order to strengthen the technical capability of the JHSC, the
bill required that at least one worker member and one employer member be specially trained and certified. Furthermore, the Workplace
Health and Safety Agency was set up to oversee the training of and
establish certification criteria for JHSC representatives.

TABLE 7.1
Ontario Ministry of Labour field-visit and enforcement activity (1988/89–1995/96)

Year	Inspection-related field visits	Investigative field visits	Consultative visits	TOTAL VISITS	Stop-work orders issued	All other orders issued	TOTAL ORDERS
1995/96	28,575	12,308	4,568	45,451	2,046	33,984	36,030
1994/95	30,926	12,415	6,015	48,728	2,304	37,394	39,698
1993/94	34,076	11,699	7,840	52,537	2,473	40,776	43,249
1992/93	39,837	11,136	7,002	57,975	2,959	48,562	51,521
1991/92	38,701	9,199	4,830	52,730	2,167	46,187	48,354
1990/91	51,106	8,712	2,276	62,094	3,095	52,130	55,225
1989/90	65,381	8,969	1,782	76,132	3,737	69,825	73,562
1988/89	66,404	8,214	1,598	76,212	5,064	70,683	75,747

Source: Ontario Ministry of Labour

A review of the relevant literature reveals some evidence of positive effects of the IRS on workplace-injury prevention. Tuohy and Simard (1992) examined survey data from approximately a thousand workplaces in Ontario and Quebec along with administrative data to study the effect of workplace JHSCs on injury rates, enforcement rates, and problem solving at the workplace. Both the Ontario and Quebec portions of the study produced generally similar findings regarding the effectiveness of joint health and safety committees. They conclude that JHSCs with bipartite structures, broad scopes of activities, and institutionalized procedures reduce workplace injuries. In a similar study, Shannon et al. (1992) studied a broad set of structural characteristics of JHSCs. They concluded that JHSCs that were forced to resort to external problem-solving mechanisms were least likely to record relatively low injury frequency rates. Finally, a study conducted by the Workplace Health and Safety Agency (1994) compared accident frequency rates in Ontario before and after 1979 (i.e., implementation of Bill 70) in order to assess the effect of JHSCs. The study reported that, while there was no noticeable change in trend for lost-time accident claims, the reduction in total claim frequency (i.e., lost-time plus no-lost-time claims) was more rapid following the implementation of Bill 70.

Dewees and Genesove (1988) studied the impact of a specific safety regulation, namely the enforcement activities of the Ontario Ministry of Labour with respect to exposure to asbestos and vinyl chloride. They concluded that safety-enforcing measures did not reduce exposure to these substances. Other non-quantitative studies (i.e., based on interviews or case studies) by Walters and Haines (1988) and Bryce and Manga discussed the effectiveness of the 'right of work refusal' policy and health and safety committee policy without demonstrating any quantitative effects of these policies on workplace safety. Walters and Haines show that the right of refusal is not used very often in Ontario largely owing to the worker's lack of knowledge of these rights.

In a recent study, Lewchuk, Robb, and Walters (1996) provide an empirical investigation of the impact of the IRS, and the associated JHSCs, on firm-specific safety performance in Ontario. They compared the safety performance, as measured by injury frequency rates, of over two hundred firms before and after the introduction of the Occupational Health and Safety Act, and before and after the creation of a JHSC at the workplace. Their study merged data collected by surveys of employers in the manufacturing and retail sector and WCB administrative records for the period 1976–89. The results of their regression analysis revealed that the introduction of Bill 70 and JHSCs has had a beneficial impact on lost-time injury frequency rates for key industrial sectors in Ontario. Specifically, the introduction of JHSCs has reduced lost-time injury frequency by up to 18 per cent.

Economic Incentive Approach to Workplace Health and Safety

North American studies have so far found that occupational safety regulations have had only a minimal effect on workplace safety performance. Therefore, it is worthwhile to consider alternatives to the regulatory approach to enhance workplace safety performance. One such alternative consists of financial or monetary incentives provided through the workers' compensation insurance-premium pricing mechanism. In addition to the compensatory role, the workers' compensation system is charged with the responsibility of endeavouring to reduce the social costs of employment-related injuries through incentives for accident prevention. The common response has been experience rating of insurance premiums. U.S. research suggests that workers' compensation experience rating provides market-based incentives for safety, the effects of which dwarf those of the regulatory alternative of direct controls, fines, and inspections carried out under occupational health and safety legislation.

It is instructive to compare workers' compensation experience rating incentives with the principal regulatory alternative, occupational health and safety regulations. Most economists argue that the injury-tax approach, experience rating, is preferred to direct standards or controls. Experience rating alters the incentives for health and safety in the desired direction, leaving the particulars of how best to achieve the optimal level of safety to employers and workers. Standards, by contrast, cannot do better economically and, as experience with OSHA in the United States indicates, they will often do worse.

The most compelling reason for using workers' compensation experience rating to regulate workplace safety is that the firm is free to choose the most cost-effective means of removing the risk. This is in sharp contrast to the command-and-control approach of OSHA.

Experience-Rating Mechanism

Over the last decade or so, it has been recognized by most provinces that the collective or 'no-fault' pooled-risk approach to workers' compensation insurance pricing resulted in financial disincentives in the area of occupational health and safety. The pooled-risk mechanism provides no, or very little, incentive for individual firms to allocate resources to activities that reduce workplace hazards or to monitor injured workers' progress, since the insurance premium is based on the claim cost experience of the *industry* group average rather than on the individual firm's own experience. Experience rating shifts the responsibility for at least some workers' compensation costs from the industry group to the particular employer incurring the accident costs. Firms with high accident rates will incur higher premium costs, creating a monetary incentive for them to reduce accidents (as well as incentive contest claims, as discussed subsequently).

By increasing the premium costs of employers with higher accident rates, experience rating can have a variety of incentive effects, some desirable, others not so desirable. It can encourage employers to take safety precautions and reduce accidents. It also encourages them to contest claims, and while some of this appeals activity may be legitimate in deterring frivolous or even fraudulent claims, some may thwart legitimate claims, leading to the problem of the 'walking wounded.' Experience rating may also encourage employers to hire only low-risk employees. It can also be a costly process, with the costs going to the legal system, rather than being a transfer of costs whereby, when one party loses, another gains. Clearly difficult trade-offs are involved; hence, the importance of knowing the empirical magnitude of the different effects.

Workers' compensation premium experience rating is available in some form to at least some industry groups in most Canadian jurisdictions. The majority of these programs have been set up or have undergone major revisions in the last decade. Unlike in the United States, the broad application of workers' compensation experience rating is a relatively new feature of the Canadian system.[5] In Ontario, almost 80 per cent of employers are experience-rated. In 1996, Ontario had two experience-rating programs in operation for different industry groups: New Experimental Experience Rating (NEER) program; and Council's Amended Draft-7 (CAD-7) program, which applies exclusively to employers in the construction industry.[6] Up until 1995, in Ontario, experience rating was elective by industry rather than mandatory as in most other jurisdictions. However, in 1995, it became compulsory for most employers.

There are a number of major differences between CAD-7 and NEER.

These variations in program features may cause participating employers to react differently to the financial incentives that these programs create. The main difference in program features is the frequency component in CAD-7, which produces one-half the refund or surcharge a firm receives. The CAD-7 formula compares the number of lost-time injuries reported during two prior years to an expected number of lost-time injuries based on industry averages. The NEER program does not directly use injury frequency to determine refunds and surcharges.

CAD-7's use of frequency provides an additional incentive to firms to reduce their new injuries in various ways: under-reporting of claims; inappropriate next-day return-to-work programs (thereby 'converting' a lost-time claim into a no-lost-time claim that is not included in the experience-rating formula); and the reporting of new injuries as recurrences. A concern with using frequency is that it makes no distinction between minor and very serious injuries. A three-day lost-time injury receives the same weight as a thirty-day lost-time injury in terms of frequency.

The other major difference between the CAD-7 and NEER programs is that NEER uses the lifetime costs of a claim, with future costs estimated by applying special reserve factors to actual costs incurred to date, while CAD-7 uses only actual costs in its calculations.

The data provided in table 7.2 indicates that NEER is a much more aggressive program financially than the CAD-7 program. Overall, since the inception of the NEER program, the average surcharge faced by employers has exceeded the average refund by almost 300 per cent.[7] By contrast, the financial impact on construction-industry employers of CAD-7 has been considerably milder, with average surcharges exceeding refunds by 60 per cent. In addition, the absolute value of the average surcharge and refund is significantly higher for NEER than for CAD-7. In 1996, over 132,000 or 75 per cent of Ontario employers were directly impacted by experience rating, that is, they either received a workers' compensation assessment refund or a surcharge.

We can also see from figure 7.1 that the NEER program off-balance, the difference between total surcharges and refunds, has skyrocketed since 1991, reaching almost $260 million in 1996.[8] This has generated much concern and discussion of reform for the program by interested stakeholders. The CAD-7 off-balance, which totalled $13.5 million in 1996, has been decreasing during the same period. Table 7.2 indicates that approximately 88 per cent of firms impacted by NEER receive a premium refund, and, similarly, that about 75 per cent of CAD-7 firms

TABLE 7.2
NEER and CAD-7 experience-rating program summary statistics, 1983–1996

	NEER program					CAD-7 program				
Year	No. of firms	Average surcharge ($)	Average refund ($)	% rec'd refund	Off balance* ($ 000)	No. of firms	Average surcharge ($)	Average refund ($)	% Rec'd refund	Off balance* ($ 000)
1983	n.a.	n.a.	n.a.	n.a.	n.a.	25,762	1,022	420	80.8	−3,680
1984	n.a.	n.a.	n.a.	n.a.	n.a.	27,068	1,122	476	80.9	−4,637
1985	1,389	8,395	3,191	73.0	−88	26,308	1,510	661	70.3	−435
1986	2,812	11,179	3,247	78.6	−457	25,981	1,677	1,039	66.9	−3,500
1987	11,979	11,739	2,876	87.4	−12,323	33,884	1,856	1,013	75.7	−10,728
1988	22,463	10,630	2,652	87.6	−22,599	37,474	1,726	1,347	77.0	−23,949
1989	17,069	6,714	647	91.9	−801	50,783	1,474	1,327	77.4	−35,303
1990	32,091	9,626	2,896	84.8	−32,106	38,064	2,180	2,008	79.2	−43,302
1991	38,350	13,351	2,499	84.6	−2,407	27,203	2,776	3,127	75.7	−43,300
1992	72,925	9,785	1,636	90.7	−42,066	29,256	2,642	2,365	75.3	−29,598
1993	72,122	8,330	3,741	87.0	−156,637	30,019	2,646	1,684	74.0	−14,172
1994	91,857	5,072	4,075	85.1	−248,861	28,843	2,395	1,375	74.7	−10,443
1995	101,026	8,160	3,279	87.9	−191,138	28,120	2,219	1,513	75.1	−13,458
1996	104,213	7,557	3,827	88.1	−257,436	n.a.	n.a.n.a.	n.a.	n.a.	

Source: Ontario Workers' Compensation Board
*Off balance = total surcharges less total rebates, with a negative figure indicating that rebates exceed surcharges.

FIGURE 7.1 NEER program off-balance,* 1985–1996

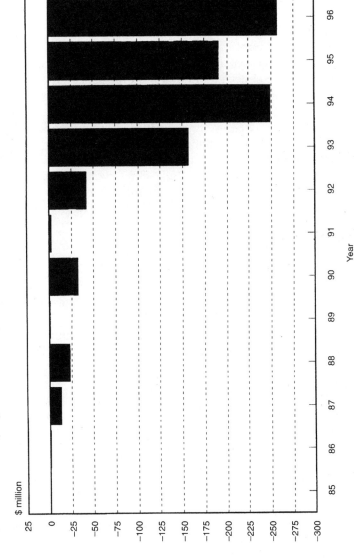

*Off-balance = surcharges less rebates (negative sign indicates that rebates exceed surcharges)
Source: Ontario Workers' Compensation Board, Annual Report, 1996

receive a refund. This may in large part contribute to the high level of support for these experience-rating programs that is found in the employer community.

Theoretical Perspective

A conceptual behavioural model of firm behaviour when faced with workers' compensation experience rating is presented in Kralj (1995b).[9] The neoclassical economics model of the profit-maximizing employer predicts that employers will respond to the economic incentives provided by experience rating by allocating resources to activities that lower their workers' compensation accident costs up to the point where their marginal benefits equal their marginal costs. The employer can either allocate resources to safety practices (i.e., prevention) or pay the costs associated with work injury. Profit-maximizing firms, operating in competitive markets, strive to minimize the sum of the cost of workplace accidents and the costs of preventing injuries. The former consist of workers' compensation premium payments, including experience-rating surcharges/rebates, in addition to material costs, fixed employment costs, lost production time, and damage to equipment.

The firm can also reduce its costs of occupational injuries by engaging in activities that minimize the costs of accidents after they occur. Activities that were *intended* to be generated by experience-rating programs are actions that minimize the severity of the injuries likely to be caused by an accident as well as activities aimed at minimizing the injured workers' duration of absence from employment. These may include the provision of protective equipment such as machine guards and safety goggles as well as medical rehabilitation, retraining, and job-modification activities. *Unintended* employer activities that can reduce accident costs include excessive claims management, subcontracting of most dangerous activities, excessive or frivolous protests, and appeals of injured workers' claims.

In many circumstances a firm would invest in all of these types of activities; however, the optimal mix of resources allocated to each will be determined by the costs of each option relative to the benefits – reduction in expected total cost of accidents – that it achieves.

The economic stimulus offered by experience rating is hypothesized to spur employers to adopt practices or strategies to improve their accident performance by focusing their attention on their accident record relative to the industry average. Over time these practices are expected to affect final safety performance measures such as injury rates and duration of benefits. If the financial incentive provided by experience rating is sufficient in magnitude, an intermediate result would be a change in employers' safety-related practices. Modification of firm behaviour is a precursor to observing any impacts of experience rating on final outcome measures. While it is important to determine whether or not experience rating affects final outcome measures, it is equally important to ascertain how the result is achieved.

Impact of Experience Rating on Injury Frequency Rates and Disability Spell Duration

Much of the past empirical workers' compensation literature, focusing primarily on the U.S. system, uses aggregate data. However, a handful of more recent investigations present micro-level analysis of individual firms and worker-based data sets. These studies, which are consistent with the more recent theoretical models incorporating both firm and worker optimization decisions, have the advantage of being based explicitly on individual behaviour by controlling for detailed worker characteristics as well as employer characteristics in their empirical specifications (for example, Kralj, 1995b). Despite the pervasiveness of workers' compensation experience rating across the United States and Canada, the economic impacts of these programs on employer behaviour have until recently received little attention from empirical researchers. There are a limited number of published studies that examine the impact of experience rating, and only a handful of these examine the Canadian experience.

An empirical linkage between experience rating and workplace safety has proved to be elusive. As indicated in table 7.3, a number of studies have suggested that there is minimal or no evidence that experience rating has any effect on workplace safety. Generally, though, the empirical evidence is supportive of a positive effect on reducing injury frequency rates.

Typically, in order to gauge the impact of experience rating, U.S. studies have exploited the institutional characteristic that larger firms tend to be more highly experience-rated. They test the hypothesis that the positive relationship between workers' compensation benefits and injury rates is smaller for larger firms. These studies include separate controls for benefit levels, firm size, and an interaction between firm size and benefit levels. As shown by Ruser (1985), it is this latter term

TABLE 7.3
Summary of studies on the impacts of experience rating on injury frequency rates

Study	Data/jurisdiction	Methodology/analysis	Impact of experience rating
Chelius & Smith (1983)	1979 data on injury rates for 15 two-digit U.S. industries in 37 states.	Ordinary Least Squares estimation of injury rate equations.	Decreased injury rates in 2 of 15 industries.
Ruser (1985)	Pooled cross-sectional and time-series data on 25 U.S. manufacturing industries in 41 states, 1972–9.	Ordinary Least Squares and Generalized Lease Squares estimates of injury rate equations.	Decrease injury frequency rates.
Worral & Butler (1988)	Pooled cross-sectional data on 15 South Carolina industries, 1940–71.	Two-stage Least Squares to examine permanent partial, temporary total, and an index of all indemnity claim rates.	Decreased permanent disability claims and all claims, but not temporary total claims.
Chelius and Kavanaugh (1988)	Time-series quarterly data injury frequency rates, 1979–84, for two New Jersey community colleges. Small sample of 54 observations.	Ordinary Least Squares estimates of injury-rate equation to measure impact of switch in insurance arrangements to self-insurance.	Decreased injury frequency rates.
Kniesner & Leeth (1989)	Early 1970s U.S. manufacturing-sector data.	Numerical simulation model to investigate linkages between WC system and labour-market outcomes.	Decreased injury frequency rates.
Ruser (1991)	Longitudinal micro data for about 2800 U.S. manufacturing establishments, 1979–84.	Ordinary Least Squares, Weighted Least Squares, and count data models.	Decreased injury frequency rates.

TABLE 7.3 – concluded
Summary of studies on the impacts of experience rating on injury frequency rates

Study	Data/jurisdiction	Methodology/analysis	Impact of experience rating
Moore & Viscusi (1990)	About 1200 observations of data collected by National Traumatic Occupational Fatality Project, 1980–5, Panel Study of Income Dynamics, and the Quality of Employment Survey.	Ordinary Least Squares estimation of fatality-rate equations. Fatalities used to avoid any moral-hazard effects of WC benefits on reported injury rates.	Decreased hazard levels and decreased risk of fatalities.
Chelius & Smith (1992)	Industry-level data, disaggregated for seven firm-size categories, for Washington state, 1979–81.	Ordinary Least Squares estimation of regression equations.	No effect on injury frequency rates.
Ruser (1993)	Longitudinal data of 2798 U.S. manufacturing establishments.	Count data models of injuries. Extension of Ruser (1991) to consider distribution of injuries by severity.	Decreased non-lost-workday and days-away-from-work injuries, but no effect on restricted workday injuries or fatalities.
Bruce & Atkins (1993)	Annual fatality-rate data for the forestry and construction industries in Ontario, 1951–89.	'Before and after' test to gauge impact of ER introduction using co-integration analysis.	Decreased fatality rates.
Lanoie (1992a)	Two-digit industry-level data from Quebec, 1983–7.	Ordinary Least Squares estimation, adjusted for heteroscedasticity, of frequency equation.	No statistically significant effect on injury frequency rates.
Kotz & Schafer (1993)	Annual data from the German sugar industry, 1955–80.	Ordinary Least Squares estimation of accident frequency rate equations.	Decreased injury frequency rate.
Kniesner & Leeth (1995)	Parameters of underlying structural model intended to reproduce U.S. labour market at the end of the 1960s.	Numerical simulation of labour market to investigate WC and OSHA policy changes.	Decreased injury frequency rate.

that is intended to pick up the effects (indirectly) of experience rating. If experience rating does lead to the hypothesized reduction in injury rates, the interaction term coefficient should have a negative sign.

One major limitation of using data from the United States to test the hypothesized relationship between experience rating and workplace safety is that no direct measure of the degree of experience rating employed by private insurers is available. As a result, most United States studies utilize the firm size and benefits proxy described above. It would be more useful to obtain data that would allow for a direct comparison of experience-rated with non-experience-rated firms. The Canadian experience allows for such pre- and post-experience rating comparison given that the vast majority of Canadian jurisdictions have only introduced experience rating within the last decade and that not all firms are necessarily experience-rated. As a result, Canadian data may provide a better, more direct, test of the economic model's hypotheses than have the U.S. data.

There are even fewer studies that examine the impact of experience rating on the duration of injured workers receiving workers' compensation benefits than there are on the impact on injury incidence rates, and the results are more ambiguous. In fact, there are only five such studies and only two of them use Canadian data. The U.S. literature finds evidence of reductions in duration, while the Canadian studies conclude the opposite unexpected result, that is, that experience rating increases claim duration. A summary of the literature on the impact of experience rating on disability-claim duration is provided in table 7.4.

Other Impacts of Experience Rating

Traditionally, organized labour has been opposed to the concept of experience rating. They claim that experience rating does not improve workplace health and safety but only generates other effects, such as employer challenges to workers' entitlement to benefits and an inappropriate emphasis on claims-control activities.

Ison (1986) argues that there is no conclusive empirical evidence to support the claim that experience rating promotes workplace health and safety by providing increased incentives. According to Ison, economic incentives for accident prevention are already in place – cost to employers of accidents (i.e., lost production, damage to equipment, etc.) is probably in excess of workers' compensation assessments – and that any further investment in safety is likely uneconomical. Claims

TABLE 7.4
Summary of studies on the impacts of experience rating on duration of disability benefits

Study	Data/jurisdiction	Methodology/analysis	Impact of experience rating
Chelius & Kavanaugh (1988)	Time-series quarterly data injury-frequency rates, 1979–84, for two New Jersey community colleges (54 observations).	Ordinary Least Squares estimates of claim duration equation to measure impact of switch in insurance arrangements to self-insurance.	Decreased duration of disability benefits.
Krueger (1990a)	Approximately 27,000 temporary total disability claims from administrative records in Minnesota.	Ordinary Least Squares estimation of claim duration equations.	Decreased duration of disability benefits.
Lanoie (1992a)	Two-digit industry level data from Quebec, 1983–7.	Generalized Least Squares estimation of injury severity or duration equations.	Increased duration of disability benefits.
Cheadle et al. (1994)	Sample of all workers' compensation claims from Washington State, 1987–9.	Survival analysis using the Cox proportional hazards specification of disability spell duration.	Decreased duration of disability benefits.
Kralj (1995)	Approximately 4400 temporary total disability claims in the Ontario construction industry, 1983 and 1988.	Ordinary Least Squares estimation of claim duration equations.	Increased duration of disability benefits.

management, however, offers considerable paybacks to experience-rated firms. Ison hypothesizes that experience-rating formulas based on a firm's actual claims experience gives firms more incentive to suppress or dispute claims than to avoid or prevent injuries. In addition, he claims that experience rating provides incentives for employers to institute elaborate claims monitoring and control systems that attempt to reduce the recorded claims cost experience and hence lower assessments. Claims management, he argues, often results in diminished safety activity efforts, and in reintroducing into the workers' compensation system the delays, costs, and therapeutic damage of an adversary system.

Kralj (1994) analyses the impact of the introduction of workers' compensation insurance experience rating on employer behaviour in Ontario. Unlike previous research, which focused on impacts on final outcome measures, Kralj attempted to identify noticeable incremental effects on intermediate safety behaviours by employers. His analysis is based on information collected by random sample surveys and from detailed personal-interview case studies of employers. Empirical results reveal that the economic incentives provided to employers by experience rating in the form of premium refunds and surcharges exert a powerful positive influence on the likelihood of changes in employer safety behaviour. Experience rating increased firm awareness and focus on controlling workers' compensation claim costs so as to reduce experience-rating costs. Claims costs (and hence experience rating costs) can be reduced by claims-management procedures (e.g., claims monitoring and appeals) and accident-prevention activities. In essence, experience rating does lead to reductions in claims costs through both greater stringency in claims management and accident-prevention, although the former effect is greater than the latter.

Hyatt and Kralj (1995) provide the first empirical investigation of the relationship between experience rating and employer appeals of workers' compensation decisions. Applying multivariate regression techniques to a large workers' compensation claims database from Ontario, they find that while the total volume of employer-initiated appeals in not large, experience-rated firms are significantly more likely to appeal a claim than are non-experience-rated firms. This is so because firms have a monetary incentive to appeal claims under experience rating. This effect of experience rating is greater for larger firms than for smaller firms, with large firms having a greater incentive to appeal because the consequences are amortized over a larger number of workers.

In a subsequent study, Hyatt and Kralj (1996) investigate the relationship between experience-rating of accident employers and the probability that an injured worker's compensation appeal will be successful. Their data consists of 3837 cases between 1980 and 1989, drawn from files maintained by the Ontario Workers' Compensation Board. Multinomial logit regression results revealed that experience rating had no significant relationship to a worker's appeal being granted.

Baldwin and Johnson (1990) employ numerical simulation to examine the impact of the introduction of Ontario's New Experimental Experience Rating (NEER) program. NEER uses claim cost rather than claim frequency as the basis for experience rating. Baldwin and Johnson's results indicate that firms can reduce the costs of accidents by reducing their severity even if they do not reduce the frequency of accidents.

Kahley and Sornberger (1994) report on the results of a telephone survey conducted by the National Council on Compensation Insurance to determine whether experience rating provides effective safety incentives to employers. Management officials at 150 mid-sized Illinois employers were interviewed and asked about their workers' compensation cost-control measures. Given the relatively small sample size, non-random sample, and low response rate the survey results must be regarded with caution. Nevertheless, Kahley and Sornberger found evidence that experience-rated employers feel that safety in the workplace is a highly important and effective means of lowering workers' compensation costs and that experience rating does affect employer safety behaviour.

The type of survey analysis conducted by Kralj (1994, 1995b) and Kahley and Sornberger (1994), with their emphasis on directly measuring a spectrum of employer behaviours and opinions, has opened an avenue of research that will be much more useful to policy makers in addressing the incremental effects of experience rating than many of the studies that have been conducted to date focusing only on final outcome measures, namely, injury frequency rates and claim duration.

Recent Developments and Potential Reforms in Ontario

Effective January 1997, the Ontario WCB implemented a three-year pilot of a new community-based group rating program aimed at small and medium-sized Schedule 1 firms. This program, known as the Safe

Communities Incentive Program (SCIP) is a voluntary program open to groups of employers, organized on a community basis, who are currently registered with the WCB and who have an annual assessment of less than or equal to $90,000. Employers who are already covered by either the NEER or CAD-7 experience-rating programs will also be permitted to participate in SCIP. Once participating employers in a community are identified, a workplace-injury claims cost target for the community, based on the previous accident claims record of the enrolled firms, is established. Actual accident costs for the group are then compared to the group target. If actual costs are less than target costs, the group receives an assessment refund equal to 75 per cent of the cost savings (i.e., the difference between target and actual accident claims costs). The refund amount is distributed to the individual firms in the group in proportion to each firm's share of the total WCB assessment for the group. This refund is distinct from, and additional to, any NEER or CAD-7 program refunds or surcharges. The SCIP program does not generate a surcharge or penalty; if accident claims costs exceed the target costs, then no refund is issued.

In its July 1996 report entitled *New Directions for Workers' Compensation Reform*, the Ontario government outlined its proposed initiatives with respect to reforming the workers' compensation system including experience rating. Specifically, it recommended that the WCB review a number of funding and assessment issues, such as measures to improve experience rating, including steps to eliminate any technical or methodological problems that are giving rise to an off-balance.

The growing NEER program off-balance, the extent to which total rebates exceed surcharges, has served as the catalyst for minor technical changes to the program in recent years as well as for extensive discussion with stakeholders. However, in addition to resolving the off-balance issue, the proposed review provides an opportunity to examine other more fundamental features of experience rating. These should include the development or examination of prospective experience rating for large employers and separate programs or mechanisms aimed at encouraging workplace health and safety for smaller employers. Experience-rating program changes aimed at simplifying the relatively complicated programs such as NEER should be undertaken for both program administration and program effectiveness reasons (i.e., generating modification in appropriate employer behaviours).

Specifically, it is the author's view that the following changes would enhance the effectiveness of the experience-rating mechanism in

Ontario in providing incentives for improved workplace health and safety:

1   The NEER program should replace all other merit rating programs. The program should be made more aggressive through experience-rating the entire assessment premium, as was the case when it was originally introduced. Furthermore, NEER should be based on prospective rating rather than retrospective rating as is the case currently. Prospective rating consists of a review of each employer's performance over a previous period of time and establishes an actuarially appropriate premium, based on performance, for the upcoming year. Firms with good past performance are assumed to be more likely to have a continuation of this experience, and pay a lower initial assessment premium than those in the opposite situation (i.e., poor past performance) and than would be the case with retrospective rate setting. With retrospective rate setting, all employers in a particular rate group pay the same initial assessment premium, irrespective of their previous individual accident performance.

2   The NEER program should only apply to larger firms, specifically those employing in excess of 100 workers. As depicted in figure 7.2, the vast majority (i.e., 80 per cent) of Ontario Schedule 1 firms are very small, employing fewer than ten employees and accounting for a relatively small share of total employment. However, the approximately 4500 firms, or 2.3 per cent of all Schedule 1 firms, that employ in excess of 100 workers account for the majority of total employment (i.e., over 60 per cent). Large employers are much more likely to have the resources, in terms of safety personnel and knowledge, to undertake appropriate activities in response to the incentives provided by experience rating. In addition, given that larger employers tend to be relatively more concerned with their public image and more likely to have workforces that are unionized, the likelihood of inappropriate claims-management activities would be minimized.

3   While the opportunity to experience-rate smaller firms on the basis of their own accident record is limited, a new pilot program aimed at smaller employers should be designed. Since relatively sophisticated and complex programs such as NEER have not proved to be a very effective means to experience-rate smaller firms, a simpler, more straightforward approach is warranted.

FIGURE 7.2 Schedule 1 employers and covered employment, 1995 (by firm size category, per cent of total)

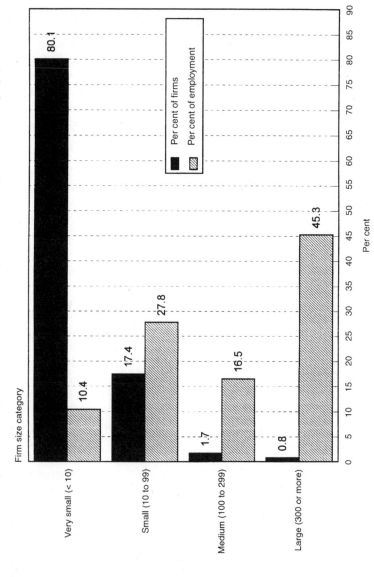

Source: Ontario Workers' Compensation Board

One possible approach would be to provide assessment premium rebates for small firms that exhibit accident-free experience over a period of two or three years. The use of claim deductibles offers another way to apply experience-rating principles to small firms in a relatively simple manner.

Concluding Remarks

Overall, the empirical evidence on the impact of occupational health and safety regulations is mixed, generally indicating that the regulations have little or no impact on outcomes. The limited Canadian evidence tends to find the internal responsibility system to have a positive effect on improving workplace health and safety. The evidence also suggests that economic or market incentives through experience rating of workers' compensation have a more pronounced effect on improving workplace health and safety, since employers have a monetary incentive to reduce accidents and hence their premiums. Market incentives through experience rating are particularly attractive since they simply raise the costs of accidents, leaving it up to the employers as to how best to reduce injuries and hence cost.

NOTES

1 Senior Director, Economics Department, Ontario Medical Association (OMA). Opinions expressed in this paper are those of the author and do not necessarily reflect the position or policies of the OMA. The constructive and helpful comments of Douglas Hyatt and Morley Gunderson are gratefully acknowledged.

2 Bruce and Atkins (1993) provide a brief summary of these arguments.

3 In the only study of the impact of OSHA penalties on the extent of employer compliance with health and safety regulations Bartel and Thomas (1985) found a strong association between compliance and the average penalty per inspection.

4 If inspections are being caused by high injury rates, this creates an obvious endogeneity problem for an analysis of the impact of inspections on injuries. OSHA inspectors review injury records as part of a routine inspection, and may be more likely to carefully scrutinize and penalize a plant that has experienced increasing numbers of injuries.

5 The Workers' Compensation Act in Ontario did not provide for experience-

rating until 1917. From then until 1938, a variety of systems were introduced, found to be unsatisfactory, and abandoned. The 1938 plan was criticized by employers when it was realized that 55 per cent of those penalized had favourable accident experience. Workers were critical of the plan, claiming that it encouraged employers to hide accidents. They felt also that many employers adopted hiring policies that favoured good risks (i.e., young, single men).

The Canadian Manufacturers Association (CMA) felt that the previous plans had failed basically because of administrative defects and, consequently, in 1948 set up a committee to study the subject and investigate the possibility of a new program. The WCB did not consider that the full effect of such plans in stimulating accident prevention had been demonstrated, and felt obliged to try at least one plan. The objectives were to provide an incentive to prevent workplace injuries and to more equitably distribute the costs of accidents. The CMA committee's recommendation was reviewed by the WCB's consulting actuary during 1952, and a revised program, which became known as the Voluntary plan, was adopted.

By 1978, a total of 41 rate groups had entered the Voluntary plan, comprising nearly 40 per cent of total assessments paid to the WCB. The Wyatt Company's report into the financial structure of workers' compensation paid particular attention to the Voluntary experience-rating plan. The Wyatt report pointed out a number of shortcomings of the plan, such as insufficient refunds and surcharges to provide meaningful incentives to employers, and recommended that a completely new plan be developed. Following from the Wyatt report's recommendations, the WCB and employer groups began to develop an acceptable replacement plan. Owing to a lack of consensus within industry, two plans grew out of the search for a better formula – the CAD-7 and NEER plans.

6 The Voluntary program was terminated as of 1 January 1992 and the industries enrolled in it were transferred to NEER.

7 However, given that the vast majority of NEER firms, about 90 per cent, receive a refund, an overall off-balance (aggregate rebates exceed aggregate surcharges) results.

8 Experience-rating program off balances contribute to the overall unfunded liability of the workers' compensation agency. A detailed analysis of the potential effects of unfunded liabilities is provided by Gunderson and Hyatt (this volume).

9 Earlier models used in workers' compensation literature such as Curington, 1986, and Carmichael, 1986, were developed in a framework where the risk and/or severity of accidents was *only affected by a firm's behaviour*. Other

authors, such as Krueger (1990), analyse the risk of accidents within theoretical frameworks where risk is influenced by *both firms and workers*. A recent study bases its empirical work on a theoretical principal-agent framework in which *both firms and workers* can influence the risk of work accidents. Specifically, in this model the firm and worker play a two-stage Stackelberg game with the firm being the leader. This important feature is not considered by other authors such as Curington (1986), whose model is based on the firm's side of the problem only. For a formal development of this type of model the reader is referred to Lanoie, 1992c. The principal-agent framework is justified by Lanoie, since it is plausible that the firm cannot observe the risk-related behaviour of its workers. It is also important, in a policy analysis, that both firms and workers be able to influence the risk and severity of accidents, since their respective risk-related behaviour could counterbalance each other and thereby undermine any safety-improving policy; for example, workers becoming less careful when the employer increases its investment in safety.

The theoretical predictions of this type of model are analogous to simpler Curington-type models, but they are derived from a more general and realistic framework. Specifically, as with simpler models, a policy shift, such as the introduction or strengthening of experience rating that increases the firm's expected cost, leads to an unambiguous reduction in workplace accident frequency, since it induces the firm to devote more resources to safety.

REFERENCES

Baldwin, M., and W.G. Johnson. 1990. 'Ontario's New Experimental Experience Rating Plan.' Mimeo, Syracuse University.
Bartel, A.P., and L.G. Thomas. 1985. 'Direct and Indirect Effects of Regulation: A New Look at OSHA's Impact.' *Journal of Law and Economics* 28: 1–25.
Brody, B., et al. 1990. 'Le Cout des accidents du travail: Etat de connaissances.' *Relations Industrielles / Industrial Relations* 45: 94–117.
Bruce, C.J., and F.J. Atkins. 1993. 'Efficiency Effects of Premium-setting Regimes under Workers' Compensation: Canada and the United States.' *Journal of Labor Economics* 11: S38–69.
Bryce, G.K., and P. Manga. 1985. 'The Effectiveness of Health and Safety Committees.' *Industrial Relations* 40: 257–82.
Carmichael, L. 1986. 'Reputations for Safety: Market Performance and Policy Remedies.' *Journal of Labour Economics* 4: 458–72.
Cheadle, A., G. Franklin, C. Wolfhagen, J. Savarino, P.Y. Liu, C. Salley, and M. Weaver. 1994. 'Factors Influencing the Duration of Work-Related Disability:

A Population-Based Study of Washington State Workers' Compensation.' *American Journal of Public Health* 84: 190–6.

Chelius, J.R., and K. Kavanaugh. 1988. 'Workers' Compensation and the Level of Occupational Injuries.' *Journal of Risk and Insurance* 55: 315–23.

Chelius, J.R., and R.S. Smith. 1983. 'Experience-Rating and Injury Prevention.' In John D. Worrall, ed., *Safety and the Work Force*. Ithaca, NY: ILR Press.

– 1993. 'The Impact of Experience-Rating on Employer Behaviour: The Case of Washington State.' In David Durbin and Philip S. Borba, eds, *Workers' Compensation Insurance: Claim Costs, Prices, and Regulation*. Boston: Kluwer Academic Publishers.

Cousineau, J-M., Sandra Girard, and Paul Lanoie. 1995. 'Safety Regulation and Specific Injury Types in Quebec.' In Richard P. Chaykowski and Terry Thomason, eds, *Research in Canadian Workers' Compensation*. Kingston: Queen's University IRC Press.

Curington, W.P. 1986. 'Safety Regulation and Workplace Injuries.' *Southern Economic Journal* 53: 51–72.

Dewees, D.N., and D. Genesove. 1989. 'The Effect of Regulation on Worker Exposure to Hazardous Substances: Two Case Studies.' Mimeo, University of Toronto.

Dionne, G., and P. St-Michel. 1991. 'Workers' Compensation and Moral Hazard.' *Review of Economics and Statistics* 73: 236–44.

Doherty, N. 1979. 'National Insurance and Absence from Work.' *Economic Journal* 89: 50–63.

Ehrenberg, R.G. 1988. 'Workers' Compensation, Wages, and the Risk of Injury.' In John F. Burton, Jr, ed., *New Perspectives in Workers' Compensation*. Ithaca, NY: ILR Press.

Gray, W.B., and J.T. Scholz. 1993. 'Does Regulatory Enforcement Work? A Panel Analysis of OSHA Enforcement.' *Law & Society Review* 27(1): 177–213.

Hyatt, D.E., and B. Kralj. 1995. 'The Impact of Workers' Compensation Experience Rating on Employer Appeals Activity.' *Industrial Relations* 34: 95–106.

– 1996. 'The Impact of Representation (and Other Factors) on the Outcomes of Employee-Initiated Workers' Compensation Appeals.' Mimeo, University of Toronto.

Ison, T.G. 1986. 'The Significance of Experience Rating.' *Osgoode Hall Law Journal* 24: 723–42.

Kahley, W., and C. Sornberger. 1994. 'Experience Rating and Workplace Safety.' *NCCI Digest* 9: 43–51.

Kniesner, T.J., and J.D. Leeth. 1989. 'Separating the Reporting Effects from the Injury Rate Effects of Workers' Compensation Insurance: A Hedonic Simulation.' *Industrial and Labor Relations Review* 42: 280–93.

– 1995. 'Numerical Simulation as a Complement to Econometric Research on Workplace Safety.' *Journal of Risk and Uncertainty* 10: 99–125.

Kotz, H., and H.B. Schafer. 1993. 'Economic Incentives to Accident Prevention: An Empirical Study of the German Sugar Industry.' *International Review of Law and Economics* 13: 19–33.

Kralj, B. 1994. 'Employer Responses to Workers' Compensation Insurance Experience Rating.' *Relations Industrielles / Industrial Relations* 49: 41–61.

– 1995a. 'Experience Rating of Workers' Compensation Insurance Premiums and the Duration of Workplace Injuries.' In Richard P. Chaykowski and Terry Thomason, eds, *Research in Canadian Workers' Compensation*. Kingston: Queen's University IRC Press.

– 1995b. 'Workers' Compensation Insurance Pricing: The Efficacy of Experience Rating.' PhD dissertation, Department of Economics, York University.

Krueger, A.B. 1990. 'Workers' Compensation Insurance and the Duration of Workplace Injuries.' National Bureau of Economic Research, Working paper no. 3253.

Lanoie, P. 1992a. 'The Impact of Occupational Safety and Health Regulation on the Incidence of Workplace Accidents: Quebec 1983–87.' *Journal of Human Resources* 27: 643–60.

– 1992b. 'Government Intervention in Occupational Safety: Lessons from the American and Canadian Experience.' *Canadian Public Policy* 18: 62–75.

– 1992c. 'Safety Regulation and the Risk of Workplace Accidents in Quebec.' *Southern Economic Journal* 58: 950–65.

Lewchuk, W., A.L. Robb, and V. Walters. 1996. 'The Effectiveness of Bill 70 and Joint Health and Safety Committees in Reducing Injuries in the Workplace: The Case of Ontario.' *Canadian Public Policy* 22: 225–43.

McCaffrey, D.P. 1983. 'An Assessment of OSHA's Recent Effects on Injury Rates.' *Journal of Human Resources* 18: 131–46.

Mendeloff, J. 1979. *Regulating Safety: An Economic and Political Analysis of Occupational Safety Policy.* Cambridge, MA: MIT Press.

Moore, M.J., and W.K. Viscusi. 1990. *Compensating Mechanisms for Job Risk.* Princeton, NJ: Princeton University Press.

Parsons, M.D. 1988. 'Worker Participation in Occupational Health and Safety: Lessons from the Canadian Experience.' *Labor Studies Journal*, 22–32.

Ruser, J.W. 1985. 'Workers' Compensation Insurance, Experience Rating and Occupational Injuries.' *Rand Journal of Economics* 16: 487–503.

– 1993. 'Workers' Compensation and the Distribution of Occupational Injuries.' *Journal of Human Resources* 28: 593–617.

– 1991. 'Workers' Compensation and Occupational Injuries and Illnesses.' *Journal of Labor Economics* 9: 325–50.

Ruser, J.W., and R.S. Smith. 1991. 'Reestimating OSHA's Effects: Have the Data Changed?' *Journal of Human Resources* 26: 212–35.

Scholz, J.T., and W.B. Gray. 1990. 'OSHA Enforcement and Workplace Injuries: A Behavioral Approach to Risk Assessment.' *Journal of Risk and Uncertainty* 3: 283–305.

Shannon, H., et al. 1992. *Health and Safety Approaches in the Workplace: Report to the Industrial Accident Prevention Association.* Toronto: APA.

Smith, R.S. 1979. 'The Impact of OSHA Inspections on Manufacturing Injury Rates.' *Journal of Human Resources* 14: 145–70.

– 1992. 'Have OSHA and Workers' Compensation Made the Workplace Safer?' In D. Lewin, O.S. Mitchell, and P.D. Sherer, eds, *Research Frontiers in Industrial Relations and Human Resources.* Madison, Wisc.: Industrial Relations Research Association.

Tucker, E. 1995. 'And Defeat Goes On: An Assessment of Third-Wave Health and Safety Regulation.' In F. Pearce and L. Snider, eds, *Corporate Crime: Contemporary Debates.* Toronto: University of Toronto Press.

Tuohy, C., and M. Simard. 1992. 'The Impact of Joint Health and Safety Committees in Ontario and Quebec.' Report to the Canadian Association of Administrators of Labour Law, Toronto.

Viscusi, W.K. 1983. *Risk by Choice: Regulating Health and Safety in the Workplace.* Cambridge: Harvard University Press.

– 1986. 'The Impact of Occupational Safety and Health Regulation.' *Rand Journal of Economics* 17: 567–80.

Walters, V., and T. Haines. 1988. 'Workers' Use and Knowledge of the "Internal Responsibility System": Limits to Participation in Occupational Health and Safety.' *Canadian Public Policy* 14: 411–23.

Weil, D. 1996. 'If OSHA Is So Bad, Why Is Compliance So Good?' *Rand Journal of Economics* 27: 618–40.

Welton, I. 1996. 'New Directions in Employer Incentives: Experience Rating at the Ontario WCB.' Paper presented at OSH 1996 Conference, Toronto.

Workplace Health and Safety Agency. 1994. *The Impact of Joint Health and Safety Committees on Health and Safety in Ontario.* Toronto: Workplace Health and Safety Agency.

Worrall, J.D., and R.J. Butler. 1988. 'Experience Rating Matters.' In D. Appel and P.S. Borba, *Workers' Compensation Insurance Pricing.* Boston: Kluwer Academic Publishers.

8 Private Participation in Workers' Compensation

DONALD N. DEWEES

The administrative arrangements for workers' compensation (WC) today range from systems that are entirely operated by government agencies to systems in which WC insurance is entirely provided by private insurers, with many arrangements in between. Throughout the 1990s there has been much criticism of the inefficiency of public bodies and the potential benefits of allowing private firms to provide some or all of their functions. On the other hand, there is the concern that the public interest may be lost in a system driven by the profit motive. This paper uses an economic framework to consider the advantages and disadvantages of allowing private firms to perform some of the functions of public WC agencies. It provides a structure for analysing these issues and identifies areas requiring research. Because there has been little study of these issues to date, few hard conclusions will be drawn here. It is, however, possible to suggest possible outcomes of some structural changes and of more detailed investigations. The focus of the paper is on Ontario, but examples and data are drawn from other provinces and from the extensive U.S. experience.

Two types of changes are examined: the allocation of certain individual functions that are normally performed by a monopoly public provider to the private sector; and the introduction of private insurers where only a public insurer operates. Four distinct models of the role of public and private insurers are identified:

1 monopoly public provision, in which a single public organization performs all functions (as in ten provinces, six states, and some federal areas of jurisdiction);

2 public and private provision, in which private firms are allowed to compete with the public provider (as in 18 states);
3 purely private provision, with strict rate regulation (manual rates); and
4 purely private provision, with no rate regulation (open competition).

In all cases, governments set the eligibility conditions and benefit levels. This paper explores the effects of allowing private firms to compete with the WCB, the mixed system of model 2, and of eliminating the public provider entirely and replacing it with private insurers with open price competition, model 4.

Economists have conducted numerous studies over many years of the relative performance of the public and private sector for providing a number of services. Sectors studied include fire protection, urban transportation, railroads, airlines, postal service, electric utilities, water supply, and especially waste collection. A survey of this literature is contained in Dewees et al. (1993: 6.2 to 6.28). All of these sectors, like workers' compensation, have examples of public provision and examples of private provision, allowing some empirical comparison of performance. More recently, the privatization of state enterprises in the United Kingdom since 1979 and the privatization of state enterprises in Eastern Europe since the fall of the Iron Curtain have provided additional data for analysis. (See, e.g., Megginson, Nash, and van Randenborgh, 1994.)

Workers' compensation differs from most other insurance in several important ways. First, it is compulsory in every jurisdiction. WC was intended to provide prompt administrative compensation to injured workers in place of the uncertain awards of the tort system. When workers gave up their right to sue, they had to be assured that they would receive the administrative compensation. Thus, it had to be available for all workers in industries with significant health and safety risks. This rationale is somewhat different from the rationale for compulsory automobile insurance, which is intended to ensure that motorists generally pay for the costs of accidents that they cause and to ensure that accident victims who are not at fault will be compensated. Second, the legislature always sets both eligibility criteria and compensation levels. Employers gained freedom from tort liability, but in exchange they were required to pay for the WC insurance (Dee, McCombie, Newhouse, 1987: 9). Since the employer purchases insurance to compensate the workers, there is a clear conflict of interest if the employer can shop for the policy that best suits the employer rather than the employees. In order to ensure that workers are adequately protected by WC insurance, the government in every jurisdiction in North America establishes, by legislation or by regulation, the conditions for eligibility and the benefits to be paid for various injuries. Third, in a number of jurisdictions, including all Canadian provinces, the state is the insurer or, as in some U.S. states, the state is one of several insurers. Since the primary characteristics of the insurance coverage are a matter of public policy specified by law, it is a small step for the government to operate some or all of the insurance system itself. Furthermore, there is an argument that public provision of WC insurance will reduce the incentive for employers or insurers to challenge claims and will therefore support the goal of compensating injured workers.

Through the 1970s, most WC rates in the United States were manual rates set by the state's insurance commissioner. In 1981, states began to deregulate WC insurance rates, with thirty-one states having deregulated by late 1995. Studies of this experience, discussed below, have found mixed effects on both costs and rates. Furthermore, other studies, also discussed below, compare the performance of private WC insurance with mixed systems and with public systems in Canada, finding that mixed systems in the United States have higher costs than purely private systems, while the Canadian monopoly systems appear to have lower costs per unit of benefits than the U.S. systems. This paper will explore further the theoretical and empirical evidence on this question.

A summary of the financial operations of the Ontario WCB is presented in table 8.1. The benefits paid out in 1995 were $2.385 billion, administrative expenses were $339 million and expenses for other programs that legislation has imposed on the WCB were $113 million. These costs might be reduced by reducing benefit payments through accident and disease prevention, vocational rehabilitation, claims management, and return to work, or through reduced administrative costs. The costs of administration, however, represent only 14 per cent of the benefits paid in 1995 or 12.3 per cent of total expenses. To the extent that the impact of privatization is mainly through efficiency gains in administration, significant reductions in administrative costs would have only a small impact on total WCB expenditures. Major savings must be found elsewhere, most likely in loss prevention and more rapid return to work.

TABLE 8.1
Ontario Workers' Compensation Board, Summary of operations, 1986–1995 (millions of dollars)

	1995	1994	1993	1992	1991	1990	1989	1988	1987	1986
Revenues										
Assessment	2,653	2,351	2,283	2,528	2,505	2,596	2,678	2,377	2,092	1,737
Investment	593	499	521	453	450	440	409	316	272	217
Total	3,246	2,850	2,804	2,981	2,955	3,036	3,087	2,693	2,364	1,954
Expenses										
Benefits paid	2,385	2,331	2,435	2,444	2,342	2,059	1,782	1,624	1,463	1,246
Increase in benefits liability	(150)	(75)	400	760	1,440	1,220	2,117	1,443	1,096	1,304
Increase in IWRF*	49	29	30	14	2					
Sub-total	2,284	2,285	2,865	3,218	3,784	3,279	3,899	3,067	2,559	2,550
Administration	339	331	343	347	343	323	281	259	267	214
Legislated obligations	113	104	100	97	87	53	26	26	22	16
Total	2,736	2,720	3,308	3,662	4,214	3,655	4,206	3,352	2,848	2,780
Surplus (deficiency) from operations	510	130	(504)	(681)	(1,259)	(619)	(1,119)	(659)	(484)	(826)
Unfunded liability	10,892	11,402	11,532	11,028	10,347	9,088	8,469	7,350	6,691	6,207
Total assessable payroll	86,065	82,818	84,243	83,048	80,727	80,352	79,475	73,789	67,974	61,574
Average assessment (%)	3.00	3.01	2.95	3.16	3.20	3.18	3.12	3.02	2.88	2.65
WCB employees (#)	4,597	4,603	4,751	4,909	5,139	5,138	4,611	4,387	4,211	4,218
New claims (thousands)	372	370	368	377	410	473	467	490	470	442

Source: Ontario WCB 1996a: 21
*IWRF = Injured Workers Retirement Fund

As shown in table 8.1, the Ontario WCB had an unfunded liability of $10.892 billion at the end of 1995, reduced in 1996 by $432 million (Gunderson and Hyatt, this volume). This represents expected payments to workers who have been injured and are expected to remain on disability pensions in future years. It represents more than three times the total revenues of the Ontario WCB in 1995. While a variety of mechanisms exist to reduce the unfunded liability (discussed in Gunderson and Hyatt, this volume), it may be a source of pressure for reforms, including private-sector participation to force cost reductions.

The Policy Setting

In recent years policy makers have become increasingly interested in the relative merits of the private provision of services that have previously been provided mainly by the public sector. There has been debate about the merits of privatizing a number of traditionally public services, including electricity generation and distribution, the sale of alcoholic beverages, prison operations, waste collection and disposal, and others. (See, e.g., Trebilcock, 1994.) In this context, WC in Canada is an obvious candidate for consideration given its size, the implications of its premiums for employer costs, and the system's existing unfunded liability. Furthermore, private insurers already offer non-occupational disability insurance coverage. The extensive U.S. experience with private provision invites obvious comparisons.

In 1986 six U.S. states relied on a monopoly public insurer, twelve states employed mixed systems in which private insurers competed with a public insurer, and the rest relied exclusively on private insurers.[1] By 1996, one state had discontinued its public insurer and seven states had created a public insurer to compete with private insurers, so there were eighteen mixed systems.[2] At a time when much of the world has been contemplating privatization and a diminished role for the public sector, there has been growth in the use of public-sector insurance to compete with private WC insurers in the United States or to act as the insurer of last resort.

Of course the substitution of private for public providers in Canada is not the only possible solution to perceived problems with a public provider. Reform of the public provider represents a less radical change and might be able to address some of the perceived needs. Previous reform of Ontario's WC system, including retroactive indexing of permanent disability pensions and increases in benefits, contributed significantly to the unfunded liability that has been a source of concern through the 1990s (Vaillancourt, 1994; Gunderson and Hyatt, this volume). However, more recent reform efforts have sought to restrain system costs. In November 1996, the Minister of Labour tabled a bill that would amend the Workers' Compensation Act, renaming it the Workplace Safety and Insurance Act, 1996, and would make a number of changes intended to reduce the cost of WC in the province. The bill would reduce indexation of benefits for all but permanently totally disabled workers, reduce benefits from 90 per cent of pre-injury net earnings to 85 per cent, and strengthen the WCB's role in preventing injuries and illness and hastening the return to work of injured workers. Further reforms, either in the Act or in the policies and procedures of the WCB, could be undertaken to address concerns regarding its effectiveness.

When an injury results in immediate medical costs and a short absence from work, the costs of the injury can generally be accounted for in the year of the injury, and in principle the assessments in that year should cover those costs. However, when a worker suffers an injury leading to permanent partial or total disability, the payments to the worker may stretch over many years in the future. These payments will have to be made whether or not the employer continues to exist in Ontario, and indeed whether or not the industry continues to exist in Ontario. Like most insurance schemes, it is generally assumed that WC premiums paid in any year will approximately cover the full liability for all injuries suffered in that year, even if payments will be made in later years. The unfunded liability of the Ontario WCB, equal to about four years of revenues at current rates, shows that this principle has failed, at least over the last decade. This raises two policy concerns.

First, would private insurers be any less likely to give rise to unfunded liability in the future? Because such liability is an economic burden passed on to future generations in the province, it represents a future drag on the economy. Any proposal to introduce private firms into the WC insurance business would have to confront this risk.

Second, what happens to the existing unfunded liability if private insurers are allowed to compete with the Ontario WCB or if the WCB is completely displaced by private insurers? Clearly some provision must be made to pay those workers who have established entitlements under the existing system. Furthermore, the mechanism for doing this if the WCB is not the exclusive insurance provider must be worked out. This problem is analogous to the problem of 'stranded assets' that may arise if public utilities are privatized. If private firms enter the electricity-generation business, what happens to those older generating facilities that have not paid off the debt incurred in their construction and which cannot do so in competition with more efficient operators? Proposals for allowing competition in the electricity utility business have had to provide solutions for this problem, which may be instructive in considering the WCB problem. Generally these solutions have involved levying a charge on customers to write down the liability or passing the liability on to taxpayers (Daniels and Trebilcock, 1995: 37). In the case of WC, one could either impose a levy on all WC insurance premiums or the province could assume some or all of the liability and thereby pass it on to taxpayers.

To assess the prospect of private provision properly, we need to examine the full set of functions that are currently performed by the WC system and to consider who would perform them in various alternative models. Table 8.2 lists a set of functions related to WC and the individual or agency that performs that function in three types of systems: Ontario, a purely public system; Pennsylvania and Minnesota, where a public fund operates in competition with private insurers; and Wisconsin and Illinois, which are purely private. We will focus first on Ontario, then on Wisconsin, and then consider the general implications of the table.

In Ontario the basic eligibility criteria and benefit levels are set by government (Ison, 1989: 73, chap. 5). The legislation, however, is generally quite broad, so much of the law governing WC consists of the rules, orders, directives and board decisions themselves (ibid., 4). In Ontario, appeals from decisions of the board may be heard internally on an informal basis; further appeals are taken to an appeals tribunal, which is independent of the Board, and its decisions also form part of the relevant law (Chaykowski and Thomason, 1995: 10). In Ontario there is no appeal to the courts from a board *decision*, but a claimant may go to court to request judicial review of the *process* used by the board in reaching a decision, and this leads to a modest amount of litigation (Ison, 1989: 5). An injured worker is entitled to any medical aid that may be required as a result of an injury. The worker is entitled to choose the treating physician and to participate in treatment decisions as with any medical problem (ibid., 76). The board pays all costs of medical diagnosis, assessment, and treatment, except in cases where the worker does not notify the attending physician that the injury is work-related, in which case the cost is borne by the provincial health

TABLE 8.2
Workers' compensation functions and responsibility

Function	Who does it				
	Ontario	Pennsylvania	Minnesota	Wisconsin	Illinois
Set benefits, eligibility	Legislature	Legislature	Legislature	Legis., on advice of WC Advisory Council	Legislature
Set policy and procedures	WC Board (WCB)	Bureau of WC (BWC)	WC Division (WCD)	WCD on advice of WC Advisory Council	Insurers
Process claims	WCB	Insurers	Insurers	Insurers	Insurers
Investigate contested claims	WCB	BWC	Insurers	Insurers	Insurers
Hear appeals, resolve disputes	WCB, Appeals Tribunal	BWC referees, WC Appeals Board, courts	Office of Admin. Hearings; WC Court of Appeal; courts	WCD, judges; appeals to LIR Comm., courts	Ill. Indep. Comm. of Arbitrators; IIC; courts
Maintain records of claims, decisions	WCB	BWC	WCD	WCD	IIC minimal
Medical diagnosis, treatment	Employee's (EE) physician	EE's physician unless employer (ER) posts list of five	EE's physician	EE's physician; ER can choose second opinion	EE's physician
Disability assessment	WCB physician	Attending physician	Attending physician	Attending physician, schedule	Attending physician
Rehabilitation	WCB provides, pays	Not covered, sometimes offered voluntarily	Optional since 1992	Worker chooses, insurer pays	Nominally mandatory, ER pays, private providers

TABLE 8.2 – concluded
Workers' compensation functions and responsibility

Function	Who does it				
	Ontario	Pennsylvania	Minnesota	Wisconsin	Illinois
Set rates	WCB	Manual, discounts	Open rating	Insurers	Insurers
Advise employers re WC	WCB, Employers' Advisor	BWC Commun. Division	WCD Assistance and Compliance Section	Insurers, Public Service Unit of WCD	Minimal
Advise workers re WC	WCB, Workers' Advisor	BWC Communications Division	WCD Assistance and Compliance Section	Insurers, Public Service Unit of WCD	Minimal
OHS, prevention	WCB, MoL	U.S. OSHA; Pa. Dept. Labor & Ind.	U.S. OSHA; Minn. Dept. Labor & Ind.	U.S. OSHA; Wis. Div. Safety & Bldgs	Not IIC
Research on injuries, compensation	WCB	BWC	WCD	Insurers, WCD	Not IIC
Marketing and promotion	None	Insurers	Insurers	Insurers	Insurers
Establish reserves	WCB	BWC	Dept. Commerce	Insurers	None
Name of fund	WCB	State Workmen's Insurance Fund	Minn. State Fund Mutual Ins. Co.	None	None
Administrative functions: actuarial analysis, accounting, computing/ communications, provision of office space, legal services	WCB	Dept. Labor & Ind., except litigation	Generally WCD, insurers; actuarial studies contracted out; office space leased	Generally WCD, insurers; actuarial studies contracted out	Generally insurers, IIC

Sources: Ontario: Dee, McCombie, and Newhouse, 1987; Ison, 1989. Pennsylvania: Ballantyne and Telles, 1991a. Wisconsin: Ballantyne and Telles, 1992. Illinois: Ballantyne and Telles, 1991b. Minnesota: Ballantyne and Telles, 1991a. Wisconsin: Ballantyne and Telles, 1992. Illinois: Ballantyne and Joyce, 1996. Various: AASCIF, 1995.

plan. The board will generally accept the treatment decisions of the worker and attending physician, but it has some authority to question some decisions (ibid., 77). Indeed, the board may reduce or suspend compensation if workers reject treatment that the board believes is reasonably necessary for their recovery. The board employs its own medical staff, who advise claims adjudicators regarding evidence in a file or who may examine a claimant. In cases of permanent disability, the board's physicians will determine the degree of physical impairment (ibid., 215). The board is authorized to provide rehabilitation assistance to an injured worker. Workers may decide what advice and rehabilitation they want, and the board will decide what it will provide or pay for. While rehabilitation is voluntary, the board may decide to reduce payments to claimants if they refuse to follow a recommended vocational rehabilitation program, in which case VR is essentially mandatory (Allingham and Hyatt, 1995: 164–6). The rates in Ontario and other provinces are set by the board itself under statutory guidance that the revenues should equal the payments by the board (Ison, 1989: 261). All jurisdictions have an agency charged with regulating occupational health and safety (OHS); in some cases, such as British Columbia, this agency is the WCB, while in others the board plays a supporting role in OHS regulation.

Turning to the private systems in the United States, the Wisconsin legislature sets benefits and eligibility as well as a number of policy matters, acting on the advice of the Worker's Compensation Advisory Council, composed of labour and management representatives (Ballantyne and Telles, 1992: 11).[3] Policies and procedures are established by the Worker's Compensation Division (WCD) of the Department of Industry, Labor and Human Relations (DILHR), again on the advice of the WC Advisory Council. Claims are adjudicated by the private insurers, or by self-insured employers. The worker may appeal the insurer's decision to an Administrative Law Judge (ALJ) in the Bureau of Legal Services of the WCD, who will issue a decision after a hearing. The decision of the ALJ may be appealed to the three-member Labor and Industry Review Commission, and then to the Circuit Court of Appeal (Ballantyne and Telles, 1992: 64–73). Workers may choose their own physician, but the employer may also require workers to submit to an examination by a physician of the employer's choice (ibid., 19). With respect to choice of physician, Wisconsin is typical of twenty-seven states in which the employee makes the initial selection; in a number of others the employee may choose from a list provided by the employer, and in some the employer chooses the physician (Boden, DeFinis, and Fleischman, 1990: 29). The insurer pays all reasonable and necessary costs of medical treatment and supplies. The extent of disability is determined by the attending physician with reference to a schedule of injuries. A disabled worker may be entitled to vocational rehabilitation services provided either by the Division of Vocational Rehabilitation of the Wisconsin Department of Health and Social Services or by a private provider, and paid for by the insurer (Ballantyne and Telles, 1992: 9). The cost of running the state WC system is funded by an assessment on insurers and self-insured employers. The WCD has 101 full-time staff members (ibid., 12). Advice to workers and employers regarding WC issues is provided by insurers, by the Bureau of Claims Management of the WCD, and by its Public Service Unit (ibid.). Research on WC issues is performed by the Bureau of Claims Management.

Table 8.2 reveals a surprising feature of these varied WC systems: the similarity of the allocation of powers and duties among them. In all jurisdictions, whether monopoly public, mixed, or purely private, the basic eligibility criteria and benefit levels are set by government, often in the legislation itself. In most cases, policies and procedures are set by the provincial or state WC agency. Any claim that is contested goes to a provincial or state WC mediation or hearing process and then to a WC appeal body, and then, except in Ontario, to the courts. The WC agency, except in Illinois, maintains records of larger claims and the outcome of disputes. This handling of disputed claims yields uniform outcomes across the jurisdiction, so that the outcome of an appeal should depend relatively little on which insurer is chosen, although some insurers may contest more claims than others. In many cases, the employee's physician provides diagnosis and treatment and even an assessment of disability, although generally the insurer may secure a second opinion by a physician of its own choosing. The provincial or state agency generally provides information to employees and employers regarding WC and performs research on occupational health and safety as well as on WC matters. It appears that the difference between public and private provision of WC is in the details and not in the fundamental structure of the system. The state is involved in setting many parameters of the WC system, in establishing policies, in adjudicating disputes, and in regulating the insurers, just as it regulates other types of insurers operating in the state. Some functions are performed by the public sector in all jurisdictions and some by the private sector in all jurisdictions, with a substantial number that could be done by either. It would be a mistake to think of the private operation of WC in the same terms as the privatization of a previously national-ized state oil company or automobile manufacturer, although even in these cases the private firms are subject to substantial regulation concerning environmental pollution, occupational health and safety, financial reporting, and so forth.

While the allocation of powers and duties of most systems seems sim-ilar, the results need not be. It is entirely plausible that the presence of private insurers lobbying for their interests might yield a different out-come from the state's determination of eligibility criteria and benefit levels, or other parameters of the system, than when there is no compet-itive industry to present its view. If such differences exist, it remains to be determined which best secures the overall public interest.

In Canada health care is paid for by the provincial health-care sys-tems, while in the United States it is paid for by individuals or their private insurers, many of whom are funded through employee health plans. In the United States, a worker has an incentive to make a WC claim in order to recover health-care costs, while in Canada the worker has no liability for health care regardless of the origin of the injury. This reduces the inclination to file WC claims by Canadian workers who have not lost wages as a result of their injury, and it reduces the incen-tive to dispute WC decisions in similar situations. However, the real resource costs of health care still exist in Canada, so we should be con-cerned with the extent to which the existing system or any alternative tends to ensure that appropriate health care is delivered to injured workers in the most cost-effective fashion.

Theoretical Evaluation of Modes of Provision

Criteria

An important criterion for evaluating the performance of workers' compensation systems is economic efficiency. Efficiency refers to the ability to maximize the welfare of the populace by providing goods or services that match the desires of consumers at the lowest cost. Effi-ciency can be measured in both static and dynamic terms.

Static efficiency generally requires that prices of goods and services be set at the marginal cost of producing those goods and services and that there be no slack in the economy. Slack occurs when resources are not fully utilized so that the same output could be produced using fewer resources. Thus, a change that allows us to provide the same services at a lower cost will increase efficiency, as will a change that provides better service at the same cost. Since cost saving is an important measure of efficiency, it is important to look carefully at how this should be measured and at problems in its measurement.

Most costs of WC agencies, unlike many functions analysed for public-private provision, are represented by payments to claimants. Typically in public systems in Canada only 15 per cent of total expenditures are for administration. This means that efficiency gains in administration can only save a fraction of 15 per cent of total WC costs. A 10 per cent improvement in administrative efficiency would save only 1.5 per cent of total WC costs. It follows that large financial savings will only arise from reducing injury rates, decreasing the frequency and severity of claims, or increasing the speed of workers returning to work. These issues must therefore be a central consideration in this analysis. We will also consider the extent to which better administration might be able to promote such savings.

Another problem is that efficiency measures the overall use of resources in the economy rather than looking specifically at who pays the costs of those resources. A cost saving improves efficiency if it represents a reduction in the real resource costs of producing the output. A cost saving that results from shifting costs from one agency to another has not reduced total resource costs in the economy and would not represent an increase in efficiency. For example, an agency that succeeded in shifting medical costs for injured workers from the WC system to the public health-insurance system would appear to have saved money, but in fact would have saved nothing for the economy as a whole; it has just transferred the liability from one agency to another. As a second example, if a worker has suffered genuine wage losses as a result of a workplace accident, denial of her claim by the WC agency will simply shift the burden of this loss to the individual or even to the welfare system. Again, this is not a saving of social resources, it is simply a transfer from one agency to an individual or another agency. We must therefore be careful in assessing the efficiency of WC to remember its mission and to focus on resource costs not just accounting costs.

How could we measure the static efficiency of the workers' compensation system? Efficiency might be measured in part by the proportion of premium dollars that are paid out to injured workers. But by this measure, an agency that paid all claims without scrutiny would be seen as a good performer, although it might in fact be subject to serious abuse. A second measure might be the average claims cost per injured worker. Of course, such a measure would reward an agency that routinely denied legitimate claims, also not a desirable outcome. Third, we might look at the cost of the WC system per insured employee. But injury rates vary greatly among sectors of the economy, so jurisdictions with a higher proportion of low-risk industries would automatically look more efficient. This problem might be solved by comparing costs per employee in each sector, where sectors are categorized by risk level. Again, however, a low-cost jurisdiction might be one that routinely denied legitimate claims. Perhaps looking at cost per worker and at the proportion of claims settled in full would provide a measure of both thrift and client satisfaction.

Despite these problems, there must be a legitimate role for reasonable cost control or claims management. Two plausible areas for cost control relate to the duration of temporary-disability claims and the proportion of temporary-disability claims that become permanent. In Ontario, the average duration of temporary-disability claims in the current year rose from 29 days in 1986 to 41 days in 1991, then declined to 32 days in 1995 without any change in workplaces that could account for this change (Ontario WCB, 1996b: 17). It seems possible that this increase arose from inadequate attention by the WCB in managing the various phases of claims: bringing medical, psychological, and other therapeutic skills together with the claimant to examine the problem; identifying the best treatment; and determining the earliest time when the claimant can reasonably be expected to return to work. Furthermore, between 1986 and 1992 the number of permanent-disability pensioners increased by about 60 per cent also without apparent reason (ibid., 22). Again, better claims management might have reduced or avoided this increase. A legitimate measure of the effectiveness of WC might be seen in the minimization of claims costs subject to some confidence that claims were being dealt with reasonably and fairly.

Dynamic efficiency refers to the ability of the economy to improve its performance over time. Improvements in performance can be measured by improvements in the productivity of resources: increases in output without increased inputs. Technological progress has greatly improved our standard of living over the years, so the ability of social institutions to encourage technological progress is an important consideration in promoting dynamic efficiency.

Workers' compensation is different than the production of widgets in a widget factory, and this difference leads to some additional important criteria for measuring the performance of a workers' compensation system. These criteria include prompt response to and disposition of inquiries and claims by clients; involvement of and responsiveness to stakeholders in developing policies and procedures, adjudicating claims, and evaluating performance; horizontal equity, so that similarly situated workers are treated in a similar fashion; control over the accumulation of unfunded liability and the ability to deal with the existing unfunded liability of the WCB; assurance that injured workers will receive their compensation if an insurer should fail; and flexibility and reversibility of policies and decisions, so that the institution can respond to an ever-changing workplace and claims environment. We will consider each of these in turn.

Prompt response to and disposition of inquiries and claims is often cited as a concern by both workers and employers. A worker who has made a claim is clearly better served by learning of the outcome of her claim sooner rather than later. Furthermore, an institution that can respond promptly to inquiries by, for example, informing the claimant as to the status of an unresolved claim, can reduce the anxiety associated with waiting for the outcome. As the service sector of the economy has grown over the last quarter-century, providing good service has become an important competitive tool, reflecting the importance of service to the public. In the case of an injured worker whose economic circumstances may have become desperate as a result of an injury, long delays in awarding compensation exact a heavy toll. Indeed, in some circumstances employers or insurers have been accused of using delay as a tactic to cause the claimant to settle for a lesser amount than initially requested. Furthermore, the historic shift from the tort liability system to WC was motivated, in part, by a desire to reduce the long delays inherent in the judicial process, recognizing that 'justice delayed is justice denied.' An evaluation of performance should therefore include some measure of the time between filing a claim and the various stages of satisfaction of that claim.

Involvement of stakeholders in the development and implementation of policy and procedures may be valued by those stakeholders entirely aside from the substantive outcome of the process. Participants in the WC process attach a great deal of importance to having the opportunity to express their view or argue their case, to ensure that their concerns have been heard. Whether or not their input is ultimately persuasive, some value is attached to a process in which the stakeholders have a chance to be heard. This is true for policy formulation, the adoption of administrative procedures, and the adjudication of individual claims. Stakeholders are more likely to accept and live with a decision when they have had a meaningful input into the process, in part because they are more likely to understand the constraints under which such decisions are made.

Horizontal equity requires that similarly situated individuals be treated in a similar fashion. Workers require some assurance that the benefits of a system for which they have fought over the years will be distributed fairly, so that two injured workers who are in similar situations will receive similar benefits. Employees may become concerned if the system is thought to be arbitrary, making large payments to some and small payments to others who are similarly situated. Employers, too, have an interest in a system that imposes costs on them fairly, such that employers in the same industry and with the same accident record should pay the same assessment.

The principle that injuries should be paid for in the year in which they occur raises two related objectives. First, any system should have controls that minimize the risk that a significant unfunded liability will accumulate. Second, in the case of Ontario, any changes to the present system should preserve the ability to deal with the unfunded liability currently on the books of the WCB. This liability, which grew almost entirely during the 1980s, represents estimates of the permanent disability pensions owed today as a result of injuries that occurred in the past. In theory, one might wish to retroactively assess the employers of the workers at the time that they were injured, but this is impractical. If the WCB continues to be a monopoly provider, it will likely make assessments larger than necessary for current liabilities in order to pay down the unfunded liability. Any proposal to allow private firms to write WC insurance must be assessed in part on its provisions for a mechanism for retiring the board's unfunded liability.

WC insurance is paid for by the employer for the benefit of the worker. Since the purpose is to compensate injured workers, it is essential that their compensation not be put at risk by the failure of their insurance carrier. It is assumed that the government of Ontario stands behind the WCB, so concern about its unfunded liability does not raise concerns that the injured will not be paid. If private firms are allowed to provide WC insurance, the security of the benefits of injured workers must not be reduced.

Flexibility and responsiveness to a changing environment are also important. Legislatures are loath to make significant changes to WC laws and regulations in part because any change is likely to open up a variety of issues on which stakeholders have strong preferences. Yet the nature of the workplace is constantly changing, new occupational risks arise or are discovered, and our medical knowledge about both the causes of some conditions and of the feasibility of treating them are under constant revision. The WC system will perform better if it is designed to be responsive to these changing conditions – if it has the ability to adapt its policies and procedures as needed, rather than being ruled by the dead hand of the past.

With these criteria for evaluating proposals to reform or privatize workers' compensation in mind, we turn next to what economic theory says about the ability of public and private institutions to meet some of these criteria.

Theoretical Framework

Two sets of economic theories are relevant to the question of whether some WC functions could or would be better provided by the private sector. In the following three subsections we examine agency cost theory to determine whether or not the private sector is likely to be more efficient than the public sector in general and why; we consider the theory of the firm to determine the circumstances under which efficient private-sector firms decide to contract out for needed inputs (the factors considered by the private sector in reaching a contracting-out decision should be equally important to the public sector in deciding the functions that might be contracted out to the private sector); and we combine agency cost theory and the theory of the firm in order to determine which functions of the WC system might theoretically be best provided by the private sector.

AGENCY COST THEORY

Jensen and Smith (1985: 96) defined agency costs as costs arising whenever one person or organization (the principal) contracts with another person or organization (the agent) to perform a service for the principal, and the performance of this service necessitates the delegation of some decision-making authority from the principal to the agent. The agency problem is the difficulty of ensuring that the principal is faithfully served and that the agent is fairly compensated in situations where the agent's interests do not coincide with those of the principal, where the principal has incomplete control over the agent, and where the agent has incomplete information about the principal's interests (Donahue, 1989: 38).

Jensen and Smith identify three types of agency costs. First, there is the cost of structuring the contract so as to require the agent to perform the desired service for the principal. Second, there is the cost of enforcing the contract. This includes monitoring costs (actions taken by the principal in order to ensure that the terms of the contract are adhered to) and bonding costs (actions taken by the agent to restrict his/her ability to act against the principal's interest). Third, there are residual losses. There will always be some residual loss by the principal when the contracting, monitoring, and bonding costs do not ensure that the agent acts as a perfect proxy for the principal (Jensen and Smith, 1985).

Donahue (1989: 49) describes a further component of agency cost, which he calls 'slack.' Slack is the gradual increase in agency cost components as a result of a lengthy agency relationship. When an agency relationship is first established, the agent's role and the principal's expectations from him/her are usually clear, and adequate monitoring and bonding provisions are established. With time, however, this initially tight relationship tends to loosen. As objectives and tasks are modified, they must be restated for the agent, and new monitoring and bonding provisions must be established. Often, this restatement of roles and these new monitoring and bonding provisions are not as effective as those in the initial relationship. Furthermore, monitoring, even if it is stringent at first, has a tendency to become less stringent with time as the relationship becomes more relaxed and less formalized. Both of these factors result in a gradual increase in agency costs referred to as slack. Slack will continue to grow in magnitude unless properly controlled.

Agency Costs and Organizational Structure
Different organizational arrangements have different inherent incentive structures that yield different agency costs. We can explore these incentive structures by considering the principal type of competitive private-sector organization and the incentive structure it entails: firms that are managed by professional managers and in which the owners (shareholders) have little involvement in day-to-day control of organizational activities.

Most companies where ownership and management are separated are companies whose stock is publicly traded on the open market. Such companies have many owners who collectively delegate management responsibilities to professional managers. The agency problem arises because the managers will often be tempted to act in their own self-interest, not in the best interests of the company. Furthermore, there is no owner actively involved in management who can minimize agency costs (Fama, 1980). Most shareholders only hold a small number of shares and therefore have little influence over managers. While shareholders with large blocks of shares (such as institutional investors) are not uncommon, the amount of control they exert over management is tempered by the fact that they find it difficult to acquire needed information about most issues facing management. Thus, in practice, management often has substantial discretion and freedom in running such a company.

However, since such companies continue to exist, there must be some mechanism, other than the owner-entrepreneur, that controls agency costs. According to Easterbrook and Fischel (1991: 4), agency costs are controlled by the 'invisible hand' of the market that causes managers to act as if they had investors' interests at heart. The literature on the factors that drive this 'invisible hand' has identified three principal factors.

First, competition among managers encourages greater efficiency, greater innovation, and lower agency costs in publicly traded corporations. Managers, in a quest for promotions, will attempt to outperform their rivals. Furthermore, as a result of this competition, managers are interested in the behaviour of both their subordinates and their supervisors, both of which will affect the manager's apparent productivity, and will both monitor and correct this behaviour when necessary (Fama, 1980: 292–3).

Second, the mere existence of competition among firms in their output markets requires firms to act efficiently if they are going to survive and managers are to retain their jobs. In fact, competition is a central factor in the control of agency costs and the enhancement of the efficient operation of a firm.

Finally, open-market trading of shares contributes to the minimization of agency costs. In part, this is because senior management is frequently rewarded, at least partially, based on stock performance. Furthermore, companies considering hiring new managers typically evaluate candidates based on their previous performance with other companies. Consequently, even if managers are not rewarded immediately based on stock performance, ultimately their future job prospects will be affected by their current performance as measured on the stock market (Fama, 1980: 241). As a result, the company's interest and the manager's self-interest become more closely aligned and agency costs are reduced.

A second incentive arises from open-market trading of stocks.[4] The fact that a company has shares traded on the stock market means that corporate take-overs can occur whenever that company is undervalued. Since such take-overs often result in management being replaced by a new team, existing managers will be motivated to strive for improved efficiency so as to ensure that a take-over, with the resultant managerial job loss, does not occur.

Thus, in the case of professionally managed firms, three factors are key in minimizing agency costs: first, managers compete among themselves; second, these firms usually face strong competitive pressures from other firms in their output markets; third, the shares of these firms are usually traded on the stock market, creating competition for corporate control. These three factors also work to limit the development of slack within professionally managed firms.

Agency Costs and the Public Sector
The problem of agency costs increases greatly in the public sector. First, the owners of public-sector enterprise, the electorate, exert little control over the managers of public-sector enterprises and are therefore ineffective at minimizing agency costs. Their control over management is even weaker than that of shareholders in large publicly traded corporations, primarily because of the extremely diffuse nature of ownership in public enterprise. Each elector owns in effect but one share. In the case of the Workers' Compensation Board, employers and employees have a far greater stake in the performance of the board than does the general public, but the same problems arise, as each worker and each employer has little stake and influence. Furthermore, unlike shareholders in publicly traded corporations, electors or stakeholders cannot purchase large numbers of shares so as to increase their influence over management.

Electors or stakeholders could increase the control they exert over management by banding together in large, powerful groups. However, they have little incentive to do this in pursuit of efficiency because their individual share of the cost of the enterprise's inefficiency is infinitesimally small and unlikely to motivate action (Donahue, 1989: 49–51).

Thus, the situation with public enterprise is inferior to that of large publicly traded corporations in terms of the ability of 'owners' to exercise control over management and to minimize agency costs and inefficiency. Furthermore, the other factors that successfully work to minimize agency costs in large publicly traded corporations are not as strong in the public sector. First, competition among managers is muted by the existence of highly formalized rules for promotions. Second, public-sector enterprises rarely face competition in their output markets. Therefore, they cannot be driven out of business by competition nor can the taxpayer easily compare the cost of their public services with those of other jurisdictions. Finally, shares in public-sector enterprises are not traded on the open market. Consequently, there is no risk of corporate take-over. This last factor makes it difficult for senior management's pay to be dependent on their performance, for without the aid of the stock market, evaluating this performance can be quite difficult. Thus, it is likely that agency costs will be significantly higher in the public sector than in the private sector.

Some may argue that politicians serve a controlling role in public enterprise and work to minimize agency costs. In reality, however, it is highly unlikely that the politicians who oversee public enterprise will have major stakes in minimizing agency costs. Politicians are motivated by popular support and the public is often resigned to the existence of high agency costs in the public sector. The public also tends to be unaware of whether or not politicians are undertaking serious efforts to control agency costs. The absence of competition deprives the taxpayer of a benchmark for comparing the cost of the publicly provided service. Finally, for many electors, public-sector inefficiency is not a key issue on which voting decisions are made. On the other hand, public servants, who may benefit from public-sector inefficiency, represent a powerful interest group and may prefer that politicians do nothing in response to the agency problems of public enterprises or institutions (Bush and Denzau, 1977: 90). The result is that politicians may not be particularly interested in controlling agency costs within the public sector.

The agency relationship in public enterprise also results in lower rates of innovation. The private sector is motivated by profits to innovate and develop new, cheaper operating procedures or new, less-expensive or higher-quality products. In the public sector, by contrast, there is less motivation to innovate since profits play a less central role.

Furthermore, managers in the public sector are often primarily interested in maintaining their jobs or gaining promotions. The promotion policies within the public sector are highly formalized (Trebilcock and Prichard, 1983). Consequently, public-sector managers tend to be risk-averse and prefer not to innovate, for innovation that does not succeed may adversely reflect on them, while missing an opportunity to innovate is unlikely to be noticed.

We conclude that, in theory, public-sector enterprises are likely to be less efficient and less innovative than their private-sector equivalent. However, as we noted earlier, competition in output markets is a major factor that encourages efficiency and minimizes agency costs among publicly traded companies. Thus, it may follow that when a public-sector enterprise is forced to compete with private-sector enterprises, it will become more efficient. When the public-sector enterprise is forced to compete for its very survival, it becomes in management's self-interest to become more efficient. After all, they can now be evaluated based on their market performance. Furthermore, and most importantly, their job, pay, power, and prestige depend on successful competition. Borcherding (1983: 136) argues that 'subject to sufficient competitive pressures and absent subsidies, public and private supplying firms need not differ markedly in their efficiencies.' Donahue also adopts this view: '[T]he fundamental distinction may be more between competitive output based relationships and non-competitive input based relationships rather than between profit-seekers and civil servants per se' (Donahue, 1989: 82).

Conclusion
Agency cost theory supports the proposition that the private sector is likely to be more efficient than the public sector, in both cost and performance. In the private sector, there are inherent incentive structures that help reduce agency costs. To a large extent, these incentives are absent in the public sector and result in a less-efficient, less-innovative public sector. However, when the public sector is forced to compete with the private sector for its survival, it is likely to become more efficient than when it does not compete, approaching private-sector efficiency.

THE THEORY OF THE FIRM

Economic literature on the theory of the firm has attempted to explain why some private-sector economic activity is organized in firms and other through the market (Hart, 1988). For example, if GM needs tires for its cars, should it purchase them from a tire manufacturing company or should it create its own tire manufacturing division? More generally, why do we sometimes observe firms producing their own inputs and at other times see firms contracting out the provision of inputs?

Transaction Cost Theories

Coase's pioneering analysis of this question focuses on the costs inherent in organizing an activity through either the market or the firm (Coase, 1937). When a transaction is organized through the market, information on available prices and quality must be obtained. As well, contracts must be negotiated for each desired purchase. Both of these steps are costly. On the other hand, internalizing production is also costly. Borcherding (1983) noted that Coase was not very specific in detailing these costs. Simon (1961) and Williamson (1967), however, have since asserted that the information distortion caused by private bureaucratic organization is an important cost resulting from organizing activity through the firm, because information on the value and scarcity of inputs, which would otherwise be provided by the market, is replaced by less accurate internal proxies.

Coase theorized that it is desirable to provide a service, or produce a product, within a firm so long as the costs of arranging for 'in-firm' production are cheaper than the costs of purchasing the product or service through the market. Assuming that the costs of organizing additional transactions within the firm rise with firm size, the firm will tend to expand until the costs of organizing further transactions within the firm equal the costs of carrying out the same transaction on the open market (Coase, 1937: 395).

Coase's basic approach of balancing 'in-firm' and market transaction costs remains a central theoretical approach today, over fifty years after he first proposed it. However, subsequent scholars have substantially refined and expanded the types of transaction costs that must be considered.

First, it is important to evaluate carefully the contracting and negotiating components of transactions costs. When a needed input is purchased through the market, the contract must specify exactly what is required. Arriving at a clear, concise, contractually operational definition of what is needed can be difficult and expensive, especially when the need to be fulfilled is complex or evolving. In such a case, gradual fine-tuning, through 'in-firm' production, of exactly what is required may be less costly than contracting out.

Second, monitoring costs are fundamental to any discussion of the theory of the firm. Alchian and Demsetz (1972), McManus (1975), and Williamson (1975, 1979) considered this issue extensively in the 1970s. Monitoring costs are a result of the risk of 'chiselling' or 'opportunism.' McManus (1975) argues that under both employment contracts within a firm and purchase contracts through the market, parties to the contract will tend to take advantage of opportunities to act in their self-interest for which they will not be held accountable. As an example, McManus cites the relationship between a truck owner and a driver. If the owner rents the truck to the driver, the driver's income depends on his rate of output. As a result, the driver may abuse the truck by driving too hard unless he is held accountable for depreciation. Since depreciation is hard to measure, this will be very difficult to do. On the other hand, if the driver is hired by the truck owner as an employee and paid on a per-day basis, the driver's income is no longer dependent on his/her productivity. Now, the driver will not abuse the truck, but he will also not be motivated to work as diligently or as efficiently. Thus, under both market and firm organization, the driver will be motivated by opportunism to chisel on his contract and behave inefficiently unless he can be monitored and held accountable for his action.

To control this chiselling, the principal must institute monitoring arrangements. Therefore monitoring costs and the effectiveness of monitoring efforts must be considered in addition to Coasian transaction costs in determining whether market or firm organization is ideal (Borcherding, 1983: 155). If under a market arrangement it is prohibitively expensive to monitor against potentially costly chiselling or it is impossible to fully eliminate such chiselling, it may be preferable to internalize production within the firm. Similarly, if within a firm employee chiselling is costly and it is not feasible to control it, market arrangements may be preferable.

Property-Rights Theories
In the late 1980s, Grossman and Hart (1986), Hart (1988), Hart and Moore (1988), and Holmstrom and Tirole (1989) proposed a further addition to the theory of the firm: the property-rights theory of the firm. Under this approach, the choice between market and firm organization is thought to be explained by the differing ownership patterns under each arrangement. The property-rights theorists define owner-

ship of a firm as the possession of residual rights of control over the assets of a firm. In other words, the owner has the right to use the firm's assets in any way that is not inconsistent with existing contracts.

The direct implication of this approach is that when a need is constantly evolving or is very difficult to specify in contractual terms, it may not be desirable to satisfy it through the market. This is because if the need is satisfied through a purchase in the market, all details concerning what is needed must be specified in advance. When the need is complex, this can be quite costly to accomplish. Furthermore, if changes in the desired input develop at a future date, the firm will have to renegotiate the contract, often at significant expense. However, by producing the desired product or service 'in-house,' the firm retains residual control and can make alterations in the input being produced when these are required. Through in-house production, changes in input needs can be dealt with by altering instructions given to employees on how to use the organization's assets. Under employment contracts, the agent agrees to follow the instructions of the principal, within specified limits and for a specified time (Donahue, 1989: 44). This flexibility, inherent in employment contracts, is not as easily available in market transactions.

The property-rights approach to the theory of the firm also emphasizes the effects of ownership on incentive structures. For example, contracting out is thought usually to provide greater incentives for efficiency and innovation than in-firm organization, because contracting out avoids creating large bureaucratic structures where senior management and owners have little direct connection with the production of the needed input and large agency costs exist. These incentive effects must also be considered in determining when firm organization or when market organization should be employed.

Conclusion
Market provision of needed inputs becomes preferred when needs can be easily specified and are relatively constant; when compliance with contractual terms is easily monitored; when there is little possibility for 'chiselling' by contractors; when negotiation of contracts is relatively inexpensive; and where highly differentiated inputs with few economies of scale and scope but large returns to specialization are entailed. On the other hand, 'in-firm' production becomes preferred when needs become more difficult to specify or are in a state of continuous evolution and change; when compliance with contractual terms becomes

harder to monitor; when there is an increased risk of chiselling by contractors; and when contract negotiations become more complicated, lengthy, and expensive.

APPLICATION OF THEORY TO THE PUBLIC / PRIVATE CHOICE IN GENERAL

Economic theory suggests that in general the private sector is likely to be more efficient than the public sector, particularly if the private sector is competitive. As a result, service provision is generally cheaper when undertaken through the private sector. However, there are costs associated with private-sector service provision. First of all, program objectives, requirements, and procedures must be specified in contractual or regulatory terms. This is particularly costly when these objectives, requirements, or procedures are complex or rapidly changing. In the case of WC, the service is complex and many-faceted, including involvement of stakeholders in setting policy and in adjudicating claims, and there is the need to balance the satisfaction of claimants with controlling costs. Second, compliance with program specifications must be monitored, which may be expensive or in some cases impossible. This is especially true as the program becomes increasingly complex. Again, with WC, the operations are complex, and there is an enormous variety of cases to be adjudicated consistently, so substantial effort will be required before a government could ensure that the intended policies were being followed. Unlike many of the services that studies have shown the private sector can provide at lower cost, complex rules and institutional structures will be necessary to ensure that a private provider satisfies the objectives of the WC system, and this reduces the likelihood of substantial cost savings. In arriving at a judgment, the magnitude of the efficiency gains and the costs of private-sector service provision must be balanced and compared with the achievement of the criteria for evaluating modes of provision specified above.

Empirical Evidence

While the theoretical literature strongly suggests that competition should improve both static and dynamic efficiency, the empirical literature is less clear. First consider evidence from fields other than WC, which is suggestive if not directly relevant. Evidence is available from studies of the privatization of public firms of many types, in some cases representing the privatization of a public firm that faced private competition. West (1997) analysed the privatization of Alberta liquor stores and found mixed results, concluding that prices have risen, product selection has increased, wages have fallen greatly, and employment has increased. Day (1997) concludes that privatization in the United Kingdom transformed firms that required massive public subsidies into firms paying taxes, but he presents no empirical data on performance before and after privatization. He also notes that labour-law reforms enacted at the start of privatization dramatically shifted the balance of power in labour relations away from labour for all United Kingdom firms, private and public. Bernier (1997) finds that the effects of privatization in the United Kingdom were mixed, and that competition is more important than ownership in determining productivity. He also examines privatization in Quebec and concludes that the impact on performance is mixed; it does not clearly increase the return on assets. The most complete study, by Megginson et al. (1994), studied privatization in many countries, including the United Kingdom and Eastern Europe, and found that privatized firms increased their sales, improved operating efficiency, and increased their work forces. No data were available regarding the relative quality of service before and after privatization. These studies together support the theoretical literature in suggesting that private firms may (but not must) be more efficient than public firms. But in general they deal with complete privatization rather than the introduction of competition by private providers. Furthermore, they do not offer any indication of the institutional context that would be necessary to ensure an essential goal, that the particular objectives of the WC system be met by private providers.

Turning next to the empirical literature relating to WC, we find results that range from ambiguous to unsupportive. First, consider the effects of rate regulation. Hunt, Krueger, and Burton (1988) found that the introduction of 'open competition' in Michigan in 1981 led to a 25 per cent rate decrease in the first year, which grew to 30 per cent in the second year but dropped to only 10 to 15 per cent in the third year. While rates and presumably costs declined, some problems arose, including difficulty in securing coverage for some employers. Moreover, a later study of a number of states found that open competition is associated with increased rates and costs or did not affect them at all (Schmidle, 1995). One explanation for this distinctly ambiguous result is that regulation can protect consumers by holding rates down or the regulator can be captured by the regulated firms and act to hold rates up. If actual regulation reflects an ongoing tension between these outcomes, the elimination of regulation could decrease rates in some cases and increase them in others.

Next, consider the comparison of private WC providers with public providers. Krueger and Burton (1990: 36) analyse the determinants of WC costs in the United States and find that states with a mix of public and private providers face costs 20 per cent greater than states with a purely private system. That study does not indicate how those costs compare with a purely public system, in part because the United States has so few monopoly public systems. Hyatt (1994: 62) reports that a 1990 Alberta study that compared occupational and non-occupational disability insurance concluded that the public WCB could compete with private insurers.

Two recent studies, however, cast doubt on the efficiency of private provision. Leigh and Bernstein (1997) analyse data from the U.S. Social Security Administration on WC costs relating to public insurers, both monopolistic and in competition with private firms, and private insurers, both competing with public funds and in states with purely private systems. They focus on the ratio of benefits to premiums, the 'loading ratio,' which shows the efficiency of the system in transferring premium dollars to claimants. From 1980 to 1988, the average loading ratio was 57.6 per cent for private insurers and 73.6 per cent for public insurers, a massive advantage of 16 percentage points for the public insurers. From 1989 to 1993, the average loading ratio for private insurers was 66.5 per cent, while that of public insurers was 75.9 per cent, a difference of 9.2 percentage points. After adjusting for differential tax treatment they conclude that the loading-ratio advantage of the public insurers is between 4.9 and 11.7 percentage points. They speculate that this efficiency advantage of public insurers is one reason for the creation of six additional public funds in the United States since 1980.

The most recent study is by Thomason and Burton (this volume). They compare WC costs in British Columbia and Ontario with costs in forty-five states served by private or private and public insurers, excluding the monopoly public states in the United States. Their data span the years 1975 to 1995. After adjusting for the composition of the economy in the various jurisdictions, and for differing levels of benefits, they conclude that WC costs are lower with monopoly public provision in British Columbia and in Ontario than with competitive provision in the United States. While they emphasize that their study is not definitive, and although it is difficult to correct for all institutional differences in an international study, this is significant evidence against the proposition that introducing competition in Ontario, or any other Canadian province, would lower WC costs.

Analysis of Alternative Arrangements

Public Provision, Contract Out Some Functions

This model assumes that the public WCB continues to be the only insurance carrier in the jurisdiction, but that it contracts out some of its current functions. We examine three levels of contracting-out here.

First, we could consider contracting out the routine support and administration functions listed at the bottom of table 8.2. This should not affect performance of the system with respect to any of our criteria except for administrative costs: static and dynamic efficiency. At present private firms provide all of these services to private and public clients, both small and large. While large firms often supply their own services, some also purchase some of these services from outside providers. Contracting out these functions would raise agency problems requiring monitoring the output and performance of the outside provider, but these problems are not necessarily greater than the problem of monitoring a department within the organization. The Ontario WCB has just built and occupied its own office building, so it seems unlikely that renting other space on the open market and leasing out their new building could save money, but this could be looked into. A more modest proposal would be to consider contracting out building management, cleaning, and maintenance functions to the extent that they are not already performed privately. To determine whether contracting out this set of functions would lower costs or improve the service that the WCB enjoys it would seem reasonable to commission a study of the extent to which these services are contracted out by firms the size of the WCB, and to estimate the effects on cost and service that might result from contracting out.

Second, we could consider contracting out medical functions: medical diagnosis, treatment of injury, and rehabilitation. In Ontario, most of the diagnosis and treatment is already performed by private physicians or other providers selected by the worker; little remains to contract out. The board has staff physicians who review files and advise adjudicators, but this function involves such discretion and judgment that it seems likely to be more difficult to establish a satisfactory relationship with outside physicians than with internal staff. Furthermore, our criteria include stakeholder involvement and horizontal equity, both functions that may be served better by using WCB staff unless a very close and long-term relationship is provided with an outside provider. The board has a large rehabilitation service and the portions of this service that are performed by the board may warrant consideration for contracting out. The issue here is that an effective rehabilitation service can reduce the proportion of temporary disabilities that become permanent and may reduce the percentage of partial disability, so the provision of this service is potentially important in cost control. Clearly the provider of this service must operate under carefully crafted incentives to offer effective rehabilitation without forcing workers into programs that will not be effective or requiring them to return to work if they are really not capable. Furthermore, the criteria of stakeholder involvement and horizontal equity must again be satisfied. Theory does not dictate whether these incentives can be provided more efficiently through internal management controls or through contracting out. But this function has such a large potential effect on claims costs that it is worth studying carefully, with a view either towards contracting out or towards improving the incentives within the board itself.

Third, consideration could be given to contracting out the functions of advising employers and employees regarding WC matters and promoting OHS in the workplace. The contractor would have to be deeply involved in many aspects of the board's operations so that it was fully informed and could accurately represent board policies and safety practices. This function may be difficult to monitor; one could ask WCB clients if they were satisfied with these services, but would it be possible to determine whether this advising actually follows WCB policies or not? Would it be more difficult to manage these services through an outside contractor than through internal staff? The complexity of the policies and the discretion that these staff members would have in their work argues against being able to write satisfactory contracts for outsourcing these functions.

A fourth possibility in principle is to contract out the adjudication of claims and hearing of appeals. This, however, is at the heart of the business of the board. The adjudication of individual claims provides the information that supports the development of board policies and procedures, so that if adjudication was contracted out, it would make sense for the contractor to develop policies and procedures. Even states with only private insurers provide a public appeals process separate from the court system.

Public Provision with Private Competition

This model assumes that private insurers are allowed to compete with the Ontario WCB in the provision of WC insurance. It is assumed that while benefits and eligibility continue to be specified in provincial legislation and policies, the rates charged to employers may be set by the insurers in open competition. Regulations would require insurance firms (and the WCB) to charge rates that cover current and projected liabilities in any year, effectively prohibiting the accumulation of any significant unfunded liability. As in the United States, a shortfall in any year arising from mandatory changes in benefits could be recouped over a few succeeding years, while a shortfall not arising from such a policy change would have to be made up in one or two years. No public subsidy would be allowed to the board; it would have to compete with the private sector on a level playing field. This is not 'privatization' in that the WCB would not be sold to the private sector; on the other hand, if private firms compete successfully with the WCB, its share of the market will decline and the size of the organization will have to shrink in response.

One of the criteria for evaluating modes of provision discussed earlier was involvement of stakeholders in the development and implementation of policy and procedures and the adjudication of claims. Private insurers would have to establish some internal appeal process that allowed a dissatisfied claimant to argue his case or the government would have to offer such a process. More important, the input that labour and management have into the development of general policies and procedures under the present system would have to be replicated in the new system. This seems to occur in most of the U.S. systems, where there exists a set of policies and procedures that apply to all insurers. The process for developing these policies and procedures should be similar to the current process in terms of the involvement of stakeholders. In addition, each insurer would have to have some means of discussing its own procedures and practices with its stakeholders to ensure that they were responsive to the concerns of those stakeholders and that they were consistent with the provincial policies and procedures. It would be useful to review the U.S. experience to determine the extent to which stakeholder satisfaction in states with mixed public/private systems compares to that in states with monopoly public systems, and what methods are used to deal with this problem.

The theoretical discussion above strongly suggests that the introduction of competitive firms into the WC insurance business should improve both the static and dynamic efficiency of the industry. The board would be forced to match the price and service offered by private firms or it would lose business. This competitive pressure should tend to reduce costs and improve the service offered by the board; if not, its share of the business would shrink rapidly. If the board has already exhausted all opportunities for cost saving and service improvement, then private firms, with their marketing expenses and their need to earn a return on equity, would be unable to compete and the board would remain the dominant insurer. The U.S. experience with this model suggests that the private sector would in fact secure a significant share of the market.

The empirical evidence, as discussed earlier, is much less encouraging about the benefits of introducing competition. The monopoly public insurers in Canada seem to provide benefits at lower costs than do private insurers in the United States, while the load ratios of public insurers in the U.S. are higher than those of their private competitors, implying lower costs for the public insurers. While we have found no study of a monopoly public WC carrier being privatized or being faced with new private competition, the existing evidence does not provide reassurance that the theoretical promise will be delivered in practice. This suggests a need for realistic expectations in introducing competition in Ontario.

While the Ontario WCB has run up a large unfunded liability, it is understood that the government of Ontario stands behind the board and there is no risk that the board will fail financially or fail to compensate injured workers. With private insurers, the risk of failure arises; indeed it is the very prospect of failure that provides some of the motivation for more efficient operation. Yet it would be unacceptable in Ontario that any injured worker be exposed to the risk of not receiving compensation that was legally owed because of the financial failure of an insurer. Some means would have to be found to provide back-up insurance to cover the risk of failure of a firm, probably funded in some way by a surcharge on all WC assessments. Steps would also have to be taken to ensure that this 'reinsurance' did not reduce the incentives for firms to ensure their own continuing solvency. This problem is a recurring one in the insurance industry generally, so solutions should not be hard to find.

Another criterion for assessing modes of provision presented above was prompt response to and disposition of claims. To the extent that a private insurer's market share will benefit from this promptness, the introduction of competition should improve performance under this criterion. Certainly in a line of insurance, such as automobile insurance, where the prospective claimant chooses the insurer, service makes a difference. In WC, however, the employer buys the policy and the employee makes the claim. The employer may prefer that the insurer process claims rapidly as a means of maintaining a satisfied work force. On the other hand, some employers might prefer that claims were processed slowly as a means of discouraging them and thereby keeping insurance premiums low. It is not clear, a priori, how this would play out in the WC arena, so a study of the U.S. experience might be illuminating. If both situations occur, it would be important to determine what institutional factors support the former outcome rather than the latter.

One consequence of a new competitive environment would be that the rates charged to each sector of industry would have to reflect the actual costs in that sector. There may be some fear that the private insurers will take over the profitable lines of business, leaving the WCB with industries with high loss ratios. But if this happens, the WCB will have to try to raise the rates on those industries until they cover the losses. Cross-subsidy will be largely eliminated, because any industry that is overcharged will attract entry by private insurers looking for profits, which will drive rates down to the competitive level. An industry with a costly accident record will have to pay the full cost of that dismal record in order to attract private insurers or to allow the WCB to remain solvent if it is the only insurer of such industries. And if some industry cannot pay the full cost of current accidents and injuries to its workers without facing financial ruin, then perhaps this is an industry that should not operate. In short, safe industries should not be asked to subsidize unsafe industries.

Because administration costs represent less than 15 per cent of the total costs of WC, and because the empirical literature suggests that any administrative savings may be overwhelmed by added marketing, profit taking, and other costs, any significant savings from private competition must come from reduced payments to claimants. If such savings arise from improved loss-management programs that promote improved workplace safety, leading to fewer injuries and claims, as well as more rapid and complete rehabilitation of the disabled and their speedier return to productive work, then there is a genuine efficiency gain to the economy; the savings in WC costs reflect a reduced loss of productivity and a reduction in suffering and losses by injured workers. If reduced payments to claimants result from denying legitimate claims there is no efficiency gain, but simply a shifting of costs from the WC system to the worker, to the health-insurance system, and perhaps to other forms of social assistance. It is important to try to predict which of these is the more likely outcome.

One means of determining that an insurer was unfairly denying claims or cutting workers off from disability pensions would be to record the proportion of each insurer's claims that were appealed and the proportion that were appealed successfully. The provincial WC agency should therefore be charged with maintaining such records and with investigating cases in which unusually high rates of appeals and successful appeals occurred. The fact of an unexplained high rate of successful appeals might be publicized so that workers could bargain for avoiding that WC insurer, or some sanctions might be imposed by the province if the appeal rate exceeded some threshold. It is possible that the private-market incentives of employers who wish to maintain a satisfied workforce would be sufficient to avoid the excessive denial of claims.

Another criterion for evaluating WC systems is horizontal equity. The province-wide policies and procedures that every insurer must follow would be important in promoting horizontal equity. If each firm has some consultation with its stakeholders, this should further promote horizontal equity among firms and covered workers. However, there is always the risk that even within uniform policies and procedures different insurers may reach different results in adjudicating similar claims. This argues strongly for the continued existence of a single WC appeal agency similar to the current Ontario Appeal Tribunal. The Appeal Tribunal would hear appeals from individual claims decisions of the WCB and of private insurers. Most U.S. jurisdictions have such a WC appeal body.

A frequent complaint about the U.S. WC system is the high proportion of claims that are challenged by employers and both the high cost and the delays arising from litigation over WC claims. Canada is generally proud of having avoided these challenges, costs, and delays. The delays violate the objective of prompt disposition, and the costs violate the efficiency criterion. It would be important in any move that allowed private insurers into the WC business to avoid an escalation to confrontation and litigation. An essential part of this model would be a continuance of the existing policy in Canada that decisions on individual claims cannot be challenged in court (Ison, 1989: 3). But would stakeholders be satisfied with this policy in the context of private insurance companies? The answer probably depends on the success in establishing the stakeholder – involvement and horizontal-equity mechanisms discussed above.

Another criterion is flexibility and responsiveness. The theoretical discussion suggested that a competitive private sector should be more flexible and responsive than a monopolist, public or private. Allowing the entry of private insurers would likely improve the flexibility and responsiveness of WC service in Ontario. The principal caveat is that private carriers will be heavily regulated, will have to follow provincial policies and procedures, and their claims adjudication will be subject to appeal to the WCAT. There is always the risk that these factors will strangle flexibility and responsiveness. Therefore, the design of the policies and procedures should include serious consideration of this criterion and attempt to provide fairness and predictability without undue constraints on changing procedures.

The final problem, but not the smallest, is how to deal with the existing unfunded liability. If the WCB remained as the sole provider of WC insurance, the unfunded liability would likely be paid down by imposing a surcharge on employer assessments for a period of years as is currently occurring in Ontario. Part of it could also be paid out of general tax revenues on the grounds that it was created by government policy in retroactively raising benefits (Vaillancourt, 1995: 83, 84). If private firms are allowed to enter the WC insurance business, they should be treated just like the WCB with respect to paying down the unfunded liability. Thus, a surcharge could be applied to all WC premiums in the province, whether charged by the WCB or by private insurers; the total surcharge would be applied to paying down the unfunded liability. If some general tax revenues are to be used to retire it, this affects the total to be paid from a surcharge, but not the principle involved. Under this approach, the method of reducing the unfunded liability is unaffected by whether or not competition is allowed.

Purely Private Model

This model assumes that the WCB is replaced by private insurers with no public insurance provider remaining. The legislature would continue to set benefits and eligibility criteria. In addition, a remnant of the WCB would continue to promulgate general policies and procedures to be followed by the insurers. The remnant would also continue to operate a single province-wide appeal mechanism like the current WC Appeals Tribunal. Finally, the remnant would carry out all of the regulatory functions identified in the public/private mixed model above.

This model might be implemented in either of two ways. First, when private entry into the industry is allowed, the WCB might stop providing insurance and rapidly contract its operations until it only provided the ongoing functions listed in the preceding paragraph, as well as continuing to administer its existing pool of permanent disability cases. The unfunded liability would be taken care of as in the mixed model above, with some combination of a surcharge on all WC premiums and a transfer from the province's general tax revenues. The ongoing functions would also be paid for by a surcharge on all WC premiums. Second, the WCB might be divided into operating units, perhaps each of its local and regional offices representing one unit, and those units offered to private insurers, with arrangements regarding the retention of existing workers and coverage of existing liabilities. This second method would be a form of privatization similar to that evolved in the United Kingdom and Europe since the late 1970s. That experience has shown there are myriad ways of selling off public firms that have achieved widely varying degrees of success (Megginson, Nash, and Van Randenborgh, 1994).

It is not apparent that this model has any advantages over the mixed model in which private firms enter and compete with the WCB. In the mixed model, if the private sector is in fact more efficient than the WCB, it will garner an increasing share of the market until the board improves its efficiency enough to maintain its share of the market. If the private firms are not more efficient, their share will never grow large. But if the WCB is abolished or sold off, and if the private sector is no more efficient, or its performance is less satisfactory than that of the board, the board will be gone by the time this is known with certainty. Furthermore, the continued existence of the board in the mixed model provides the government with a window on the industry through which it can learn more about its operation than it can by gathering information from private insurance companies. This window would be closed with the abolition of the board as an insurer.

The theoretical literature suggested that most of the benefits of private operation could be secured by allowing private firms to compete with a public operator. Furthermore, the limited empirical evidence on WC suggests that private firms may have cost/premium ratios greater than in the public sector. The complexity of the objectives for the WC system and the extensive criteria by which its performance must be judged mean that abolition of the public provider and turning the business over to private firms carries much greater risks than when this is done with waste collection or other simpler services. These risks argue against full privatization.

Conclusion

While I have not gathered new data for this study and while empirical data on the relative performance of public and private WC insurers is limited, some tentative conclusions are possible.

First, even if the WCB is to remain a monopoly provider of insurance it should study carefully the possible savings that might accrue from contracting out some of its current functions. Purely administrative functions, such as those listed at the bottom of table 8.2 should be considered, although the potential savings there are small. More important, the board should carefully consider contracting out its rehabilitation service under an arrangement that offers incentives for the contractor to provide good service at a reasonable cost, to reduce the proportion of temporary claims that become permanent, and to increase the rate at which the permanently disabled return to productive work. The high cost of permanent disability claims means that a reduction in their number and duration can greatly reduce the costs of WC.

Second, it is possible, though far from certain, that allowing private insurers to compete with the WCB would reduce the costs of WC and also improve service to the clients, both employers and employees. Competition might force reductions in administrative costs that are unlikely at the board without this competitive pressure, although it will introduce new marketing and capital costs. More important, it would force a careful examination of loss-management policies and an attendant drive to reduce accident rates, improve rehabilitation, reduce the rate at which lost-time injuries become permanent disability claims, and increase the rate at which those workers assessed as permanently disabled are able to return to the work force. While public boards are working on all of these issues today, competition may force them to find ways to do better. The potential savings from such improvements are large, although the existing empirical literature gives no assurance that lower total costs will result. In this situation, further study of the introduction of private insurers of WC in Ontario seems warranted.

If private WC insurers are allowed to enter the Ontario market, this entry should be subject to procedures that would ensure the pursuit of the criteria identified: prompt response to and disposition of inquiries and claims by clients; involvement of and responsiveness to stakeholders in developing policies and procedures, adjudicating claims, and evaluating performance; horizontal equity, so that similarly situated workers are treated in a similar fashion; and flexibility and reversibility of policies and decisions. The requisite procedures should include continuing the development of province-wide policies and procedures that would be applicable to all insurers, including the WCB; ensuring a single province-wide appeal body by continuing the operation of the WC Appeals Tribunal; keeping records of the rate at which individual insurers' claims decisions are appealed and successfully appealed, and disseminating this information, as well as perhaps penalizing firms that are subject to excessive successful appeals; retaining the ban on challenges to individual WC adjudications in court; ensuring that workers are protected against any loss in the event that a private insurer fails; and paying down the unfunded liability through a combination of shifting a portion to the general tax revenues and levying a surcharge on all WC premiums in the province, whether charged by the board or private insurers. Moreover, it must be recognized that the introduction of private insurers may increase the political pressure to reduce the generosity of WC benefit levels, particularly given the high benefit levels in Ontario compared to that in most U.S. states in which private insurers currently operate.

While there may be significant benefits from allowing private insurers to compete with the WCB, it is not apparent that there are further benefits to be gained from privatizing the board so that there is no public WC insurer. If private insurers are more efficient than the board, they will take an increasing share of the market in a mixed system. And if there are serious problems in achieving Ontario's WC objectives with private insurers, these problems can be addressed in the mixed system when those firms still have a small share of the market. If the problems cannot be solved, then the private entry could be rolled back. But if the WCB is abolished or completely privatized and if serious problems emerge, there is no remaining public provider to fall back on. Moreover, there is no insurer of last resort for firms or industries that the private sector will not voluntarily insure. The omelette has been made and the eggs cannot be unscrambled. Hence, moving beyond the mixed model to full privatization of the WCB does not seem to be warranted by the available evidence.

Perhaps the greatest need, given the potential of private entry into WC insurance, is for further study of the experience in other jurisdictions that are more like Canada than the United States, such as Australia, but that have private provision of WC insurance. There is also a need for careful study to design the institutional arrangements that would achieve Ontario's WC objectives in a mixed system. Issues to be studied include the rules for covering the current unfunded liability, the rules for ensuring the financial security of workers covered by private insurers, the extent to which rates should be regulated if at all, and the arrangements for monitoring and reporting on the performance of private insurers.

NOTES

1 Monopoly public: Nevada, North Dakota, Ohio, Washington, West Virginia, Wyoming. Mixed: Arizona, California, Colorado, Idaho, Maryland, Michigan, Montana, New York, Oklahoma, Oregon, Pennsylvania, Utah.
2 Colorado discontinued while Hawaii, Minnesota, Louisiana, Texas, Tennessee, Missouri, and Kentucky created. In 1991, Maine authorized the creation of a state fund, but the legislation was repealed in 1992. In 1995, Nevada announced that a state fund would begin operation in 1999 (as it has).
3 Information in this section was gathered in part from the web site of the Wisconsin Worker's Compensation Division: 'Wisconsin Worker's Compensation Guide' at http://badger.state.wi.us/agencies/dilhr/wc/wkc18p.html in March 1997.
4 See Alchian and Demsetz, 1972.

REFERENCES

AASCIF, American Association of State Compensation Insurance Funds. 1995. 1995 Fact Book. Texas: Texas Workers' Compensation Insurance Fund.

Alchian, A., and H. Demsetz. 1972. 'Production, Information Costs, and Economic Organization.' *American Economic Review* 62: 777.

Allingham, R., and D. Hyatt. 1995. 'Measuring the Impact of Vocational Rehabilitation on the Probability of Post-Injury Return to Work.' In T. Thomason and R. Chaykowski, eds, *Research in Canadian Workers' Compensation*, 158–80. Kingston: Industrial Relations Centre Press.

Ballantyne, D., and K. Joyce. 1996. *Workers' Compensation in Illinois: Administrative Inventory.* Boston: Workers' Compensation Research Institute, WC-96-9.

Ballantyne, D., and C. Telles. 1991a. *Workers' Compensation in Minnesota: Administrative Inventory.* Boston: Workers' Compensation Research Institute, WC-91-1.

– 1991b. *Workers' Compensation in Pennsylvania: Administrative Inventory.* Boston: Workers' Compensation Research Institute, WC-91-4.

– 1992. *Workers' Compensation in Wisconsin: Administrative Inventory.* Boston: Workers' Compensation Research Institute, WC-92-7.

Bernier, L. 1997. 'The Promises of Privatization: The Idea and the Statistics.' Paper presented at the Privatization Roundtable of the Centre for the Study of the State and Market, University of Toronto, 17 January 1997.

Boden, L., J. DeFinis, and C. Fleischman. 1990. 'Medical Cost Containment in Workers' Compensation a National Inventory.' Boston: Workers' Compensation Research Institute, WC-90-4.

Borcherding, T.E. 1983. 'Towards a Positive Theory of Public Sector Supply Arrangements.' In J.R.S. Prichard, ed., *Crown Corporations in Canada*, 99–184. Toronto: Butterworths.

Bush, W., and A. Denzau. 1977. 'The Voting Behaviour of Bureaucrats and Public Sector Growth.' In T.E. Borcherding, ed., *Budgets and Bureaucrats: The Sources of Government Growth*, 90–9. Durham, NC: Duke University Press.

Chaykowski, R., and T. Thomason. 1995. 'Canadian Workers' Compensation: Institutions and Economics.' In T. Thomason and R. Chaykowski, eds, *Research in Canadian Workers' Compensation*, 1–42. Kingston: Industrial Relations Centre Press.

Coase, R. 1937. 'The Nature of the Firm.' *Economica* 4: 386–405.

Daniels, R.J., and M.J. Trebilcock. 1995. 'The Future of Ontario Hydro: A Review of Structural and Regulatory Options.' In R.J. Daniels, ed., *Ontario Hydro at the Millennium: Has Monopoly's Moment Passed?* 1–52. Kingston: McGill-Queen's University Press.

Day, Sir G. 1997. Speech given at the Privatization Roundtable of the Centre for the Study of the State and Market, University of Toronto, 16 January 1997.

Dee, G., N. McCombie, and G. Newhouse. 1987. *Workers' Compensation in Ontario.* Toronto: Butterworths.

Dewees, D.N., M.J. Trebilcock, K.B. Snell, and I. Freedman. 1993. 'The Regula-
tion of Solid Waste Management in Ontario: A Policy Perspective.' Report to
the Ontario Waste Management Association, Toronto. Mimeo.
Donahue, J. 1989. *The Privatization Decision: Public Ends, Private Means.* New
York: Basic Books Inc.
Easterbrook, F.H., and D. Fischel. 1991. *The Economic Structure of Corporate Law.*
Cambridge, Mass.: Harvard University Press.
Fama, E. 1980. Agency Problems and the Theory of the Firm.' *Journal of Political
Economy* 88: 288–307.
Grossman, S., and O. Hart. 1986. 'The Costs and Benefits of Ownership: A
Theory of Vertical and Lateral Integration.' *Journal of Political Economy* 94:
631–719.
Hart, O.D. 1988. 'Incomplete Contracts and the Theory of the Firm.' *Journal of
Law, Economics, and Organization* 4: 119–39.
Hart, O.D., and J. Moore. 1988. 'Property Rights and the Nature of the Firm.'
Cambridge, Mass.: MIT Discussion Paper.
Holmstrom, B., and J. Tirole. 1989. 'The Theory of the Firm.' In R. Schmalensee
and R. Willig, eds, *Handbook of Industrial Organization Vol. 1*, 61–133. Amster-
dam: North Holland.
Hunt, H., A. Krueger, and J.F. Burton, Jr. 1988. 'The Impact of Open Competi-
tion in Michigan on the Employers' Costs of Workers' Compensation.' In
P. Borba and D. Appel, eds, *Workers' Compensation Insurance Pricing*, 109–44.
New York: Kluwer.
Hyatt, D. 1994. 'Workers' Compensation in Canada: An Overview.' Report to
Liberty International Canada. Mimeo.
Ison, T. 1989. *Workers' Compensation in Canada.* 2nd ed. Butterworths: Toronto.
Jensen, M., and C. Smith 1985. 'Stockholder, Manager, and Creditor Interests:
Applications of Agency Theory.' In E. Altman and M. Subrahmanyam, eds,
Recent Advances in Corporate Finance, 93–131. Homewood, Ill.: Richard D.
Irwin.
Krueger, A.B., and J.F. Burton, Jr. 1990. 'The Employers' Costs of Workers'
Compensation Insurance: Magnitudes, Determinants and Public Policy.'
Review of Economics and Statistics 72: 228–40.
Leigh, J.P., and J. Bernstein. 1997. 'Public and Private Workers' Compensation.'
Journal of Occupational and Environmental Medicine 39: 119–21.
McManus, J.C. 1975. 'The Costs of Alternative Economic Organization.'
Canadian Journal of Economics 8: 334–50.
Megginson, W.L., R.C. Nash, and M. Randenborgh. 1994. 'The Financial and
Operating Performance of Newly Privatized Firms: An International Empir-
ical Analysis.' *Journal of Finance* 49: 403–52.

Ontario Workers' Compensation Board. 1996a. *1995 Annual Report*. Toronto: WCB.
– 1996b. Statistical supplement to the *1995 Annual Report*. Toronto: WCB.
Schmidle, T. 1995. 'The Impact of Insurance Pricing Deregulation on Workers' Compensation Costs.' *John Burton's Workers' Compensation Monitor* 8: 1–12.
Simon, H.A. 1961. *Administrative Behavior*. 2nd ed. New York: Macmillan.
   Trebilcock, M.J. 1994. *The Prospects for Reinventing Government*. Toronto: C.D. Howe Institute.
Trebilcock, M.J., and J.R.S. Prichard. 1983. 'Crown Corporations: The Calculus of Instrument Choice.' In J.R.S. Prichard, ed., *Crown Corporations in Canada: The Calculus of Instrument Choice*, 1–97. Toronto: Butterworths.
U.S. Department of Labor. 1987. *State Workers' Compensation Laws*. Washington: U.S. Department of Labor, Employment Standards Administration, Office of State Liaison and Legislative Analysis, Division of State Workers' Compensation Programs.
Vaillancourt, F. 1994. *The Financing of Workers' Compensation Boards in Canada, 1960–1990*. Canadian Tax Paper no. 98. Toronto: Canadian Tax Foundation.
– 1995. 'The Financing and Pricing of WCBs in Canada: Existing Arrangements, Possible Changes.' In T. Thomason, F. Vaillancourt, T.J. Bogyo, and A. Stritch, eds, *Chronic Stress: Workers' Compensation in the 1990s*, 66–91. Toronto: C.D. Howe Institute.
West, D.S. 1997. 'The Privatization of Alberta's Liquor Stores: An Overview.' Paper presented at the Privatization Roundtable of the Centre for the Study of the State and Market, University of Toronto, 17 January 1997.
Williamson, O.E. 1967. 'Hierarchical Control and Optimal Firm Size.' *Journal of Political Economy* 75: 123–38.
– 1975. *Markets and Hierarchies: Analysis and Antitrust Implications*. New York: Free Press.
– 1979. 'Transaction Cost Economics: The Governance of Contractual Relations.' *Journal of Law and Economics* 22: 233–61.

9 The Cost of Workers' Compensation in Ontario and British Columbia

TERRY THOMASON and JOHN F. BURTON, JR[1]

Workers' compensation costs merit scrutiny because they have risen markedly over the last thirty years, and there is currently considerable variation in these costs across different jurisdictions. For example, the per-employee cost of workers' compensation in Ontario rose from $149.50 in 1961 to $572.56 in 1994 (both in 1994 constant dollars). Ontario workers' compensation expenditures were about 0.57 per cent of provincial GDP in 1960, while they amount to about 1.3 per cent of GDP today. Moreover, on a per capita basis, compensation benefit costs – the costs of workers' compensation excluding administrative expenses – are higher in Ontario than in any other Canadian jurisdiction. In 1994, Ontario benefit costs were about two and a half times those of Prince Edward Island and nearly 25 per cent greater than the national average on a per capita basis (Human Resources Development Canada, 1995).

It is sometimes alleged that high compensation costs have impaired the competitiveness of Canadian firms and that these high costs are due to overly generous cash (indemnity) benefits relative to other jurisdictions. The increased flow of north–south trade following the negotiation of the Free Trade Agreement in 1989 and the North American Free Trade Agreement in 1992 have led to concerns about the costs of Canadian social programs, including workers' compensation, relative to the cost of these programs in the United States.

Despite these concerns, the issue of relative costs of Canadian workers' compensation is not well researched. In part, this is because a simple comparison of Canadian compensation expenditures or assessment revenues with comparable data from other jurisdictions is inappropriate; such a comparison does not account for differences in the industrial mix of different jurisdictions and for the fact that the risk of injury differs among industries. For example, one province may have a substantial proportion of its employment in relatively low-risk industries, such as financial institutions, while another may have a large share of employment in relatively high-risk sectors, such as mining or construction. A simple comparison of the average assessment or the average benefits paid may lead to the mistaken conclusion that compensation costs are lower for comparable employers in the former province than in the latter. An appropriate cost measure must account for differences in risk across industries.

In recent years, a debate has ensued in some Canadian provinces over the relative merits of the exclusive, monopoly provision of workers' compensation insurance through government funds. Employer groups in several provinces have endorsed proposals to privatize workers' compensation.[2] In 1996, the newly elected Progressive Conservative government of Ontario floated a proposal that would give the Workers' Compensation Board the statutory authority to implement a partial privatization of workers' compensation under the auspices of a plan known as the 'direct payment model' (Jackson, 1996). Under direct payment, the employer would be directly responsible for compensation benefits for the first six weeks of disability and would have the option of purchasing insurance that would pay for these benefits. While the proposal never made its way into legislation, it is still of policy interest.

Given the ongoing debate on these issues, a comparison of Canadian compensation costs with those of U.S. jurisdictions, where the private sector plays a much larger role in the provision of compensation insurance, seems particularly appropriate. This chapter is the first comprehensive investigation of workers' compensation costs in Ontario relative to other North American jurisdictions, using a methodology that controls for differences among jurisdictions in industrial composition. Our empirical work is based on two Canadian jurisdictions. Ontario is the largest jurisdiction in Canada and uses a form of wage-loss compensation for permanent disabilities.[3] British Columbia is the third largest and pays permanently disabled claimants a pension based on functional impairment. Both are under intense policy scrutiny, with a royal commission on workers' compensation recently examining the program in British Columbia. Specifically, we compare Ontario and BC compensation costs with those paid by employers in 45 U.S. states[4] for the years 1975 through 1995. In addition, for this same period, we construct an indemnity benefit index that allows us to compare the generosity of compensation benefits across jurisdictions and to explore the relationship between compensation benefits and costs.

The remainder of the chapter proceeds as follows. In the next section we discuss the relevant institutional and theoretical considerations involved in a U.S.-Canada comparison of workers' compensation. Specifically, we present a theoretical model of compensation costs, and discuss the differences in the institutional regimes that may have an impact on such costs. We then describe the methodology used to estimate compensation costs for employers in the two countries. Multivariate regression analysis is used to examine the determinants of the variation in costs, including benefit generosity. Finally, we describe and apply a procedure to compare U.S. and Canadian compensation costs under different institutional regimes, holding the effects of other variables constant, and present the results. We find that the costs of workers' compensation in Canadian jurisdictions compare favourably with costs in U.S. jurisdictions. Summary comments conclude the chapter.

Institutional and Theoretical Considerations

Workers' compensation programs are financed through employer payroll assessments or insurance premiums that are based on a firm's payroll and the relative risk of injury of the industry and of the firm, as measured by prior benefit payments. Specifically, in all North American jurisdictions, employers are assigned to risk categories based on the firm's occupation or industrial sector. Base (or manual) assessment rates, expressed as a percentage of firm payroll, are calculated for each rate class, using historical data on the relative frequency and severity of injuries experienced by employees in the category.[5] Individual assessments paid by firms may vary from these manual rates owing to a variety of other factors, including firm-level experience-rating modifications, which are designed to align firm compensation costs with accident experience. As a result, individual assessment rates are greater for firms with higher than average accident rates compared to other firms in the industry and vice versa.

Theoretical Model

The previous description of the workers' compensation funding mechanism suggests the following simple model of compensation costs (see Krueger and Burton, 1990). Ignoring administrative expenses (and, in the case of privately provided insurance, marketing costs and profits) the expected surplus or deficit in workers' compensation accident reserves for each covered worker (E[P]) are:

$$E[P] = (1 - p)C + p\,(C - B)$$

where p is the probability of injury, C is the per-worker cost of workers' compensation insurance (alternatively, the per-worker assessment on the employer), and B represents compensation benefits paid. If compensation insurance is actuarially fair, then C = pB.

We may consider administrative costs by allowing for a loading factor that is proportional to workers' compensation rates, so that in an actuarially fair system C = ϕC + pB, where N is the loading factor, or C = pB/(1 − ϕ). Taking the natural log of costs, we have

$$\log (C) = -\log(1 - \phi) + \log (p) + \log (B).$$

This suggests that a regression specification estimating compensation costs should (1) include measures of the probability of injury, p, and expected compensation benefits, B, and (2) assume a log-log functional form. Of crucial importance to our analysis, this equation also suggests that the intercept term provides an estimate of the impact of different institutional arrangements in each jurisdiction and time period, after controlling for differences in benefit generosity, B, and risk levels, p. As discussed subsequently, our empirical work involves relating aggregate measures of workers' compensation costs, C, in different jurisdictions and time periods, to various institutional arrangements that can affect these costs, after controlling for differences in the injury rate, p, and benefit generosity, B, in those jurisdictions.

Relevant Institutional Considerations

Despite certain similarities in pricing procedures, there are significant institutional differences between compensation programs in the United States and Canada. The most important is the extent of private-sector involvement in the provision of compensation insurance. In all Canadian provinces, benefits are provided by a monopolistic government fund; only six U.S. states have a similar arrangement. In the remaining states, private insurance companies are responsible for the largest share of benefits paid to compensation claimants. Data from 1995 indicate that private carriers paid 50.7 per cent of all benefits paid in the United States, while state funds and self-insured employers paid 23.6 and 25.7 per cent of benefits, respectively (National Academy of Social Insurance, 1997: table 4).

The institutional characteristics of the private insurance market vary substantially across those states. In particular, there is significant variation with respect to two institutional features: (1) the extent to which compensation rates are regulated by state regulatory bodies and (2) the extent to which firms can voluntarily leave the insurance market through self-insurance. Both have important cost implications.

Rate Regulation in the U.S. Insurance Market

Historically, the price of workers' compensation insurance has been regulated by state insurance commissions. Policy makers introduced insurance regulation initially because of concerns that excessive competition among insurance companies caused carriers to set premiums too low, which led to widespread insurer insolvency and substantial losses for policy holders (O'Connor, Domagalski, and Walters, 1995). More recently, rate regulation has been justified on the grounds that legally mandated compensation insurance imposes an obligation on the state to determine that rates are reasonable. Ratepayers have argued that oligopolistic pricing by insurers, coordinated by ratemaking bureaus (see below), results in supra-competitive compensation insurance prices.

Under traditional rate regulation, rating bureaus – organizations created and funded by the insurance industry – collected historical data on losses and administrative expenses, which were used to construct rates, including a provision for reasonable profits.[6] These rates were submitted to the state insurance commission for approval, which was required before insurers could use them. At its discretion, the commission could reject the proposed rate structure and substitute another. Once this rate schedule was approved, insurers were required to adhere to it and to adjustment factors, such as experience-rating formulas, that were uniform for all carriers.

By the early 1980s policy makers began to question the usefulness of traditional rate regulation. Several states enacted legislation designed to encourage competition. The legislation took several forms. In some jurisdictions, insurers were allowed to deviate generally from bureau rates upon approval of the insurance commission or to use schedule rating, which selectively reduces rates for individual risks. Other states have adopted more far-reaching legislation, sometimes called 'open competition,' that substantially eliminates rate regulation altogether, permitting insurers to set rates without first seeking commission approval.

Rate regulation potentially has a significant impact on employer compensation costs (Schmidle, 1994 and 1995). However, economic theory offers no unambiguous predictions concerning the nature of its effects. Rate regulation is a political process. Regulated rates may either be lower, higher, or the same as those charged in a competitive market, depending, among other things, on the political agenda of the regulatory agency. A regulatory agency that has been 'captured' by insurers will set rates above their competitive levels, while an agency that is overly influenced by policyholders (employers) will set rates below the market price (a condition known as rate suppression). Even when the agency pursues a public-service objective – attempts to set rates at competitive levels – in the short run, it may not succeed, owing to the delay between changing market conditions and the agency's response, a phenomenon known as regulatory lag.[7]

Self-Insurance

Under certain conditions, employers in the United States may choose to self-insure rather than purchase compensation insurance.[8] In the past, this option was limited to relatively large employers who could satisfy certain financial requirements. More recently, most states have allowed employers to form self-insured groups. Most states also permit insurers to offer policies with deductibles, a form of partial self-insurance. It is possible that there is a relationship between the extent of self-insurance and the cost of insurance in the voluntary market. Self-insured employers are typically large firms that are likely to be less risky than smaller companies owing to economies of scale in accident prevention. In addition, these firms are likely to have more highly developed internal labour markets; such firms have a greater incentive to avoid the loss of specific human capital through occupational accidents. For both reasons, insurance rates may be higher in jurisdictions where self-insurance is permitted, since low-cost employers choose to opt out of the insurance market.

Cost Methodology

As previously noted, the initial step in computing meaningful employers' costs of workers' compensation insurance in both Canada and the United States is the construction of a uniform set of industrial and occupational categories. Then for each of the insurance classifications contained in the set of classes to be compared, an appropriate initial insurance rate (the manual rate) can be located in the jurisdiction's manual rate schedule. Manual rates are specified as a certain number of dollars per $100 of weekly earnings for each employee.

Manual rates are only the first step for making comparisons that accurately reflect employers' actual costs. The weekly workers' compensation premium for most employers is *not* simply the product of their manual rate and weekly payroll. Rather, costs are affected by myriad modifying factors, which vary significantly between Canadian jurisdictions and most U.S. states. In the section that immediately follows, we will describe the procedure used to construct compensation-cost measures for U.S. jurisdictions. We then turn our attention to Canadian cost measures.

U.S. Compensation Costs

Table 9.1 provides a guide to the eleven-step procedure used to determine adjusted manual rates for most U.S. states, which represent the percentage of payroll expended by an employer on workers' compensation insurance (see Burton, 1966; Burton and Krueger, 1986; and Burton and Schmidle, 1990, for further details).[9] These adjusted manual rates can also be termed the measurable net costs to policyholders.

As can be seen, the rate-setting process begins with the calculation of pure premium rates, which are the expected losses per $100 of payroll for employers in a particular insurance class. Pure premiums are essentially reserves established by insurers to allow the payment of all cash benefits, medical care, and rehabilitation for all injuries that occur in a policy period.[10] Pure premiums also include (in most jurisdictions) the costs incurred by insurers in the claims-adjustment process, which are also termed loss-adjustment expenses. Pure premiums are adjusted by a *loading factor*, to obtain *manual rates*. The loading factor covers other insurance-carrier expenses, such as general administrative expenses, commissions, profits, and contingencies.

Manual rates are then adjusted by a number of factors to pro-

TABLE 9.1
Derivation of the employers' cost of workers' compensation insurance

	1	Pure premiums
X	2	Adjustment for loading factor
=	3	Manual rates
X	4	Experience-rating modification
=	5	Standard earned premium excluding constants
/	6	Adjustment for expense constant
=	7	Standard earned premium including constants
X	8	Adjustment for premium discounts, retrospective rating, schedule rating, and deviations
=	9	Net earned premium
X	10	Adjustment for dividends to policyholders
=	11	Adjusted manual rates

duce the rate actually paid by the employer. The first of these is the *experience-rating modification*, which is multiplied by the manual rate to produce what is termed the *standard earned premium excluding constants*. The experience-rating modification accounts for the fact that manual rates for large employers are adjusted to reflect the employers' own accident experience. This means that employers whose experience is worse than average have their rates adjusted upward, while employers with below-average experience have their rates reduced. (Experience rating is discussed in Kralj, chapter 10, this volume.)

The employer's premium may then be modified by the addition of flat charges that are assessed on a per-policy basis and are known as *expense or loss constants*. Expense constants are designed to cover the minimum costs of issuing and servicing a policy, while *loss constants* are intended to compensate for the generally inferior safety record of small businesses. When the standard earned premium excluding constants is adjusted to reflect the additional costs of these charges, the result is termed *the standard earned premium including constants*.

The standard earned premium including constants may be further adjusted by a number of devices. Owing to economies of scale large employers may be entitled to either *premium discounts or retrospective rating*. Retrospective rating is a form of experience rating whereby the firm's rate is determined by its experience under the current policy on an ex post facto basis as compared to a prospective adjustment based on experience from previous periods.[11] In some states, rates may be further modified by the use of *deviations* and *schedule rating*, which are pricing devices designed to introduce competition into the regulated rate-making process. Recall that, historically, workers' compensation rates for individual insurers were set by a rating organization, subject to approval by the state regulatory agency. A deviation is a departure from the rating organization's rate. It typically must be applied on a uniform basis to all insureds covered by the insurer and is also subject to regulatory approval. Under a schedule rating plan the individual employer's rate is increased or decreased based on a subjective evaluation of factors such as the employer's loss-control program.

Adjusting the standard earned premium to account for these premium discounts, retrospective rating, schedule rating, and deviations results in the *net earned premium*. Finally, a substantial proportion of workers' compensation insurance in the United States is written by mutual companies or stock companies with participating policies. While these companies normally use a quantity discount schedule that is less steeply graded than that of the non-participating stock companies, they also pay dividends that usually decrease policyholders' net costs to levels below those charged by non-participating stock companies, especially for large employers. Thus, to produce the *adjusted manual rates*, which can be interpreted as the percentage of payroll actually expended on workers' compensation by employers, it is necessary to subtract *dividends to policyholders* paid by mutual and participating stock companies from the net earned premium.

Aggregate measures, by state and year, of adjusted manual rates serve as one of our cost measures for U.S. states and as a dependent variable in our regression analyses. This aggregate measure is a weighted average, which was computed using data on 71 individual rate classes. The proportion of total U.S. payroll attributable to the rate group is used as weights. Data on manual rates and modification factors necessary to calculate adjusted manual rates were obtained from the NCCI and independent state rating bureaus. These 71 classifications were chosen because they are common to most jurisdictions, account for a substantial proportion of total payroll, and represent a broad spectrum of industries.[12] A second dependent measure, called *net costs*, is obtained by multiplying this rate measure by an average weekly wage in 1995 dollars.

Canadian Compensation Costs

The rate-setting process in Canadian jurisdictions is much simpler.

Base assessment rates – which are similar to manual rates – are first constructed to reflect both losses, in terms of benefits paid to injured workers, and administrative costs. In most Canadian jurisdictions, these base rates are then adjusted by an experience-rating modification to produce the rate actually charged to employers. With the exception of Quebec, which charges an expense constant and has a retrospective plan for large employers, no further adjustment to the base rate is necessary.

Data on assessment rates were obtained from the Workers' Compensation Boards of Ontario and British Columbia for the period 1975 to 1995. Data obtained from British Columbia reflect the effect of experience rating. An experience-rating modification factor was calculated for Ontario using off-balance data provided by the Ontario Workplace Safety and Insurance Board.

Canadian-U.S. cost comparisons raise three additional issues.

1. *Comparability of rate groups*: For the most part, U.S. jurisdictions used a stable and uniform set of approximately 550 rate classes during this period. Unfortunately, Ontario and British Columbia rate classifications are not only different from those used in the United States, but they vary over time. British Columbia used 86 groups at the beginning of the period and 93 groups at the end. Currently, Ontario uses 219 rate groups. Up until 1992, the province's classification scheme included slightly more than 100 rate groups. Consequently, it was not possible to obtain manual rates for classes that correspond exactly to U.S. rate groups.

Our strategy was to identify corresponding Ontario rate groups for each of our 71 U.S. classes by asking the following question: if a firm from one of our U.S. classifications were to move, to which Canadian classification would it be assigned? Since Canadian rate groups were much broader than those in United States, it was a relatively easy matter to identify corresponding Canadian classes for each U.S. rate group. However, in a few instances a U.S. rate could reasonably be assigned to two or more Canadian categories. When this occurred we computed a weighted average of the rates charged by the Canadian classes, using the proportion of Canadian payroll as weights. This process yielded a set of assessment rates that corresponded to our 71 U.S. rates that were then aggregated into a single average measure using U.S. payroll proportions as weights.[13]

A problem with this methodology is that if rate groups do not correspond exactly, then cost differences could be attributed to differences in the nature of the underlying risks. However, the impact of this 'composition effect' on price variation is minimized as the number of rate groups increases.[14] As indicated, we use 71 rate groups that are common to most jurisdictions and account for a substantial proportion of total payroll, so that aggregate measures should provide a reasonably accurate index of compensation costs.[15]

2. *Limitations on assessable payroll*: Unlike U.S. jurisdictions during this period, Canadian workers' compensation programs have limitations on assessable payroll (i.e., the total of annual wages paid to employees that is less than or equal to the maximum assessable wage). Consequently, taking the ratio of assessments charged to assessable payroll will overestimate 'adjusted manual rates' for Canadian jurisdictions relative to U.S. rates.[16] The Workers' Compensation Board of British Columbia provided us with information on total payroll by rate group, which allowed us to compute the 'total payroll' adjusted manual rate directly. Unfortunately, we were unable to obtain similar data from Ontario.

To correct for this problem we estimated total payroll for Ontario using a wage distribution obtained from the Labour Market Activity Survey and the industrial aggregate average weekly wage for Ontario from the Labor Force Survey.[17]

3. *Deficit financing*: In recent years, several Canadian provinces, including and most notably Ontario, have experienced sizable annual budget deficits, so that employer assessments do not reflect the true cost of workers' compensation in those provinces. (Problems relating to the Ontario data are discussed in Gunderson and Hyatt, chapter 6, this volume.) Since workers' compensation is, by and large, privately provided in the United States, similar deficits do not occur over a sustained period, so that adjusted manual rates are a more accurate estimate of 'true' costs. Canadian assessment rates were adjusted on an annual basis to reflect these shortfalls, so that rates were raised in those years where expenses exceeded income and reduced when there was an annual budget surplus.[18]

It is important to note two things about these adjustments. First, while in the long run U.S. insurers cannot sustain deficit funding, they can incur deficits in the short run; throughout the late 1980s and early 1990s, U.S. insurers experienced substantial underwriting losses in the workers' compensation line. To the extent that we have not accounted for these losses, we have underestimated U.S. costs relative to adjusted

Canadian costs. Second, our adjustments do not account for that part of the deficit that is due to legislated benefit changes that applied retroactively, that is, changes in benefits paid to workers who had been injured in prior years. These benefit changes were responsible for a substantial proportion of the deficit in some years.

Figures 9.1 and 9.2 show the impact of these adjustments on the assessment rates for British Columbia and Ontario, respectively. These data show that when considered separately, these adjustments, and in particular the payroll adjustment, have a much greater effect on Ontario rates than on rates in British Columbia. Figure 9.2 also shows that the effects of the deficit and payroll adjustments are often offsetting, particularly in Ontario in recent years. Comparing payroll adjustments for British Columbia and Ontario, the data indicate that the impact of this adjustment is much more profound in Ontario. This is somewhat troubling since the Ontario adjustment was calculated using the provincial wage and a contrived wage distribution, while the BC adjustment was based on rate-group data on total and assessable payroll. This would suggest that the Ontario payroll adjustment is too great, and that we are underestimating the 'true' assessment rate.[19]

Figure 9.3 presents comparative data showing the adjusted manual rates for British Columbia, Ontario, and the United States for the period 1975–1995. U.S. data are employment-weighted national averages. These data indicate that for most of this period, Canadian rates, and in particular the rates in British Columbia compared favourably with the U.S. national average. Except for 1982 and 1983, the rate in British Columbia was lower than that for the United States for the entire period. Ontario rates were lower than the average U.S. rate from 1975 through 1984. In 1985, Ontario rates rose sharply, exceeding the U.S. rate in that and the next three years. Since 1987, Ontario rates have been consistently lower than the U.S. national average, and data for 1995 indicate that the gap between the U.S. and Ontario rates has increased.

In addition to the rate measure, we also calculated an employment-weighted average of the weekly workers' compensation assessment per worker in 1995 U.S. dollars. Canadian costs were converted to U.S. dollars using the Index of Purchasing Power Parity for GDP (OECD, 1997). Figure 9.4 presents comparative data showing weekly per-worker net costs for the three jurisdictions. These data tell a similar story to that depicted in figure 9.3. For most of the period, workers' compensation costs in British Columbia are substantially lower than

FIGURE 9.1 British Columbia assessment rates, 1975–1995

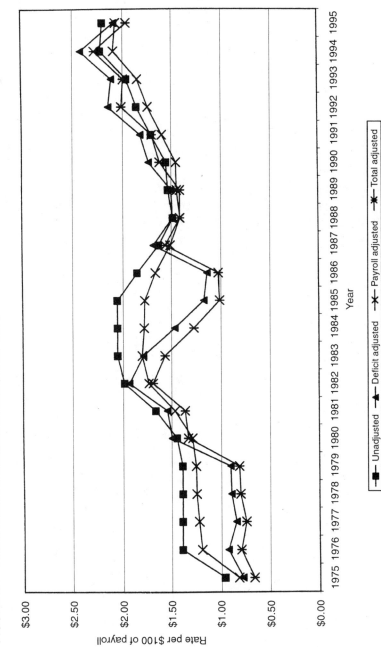

Rate per $100 of payroll

1975 1976 1977 1978 1979 1980 1981 1982 1983 1984 1985 1986 1987 1988 1989 1990 1991 1992 1993 1994 1995

Year

■— Unadjusted ▲— Deficit adjusted ✳— Payroll adjusted ✳— Total adjusted

FIGURE 9.2 Ontario assessment rates, 1975–1995

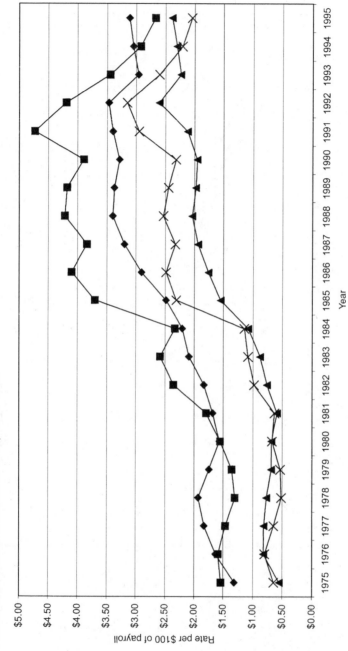

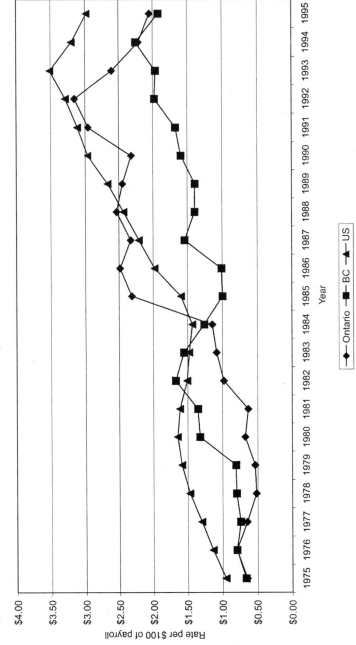

FIGURE 9.3 British Columbia, Ontario, and U.S. average assessment rates, 1975–1995

Rate per $100 of payroll

Year

◆ Ontario ■ BC ▲ US

the average rate in the United States. Ontario costs also compare favourably with those in the U.S., particularly in the early part of the study period.

Determinants of Workers' Compensation Costs

Differences in gross costs are not fully informative for many of the important public-policy questions that we seek to address. Ideally, we would like to know the reasons for inter-jurisdictional cost variation. In particular, we would like to know whether the private provision of compensation insurance is more expensive or less expensive than public funding. (A more exhaustive treatment of this topic may be found in Dewees, chapter 8, this volume.) On the one hand, we might expect that private provision will result in greater costs than public funding for two reasons: (1) a monopolistic public insurer will be able to capture certain economies of scale not available to private insurers in a competitive market and (2) unlike private insurers, a monopolistic state fund will not incur marketing costs or require profits. On the other hand, we may expect that competitive pressures for private insurers will reduce administrative costs to levels below those incurred by monopolistic public insurance funds. In addition, competitive pressures provide an incentive for insurers to engage in preventative actions that can reduce claims and to be vigilant in areas such as claims management and vocational-rehabilitation expenses.

Our theoretical model suggests that inter-jurisdictional cost variation is partially affected by differences in benefit levels. We may also expect that certain differences in institutional arrangements among jurisdictions, such as the scope of workers' compensation coverage, also have an impact on relative costs. This suggests a multivariate analysis that would control for these factors. In this section, we describe the variables to be used as regressors in our analyses.

Cash-Benefit Levels

Workers' compensation programs pay two types of benefits to injured workers: cash payments to compensate for the loss of wage income, and medical benefits to pay for the cost of hospitalization and medical care. Cash benefits take the form of either benefits paid to disabled workers or survivor benefits, including an allowance for funeral

FIGURE 9.4 Net weekly employer compensation costs, 1975–1995

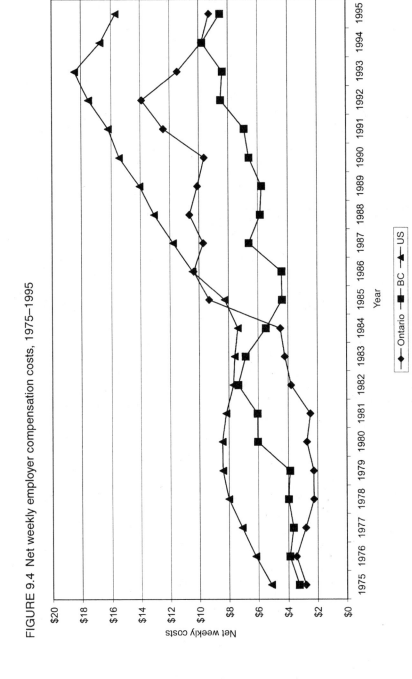

expenses, paid to the dependent survivors of fatally injured workers. It is often asserted that Canadian compensation programs pay cash benefits that are considerably more generous that those paid by U.S. programs, so that it is important to control for this source of variation when comparing employer costs.

To control for variation in cash-benefit levels across jurisdictions, we constructed a denomination-free index that measures the generosity of each jurisdiction's benefits relative to a uniform standard. This was done using a three-step procedure. First, we calculated the benefits that the average compensation claimant would receive in each jurisdiction as the result of a work injury. This variable, which we will designate B_{it}, is a weighted average of benefits that the claimant receives for each of four types of injury: temporary total, permanent total, permanent partial, and fatal.[20] For each type, we estimate the weekly benefit amount, which is typically a proportion of the claimant's pre-injury wage subject to a minimum and a maximum, and the expected duration of benefits.[21] Benefit duration is actuarially determined, subject to statutory limitations.[22] In addition, we account for benefit reductions owing to social security offsets and for benefit increases owing to cost-of-living adjustments.

Second, we calculate a 'standard benefit,' S_{it}, for each jurisdiction. This standard represents the benefits that would have been paid in each province and state, if the jurisdiction had adopted the 'Model Act' that was promulgated by the Council of State Governments in the mid-1970s (Council of State Governments, 1974).[23] Computation of the standard benefit was identical to that for B_{it}, after substitution of Model Act statutory parameters for those of the relevant jurisdiction.[24] Finally, we derive the index used in our regression analyses by taking the ratio $I_{it} = B_{it}/S_{it}$.

Figure 9.5 depicts these indices for British Columbia and Ontario as a proportion of the U.S. national average. As can be seen, benefit levels in Ontario were almost three times as generous as the U.S. national average during the period from 1975 to 1984. In 1985, benefits rose to about four and one-half times the U.S. average. This jump was primarily due to the implementation of benefit indexation in Ontario, whereby compensation benefits for long-term disability were automatically adjusted to reflect changes in the cost of living. Throughout this period, benefit levels in British Columbia were about five times their levels in the United States. Once again, much of the difference between

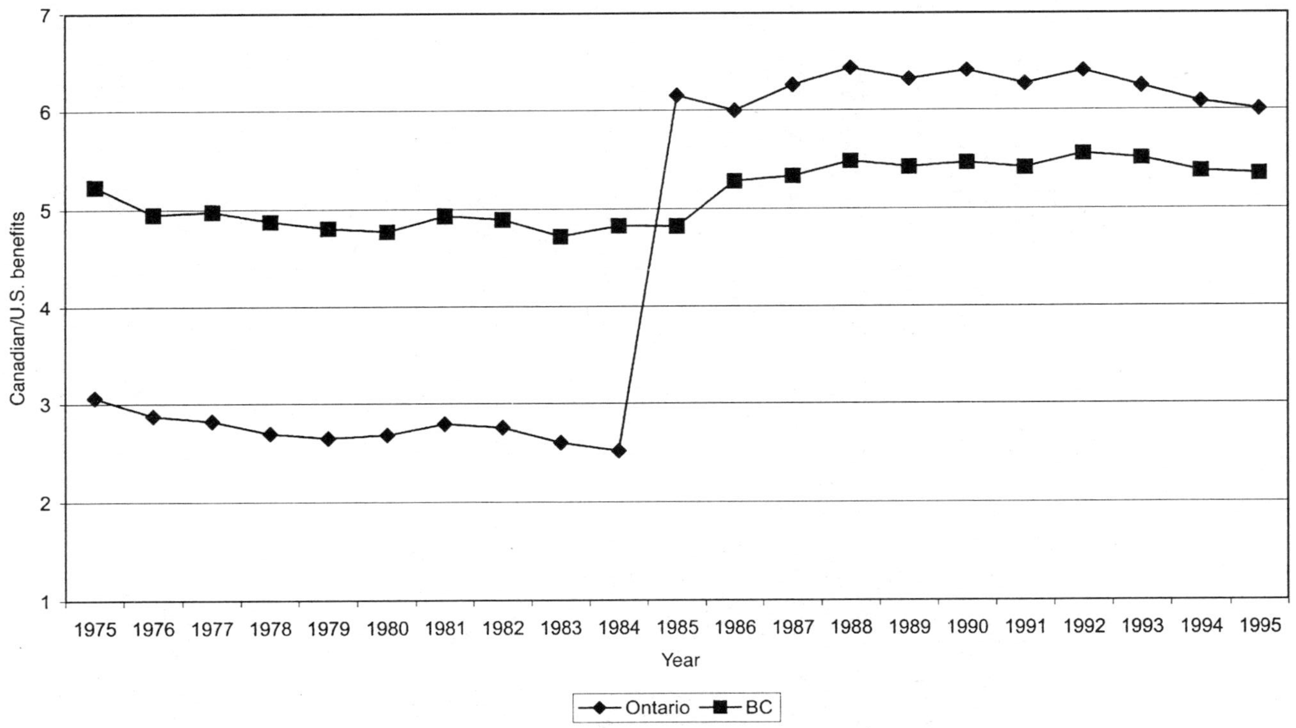

FIGURE 9.5 Ratio of Canadian to U.S. statutory benefit generosity

benefit levels in British Columbia and the average U.S. jurisdiction is due to automatic cost-of-living adjustments in BC, which are not common in U.S. workers' compensation programs.

Medical Benefit Index

Workers' compensation programs in North America pay for the cost of all medical and hospital expenses incurred by the injured worker as a result of his or her occupational accident. However, there are substantial differences between health-care systems in the two countries that could significantly affect the cost of medical benefits. Health care in Canada is publicly funded, while it remains a private system in the United States. These institutional differences in the broader health-care environment have significant implications for the cost of medical benefits paid by workers' compensation programs (Pozzebon and Thomason, 1994). It is sometimes alleged that less-extensive coverage for nonoccupational illnesses and injuries leads to cost-shifting into workers' compensation in the United States. In addition, per capita health-care costs are approximately half as great in Canada as in the United States (ibid.).

Medical-benefit costs for workers' compensation programs have grown at a substantially greater rate in the United States than in Canada in recent years, and health-care benefits account for a much smaller proportion of total benefit costs in Canadian programs.[25] Nevertheless, medical and hospitalization payments are a substantial component of total workers' compensation benefits in both countries. We therefore include a measure of the cost of medical benefits paid by jurisdiction that should be positively associated with employers' costs.[26]

Injury Rate

Variation in risk levels is at least partially controlled through the cost methodology; cost estimates use a standard set of rate groups, which are combined into an aggregate measure using identical weights for all jurisdictions. However, following Krueger and Burton (1990), we include an injury-rate variable in some of our equations for two reasons. First, if high injury rates result in political pressure to increase benefit levels, omission of an injury-rate variable will bias benefit elasticity estimates. Second, inclusion of the injury-rate variable will improve the precision of our estimates. However, if higher benefits increase the probability of injury, then the injury rate should be excluded, as it will capture some of the cost variation attributable to indemnity benefits. For these reasons, we estimate our equations with and without this variable.[27]

PPD Proportion

Permanent partial disability (PPD) claims account for a substantial proportion of total indemnity benefits paid by state and provincial workers' compensation programs. In addition, there is substantial variation across jurisdictions with respect to the way that PPD claims are processed, and anecdotal evidence suggests that there are also variations in both the probability and size of PPD awards that workers receive for identical injuries. To control for potential variation in the manner in which PPD awards are determined, we include a measure of the ratio of the frequency of PPD awards to total claims.[28]

Union Membership Rate

Several studies have found a positive relationship between union status and payment of workers' compensation benefits. Most notably, Hirsch, Macpherson, and Dumond (1997), using CPS (Current Population Survey) data, recently found that unionized workers were substantially more likely to receive workers' compensation benefits than non-union workers, after controlling for a variety of demographic, occupational, and industrial characteristics. Similarly, Thomason and Pozzebon (1994) used data from the Labour Market Activity Survey and found that union membership was positively associated with the probability of a workers' compensation claim in Canada.

There are several possible explanations for these results. Employees who work in risky establishments may be more likely to form or join a labour union. Alternatively, unions may provide claimants with information and legal assistance that is helpful in the pursuit of compensation claims. Furthermore, unionized workers may be less likely to fear employer recrimination that could result from filing a workers' compensation claim. Given the substantial differences in union density between Canada and the United States, we include a variable measuring the proportion of the workforce in each jurisdiction that is covered by a collective-bargaining agreement. U.S. data consist of CPS estimates, while Canadian data were taken from Statistics Canada.[29]

Workers' Compensation Coverage Rate

Historically, there has been considerable variation across U.S. jurisdictions with respect to the scope of workers' compensation coverage. Firms with small numbers of workers, as well as certain types of employment (frequently, farm workers, domestic workers, and casual employment), are often exempted. Canadian workers' compensation laws tend to be more inclusive. To the extent that employees in exempt categories are more likely than employees in the covered categories to sustain workplace injuries, then an extension of coverage to these exempt employees will be positively related to employers' costs of workers' compensation insurance. To the extent that these workers sustain fewer occupational injuries, then the extension of coverage will be negatively related to compensation costs.

To control for these effects, we utilized a set of dummy variables that indicates the extent to which a jurisdiction was in compliance with the eight essential recommendations of the National Commission on State Workmen's Compensation Laws. These coverage recommendations are listed in table 9.2. Data on U.S. compliance were obtained from the U.S. Department of Labor. The extent to which Canadian workers' compensation laws were in accord with these standards was determined by the authors using Ontario and British Columbia statutes and regulations in effect during the study period as well as various issues of the U.S. Chamber of Commerce publication *Analysis of Workers' Compensation Laws*.

Table 9.3 reports means, standard deviations, and a count of the number of observations with missing values for each of the variables used in our regression analysis. For a number of jurisdictions we lacked data on the dependent variable for one or more years during the study period, which reduced the total sample to 950 observations. These data are reported for the total sample and for the United States and Canada separately. In addition to these variables, we also took advantage of the panel nature of our data set to control for unobservable state-specific, time-invariant variation in our dependent cost measures using dummy variables that identified the state or province. We also controlled for unobservable time effects using a set of year

TABLE 9.2
Essential recommendations of the National Commission on State Workmen's
Compensation Laws respecting coverage

Recommendation	Description
Compulsory coverage	Coverage by workers' compensation laws is compulsory.
No waivers	No waivers are permitted.
No size exemption	Employers are not exempted from workers' compensation coverage because of the number of their employees.
Farmworkers	Farmworkers are covered on the same basis as all other employees.
Household & casual workers	Household workers and all casual workers are covered under workmen's compensation at least to the extent they are covered by Social Security.
Government employees	Workers' compensation coverage is mandatory for all government employees.
No occupational exemption	There are no exemptions for any class of employees, such as professional athletes or employees of charitable organizations.
Filing choice	Employees or survivors are given the choice of filing a workers' compensation claim in the state where the injury occurred, or where the employment was principally localized, or where the employee was hired.
Disease	Full coverage for occupational diseases.

dummy variables. Regression equations that included these dummies
were estimated with a random-effects model.

Regression Estimates

Table 9.4 reports the results for regressions predicting adjusted manual
rates, while Table 9.5 reports the results for regressions predicting
weekly net costs per worker. In accordance with the theoretical model
described above, log-log specifications were estimated with respect to
the cash-benefit and injury-rate variables.

For our key variable of interest, cost differences between U.S.
jurisdictions and the Canadian ones of Ontario and British Columbia
were captured by dummy variables indicating the identity of the
Canadian jurisdiction. The coefficient for the British Columbia variable
was negative in all equations and was statistically significant in all
models except those controlling for jurisdiction, but not for time effects.

TABLE 9.3
Means, standard deviations, and missing observations

Variable	Total sample (N = 950)			U.S. sample (N = 908)			Canada (N = 42)		
	Mean	S.D.	Number missing	Mean	S.D.	Number missing	Mean	S.D.	Number missing
Adjusted manual rate	2.00	1.01	0	2.02	1.02	0	1.52	0.74	0
Net costs	10.44	5.31	0	10.61	5.32	0	6.51	3.11	0
Cash benefit index	0.62	0.52	0	0.55	0.36	0	2.40	0.65	0
Medical benefits	986.30	776.77	236	1000.98	780.50	236	751.34	680.39	0
Injury rate	8.89	1.59	275	8.81	1.52	257	11.13	1.77	18
PPD proportion	23.03	9.75	206	24.01	9.09	205	6.20	3.24	1
Union density	17.06	8.00	112	16.30	7.03	106	33.91	9.60	6
Compulsory coverage	0.94	0.24	0	0.93	0.25	0	1.00	0.00	0
No waivers	0.50	0.50	0	0.48	0.50	0	1.00	0.00	0
No size exemption	0.71	0.46	0	0.69	0.46	0	1.00	0.00	0
Farmworker	0.31	0.46	0	0.28	0.45	0	1.00	0.00	0
Household & casual	0.04	0.20	0	0.02	0.15	0	0.50	0.51	0
Gov't employees	0.61	0.49	0	0.59	0.49	0	1.00	0.00	0
No occ. exemption	0.33	0.47	0	0.34	0.47	0	0.00	0.00	0
Filing choice	0.57	0.50	0	0.56	0.50	0	0.71	0.46	0
Diseases	0.99	0.09	0	0.99	0.09	0	1.00	0.00	0

TABLE 9.4
Determinants of adjusted manual rates (*N* = 950)

Variable	I	II	III	IV
British Columbia	−0.4857*	−0.5924*	−0.4453*	−0.8039*
	(0.094)	(0.096)	(0.216)	(0.215)
Ontario	−0.2575*	−0.3324*	−0.0889	−0.2979*
	(0.069)	(0.070)	(0.166)	(0.163)
Log (benefits)	0.2494*	0.2475*	0.1764*	0.1686*
	(0.020)	(0.020)	(0.032)	(0.030)
Log (medical benefits)	0.7973*	0.7015*	0.7824*	0.4999*
	(0.019)	(0.029)	(0.025)	(0.042)
Log (injury rate)	0.3296*	0.3697*	0.5916*	0.7382*
	(0.056)	(0.057)	(0.076)	(0.082)
PPD proportion	0.5137*	0.4952*	0.4089*	0.5140*
	(0.115)	(0.115)	(0.157)	(0.157)
Union density	0.4478*	0.5627*	−0.0496	0.6332*
	(0.143)	(0.144)	(0.255)	(0.269)
Compulsory coverage	−0.0439	−0.0635	−0.0474	−0.0968
	(0.042)	(0.041)	(0.085)	(0.082)
No waivers	0.0246	0.0177	0.0051	0.0004
	(0.020)	(0.019)	(0.032)	(0.031)
No size exemption	−0.0378	−0.0388*	0.0133	−0.0173
	(0.020)	(0.020)	(0.043)	(0.041)
Farmworkers	0.1655*	0.1762*	0.0642	−0.0707
	(0.022)	(0.022)	(0.042)	(0.041)
Household & casual	0.1090	0.1012	0.2600	0.2158
	(0.065)	(0.064)	(0.137)	(0.131)
Gov't employees	0.0440*	0.0396*	−0.0017	−0.0133
	(0.019)	(0.019)	(0.043)	(0.041)
No occ. exemption	−0.0919	−0.0969*	−0.0922*	−0.0938
	(0.019)	(0.019)	(0.046)	(0.044)
Filing choice	−0.0570*	−0.0680*	−0.0428	−0.0509
	(0.018)	(0.018)	(0.037)	(0.035)
Diseases	−0.1797*	−0.2968*	−0.0534	−0.1717*
	(0.086)	(0.086)	(0.081)	(0.078)
Jurisdiction effects	No	No	Yes	Yes
Year effects	No	Yes	No	Yes
R-Square	0.7905	0.8060	0.7681	0.7719

Note: Standard errors are within parentheses.

*Indicates that p < .05, two-tailed test.

TABLE 9.5
Determinants of workers' compensation net costs (N = 950)

Variable	I	II	III	IV
British Columbia	−0.6657* (0.093)	−0.7577* (0.095)	−0.6333* (0.216)	−0.9622* (0.215)
Ontario	−0.4915* (0.068)	−0.5588* (0.070)	−0.3171 (0.167)	−0.5189* (0.163)
Log (benefits)	0.2495* (0.020)	0.2483* (0.020)	0.1728* (0.031)	0.1702* (0.030)
Log (medical benefits)	0.7923* (0.019)	0.7057* (0.029)	0.7775* (0.025)	0.5114* (0.042)
Log (injury rate)	0.3610* (0.055)	0.3660* (0.057)	0.6709* (0.075)	0.7307* (0.082)
PPD proportion	0.5208* (0.114)	0.4972* (0.115)	0.4259* (0.155)	0.5157* (0.157)
Union density	0.4554* (0.142)	0.5618* (0.143)	−0.0192 (0.252)	0.6201* (0.269)
Compulsory coverage	−0.0484 (0.042)	−0.0625 (0.041)	−0.0555 (0.085)	−0.0954 (0.082)
No waivers	0.0259 (0.019)	0.0180 (0.019)	0.0085 (0.032)	0.0004 (0.031)
No size exemption	−0.0385* (0.020)	−0.0386* (0.020)	0.0162 (0.042)	0.0182 (0.041)
Farmworkers	0.1656* (0.022)	0.1757* (0.022)	0.0593 (0.042)	0.0697 (0.041)
Household & casual	0.1052 (0.065)	0.1012 (0.063)	0.2498 (0.136)	0.2158 (0.130)
Gov't employees	0.0406* (0.019)	0.0399* (0.019)	−0.0109 (0.043)	−0.0128 (0.041)
No occ. exemption	−0.0921* (0.019)	−0.0968* (0.019)	−0.0880 (0.046)	−0.0939* (0.044)
Filing choice	−0.0567* (0.018)	−0.0665* (0.018)	−0.0340 (0.036)	−0.0451 (0.035)
Diseases	−0.2062* (0.085)	−0.2955* (0.085)	−0.0744 (0.080)	−0.1683* (0.078)
Jurisdiction effects	No	No	Yes	Yes
Year effects	No	Yes	No	Yes
Adjusted R-Square	0.7967	0.8091	0.7713	0.7759

Note: Standard errors are within parentheses.

*Indicates that $p < .05$, two-tailed test.

These results suggest that compensation costs in BC were less expensive than those of comparable U.S. jurisdictions, after controlling for other factors that affect costs. The results for the Ontario dummy are mixed; the coefficient is negative in all equations, although it does not reach statistical significance at the 0.05 level in adjusted manual-rate Models III and IV or in net-cost Model III. While Model IV is our preferred equation, we conclude that Ontario costs are also lower than the U.S. average after controlling for other variables affecting costs.

The magnitude of the coefficients for the British Columbia variable averages around –0.67 across the eight specifications of tables 4 and 5, ranging from –0.49 to –0.96. Ontario coefficients range from –0.09 to –0.56, averaging about –0.36. Since the dependent variables are in log form, this suggests that adjusted manual rates (table 9.4) and net costs per worker per week (table 9.5) are approximately 49 per cent lower in British Columbia than in the United States, and about 30 per cent lower in Ontario, after controlling for other determinants of such costs. These are substantial magnitudes.

For the most part, results for other variables indicate that the regression models behave as expected. Higher cash and medical benefits, a high ratio of PPD awards to total claims, greater union density, and a higher injury rate all give rise to higher workers' compensation costs, whether measured as adjusted manual rates (table 9.4) or net costs (table 9.5).

Several of the coverage dummies are significantly different from zero at conventional probability levels. These results indicate that farmworker coverage is positively related to compensation costs, while disease coverage is negatively related to costs. In addition, jurisdictions that give employees the choice of jurisdiction have lower costs than those that do not. These results contradict expectation. It is possible that these dummy variables capture the effect of unobserved factors affecting workers' compensation costs.

Insurance Regulation and Self-Insurance

As indicated, compensation-cost differences between Canada and the United States may be due to differences in the institutional features of workers' compensation programs of the two countries. In particular, these results suggest that the public provision of compensation coverage by a monopolistic provincial fund in Canada may be more efficient than the private provision of compensation insurance in the United

States. However, our analysis thus far fails to account for two other important institutional features that may affect our results: insurance regulation and the self-insurance option. As discussed previously, deregulation and more open competition in the rate-setting process could increase or decrease workers' compensation costs, while allowing self-insurance is expected to increase costs for those who remain in the system, since the low-costs firms are more likely to 'opt-out' and self-insure.

Unfortunately, it is not possible to control for these features in a regression equation, since there is little variation in these features within or across the Canadian jurisdictions. To solve this problem we adopt the following three-step strategy:

1 Using the U.S. sample we estimate an additional regression equation predicting adjusted manual rates that includes two variables measuring the effects of insurance regulation and self-insurance. The effect of regulation is captured by a dummy variable indicating whether a particular jurisdiction has enacted 'open competition' legislation, using NCCI data (NCCI, 1996: exhibit II), while the impact of self-insurance is controlled by a variable measuring benefits paid by self-insured employers as a proportion of total benefits.[30]

2 Using coefficients from this equation, we then estimate predicted adjusted manual rates for U.S. states under three assumptions. First, we assume that all states adopt policies prohibiting self-insurance, that is, we assume that the value of the self-insurance variable is zero. Second, we assume that states deregulate worker's compensation insurance markets adopting 'open' competition, that is, that the value for the open-competition variable is one. Third, we assume that states both prohibit self-insurance and adopt open competition, that is, we assume that the value for self-insurance is zero and the value for open competition is one. Costs under these three assumptions are then compared with cost predictions based on actual sample characteristics, that is, those that use the actual values of the variables in the equation.

3 The ratio of these costs predictions – that is, the ratio of predicted costs assuming a policy prohibiting open competition and no self-insurance to predicted costs assuming current policy – are then used to adjust predicted manual rates for the U.S. using coefficients-regression equations from Model VI of table 9.4.

Figure 9.6 depicts predicted costs of workers' compensation for the United States based on the Model VI regression coefficients as well as the actual compensation costs in British Columbia and Ontario. Four U.S. rates are shown. The line labelled 'U.S.' depicts the predicted rates before they are modified to reflect the assumed policy changes – no self-insurance and open competition. The 'U.S. Mod. – Self-Ins.' line shows predicted rates assuming that self-insurance is prohibited there, the 'U.S. Mod. – Dereg.' line depicts predicted rates assuming that the insurance market is deregulated, and the 'U.S. Mod. – Total' line shows predicted rates under both assumptions.

The total modified rate for the United States ranges from 1.5 to 14.5 per cent less than the unadjusted rate during this period. Both modifications reduce the predicted adjusted manual rates relative to the unmodified predicted rate. Most of the reduction is due to the prohibition of self-insurance, the effect of which increases throughout the study period – from a 3 per cent in 1975 to over 12 per cent reduction in 1995. This trend reflects an increase in the proportion of self-insured payroll in the United States during that time.

Taken together, these results indicate that U.S. costs would be reduced by eliminating the self-insurance option and adopting deregulation. Since the overwhelming majority of Canadian firms are unable to self-insure, a portion of the higher costs found in U.S. jurisdictions may be attributed to the fact that low-cost firms have self-insured and opted out of the system. Conversely, a substantial proportion of any cost advantage of the Canadian system would likely disappear if more low-cost firms were allowed to opt out and self-insure.

It should be noted that our benefit variable is a measure of the *expected* benefits according to the provisions of the relevant workers' compensation statute. These expected benefits can diverge from actual benefits paid – the ideal measure of benefit generosity – owing to differences in benefit administration. If, for example, the workers' compensation board adjusted its assessment of permanent partial disability in response to an increase in statutory benefits, then our benefit variable would overestimate the change in generosity. While we endeavour to control for these differences with other variables, such as union density and PPD costs as a proportion of total, these controls are obviously imperfect.

However, there is an important caveat. It is likely that both self-insurance and deregulation are endogenous. That is, employers are more likely to exercise the self-insurance option as insurance costs rise. Similarly, high insurance costs are likely to prompt legislators to deregulate insurance markets in response to complaints by small employers who are unable to self-insure. If high insurance costs lead to

FIGURE 9.6 Predicted assessment rates, 1975–1995

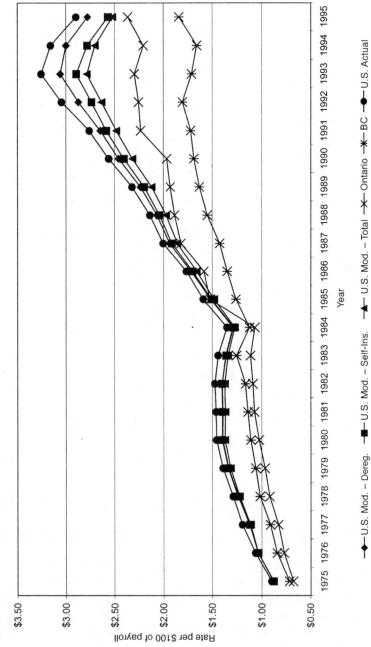

Rate per $100 of payroll

Year

◆ U.S. Mod. – Dereg.   ■ U.S. Mod. – Self-Ins.   ▲ U.S. Mod. – Total   ✕ Ontario   ✳ BC   ● U.S. Actual

deregulation, then our estimates of the impact of self-insurance and deregulation on workers' compensation costs should be considered as upper-bound estimates of these effects.[31]

Conclusions

In this chapter, we adduced evidence indicating workers' compensation programs in Canada, and the British Columbia program in particular, enjoy a relative cost advantage when compared to those in the United States. That is, the employers' average cost of workers' compensation, in terms of both assessments per $100 of payroll and weekly premiums after controlling for industrial composition, appears to be less in British Columbia and Ontario than it is in the average U.S. jurisdiction. This relative cost advantage was found both before and after controlling for a number of determinants of compensation costs, including benefit levels, compensation coverage, injury rates, the proportion of PPD claims, and union density. However, attempts to control for two institutional features thought to influence costs – self-insurance and open competition – reduced the Canadian-U.S. differential. In fact, the differential would appear to disappear altogether for Ontario.

One implication of these analyses may be that the public provision of insurance is at least as efficient as private provision. Nevertheless, there are a number of reasons why these results should be interpreted cautiously. First, note that we obtained very inconsistent and statistically insignificant results for Ontario. Furthermore, these results are inconsistent with those from previous studies examining U.S. data. Specifically, both the Krueger and Burton (1990) and Schmidle (1994 and 1995) studies, which used a similar methodology as that employed here, found that the presence of a competitive state fund in states that allow private workers' compensation insurance was associated with higher compensation costs than in those states that only relied on private provision.

In addition, our analyses have several limitations. First, our Canadian data come from only two provinces, so that is uncertain whether these results may be generalized to other Canadian jurisdictions or to other jurisdictions with a monopolistic public provider. Second, there are reasons to wonder whether our Ontario rates accurately reflect the true costs of workers' compensation. In particular, a comparison of the payroll adjusted rates for British Columbia and Ontario suggests that the adjustment for Ontario may have been too large. Third, while we attempted to derive independent variables, such as the injury rate or the PPD percentage, for Ontario and BC that were comparable to those for our U.S. sample, these data come from completely different sources. They may be sufficiently different to affect the results of our regression analyses. Finally, compensation costs in either of the two countries may be affected by factors not considered in our analyses.

Thus, definitive answers to the question of the relative costs of workers' compensation in Canada and the United States await further research. We are currently working on a major study of workers' compensation costs in the United States that will include Ohio and West Virginia, two states with monopolistic state funds. An analysis of this expanded data set, which will include more refined variables measuring the nature of the regulatory environment, will undoubtedly shed further light on these issues.

In the absence of new information to the contrary, and subject to the caveats outlined, our analysis suggests that workers' compensation costs under the provincial monopoly systems of Ontario and British Columbia are not higher, and indeed may well be lower, than they are in the more private, competitive systems that exist in the United States. This conclusion prevails both before and after controlling for a wide range of other factors that influence workers' compensation costs. While it is not a result that we expected, it suggests that cost reductions need not occur – indeed costs may increase – by shifting from monopoly provision to a U.S. model of private insurance. Accepting these results at face value, a major implication is that the cost of workers' compensation in Canada has not impaired the competitiveness of Canadian firms versus their U.S. counterparts.

NOTES

1 The authors thank Timothy P. Schmidle for his advice as well as helpful comments on previous versions of this chapter. We also thank Don Dewees for his helpful comments on a previous draft, as well as Josh Pascoe and Natan Hamerman for their expert research assistance. The U.S. data used in this chapter were collected as part of a major study of the deregulation of workers' compensation in the United States by Burton, Schmidle, and Thomason, which was sponsored by the W.E. Upjohn Institute on Employment Research. In addition, partial funding for this project was provided by

a grant to Thomason by the Social Sciences and Humanities Research Council of Canada.

2 It is important to note that in all North American jurisdictions, benefit levels and eligibility conditions are established by statute. These statutes also create agencies charged with the responsibility of administering the program. These agencies may perform two functions: (1) adjudication of disputes over eligibility and benefit levels and (2) the collection and disbursement of funds to pay for benefits. Public and private programs are distinguished with respect to the latter function. In public programs, a monopolistic state agency sets rates, collects benefits from employers, and disburses benefits to eligible claimants. In private programs, these activities are performed by private insurers. Thus, the term 'privatize,' as it is used in this chapter, refers to the transferral of the financial function from a state agency to private insurers.

3 Ontario does not have a pure wage-loss system, since wage-loss experience is evaluated at only two discrete points following maximum medical improvement.

4 U.S. jurisdictions include all states where private carriers provide workers' compensation as well as the District of Columbia. The six states that offer workers' compensation through an exclusive state fund – Nevada, North Dakota, Ohio, Washington, West Virginia, and Wyoming – are excluded.

5 In addition, rates based on past accident experience are adjusted to account for anticipated changes in the benefit structure.

6 The largest of these bureaus is the National Council of Compensation Insurance (NCCI), which acts as the primary rate-filing organization in 32 states. Other non-exclusive state-fund states use independent state rating bureaus.

7 This assumes that regulatory bodies are unable to respond as quickly to market changes as private actors, a reasonable assumption given that the agencies are one step removed from the market. An alternative assumption, however, is that private actors may overreact to changes in underlying market conditions, thereby magnifying fluctuations in the price and profitability of workers' compensation insurance.

8 While certain Canadian organizations self-insure, it is not a matter of employer choice, but of legislative fiat. By and large, self-insurance in Canada is limited to governmental bodies, such as municipalities, school boards, and the federal and provincial governments, and certain large private employers, such as the Class 1 railways.

9 This procedure is used to calculate employer compensation costs for all jurisdictions that use the NCCI as a rating bureau and for eight states with

independent rating bureaus that use the NCCI classification scheme. The remaining states use a somewhat different procedure, as described in Burton and Schmidle, 1990.

10 The payments for injuries incurred during a policy year may extend over decades in the future. Pure premiums include present-value estimates of these future benefit payments.

11 Unlike prospective programs, the effect of retrospective experience rating is not included in the experience-rating modification used to obtain the standard earned premium excluding constants.

12 These classifications include both durable and non-durable manufacturing industries (e.g., foundries and newspaper publishers), construction (e.g., masonry), utilities (e.g., electric light or power companies), retail and wholesale trade (e.g., gasoline or oil dealers and gasoline stations), and services (e.g., laundries).

13 U.S. payroll weights were used to ensure uniformity in our aggregate cost measures between the two nations. Given the similarities in the Canadian and U.S. economies, this should not significantly bias our estimates.

14 If we used all U.S. rate classifications, price variation owing to rate-group composition is eliminated.

15 Perhaps the most troubling aspect of this general problem is the fact that the 71 U.S. rate groups include four occupational classifications – clerical office employees, outside salesmen, collectors and messengers, truckmen, and chauffeurs and drivers – for which there are no comparable Canadian classes, since Canadian rate groups are based on industrial sector rather than occupation. In other words, Canadian rates for Canadian rate groups are a weighted average of the corresponding industrial rate and the rates for these four occupational groups. If the occupational composition of the 67 U.S. industrial classes (with respect to these four occupational rate groups) is approximately the same as that which exists in the economy as a whole, then the payroll weighted average rates in the two jurisdictions are comparable. To the extent that occupational composition varies between these classes and the economy as a whole, then, Canadian rates are not comparable to the U.S. rates.

16 Since assessable payroll is less than total payroll, manual rates must be higher in Canada to generate premiums equivalent to those paid by U.S. firms who are in identical classifications with identical total payroll.

17 The method for obtaining total payroll from assessable payroll is known as the limit factor method. A standard wage distribution is created using national wage data and is normalized so that the average wage is equal to one. A wage distribution for the province is created by multiplying the

industrial average wage for Ontario by the normalized wage for the standard wage distribution. Using this 'provincial' wage distribution, we may determine the proportion of wages below the maximum assessable wage. We obtain total payroll by multiplying the assessable payroll by the inverse of this proportion.

18 Income and expense data were obtained from annual reports. The adjustment factor (F) was equal to:

$$F = 1 + ((E - A)/A)$$

where A is assessment income and E is expenses. Expenses due to legislated amendments that raised benefits retrospectively were excluded from the calculation since these are not reflected in our benefit measure. (This only affects the Ontario calculation, since British Columbia did not provide any retrospective adjustments to benefit levels during this period.) Expenses were also adjusted to account for lost investment income that would have accrued in the absence of a deficit. The ratio of investment income to investment assets was used to obtain an annual average interest rate for this calculation.

19 However, it should be noted that the maximum assessable wage in British Columbia was indexed to the provincial average weekly wage throughout the period, while there was no similar indexation in Ontario until 1985. Nonetheless, this would not account for the persistence of the gap between the payroll adjusted rate and the unadjusted rate that persists beyond this point.

20 More specifically, B_{it} represents the expected value of benefits paid to the average workers' compensation claimant in the i th jurisdiction and the t th year.

21 The average state or provincial weekly wage adjusted for inter-jurisdictional differences in industrial composition is used as a proxy for average claimant wage.

22 U.S. national injury distributions obtained from the NCCI are utilized. For example, a permanent partial disability (PPD) distribution is used that itemizes relative frequency, average degree of functional impairment, and average age by type of injury (dismemberment or loss of use) and body part. Computed duration for long-term disability and survivor benefits are discounted at 3.5 per cent per annum and account for benefit cessation owing to claimant mortality.

23 We modified the Model Act benefit parameters slightly. The Model Act calls for Social Security Benefits to offset survivor benefits in the case of a fatal injury. To simplify calculations, we ignored this provision.

24 Importantly, maximum and minimum benefits are expressed as a function of the state average weekly wage, so that it was possible to compute 'denomination free' minimums and maximums.

25 Health-care costs accounted for approximately 26 per cent of total benefits for combined Canadian workers' compensation programs in 1993 (Human Resources Development Canada 1995: table 2), compared to nearly 41 per cent for U.S. programs (Social Security Administration, 1995: table III.B.13).

26 This measure is the average medical benefit paid per claim. Canadian data were converted to U.S. dollars using the OECD Purchasing Power Parity Index. All data are in real 1995 (U.S.) dollars. Missing data were a problem for the U.S. data. Missing values were interpolated using the U.S. Consumer Price Index.

27 Average injury rates were computed for each jurisdiction using injury rates disaggregated at the level of major injury division (agriculture, forestry and fishing, mining, manufacturing, etc.), using U.S. employment as weights. Unfortunately, the only disaggregated data available for British Columbia or Ontario were lost-time rates between 1983 and 1994 (inclusive). Consequently, weighted lost-time rates for the two Canadian provinces were adjusted by multiplying them by the province-wide ratio of total accepted injuries to lost-time injuries. The U.S. data were also missing values for many observations. In both cases values for the missing observations were imputed using a procedure described in Thomason, Schmidle, and Burton (forthcoming).

28 A subtantial proportion of observations were missing data for this variable as well. Values were imputed using a procedure described in Thomason, Schmidle, and Burton (forthcoming).

29 Unfortunately, Statistics Canada stopped publishing union membership data in 1993, so that it was necessary to impute missing values using the methodology discussed previously. In addition, several U.S. states were missing density data for the pre-1983 period, which also required the implementation of this missing value strategy.

30 As indicated by our previous discussion, this is a relatively crude measure of the regulatory environment. We are currently working on a major project for the W.E. Upjohn Institute on Employment, for which we are developing more refined measures. Unfortunately, these measures, which we are gathering through a survey of state insurance commissions, were not available in time for writing this chapter.

31 Alternatively, if regulatory agencies suppress rates, then pressure by insurance carriers may lead legislators to enact open-competition legislation when rates are unusually low. If so, the effects of endogeneity bias for the self-insurance and deregulation variables would be offsetting.

REFERENCES

Burton, Jr, J.F. 1966. *Interstate Variations in Employers' Costs of Workmen's Compensation*. Kalamazoo, Mich.: W.E. Upjohn Institute for Employment Research.
Burton, Jr, J.F., and A.B. Krueger. 1986. 'Interstate Variations in the Employers' Costs of Workers' Compensation, with Particular Reference to Connecticut, New Jersey, and New York.' In J. Chelius, ed., *Current Issues in Workers' Compensation*, 111–208, Kalamazoo, Mich.: W.E. Upjohn Institute for Employment Research.
Burton, Jr, J.F., and T.P. Schmidle. 1990. 'The Employer's Cost of Workers' Compensation in Michigan and the Nation.' Mimeo, Workers' Disability Income Systems.
Council of State Governments. 1974. *Workmen's Compensation and Rehabilitation Law, Revised*. Lexington, Ky.: The Council of State Governments.
Hirsch, B.T., D.A. Macpherson, and J.M. Dumond. 1997. 'Workers' Compensation Recipiency in Union and Nonunion Workplaces.' *Industrial and Labor Relations Review* 50: 213–36.
Human Resources Development Canada. 1995. *Occupational Injuries and Their Cost in Canada, 1990–1994*. Ottawa: HRDC.
Jackson, C. 1996. 'New Directions for Workers' Compensation.' Report of The Honourable Cam Jackson, Minister without Portfolio Responsible for Workers' Compensation Reform. Toronto.
Krueger, A.B., and J.F. Burton, Jr. 1990. 'The Employers' Costs of Workers' Compensation Insurance: Magnitudes, Determinants, and Public Policy.' Review of Economics and Statistics 72: 228–40.
National Academy of Social Insurance. 1997. *Workers' Compensation: Benefits, Coverage, and Costs, 1993–1995: New Estimates*. Washington: NASI.
National Council on Compensation Insurance. 1996. *Annual Statistical Bulletin*. New York: NCCI.
O'Connor, P.R., J.L. Domagalski, and J.L. Walters. 1995. 'Competitive Pricing in the Workers' Compensation Industry and Marketplace: Policy Implications for Massachusetts.' Mimeo, Palmer-Bellevue (a division of Coopers & Lybrand, L.L.P.). Chicago.
OECD. 1997. *National Accounts: Main Aggregates* 1: 162–3.
Pozzebon, S., and T. Thomason. 1993. 'Medical Benefit Costs of Workers' Compensation in Canada: A Comparative Perspective.' *Benefits Quarterly* 9(4): 32–41.
Schmidle, T.P. 1994. 'The Impact of Insurance Pricing Deregulation on the Employers' Costs of Workers' Compensation Insurance.' PhD dissertation, Cornell University.

– 1995. 'The Impact of Insurance Pricing Deregulation on the Employers' Costs of Workers' Compensation Insurance.' *John Burton's Workers' Compensation Monitor* 8(5): 1–12.

Social Security Administration. 1995. *Social Security Bulletin, Annual Statistical Supplement*. Washington: SSA.

Thomason, T., and S. Pozzebon. 1993. 'The Effect of Compensation Benefits on Claims Incidence in Canada: A Micro-Level Analysis.' Mimeo, McGill University.

Thomason T., T. Schmidle, and John F. Burton, Jr. Forthcoming. *Workers' Compensation: Adequate Benefits, Affordable Costs, and Safety Incentives under Alternative Insurance Arrangements*. Kalamazoo, Mich.: W.E. Upjohn Institute for Employment Research.

10 Appeals Litigation: Pricing the Workplace Injury

DAVID K. LAW

Workers' compensation operates in over seventy North American jurisdictions.[1] It is a particular, and sometimes peculiar, institution mandating the distinct treatment of workplace accidents for purposes of insurance and liability. The unique specifics of workers' compensation systems appear to be these:

- Limited insurance is mandated for a large part of the workforce.
- It is provided either by a state monopoly, or required of employers.
- Workers exchange their rights of legal action for this insurance.
- Employers are exempt from direct liability.
- Decision making is a mix of 'administrative adjudication' and standard litigation.

Insurance systems vary among jurisdictions (most U.S. states mandate that employers obtain insurance from private carriers,[2] while Canadian provinces have agencies to offer the insurance), as do legal systems, but in their essence, these systems are expected to result in substantially lower 'decision-making' costs (i.e., less litigation thanks to administrative adjudication processes), thus being 'more efficient' than the courts.

If that historical assumption is correct, then it will best be illustrated by the largest North American jurisdiction with the best combination of a sizeable workforce and narrow channels of decision making: the Canadian province of Ontario. There all workers' compensation is paid by a single insurer, the state monopoly agency (the 'Workers' Compensation Board' or 'WCB' up until 1 January 1998; the 'Workplace Safety and Insurance Board' or 'WSIB' since that date). That insurer decides all claims, with no recourse to the courts. A small external administrative law tribunal, created in 1985, adjudicates board decisions under appeal. The enabling legislation, formerly the Workers' Compensation Act and now the Workplace Safety and Insurance Act, creates the board, the appeals tribunal, and their mandates.

One of the peculiarities of Ontario's workers' compensation system is that in the last fifteen years it has undergone several distinct periods of statutory and administrative reform, during which there was a substantial growth in the volume, frequency, and intensity of participation by the parties. This paper explores why a workers' compensation jurisdiction with relatively narrow confines for appeal was converted, in just over a decade, into a veritable litigation mill.

Law as a Market Mechanism for Pricing Opportunities

Workers' compensation is a legal mechanism by which human injury and economic opportunity is priced. The premise is straightforward: in a market economy, everything has its price. Since the dawn of civilization human beings have evaluated the worth of items and lives and based their actions upon those determinations. The 'justice' system is, in large part, a consensual public mechanism for those calculations – weighing the currency value of violated contracts, the future earnings of injured persons, and the criminality of conduct according to elaborate processes and rules.

'Justice,' in this analysis, can best be understood as a form of relational equilibrium, wherein actors set rules that permit the distribution of opportunities. Where one person's act or omission costs another her opportunities, 'the justice system' operates to redress the injured party by providing her some other opportunity.

Justice systems can be self-operated (robbing the neighbour who robbed you), but in modern times we tend to establish rules for the distribution of opportunities, for their protection from incursion, and for their replacement. These rules are usually called 'the law,' and in the province of Ontario it is administered by a set of courts, police, and civil authorities acting with the authority of the Crown as determined by the elected legislature. Ontario is of course a common-law jurisdiction, most directly an offshoot of the British tradition of common law, but influenced more and more by the combined Anglo-American view of justice. In such common-law jurisdictions the questions of personal injury and loss of opportunity are governed by the law of personal injury, either tortious or in the context of a contractual relationship.

What the law does in these latter situations is to place an economic value on the harm (be it physical injury and/or lost opportunity). In short, *the effect of the law is to place a price on the harm*, and to require payment of that price by whichever actors are responsible for it. To achieve this end, the law identifies the party responsible for the harm, the mechanism by which they owe a duty of care to the injured party, the degree of their responsibility, and how that translates into a 'price.' In the criminal context the 'price' can be imprisonment; in the 'civil' arena the price inevitably is cast in monetary terms.

The civil arena tries to split duties and relationships into those that are explicitly and intentionally defined (contract) and those that are implicit and generally imputed to actors (tort). 'Tort' is an anglicized word for 'wrong' taken from the Latin word 'tortus,' describing something crooked or twisted. In the Anglo-American common-law experience, tort is a system of identifying injuries, apportioning responsibility, and instructing people to pay for the consequences of their actions.

According to a noted Ontario expert, Allen Linden[3] (formerly of the provincial supreme court), the law of tort has these functions:

- to compensate the injured, or 'wronged,' party
- to deter hazardous behaviour by making individuals pay
- to create 'market deterrence' by increasing the price, generally, of hazardous behaviour
- to educate the parties, and others, both about risks and about values
- to appease the sense of grievance resulting from harm
- to advance social change

The compensation, deterrence, education, appeasement, and social-change effects of tort law take their power not only from the dollar value of awards issued at the end of a case, but also from the costs and effects of the process through which the parties must take their cases. This is critical to an understanding of tort and, in this study, to our analysis of an alternative system adopted in Ontario in the second decade of the twentieth century: namely, 'workmen's compensation.'

Pricing the Workplace Injury

The personal-injury case in the workplace was recognized as a unique situation by nineteenth-century policy makers. The industrial revolution, literally and figuratively, created a new landscape. Mechanization produced different problems for the nineteenth-century worker. First, of course, it was often dangerous and operated at a pace outside the experience of most people; whereas tradesmen had previously controlled the pace of work and the tools employed, factory life removed both aspects of work from the worker's hands. Second, mechanization drew large numbers of labourers into the realm of risk, working with fast-paced and dangerous machines in noisy, unnatural environments. Finally, the experience of working in modern factory environments 'de-skilled' the working-class population, producing two effects: individual labourers were less prized for their talents, and workers had fewer transportable skills than their tradesmen forbears. This de-skilling in turn reduced their options for alternative employments.

Those workers, shorn of their economic opportunities because of injury, brought suit in the courts of law (attempting to establish a 'price' for the harm done them). The courts responded with a creative and vigorous defence of employers, erecting a series of barriers such as the 'unholy trinity' (co-workers' liability, assumption of risk, and contributory negligence). Injured workers were effectively restricted in their pursuit of a fair price for their losses. There was also the simple technical problem of determining 'fault' – who was to blame for the workplace injury when an employer, a third party, a worker, or co-workers might all share to some degree in the origins of the accident?

Beyond the problem of assessing responsibility was the sheer burden of process – court cases have always been expensive to pursue, laden as they are with often practical, but almost always arcane, procedural activity. This in itself was an almost implacable barrier to the individual plaintiff initiating a claim, never mind seeing it through to the end. The combined result was that the likelihood and severity of injury stood to increase, while the worker's post-injury prospects of recovering earning ability dimmed.

Yet the employers benefiting from these barriers sometimes suffered by them too: they had to face the same costs of litigation, and when they lost, bore an unpredictable and perhaps crippling liability. What is well documented is that many parties – legislators, employers, trade unions, 'friendly societies,' and the citizenry generally saw the value in cleansing society and the economy of the uncertainties and risks inherent in leaving workplace injury in the courts.

It was into this breach that the remarkable idea of 'no fault' insurance was thrown – a system of insuring solely against results, rather than attributing responsibility.

The North American workers' compensation regimes share core principles and attributes, including 'no fault' attribution of injuries to work, limited benefit schedules, insurance-based adjudication methods for determining entitlement, and public regulation. The overriding purpose of the systems, it could be said, has been to give workers and employers certainty of process, predictability of result, and control of cost; in so doing, these regimes produce goods such as social stability, injury-prevention incentives, and an economic flow-through of cost from the injured to the market as a whole.

At the heart of the process, both as an implement of the system and as an outcome, is a unique approach to litigation. Litigation, defined, is the process of resolving disputes between adverse parties by means of adducing evidence and argument before an impartial third-party decision maker. In common-law jurisdictions private parties, and the state, have available to them litigation processes defined by tradition, statute, and regulation. The use (and sometimes abuse) of these processes is complex, time-consuming, costly, and oftentimes exhaustive in eliciting information relevant to an issue.

In workers' compensation systems, it is fair to say that the original intent was to reduce, if not eliminate, the litigation process as a means of resolving questions. The first mechanism was to change the key question from 'Who is at fault?' to 'Is the injury a result of a work-related accident?' – a change that effectively neutralized the moral and legal implications of the answer. By so neutralizing the enquiry, the workers' compensation regime sharply reduced the value and desire of parties to pursue and defend these cases. By reducing worker incentives to claim and the absolute cost of individual claims, employer incentives to resist claims were also neutralized.

That last feature of the workers' compensation system was achieved by legislative attempts to effectively replace 'litigation' with an alternative method of decision making, 'adjudication.' The typical adjudication model aped the insurance system, wherein claims adjusters collect evidence (typically through telephone enquiry and investigation), filter the facts through guidelines governing decision makers and issue rulings on entitlement.

That at least was what the founders of North American compensation regimes intended: a claimant provides evidence in support of the claim, while the impartial adjudicator assesses those facts and any-thing else relevant to the case in light of decision-making rules. There is little or no role for the 'premium payer' and, as a result, no need to rely upon or use the diverse armoury of legal weapons upon which employers depended in the pre-workers' compensation system. Yet any observer of North American workers' compensation today knows that the non-litigious adjudicative model is at best only the 'first step' in the life of a workers' compensation claim. What has happened? In short, the following:

- Workers enter a host of claims never envisaged at the outset of the twentieth century.
- Employers vigorously defend the insurance funds against claims.
- Insurers, public and private, have developed elaborate multi-stage decision-making systems that include formal hearings.

The result is a litigation-laden web of adjudicative and tribunal-based decision making, with radically reduced degrees of certainty and predictability in conjunction with increasing administration and party costs.

Fundamentals of the Ontario Workers' Compensation System

The Ontario system was founded, and remains built upon, these basics:[4]

- Most employers are organized into clusters premised on industry type, and pay premiums based on the board's assessment of the degree of risk in that industry; these employers are labelled 'Schedule 1.'
- Schedule 1 employers have no direct liability to either their work-ers or the board in respect of a specific claim, although claim costs can affect premium levels.
- Certain employments are arbitrarily set apart into a form of self-insurance, whereby the board pays claim costs and collects those expenses (plus administrative charges); these are 'Schedule 2' employers.
- The board is responsible for maintaining the solvency of the acci-dent fund to meet present and future obligations; this is achieved through actuarial analysis, determining relative risk levels among employment types and prospective costs.

- Workers claim against the fund; there are also administrative funds set aside by the board to meet its needs in managing and supporting the fund.
- Further, the board established a 'Second Injury and Enhancement Fund' (SIEF) system to subsidize claim costs for employers who had employed previously injured persons (typically veterans) only to see those persons further injured on the job.
- Income-replacement benefit levels are capped (75 per cent of gross earnings before 1985, 90 per cent of net from 1985 through 1997 and 85 per cent of net since 1 January 1998) and subject to maximum and minimum rules. There is no schedule of time limits for collection of benefits, a fact that has inspired a series of statutory and policy initiatives designed to get people back to work sooner.
- Up until 1990 the permanently injured worker was eligible for a lifetime pension, calculated by cross-referencing the percentage of functional impairment against pre-injury earnings; in 1990 that was replaced with a 'dual award system' (more on that below) separating compensation for income loss from that paid for permanent injury.
- The accident fund is responsible for medical aid and other rehabilitation costs necessitated by injuries.

Remarkably, this basic mandate and the core characteristics of Ontario workers' compensation have changed little since the initial report of Sir William Meredith recommended a program of 'workman's compensation' during the First World War.[5] In terms of executing the mandate, the board began its life by actually having a board hear and determine cases. Adjudication was performed around a conference table by sage hands, empowered by a liberal humanist mandate: 'justice, humanely and speedily rendered.' Over the decades it grew into an insurance company, but the basic principles of administrative decision making were still said to govern.

The Situation in the Early 1980s

It is fair to say that by the end of the seventies, the Ontario WCB, like its sister agencies, public and private, across North America, was never well liked. This was in part inherent in its mandate: on the one hand, the board collected funds from employers who were sceptical of it and of its allowance of claims, while, on the other hand, workers were routinely shut out from benefit entitlement with little explanation. Certainly by the early 1980s it was evident that the Ontario system required an overhaul, not only to its statutory provisions but also to its means of service delivery. The key concerns, captured in a set of observations and recommendations by Harvard's Paul Weiler,[6] can be summarized as follows:

- Policy making within the WCB was unpredictable, exclusive of stakeholder input, and unreceptive to change.
- Decision making within the WCB was perceived to be arbitrary, adhering to internal dictates as opposed to the manifest requirements of fairness.
- Client service was organized in a bureaucratic fashion, with claims allocated to departments without regard to the impact on either workers or employers.
- In terms of the substantive law, workers were ill served by the pension system, which calculated lifetime awards according to the terms of an arbitrary 'meat chart' and ignored the actual effects of injury on earning ability (this, along with the re-employment rules first mooted in the 1980–3 period, were not addressed until the end of 1980s, however, following Weiler's second report).[7]
- Severe inequities had developed in the funding system, as 'bad actors' within classification groups continued to produce claims (and, thus, costs) that affected their entire group, denying responsible employers fair reward for their investments in accident prevention.
- Employers began to rely more heavily upon the 'Second Injury and Enhancement Fund' to shift costs from their own classification groups into a generic account funded by all employers; by the end of the 1980s over 15 per cent of all costs to the system were charged to the SIEF, three times the historic average.
- Problems with the board, particularly those experienced by workers, led to a heavy reliance upon external intervention (typically by members of the provincial legislature on behalf of constituents, later by the provincial Office of the Ombudsman) to wrench better-rationalized decisions from the board's adjudicators.

Summarizing these problems, it can be said that by the mid-1980s the Ontario workers' compensation system was perceptibly arbitrary, had few channels of genuine relief from injust decisions, based its policy on its own precedent and internal culture, and was organized in a fashion that maximized the convenience of its own staff rather than that of the client public. Further, the law itself was static, frozen in a mould formed during the First World War that promised only further inequity (particularly among employers funding the accident fund and workers with permanent disabilities) and offered little relief from a continual growth in accident rates and claim costs.

From the perspective of 'pricing' the injury, described above, the classic workers' compensation model at work in Ontario up until 1985 can be said to have affected the value of a workplace injury in this fashion:

- Benefit levels were known and relatively low.
- Decision making was highly predictable, in terms of types of cases readily allowed and those always denied (i.e., back injuries).
- The collectively liable employers' direct stake in case outcomes was very low, providing little incentive to participate.
- Problematic cases were readily allocated to either the SIEF or to the 'administrative fund' (where for years inappropriately allowed claims were shunted, with no effort to collect back benefits paid in error).
- The nascent 'unfunded liability' (the deficit drawn by comparing the current value of future claims to revenue expected in the same time-frame) was thus absorbing a share of costs.
- The bureaucracy insulated decision makers from accountability by prescribing strict policy, and by precluding meaningful appeal routes for aggrieved clients.
- Safety and prevention was consigned to a training and publicity function, ancillary to the compensation function.
- Very limited vocational rehabilitation (VR) functions offered primarily finite social counselling to claimants, with little focus on employment objectives.

The combined effect of these characteristics, it is submitted, significantly suppressed both the 'award value' of an injury (that is, what a claimant could hope to collect) and the 'litigation value' of a case (i.e., what a claimant or employer could expect to achieve through appealing a decision). In terms of pricing policy, the Ontario's workers' compensation system put a tight clamp on the award and litigation values of captured injury cases.

Substantive and Process Changes in the 1980s and 1990s

In response to the Weiler report, and to stakeholder pressure at large, the Ontario Legislature and the board's own administrators initiated a steady stream of reforms commencing in the mid-1980s that radically altered the structure and effect of the compensation system.[8]

The Due-Process Revolution

Following on the damning results of the Weiler investigation and widespread stakeholder discontent, the Conservative government of then-Premier William Davis initiated what we call a 'due-process revolution' into the hitherto dark and murky world of workers' compensation decision making. The key change was the creation of the separate Workers' Compensation Appeals Tribunal ('WCAT' – now the 'Workplace Safety and Insurance Appeals Tribunal'). Resisted for years by both the board and external examiners[9] this change had its greatest effect in producing an avenue for appeals outside the board. That alone would have induced more appeal litigation, but the tribunal took steps to augment that development, publishing its decisions (a first for Canadian workers' compensation rulings), assuming the full mantle of policy-making authority, diverging from past WCB practice, and greatly broadening the net of allowable claims.

The effect was electrifying for the system. First, it welcomed appellants and rewarded their efforts; this in turn turned a spotlight on the past failings of the WCB, forcing it to reorganize its policy-making organs into a more credible entity. The flood of newly allowable cases from the tribunal, while not strictly binding as precedent at the WCB, broke open the policy wall and required decision makers to explain and justify their rulings. A wave of newly allowable cases, with a more liberal interpretation of the statute, caught the attention of employers, who now found the system to be over-generous, unpredictable, and increasingly 'injust' in terms of permissiveness towards claimants. It was no coincidence that the first generation of advocates acting on behalf of employers sprang up in this era, acting not only as litigators but also as policy lobbyists.

The due-process revolution, at the appeals tribunal and later as it permeated the board, had the effect of a forest fire wiping clean a dense thicket of woods. Once the way was clear, the space became an avenue for claimants and employers to use, and as other changes followed, the road became very busy indeed.

Experience Rating of Claim Costs

Arguably the greatest single change in the Ontario system commencing in the 1980s, this act of policy (as opposed to legislative reform) fundamentally altered the perspective of an entire class of stakeholders – the employers. While various small experiments in 'experience rating' had touched the construction industry and certain voluntary players as early as the 1950s, the WCB avoided systematic reform of its assessment and premium-setting functions until the burgeoning unfunded liability and growing inequity of the old system demanded change.[10]

The objectives were both equity among employers and an increase in revenues without maintaining the indefinite escalation of the average assessment.[11] The reform began modestly, targeting a limited number of industry types with new rules that created a new scale for premium setting; depending upon an individual employer's comparative experience within its rate group, premiums could fall below (or significantly exceed) the average.

As a form of equity among employers, experience rating had the effect of quieting complaints from more pro-active (usually larger) companies that had been subsidizing less safety-conscious entities within their rate groups. For all employers, however, the new calculus of a claim (dubbed 'NEER' for 'New Employer Experience Rating') created an interest in claim costs and an incentive to reduce those costs.

To understand this change, the reader needs to know that premium costs for employers were (and still are) set on a dollar value per $100 of payroll. Against this annual fee, the WCB determines an employer's 'expected costs' based on industry averages. To exceed those expected costs shoves an employer into the dangerous territory of higher premiums and penalties; to contain costs below the average produces a refund of some portion of the assessment (which for sizeable employers can amount to hundreds of thousands, and sometimes millions, of dollars, every year). By significantly over-collecting on its initial assessment, the WCB then 'bought peace' by rewarding employers with their own money in the form of these 'generous' refunds. On the other hand, the board had to raise assessment rates repeatedly during

the 1980s and early 1990s to try and narrow the gap in its unfunded liability. Despite the refund system, the effect of rising assessments and
NEER was that more employers faced increased costs than got
rewards, and the overall result was to induce employers to create a
new class of 'WCB administrators' within benefit departments and to
ignite the growth of a private and public employer advocacy industry.

By increasing their participation in cases at all levels, and particularly in appeals, employers in turn motivated workers to become more
vigilant in ensuring claims were allowed (and stayed that way). This
spawned a more acute, and more antagonistic, attitude in the workplace on matters of workers' compensation.

It is likely that up until the 1980s Ontario employers were largely
oblivious to workers' compensation costs, because they were insignificant compared to increasing labour costs, inflated supply costs, the
devaluation of the dollar, and the relatively strong productivity growth
that preceded the late 1970s. When the NEER system, combined with
escalating assessments, produced increased costs, that occurred at precisely the moment when easy revenue growth had ceased. Despite the
relatively minimal cost of workers' compensation, even in comparison
to other forms of insurance, the effect of sharp increases (or even possible increases due to one or two expensive claims) was an attention-
getter.

It is arguable that even if there had been no other changes to the system than the creation of the appeals tribunal and the introduction of
NEER, Ontario workers' compensation would still have undergone a
transformation into a litigation culture. Those were not the only
reforms, of course, and it was the combined effect of further changes
that produced the overall result.

Free Representation for Stakeholders

The publicly mandated Offices of the Worker and Employer Adviser
(created in 1985)[12] produced a practical and intellectual stimulus for
more litigation in the system. These offices were created to provide
information and advocacy, free of charge, to interested and qualified
clients on both the worker and employer side of the system. This was
clearly more advantageous to workers, who hitherto relied upon a few
specialized agencies, pro bono work from lawyers, or an assortment of
marginally trained 'advocates,' but also offered a service to employers
who preferred not to secure their own counsel.

In addition to advocacy services, the Ontario worker and employer adviser offices, who receive their funding from the board, also act to lobby and oppose the board at every turn. While many observers would see this as an absurdity, the demand for and acceptance of such a move in the mid-1980s is a perfect indictment of the intransigence and arbitrariness seen in the WCB up to that point. The OWA and OEA had (and still have) their greatest impact in the management and litigation of claims issues. By raising the standard of advocacy (particularly on the worker side) and by simply being available to do the work at no cost, the offices suddenly offered parties a resource that enabled them to pursue their new interest in the system through the new avenues of appeal. The outcome should have been predictable: more work than either office could ever manage, and a substantial share of the appeal load that beset both the tribunal and the WCB's internal appeals process.

Re-organization of WCB Service Delivery

Beginning with a centralized office that allocated claims seemingly at random, organizational reform was a necessary step to better decision making. The first answer was to develop 'geographic catchment areas' in the province, and to situate offices in or near those catchment areas.[13] The second was to put claims and rehabilitation staff together in one office, labelled an 'integrated service unit.' The idea was to forge a coherent management of cases by making specialists work together on teams. A later step was the elimination of technically skilled managers, replacing them with anyone who had 'generic' management skills.

Decentralization exposed and exacerbated wide gulfs in philosophy and style between the different regional offices. Hence, one or two remote offices became famous (or infamous) for their rigidity, reputedly deplorable decision-making skills, and hostility to claimants. The result was a spike in the frequency of appeals in those areas, and the growth of strongly adversarial relationships between regional-office staff and local stakeholders. So serious did this situation become that by the mid-1990s the board itself was establishing special projects simply to 'manage' appeal cases coming from one regional office, so as to try and reduce the volume and complexity of appeals emitting from that office.

Another important step was the introduction of new technology –

first voice mail, and then optical-disc imaging storage of claim files. Both steps increased the amount of information available, leading to better decision making – arguably suppressing the number of issues that might be appealed. On the other hand, in the climate of litigation that was bred in the 1980s and bloomed in the 1990s, these new technologies simply sped up the claims process. It is arguable that once stakeholders caught the litigation fever, the quality of a decision would have little or no impact. It's possible, in fact, that knowing a claim would move with more speed through the claims and VR processes encouraged people to challenge rulings, because there was a foreseeable end to the process at the appeals tribunal.

'Older Worker Supplements'

It is difficult to quantify the system effects of the board's 1988–90 effort to enact new provisions governing the payment of supplements to pension-holders.[14]

Under the provisions, pension-receiving workers who had received past VR service or who were unlikely to gain 'earning capacity' with more VR, were entitled to a monthly stipend equal to the Old Age Supplement paid Canadian retirees. The purpose of the supplement was stark and simple: to permanently buy off workers from pursuing more expensive rehabilitation services. Easy access to these supplements at the outset led, on reviews several years later, to thousand of supplements being turned off, which in turn induced the previously quiescent pension recipients to appeal. Appeals resulted in extended supplements, or to the very thing the supplements were intended to avoid: a large growth in the VR population. With reviews occurring more than once, there was no sign of this claimant population being reduced, and by the mid-1990s yet another large-scale project team was responsible for managing the matter.

The Dual-Award System and Recession

As discussed earlier, the traditional model of compensation for permanent injury was a formula mixing degree of functional loss with pre-injury income. The result was a notorious, and not inconsiderable, population of lifetime pension recipients who returned to work at no wage loss. The standard example for illustrating the frailties of this system was that of the worker who loses a finger. Under the 'meat chart' system he would receive a pension equivalent to 5 or 6 per cent of his former net earnings.

For the bricklayer or labourer, the lost finger might have no effect on earnings: he would resume his paid employment in days; but for another person, a pianist, the lost finger meant a total loss of earnings. Here in a simple example were all the inequities and failings of the permanent pension system. The other problem here was that the pension system was rapidly escalating in cost, and the board had no means to staunch the flow of cash going to pension recipients.[15]

To address these problems of equity and cost, the Ontario government in 1989 adopted a 'dual award system' severing the compensation of earnings loss from that of functional loss. By focusing award dollars on the earnings side, the new system was intended to assist what was perceived to be the most serious long-term problem, the loss of earning ability, while limiting the compensation of functional impairments to a very low, often lump-sum award. This system was developed in conjunction with a new regime of worker 'rights' to vocational rehabilitation, intended to mitigate the loss of earning capacity through retraining and job placement. The intent was to offer these services to workers with an obvious loss of earnings, in hopes of replacing some or all of their earning capacity.

Events worked against the plan. First was the inevitable problem of determining a worker's ability to earn, which lead to considerable argument as to the justice of 'deeming' a person able to make a wage that he or she wasn't actually earning. While the legislation clearly empowered the board to 'deem' earning capacity, a change of government (from the Liberal authors of the 1990 legislation to the New Democratic Party) made any open deeming a political impossibility. Thus, the board was required by policy to maintain workers on long-term earning-loss supplements while attempting to place them in jobs. The second obstacle was the effect of the deepening recession, which posed a serious barrier to the re-employment of healthy workers, never mind those with permanent functional impairments.[16] The combined effect of restrictions on deeming in an environment of widespread unemployment was to give workers powerful incentives to prolong their benefit entitlement by seeking (and often obtaining) lengthy and repeated periods of vocational rehabilitation services.

This phenomenon occurred precisely at the point where the majority of employers became subject to experience rating, and the effects were considerable: workers with little competitive standing in the labour market took the rational step of falling back on a compensation system that had been advertised, and shaped to operate, as a more lasting and constructive alternative to unemployment insurance or welfare. Employers in a shrinking economy were faced with burgeoning accident cost records and consequent premium hikes. Again, this recipe bred a steady growth in the frequency and complexity of appeals.

Rehabilitation and Re-employment Appeals

As described earlier, the 1990 amendments, known as Bill 162, contained not only revisions to permanent impairment compensation, but also substantial efforts to mitigate those losses. One mechanism was a set of 'rehabilitation rights' that afforded workers the right to be assessed for, offered, and well served by WCB vocational rehabilitation staff. Twinned with these were meatier provisions requiring employers to rehire their injured staff if those workers met certain criteria. The legislative purpose was both to protect workers from the discrimination they typically met in the labour market (by giving them employment preferences) and to reduce compensation costs by giving workers incentives to demand their re-employment rights, rather than to demand more benefits.[17]

In a very real way, this new approach was the first step in what has emerged as a pattern of 'privatizing' the compensation system by imposing upon employers the rehabilitation tasks originally adopted by the board. With relatively rigorous application, and very high penalties by historic standards, the Board used re-employment as a means of drawing employers much more intensely into the task of mitigating the costs of injury.

The board was creative in its treatment of the VR and re-employment provisions, employing a unique form of 'mediation' in these cases. The reality of mediation in this context was to educate the parties as to the likely outcomes of cases when heard by adjudicators, and to persuade those same parties to agree to resolve the matter before a formal hearing. Legally this dispute-resolution effort appeared suspect, as the board at no time had statutory authority to defer to the wishes of the parties on any issue. In practice, though, the approach invited parties to take ownership of issues and to acknowledge the effect of the law rather than have it imposed upon them. This approach too fit the pattern of inadvertent 'privatization' of the system.

While the relative numbers of re-employment cases were modest, there was a perceptible ripple effect. But part of that impact was to escalate the level and number of appeals. First, the re-employment penalties sometimes exceeded $30,000 for a single transgression – unheard of in the Ontario regime. Second, a serious rift opened between the board's interpretation of the provisions and that held by the appeals tribunal (in a reversal of past pattern, it was the board that held the view more agreeable to workers). The result was a standing invitation to employers to challenge all board re-employment decisions in order to meet a less exacting legal standard at the final appeal. It could also be said that the onerous re-employment provisions tended to compel employers to obtain better-equipped representation, drawing more experienced labour practitioners more deeply into the workers' compensation system.

The Political and Policy Environment of the Early 1990s

Earlier it was discussed how the board's arbitrary internal policy engines were scrapped and replaced in the late 1980s. Leaving aside highly prescriptive, example-driven policies, the board shifted to thick binders of 'guidelines' offering decision-making principles, often in highly ambiguous language. The effect on board decision makers was often devastating, as they fumbled with new-found degrees of discretion.

One result was inconsistency: just as service delivery was decentralized to regions and integrated service units, so too were the principles and practices of decision making shifted to the front line.[18] This was not intentional, but rather was born out of necessity: decision makers needed rules by which to make decisions, and where those rules were coined in language that was too vague or legalistic for them to follow, the decision makers had first to decide what the rules said. It was a remarkable exercise in inadvertently shifting authority to the front line, a practical form of 'empowerment' predating the deliberate 'flattening' of the organizational structure in 1990–91.

Where policy changed substantively, it did so in ways that induced new claims: the early recognition of back claims, the development of a 'chronic pain' policy that accepted as a legal-medical entity a condition of ennui and depression that a generation earlier was dismissed as 'malingering.'

While the years of the Liberal government (1985–90) saw a high degree of policy change and the aforementioned Bill 162 revisions, political changes also played upon the tendency of stakeholders to challenge decisions. Principally there was the philosophy of 'bipartism,' wherein the government attempted to populate the WCB's board of directors with a group balanced between the representatives of labour and management. The intent was balance; the result was paralysis, with little substantive policy making taking place during the term of the New Democratic government (late 1990 to mid-1995). As is typical in governments, where power isn't exercised it simply moves into hands willing to use it; in this instance, stakeholders took some degree of power into their own hands and used the appeal system as a means of achieving case-specific changes that might once have been sought at a political level.

Such a phenomenon can never be quantified; it can only be observed. This writer's view is that both the appeals tribunal and the board's own internal appeals group gradually absorbed a certain degree of *de facto* policy-making power by means of decision-writing; similarly, the board's own operational 'front line' units adopted their own processes and methods of making decisions, sometimes at odds with the appeals units and with only a sidelong glance at written policy. This tendency dovetailed with, and enhanced, the growing trend towards litigating workers' compensation cases.

The Growth of Litigation

Having described at some length the conditions that created the growth of litigation in the Ontario workers' compensation system, we have only limited figures to illustrate the phenomenon. First are the statistics reflecting the emergence of the appeals tribunal as an active player in the system, which reveal substantial growth in the number of appeals each year since 1985.

The appeals tribunal's first year was marked with a high number of applications, presumably representing pent-up demand among claimants:[19] there were 2609 appeals lodged in the 1985–6 business year, with a drop to 1854 in the following year.[20] What must be remembered about those numbers is that they incorporate cases that, in the years before 1985, might not have been appealed, or perhaps would have been pursued in an ad hoc fashion through political channels.[21]

Numbers of appeals grew steadily through the late 1980s and early 1990s (escalating from 1579 cases in 1991 to just over 2300 in 1995 – about a 50 per cent increase in that time period). Then they skyrocketed, to almost 3600 for the year 1996. This growth parallels the implementation and widening effect of the Bill 162 provisions, with its multiplicity of issues, together with the concurrent expansion of NEER.

It is impossible to ever quantify the effect the appeals tribunal had upon cases that never left the board, for while the board was avowedly independent of the tribunal in matters of policy, it was the WCB that totally revamped its policy and appeal processes in the years after 1985. Further, the inevitable impact of highly publicized cases such as those emanating from the tribunal was to sway junior decision makers to adhere to the tribunal's thinking, or at least to couch their decisions in terms that might survive appeal.

It is evident that the effect of the appeals tribunal was to increase the volume of appeals overall. Nonetheless, some potential appeals were avoided by a resolution of cases within the board based on an under-standing of how the tribunal would dispose of them on appeal. We can only guess at the 'NET' change in the volume of appeals, but it would be safe to say that the result was a considerable increase.

There are few reliable sources for appeal statistics at the WCB before 1990. References to the size of appeal dockets in Weiler's 1980 report indicate that the combined paper-review functions (usually dubbed 'decision review') and the subsequent hearing process moved 21,000 'appeals.' This throughput of appeals undoubtedly captures several years' accumulation of backlogged cases, however – part of the prob-lem leading to the first recommendation for an external appeals agency.[22]

Looking at available board statistics on appeal volumes, we see that the real explosion occurred after 1990 and the implementation of dual awards, re-employment, and rehabilitation rights – just as NEER took full effect in the employer community. The total number of cases in 'paper' and/or full-hearing appeals at the WCB tripled in the period of 1990 through 1994. The numbers receded somewhat thereafter, thanks largely to internal reforms that imposed more stringent demands upon applicants.[23]

The numbers of appeals, on their own, illustrate an explosive growth in litigation. These statistics should not be read in isolation from other pertinent facts, namely, the trend in the number of claims filed with the board. From a peak of approximately 489,000 claims filed in 1988 (of which about 8 per cent were denied at the board), the numbers of new claims declined steadily through the 1990s, to about 365,000 in 1995.[24]

There followed a steep drop in 1996, to only 337,000 new cases, of which about one in six were denied or sidelined by the WCB.[25]

The clear implication is that the numbers of appeals, as a percentage of the overall 'claim population,' has sharply escalated in the 1990s. Indeed, while new claims have dropped by about 30 per cent in the period 1988 through 1996, internal appeals have tripled and appeals tribunal applications have more than doubled in the same time-frame. The best available conclusion, relying upon these statistics and the historical record of substantive and process reform, is that Ontario's considerable experimentation in workers' compensation during the 1980s and 1990s produced at least one clear result: an explosion in the frequency of parties challenging decisions to one level of appeal or another. So, while claims themselves are down, the appeals systems continue to clog with new cases and demands from parties.

Implications for Pricing Workers' Compensation Cases

At the outset of this paper, it was stated that the workers' compensation system is a means of applying price control to personal injuries sustained in the workplace. This, through 'no fault' insurance and a flexible form of collective liability, insulates employers from the costs of worker injuries. Workers' compensation offers the worker a relatively predictable recompense, or price, for the injury, at minimal cost in terms of litigation. Sceptics of the system challenge that assertion, and use the Ontario example of exponential litigation growth as a sign that the cost savings won through monopoly state no-fault insurance are on the wane.

Certainly the Ontario experience shows that parties now see greater value in their claims, and in opposing them. This is hardly surprising, as the law has realigned the allocation of resources from the functionally impaired to the earnings-impaired, while the Ontario economy has only recently begun to create jobs after years of staggering contraction in the labour market and burgeoning unemployment. The factor that must always be posited in evaluating the 'price' of an injury is that its relative value increases where the injured person's alternatives shrink. That, in this writer's view, is the other and most significant factor 'outside' the system inducing the growth of appeals litigation.

Earlier on in this paper we considered the notions of 'award value' and 'litigation value' in a claim; that is, a claim has a maximum likely dollar value, and litigation has a varying degree of impact on that value. In Ontario there has clearly been enough growth in litigation to signal that it has value to the parties in enhancing or suppressing the award value of claims, and there has clearly been expansion of the incentives both parties have to pursue or oppose the allowance of benefits under legislation. Comparing this system with that replaced by workers' compensation, namely tort liability, we see in the latter a pricing system where virtually every single claim is resisted by the defendants and where a substantial percentage of cases are settled for less than the initial 'asking price.' This means, in contrast to workers' compensation, that personal-injury cases are priced high enough to draw sufficient numbers of claims into the system, and are priced high enough to induce defendants to resist. Further, the existence of voluntary insurance coverage for defendants and/or the cost of litigation further induce many defendants to settle, rather than to fight and win the cases.

All of this means that a plaintiff is likely to be rewarded with some form of economic value, should he or she go so far as to file suit. Given the absence of both a floor and a ceiling on these values, anything can be claimed and will be if there is reason to think a court will accept it. The tort plaintiff has that advantage because there is no 'price ceiling'on the value of the claim – in contrast to workers' compensation, where the economic value of the claim is tightly controlled (being a multiple of pre-injury earnings, with strict scrutiny on the claim duration).

Like most forms of price control, the workers' compensation system creates as swiss-cheese of advantages and disadvantages, depending upon the nature of the case and the plaintiff's losses. For high-earning workers with marginal temporary disabilities, a workers' compensation claim can be disadvantageous in contrast to attempting to file an insurance claim for private disability coverage. For low-earning workers with sub-optimal vocational options, the workers' compensation system in Ontario (particularly after 1990) produced strong incentives to claim and appeal – because the 'price ceiling' in the claim is so much greater than the value of his labour in a market with shrinking demand for unskilled personnel.

On the other hand, the initial barrier to claiming in a personal-injury case is steep (one has to buy one's way into the decision-making process, whereas workers' compensation compels people to report cases of injury). Thus, there is still reason to believe that no-fault workers' compensation insurance brings about a more realistic *reporting* level of claims as compared to tort. The barriers to filing and maintaining a lawsuit have to mean that a certain number of tort cases are not pursued, creating a downward drag on the overall price of injuries as priced in the tort system. That does not exist in the workers' compensation system, because the price of the injury is impervious to demand.

What this tells us about workers' compensation as a pricing mechanism for personal injury, in the recent experience of the province of Ontario, is this:

- Seemingly more generous benefit policies, as adopted by the Ontario regime in 1990, do not significantly affect the incidence of initial reporting (at least not in a contracting economy).
- Subtle changes in the decision process, with moves towards greater transparency and better adherence to due-process principles, have had a marked effect on the likelihood of cases being appealed at various stages.
- Policy changes encouraging longer benefit durations have induced both workers and employers to participate in the system more vigorously.
- Policy changes slightly increasing employers' direct liability have had a very bracing effect on Ontario employers, motivating a degree of investment in workers' compensation cost control that might not have been warranted.
- Overall participation rates in the system have declined in terms of initial claims, but skyrocketed in terms of long-term involvement through the appeal process; this is a reflection of the real value of claims, as registered through wage-loss benefits, rehabilitation services, and re-employment costs that are all being felt on accident cost-reporting statements.

Conclusions

Given all the factors at play, it is perhaps most striking how *low* the relative number of appeals continues to be: even at the 1996 peak, appeal applications at the tribunal equal just over 1 per cent of total claims filed in that same year, and just 3 per cent of lost-time cases. While this represents a 150 per cent rise in the past decade (WCAT in 1988 received 2019 applications, equal to 0.41 per cent of the board's new-claim total that year), the ratio of appeals to new claims has not spiked astronomically; after all, 99 per cent of cases do *not* reach the appeals tribunal.

The first implication we can take from this is that most claimants, and employers, are sufficiently satisfied with the results of particular cases as not to appeal board decisions. Such a conclusion would jibe with the standard report by most Canadian workers' compensation agencies that the vast majority of claims are settled rapidly, involve a short period of temporary disability, and result in no permanent award. Typical figures indicate 70 to 80 per cent of claims being resolved satisfactorily within six or eight weeks.

From a pricing perspective, this means that workers' compensation is effective in suppressing the price of an injury in short-term claims, so that neither claimants nor employers see significant economic advantage in litigation. Understanding that workers' compensation is, first and foremost, a price-control mechanism on workplace personal injury, we are led to conclude that the Ontario system continues to achieve one of its primary objectives, at least in the majority of claims.

Yet there are other possible implications as well. If we recognize that workers' compensation is a price-control system, then we must also see that the restrictive force of the law in containing the value of an injury will affect the behaviours surrounding workplace accidents and safety. If injuries are underpriced, for example (which is probably true in comparison with the tort regime), then they lose considerable significance to the parties who might otherwise be deemed 'responsible' for the injuries (be those individuals employers, third parties, or the workers themselves). Causal behaviours simply have less meaning and gain less attention when less weight hangs on their consequences. This is something the tort system understands, as explained above.

Arguably, the Ontario system has attempted to compensate for this effect by increasing employers' share of collective liability costs through the experience rating of premiums. In Ontario this has thrown some light on the most extreme cases, attracting employers' attention particularly to the issue of benefit duration. Yet even here, with a three-year 'window' limiting the long-term effects of claims, employers have only a finite period of time during which they sustain higher cost from a claim. This window, which closes off the premium effects of claims after their third year, has become a determinative fact in how employers address claims; after three years, they usually forget about them, because there is no longer any serious cost implication. Thus, the 'litigation value' of a claim drops to nothing for employers at that point, while for workers it remains precious.[26]

Thus, Ontario created a system of varying incentives for workers and employers, incentives with greater or lesser significance depending upon the worker's characteristics, the nature of the injury, the duration of the claim, and the employer's capacity to bear premium increases. In order to keep the face (award) value of a claim relatively low and predictable, Ontario appears to have inadvertently developed a dynamic, unpredictable, increasingly complex decision-making system where employers and workers find varying degrees of value in litigation.

The ultimate question, then, is whether the costs and complexities of the workers' compensation system operating 'underground' now outweigh the advantages of controlling prices on the surface. The system controls prices and so regulates demand and reduces the relative cost of resisting individual claims; this is projected as advantageous to employers, but in truth it has been grossly disadvantageous to many employers and the system remains almost indecipherable, except to a specialized class of workers' compensation experts and professionals. Only safety valves like the three-year NEER limit and the recent legislative rollbacks of entitlement terms have contained the damage to Ontario employers. Aggressive use of the new legislation could well lead to a more serious outbreak of litigation fever among employers.

Similarly, workers in Ontario pay a high price for the system – individually, in the statutorily limited value of their claims, and collectively, in that the system is now subject to reversals of benefits and services because of a widely perceived sense that too many recipients were taking too much out of the accident fund. Further, workers have always paid the price simply in terms of having to deal with the board, which, as described above, has historically been viewed as unfriendly and foreign to working people.

While the participants pay depending on their relative positions in the market, the effect on society at large and the economy is too complex to summarize here. Suffice it to say that the price-control effects of workers' compensation appear to suppress the 'bottom-line' effects of injury in a fair proportion of cases, meaning that the productive activity of employers is not endangered by large numbers of expensive injury claims. On the other hand, by immunizing employers from direct cost the system numbs stakeholders to the effects of their decisions, altering their behaviours and, to the extent serious permanent disabilities result, creating human and economic losses that can hardly be quantified and are not being compensated.

The results are perverse and deserve more attention. Less-competitive workers with lower earning capacities see greater award and litigation value in pursuing claims, and do so to the long-term cost of other workers whose wage competitiveness makes workers' compensation a poor substitute for working while injured. The accident fund continues to subsidize the less safety-conscious and responsible employers, meaning that the workers' compensation system effectively allows the latter group to operate (and compete) for less cost than safety-conscious employers. The recent spate of litigation has, most likely, been a sign that less competitive or responsible actors are taking advantage of the system, and also that the workers and employers subsidizing all this have begun to resist. So long as workers and employers are involuntarily chained to the mandatory price-control method in place in Ontario, the volume of litigation is likely to keep growing.

NOTES

1 Thirteen in Canada, 58 in the United States. See U.S. Dept. of Labor, *State Workers' Compensation Laws*.
2 Ibid.
3 Linden, *Canadian Tort Law* (1982).
4 Sir William Meredith, *Laws Relating to the Liability of Employers*, 1913.
5 Ibid.
6 Weiler, *Reshaping Workers' Compensation in Ontario* (1980).
7 Weiler, *Permanent Partial Disability: Alternative Models for Compensation* (1986).
8 Legislature of Ontario, *Final Report of the Standing Committee on Resource Development* (1983).
9 See the 1959–60 royal commission study (the Roach report), the 1967 *Report of the Royal Commission in the Matter of Workmen's Compensation* (McGillivray report), and the WCB's 1968 'Brief to the Resources Development Committee' in reply to McGillivray.
10 The WCB's internal 'Sessions Book' for 1973, for example, discusses voluntary experience-rating approaches within Schedule 1, which were deliberately modest.
11 Note the WCB's annual reports in the period 1980–9, which show an increase in the average annual assessment from $1.65 per $100 of payroll (1980) to $2.88 by 1987.

12 McGillivray describes how the board maintained an internal worker adviser staff for many years, but this was found wanting both by Weiler (1980) and the Legislature standing committee (1983).
13 Another response to Weiler's 1980 study, this time from administrators rather than the legislature.
14 Originally section 147(4) of the Workers' Compensation Act as amended in 1990 through the Bill 162 provisions.
15 After seeing his initial recommendations for a dual-award system rebuffed by the legislature in 1984, Paul Weiler went at the matter again in his 1986 report, noting that in the period 1980 through 1985 pensions costs to the accident fund had increased almost 100 per cent.
16 *The Displaced Workers of Ontario*, published by the Ontario Ministry of Labour's Economics and Labour Market Research group in 1993, demonstrates how in the 1990–91 period economic growth fell to −10 per cent, with unemployment doubling to over 10 per cent in the short interval of late 1989 to early 1991. The number of permanently laid-off employees almost doubled from 1989 to 1990 and totalled almost 100,000 people in the first three years of the 1990s. The report concludes that healthy displaced workers suffered long-term losses of earning capacity compared to their pre-injury jobs and noted that health and skills limitations made these effects more severe.
17 This was a Weiler-based initiative considered in the 1984 reforms but deferred, and ultimately housed in sections 53 and 54 of the act as amended in 1990.
18 The board ultimately issued something of a mea culpa in this regard, in a self-critical document entitled the 'Operational Review,' produced over the course of 1992. This did not lead to significant change in policy development, however, for reasons described elsewhere in this paper.
19 The Workers' Compensation Appeals Tribunal (WCAT) 'First Report' in 1986 noted that a 'backlog of 1,100 cases existed on the Tribunal's first day of existence.'
20 WCAT 'Second Report.' 1987.
21 Wildly inappropriate and inequitable treatment was afforded appellants within the board in the 1970s, where connections and ethnic background were often determining factors in one's access to a reconsideration of the case. The board itself took another view, describing its 1965 conversion to a four-stage decision pyramid as another example of 'the Board's effort to ensure that justice continues to be a major part of the humanitarianism practised by the WCB' (1973 Sessions Book). Weiler, less glowing, thought

the quality of appeals decisions admirable by the late 1970s (after another internal reorganization), but found the delays 'intolerable.'

22 Weiler, 1980; Legislature Standing Committee, 1983.
23 Total appeals for this five-year period: 1990, 155; 1991, 815; 1992, 2088; 1993, 2506; 1994, 2355. Source: J. Slinger, Director of Client Appeals, Ontario WSIB.
24 WCB annual reports, 1984–96.
25 Ibid.
26 A good illustration of this phenomenon is apparent in the province of Nova Scotia, which caps experience-rating costs at a maximum of one year's benefits; the effect is to give employers little reason to oppose long-term benefit decisions, with the consequence of relatively low employer participation in appeals litigation.

REFERENCES

Legislature of Ontario. 1983. *Final Report of the Standing Committee on Resource Development*. Toronto: Queen's Printer.
Linden, Allen M. 1982. *Canadian Tort Law*. Toronto: Butterworths.
McGillivray, George. 1967. *Report of the Royal Commission in the Matter of Workmen's Compensation*. Toronto: The Commission.
Meredith, Sir William Ralph. 1913. *Final Report on the Laws Relating to the Liability of Employers to Make Compensation to Their Employees for Injuries Received in the Course of Their Employment Which Are in Force in Other Countries*. Toronto: L.K. Cameron.
Ontario Ministry of Labour. 1993. *The Displaced Workers of Ontario: How Do They Fare?* Toronto: Economics and Labour Market Research Group, Ontario Ministry of Labour.
Ontario Workers' Compensation Board. Various years. *Annual Report*. Toronto: Ontario Workers' Compensation Board.
– 1968. 'Brief to the Resources Development Committee.' Mimeo. Toronto: OWCB.
– 1973. *Sessions Book*. Toronto: OWCB.
Roach, Wilfred. 1960. *Report on the Workmen's Compensation Act*. Toronto: OWCB.
United States Department of Labor. 1995. *State Workers' Compensation Laws*. Washington: Employment Standards Administration, Office of Workers' Compensation Programs.

Weiler, Paul C. 1980. *Reshaping Workers' Compensation in Ontario*. Toronto: Ontario Ministry of Labour.

– 1986. *Permanent Partial Disability: Alternative Models for Compensation*. Toronto: Ontario Ministry of Labour.

Workers' Compensation Appeals Tribunal. 1986. *First Report of the Workers' Compensation Appeals Tribunal*. Toronto: WCAT.

– 1987. *Second Report of the Workers' Compensation Appeals Tribunal*. Toronto: WCAT.

11 Should Work-Injury Compensation Continue to Imbibe at the Tort Bar?

DOUGLAS HYATT and DAVID K. LAW

Workers' compensation systems bar workers and their families from bringing an action against the worker's employer, the employer's agent, or a co-worker in respect of any personal injury, disablement, or death arising out of and in the course of employment. In exchange, it is said that workers have received a form of 'social insurance.' Employers are charged with funding that insurance, but are protected from liability. This, in essence, is the 'historic compromise' – the rock upon which workers' compensation is built.

This provision, in one form or another, is contained in every North American workers' compensation (WC) statute. In Canada, we can trace this back to the report of Sir William Meredith (1913: 15) who, after enumerating the sacrifices of workers under the proposed WC insurance plan, stated the most significant one of all: 'It must be borne in mind that the workman is required, as the price of the compensation he is to receive, to surrender his right to damages under the common law, if his injury happens under circumstances entitling him by the common law to recover.'

The key logic to this sacrifice, as we know, is that the worker traded his uncertain right to greater awards for more certain entitlement to limited compensation.

To many observers concerned about the plight of workers, the system shifts risks and costs upon those who are injured (or who might be injured) and puts restrictive limits on the value of awards gained through claims for redress. Inevitably, these parties have begun to consider alternative systems that might place a higher value on the workers' health and economic prospects – a system like the tort regime. The tort regime, particularly in the United States, appears to grant substantially greater recognition to the dollar value of personal injury (particularly for non-pecuniary losses). If the degree of political heat behind 'tort reform' is any indicator, it would seem that plaintiff power in the courts has grown significantly in the past two decades. For workers afforded comparatively less insurance against workplace hazards, the option of suing one's employer becomes more appealing. This becomes even more true as WC systems clamp down on costs through benefit reductions.

For many employers, the workers' compensation system seems cumbersome, expensive, inflexible, and oblivious to the realities of the market (Koester, 1997). Absorbing a proportion of their neighbour's risk through collective liability, employers battle against escalations of their own accident costs while continuing to subsidize other companies in their risk groups. Weary of staggering annual premiums and the seeming politicization of the workplace through government intervention, employers and their advocates increasingly see advantages in wiping the slate clean and re-instituting the tort system.

The inclination to sue is already visible in the United States, where worker-plaintiffs have attempted to augment the WC benefit schedule by aggressively pursuing product liability claims against equipment providers, or suits against their employers under the rubric of a 'dual capacity doctrine' (Jackson, 1995). Efforts to sue in Canada have been thwarted by the courts' continuing deference to the legislature, but at least one appeal court ruling has explicitly stated that the constitutionality of limits on a worker's right of action will last only as long as WC provides that worker with a benefit generally comparable to that afforded in tort.[1]

If the two parties with opposing interests see salvation in the same response, should they be granted their wish? Underlying that question is another query: can both parties be right about the efficacy of the tort regime as a substitute (or supplement) for workers' compensation? We believe that the answer is 'No, they both can't be right, but they could both be *wrong.*' At a minimum, abandoning the collective liability–no fault regime, even in part, merits a closer look before leaping.

This chapter has seven more sections. We begin by describing what the workers' compensation system sought to achieve when it was established in the early part of the twentieth century. This is followed by a discussion of what employers and workers got (get) from the system, and the sources of disenchantment that are leading some in the stakeholder communities to call for a return to tort. We then contrast the wrongs addressed by tort and workers' compensation. Outcomes of the two approaches are compared in section 4, with a focus on two types of claims – back injuries and facial disfigurement – in Ontario and British Columbia. In section 5, we review recent judicial decisions that have addressed the tort bar and offer the opinion that the bar faces no serious threat. While we believe that workers' compensation is still superior to tort for most workers much of the time, we suggest in section 6 some possible areas for tort access that would not entirely abandon the historic compromise. Summary comments conclude the chapter.

1. What Did Workers' Compensation Seek to Achieve and Why?

Very often it seems that the question of cost dominates any discussion of workers' compensation administration and reform. However, the cost debate overshadows the reciprocal topic: *rewards*. The legislative founders of workers' compensation in North America built the system to deliver certain results believed to be of value both to the people of their day and to subsequent generations. By examining the putative goals of the system and, in subsequent sections, the degree to which they've been achieved, we may obtain a more complete picture of the system, its merits and faults. Then we can ponder whether to junk, re-model, or simply sustain the workers' compensation system we live with today.

What were the objectives sought in the first decade of this century, when American states and Canadian provinces began to adopt collective-liability / no-fault insurance systems for employment-related injuries? While the passage of time has resulted in many reinterpretations of its original intent, we believe that there were three overarching goals for the WC system at its inception: first, a remedy for the suffering of workers injured without insurance or chance of reasonable redress; second, protection for employers against potentially expensive and disruptive personal-injury litigation; and, third, the prevention of social instability inherent in either or both of those ills going unchecked. To appreciate how important these goals would have appeared to people at the turn of the last century, it is helpful to recall the economic, social, and legal environment at the time (Humphries et al., 1998, chapter 1).

As the last century ended, the migration of labour from agricultural, rural, and small-town life had begun in earnest, as populations shifted to larger towns and industrial activity. The emergence of technologies and methods of mass production had been cemented, with a permanent shift from craft to unskilled labour. Machines posed new hazards, and imposed accelerated rates of production – both of which invited accidents and injuries.

At the same time, working people had begun to see themselves (and to be seen) as a separate class, with interests different from (and frequently in conflict with) those of their employers. Workers formed organizations to represent them collectively, and created self-insurance associations such as 'friendly societies' to attend to their common concerns and bargaining efforts with employers.

The courts, however, along with the legal system they administered, did not immediately absorb or understand the scope of change in the economic life of employer and worker. Being lawyers, judges tended to adhere to established principles, precedents, and rules in coming to an understanding of the rights and responsibilities of the parties to an employment contract. That is why, for example, the courts (and the state) were so ready to view collective bargaining as a form of criminal conspiracy before the legislative introduction of trade-union laws in the nineteenth century.

Drawing on the rich reservoir of legal literature, the courts saw the late-nineteenth-century employment arrangement through the prism of the class-based 'master-servant' relationship. Similarly, where a worker sued his employer for damages resulting from an accident at work, the courts managed the issue of workplace hazards and injuries with the traditional methods of adjudicating any personal injury – applying normal principles of contributory negligence, assumption of risk, the joint responsibility of co-workers, and even the payment of 'danger pay' to the case. Thus, workers faced considerable legal hurdles to securing fair redress for injuries incurred in circumstances where they had little or no real power.

The barriers to a worker's claim lay in stark contrast to the employer's almost complete power over the workplace, safety behind legal barriers, and comparatively ample resources in defending itself against suit. It is very important, at the end of the twentieth century, to try and capture a sense of the situation facing the injured worker ninety years ago. Bereft of most institutional supports, a worker disabled from working immediately fell upon his own resources – savings, at first, then (maybe) the earnings of a spouse. Churches and other charitable organizations might have interceded in the case of an injured man unable to support his dependents. Relatives, if they had money or a room, might also support the injured person and his family. A prolonged recovery from work-related injury could readily rob a man (and it was usually men in this situation) of his home, family, and place in social life. It is not insignificant, too, that the injured man's 'role' in life was irreparably damaged, and that he and his family would suffer the indignity of falling back upon the wife's ability to earn, or the support of a charity.

In economic terms, a series of negative outcomes flowed from a worker's prolonged illness after a work-related accident. First, the worker's capacity to act as a consumer was reduced or eliminated, affecting everyone in the 'food chain' of that worker's spending decisions. Second, the need to hoard resources (savings) in case of a rainy day reduced the pre-injury consumption of the family, and given that this requirement fell upon everyone in the economy (for everyone is a potential injured worker and must, to the degree they're interested, plan for bad luck), the overall effect was likely to keep savings rates higher than truly necessary. Further, in that these savings would often be utterly unable to meet the needs of the injured person and his dependents, this hoarding of resources was ultimately futile anyway.

Fourth, the effect of impoverishment and the loss of social standing is devastating to anyone, including the families of injured workers. It is a galling and distasteful thing to see one's lot in life diminished owing to circumstances outside one's control (workplace hazards) and to have almost no recourse. The general effect of such suffering is for one to become disenchanted with, and hostile towards, the governing political and economic order.

Fifth, a typical outcome in these cases would be that the injured worker would return to the economy, in some alternative employment within his physical ability, usually at reduced pay and status. This effort at mitigating the wage loss was (and is) laudable and morally preferable to having the worker languish in impoverished victimhood, but was in the most practical terms a poor use of 'human resources' – that is, the accident employer's and the worker's investment of time and training in the pre-injury occupation was lost forever to the permanent injury.

Finally, a society that tolerates a corrosive, destructive injustice will ultimately be devoured by that injustice. Informed individuals early in this century understood that the survival of 'civilization' (as they knew it), and more specifically, the endurance of capitalism and the existing social order, depended upon the capacity of the new economy and its institutions to win the loyalty and commitment of the working classes. There were simply too many workers to be ignored, and too much risk of instability and social disorder if gross inequities (such as the treatment of injured workers) went on unaddressed.

The inequity of the situation was not lost on observers, who began to champion the cause of expanded worker rights – first through a stripping away of employer defences, then by the introduction of a form of 'social insurance.' By enacting legislation removing employer common-law defences, the state legislatures and provincial assemblies began a slow shift of power in workplace injury cases towards the injured party. While this development offered a theoretical advantage to the worker, the fact of having to wait months or years for success in lawsuits and the prohibitive cost of these actions (this was long before the days of contingency-fee legal services) still posed a practical wall the injured worker found hard to scale.

In the end, of course, every North American jurisdiction adopted some scheme for the specialized treatment of employer liability and worker compensation. Workers and employers entered into what history has come to call the 'historic compromise,' where workers exchanged their rights of action for reliable insurance, and where employers traded their freedom to contest claims for cost-effective collective liability. The tort regime was ousted, and with it all its attendant evils to workers and risks to employers, and replaced with the promise of a smooth, 'automatic' insurance scheme (the insurance being offered by the state itself, or through private carriers with which employers were required to contract).

In time, these WC systems inevitably shared certain characteristics: benefits determined as a function of earnings; waiting periods for workers following the day of accident; statutory maximums and minimums on benefits; administrative adjudication by insurance-style organizations; employer premiums based on industry experience; a collective-liability pooling of premiums into a 'fund' to support the benefit regime; coverage of medical costs related to the injury; long-term pension awards for the permanently disabled; and some form of 'vocational rehabilitation' service to those in need of help in resuming gainful employment. The key to all this, of course, was the employer's total liberation from any liability due to the accident – it was a 'no fault' system of compensation. Further, and of great importance to the viability of the system, workers and employers were generally forbidden from entering into any private arrangements regarding employer liability and worker compensation.

The effect, over time, of these reforms was to achieve each of the three main objectives of the WC system. Workers had a prompt, responsive resource to turn to in times of medical emergency and disability arising from work; many of the most dire consequences of an injury were delayed, defrayed, or avoided outright by dint of the WC system's delivery of medical aid and income replacement to the injured worker. This in turn reduced the pressure upon workers either to save in anticipation of disaster or to resort to friends, family, and institutions for support. Just as important, when, later in the twentieth century, governments began to offer unemployment insurance, pensions, and welfare, the rate with which people took up those programs was reduced to the extent those individuals could rely upon the more appropriate, and usually more generous, terms of workers' compensation. All of these salutary outcomes meant that working people were more dependable consumers, needed to save less, and were able to rely less upon private and public charity.

In adopting collective-liability, no-fault insurance in these cases, North American jurisdictions assumed an instrument that actually met its general goals (notwithstanding the many failures those systems may have also suffered along the way). To the extent we can extrapolate from the advantages won for workers and employers, it is possible to read into workers' compensation a method for the overall reduction of class conflict, glaring injustice, and destabilizing economic nuisances such as over-saving, the breakdown of nuclear families, and the hazard of large-scale employer liability.

2. What Was In It for Employers and Workers and Why Do They Want Out?

As traditional tort defences were gutted, employers had to take notice of their worsening legal position; as they sought private-market insurance against the cost of injury claims, employers began to get a taste for the cost that workplace injury cases could inflict. The threat of lawsuits in the workplace, particularly those promising reward to worker plaintiffs, was a significant intrusion itself into the traditional master-servant relationship; in some ways, shifting the management of workplace injury to a neutral third party (such as the state) would remove the adversarial quality of litigation and inoculate the employer against the effects of an emboldened, 'empowered' workforce.

More important, a social-insurance scheme would also immunize the employer against the worse risk of rising injury claim costs. By confining those costs to predictable insurance, as opposed to the vagaries of the judiciary or juries, employers could establish some degree of regularity to workplace injury claims. By ensuring that worker-plaintiffs or their survivors had circumscribed benefits, the more extreme forms of damage award could be avoided. By eliminating, outright, the employer's liability to the worker and his dependents for the effects of injury, the employer was free of having to invest more time and money in the prevention of accidents. This gave the employer the ability to focus energy and resources on investments that increased productivity and profit, as opposed to containing cost.

The predictable, reasonably cost-effective method of paying payroll taxes (or premiums) to the insurer replaced the price paid in legal fees, settlements, and awards. Employers also enjoyed the advantage of being able to conduct their affairs with perhaps less attention to the matter of safety and injury avoidance, knowing that the cost of the claim (and the worker's ability to get help) were guaranteed by the insurance scheme.

Perhaps most important, workers' compensation pooled injury-claims cost risk across employers and, subject perhaps to some experience rating, to a very large extent took injury costs 'out of competition.' A firm was not placed at risk of its very survival in the event of expensive work-injury compensation claims.

Furthermore, the cost of injury compensation is passed, in whole or in part, onto workers – not so much those who collect benefits, but all who work in an establishment that is covered by the workplace-injury insurance scheme. This result, while not necessarily sought by the founders of the WC system, was certainly well within the realm of possibility (Meredith, 1913: 15): 'The burden that the workman is required to bear (as a result of a workplace injury) he cannot shift upon the shoulders of anyone else, but the employer may and no doubt will shift this burden upon the shoulders of the community, or if he has difficulty in doing that will by reducing the wages of his workmen compel them to bear part of it.'

Given that wage reductions are allocated broadly among workers in employments susceptible to these changes in the price of labour, it can be said that *non*-injured workers, earning a reduced wage in light of

WC payroll taxes, are subsidizing almost all of the benefits and services afforded to injured workers. While historians tend to trace the fundamental compromise of workers' compensation back to the decision to take rights away from workers and employers (see above), there is reason to believe that the more meaningful trade-off may have occurred elsewhere: between workers.

What's in it for employers? They remain immune from liability to anyone as a result of workplace injuries and diseases, and are free to operate their businesses without the moral or economic check imposed by such liability. Thus, while employers gave up their freedom to directly contest the claims of injured workers and allegedly adopted the cost of social insurance, we can see that by maintaining their relatively firm hold over wages employers have simply been able to transfer these costs onto others, while keeping their liability protection intact. The workers continue to face the hazards of the workplace, to sustain the injuries resulting therefrom, and to fund most of the cost of compensating and treating the victims. In this way, the real 'historic compromise' of North American workers' compensation appears not to be one between workers and employers, but rather a bargain struck among workers themselves.

What Do Workers Get?

In light of the recognizable cost burden imposed upon workers in the form of reduced wages, and the significant limitations of workers' compensation as a form of insurance (with maximum benefit levels, time limits on certain benefits, relatively miserly non-pecuniary loss provisions in certain jurisdictions, etc.), the open question for workers and their advocates must be whether there is value in remaining within the traditional workers' compensation system.

Workers and their organizations have in recent years begun to search for means of either broadening the available awards linked to injury (by adding certain lawsuits to existing WC claims) or replacing WC altogether with civil-liability actions. This change should not be surprising in an environment where repeated studies show workers paying up to 85 per cent of system costs yet garnering awards that seem to be a fraction of those paid in cases of similar injury sustained outside the workplace.

The value of workers' compensation to workers can be measured in many ways, including:

- removing the need for self-insurance or saving against hardship;
- removing the burden of choosing, administering, and negotiating insurance terms with a carrier;
- providing some sense of security against the unknown (or known) risks of employment;
- eliminating, or reducing, the need to contest or litigate claims subsequent to an event that has left the injured worker less healthy and able to function;
- reducing an employer's incentives, and avenues, to contest a claim;
- the immediate introduction of a neutral third party, temporarily at least, into the employment relationship to manage and mediate any areas of dispute or friction between worker and employer regarding an accident or claim;
- affording injured workers relatively quick, simple payment of benefits after an accident;
- providing a wide menu of services, including medical treatment, counselling, and vocational rehabilitation (testing, training, placement, etc.);
- creating monetary and other incentives for employers to integrate the injured worker back into the workplace, or into alternative employments;
- offering a predictable level of income replacement, often for a predictable period of time; and
- offering a predictable level of 'non-pecuniary loss' award, varying considerably from jurisdiction to jurisdiction.

Why the Interest in a Return to Tort?

Driven by pressures to control the escalating costs of workers' compensation, there has been a steady withdrawal from the traditional notions of the collective protection of workers from the costs associated with workplace injuries. A recent study by Thomason, Schmidle, and Burton (forthcoming) includes comprehensive indices of the generosity of workers' compensation indemnity benefits in the United States, and those indices show a downward trend in partial and total temporary disability benefits for minor injuries since a peak in those rates in 1991. Given that these kinds of benefits represent the bulk of system benefit costs, the inescapable conclusion is that workers' compensation pays less to workers with a given condition than it did up to this decade.

Along with reduced benefit generosity, moreover, are signs of a reduced likelihood of benefit payment, primarily through a subtle redefinition of what constitutes a compensable injury. This takes many forms: the exclusion of specific conditions (stress, or in some instances repetitive strains); the categorization of conditions as those warranting treatment but not extended disability benefits (chronic pain in some jurisdictions);[2] the refusal to include 'latent' conditions in those meriting awards (e.g., back injuries that are temporarily asymptomatic are often excluded from pension rating systems); the elimination of coverage altogether (inducements to workers to enrol as independent contractors rather than as employees); and administrative measures designed to pose barriers to claims (time limits, reduced opportunities to appeal, etc.).[3]

Less easy to adduce from numbers, but articulated during informal discussions with system administrators and stakeholders, is the recognition that boards and other insurers are simply less friendly to claimants today than they were ten years ago. This is sharply felt in the province of Ontario, where radical statutory, policy, and administrative changes have unfolded over the last two years. Typical of any workers' compensation jurisdiction, the Ontario board (a monopoly insurer) is seen as having shifted its emphasis to responding to employer demands (for example, by reorganizing its adjudicative structure to reflect industries instead of geographic areas) and has even seen a change of name designed to 'neutralize' the institution (e.g., the 'Workers' Compensation Board' is now the 'Workplace Safety and Insurance Board'). None of these changes is necessarily bad, even for workers, but combined with benefit reductions, a curtailment of long-term wage-loss awards, the exclusion of chronic stress, and the reduction of allowances for claims of chronic pain, they create the palpable perception that the Ontario system is shifting its focus against the interests of labour. Just as serious, to workers, is the organization's very public and redoubled efforts to identify and prosecute fraud. While no one would condone fraud, making this the central public-relations sphere of the system appears to have a chilling effect upon all claimants, and to undermine public respect for the institution of public insurance against workplace injuries.

Key to a worker's evaluation of the benefits of the workers' compensation system is an appreciation of (a) the level of benefits paid and (b) the likelihood they will be paid when needed. If either, or both, of those two elements is made less attractive to workers, one can predict a reduction in their degree of commitment to the system – and that is what appears to be happening.

At the same time, North American jurisdictions have moved to give employers more reason to become involved in claims, specifically by altering collective liability so as to hinge premium levels more tightly to an individual company's accident cost. Intended to motivate employers to prevent claims, experience rating of course also induces employers to police claims – in a fashion that makes the original 'non-adversarial' model of insurance adjudication appear a relic of history. The mass outbreak of 'alternative dispute resolution' practices, offices, and rules across U.S. and Canadian workers' compensation regimes is a strong indicator of an escalating level, and incidence, of 'dispute' between workers and employers over claims. This phenomenon drives straight at the heart of the original 'bargain' struck between labour and capital over the formation of the WC system – a bargain that was intended to save both sides from the cost, torment, and unpredictability of litigation.

Thus, we see a host of factors eroding the confidence, comfort, and commitment of labour to the workers' compensation system. The commitment of employers has always been unsteady, linked as it is directly to the degree of cost-saving and other advantages that enterprise perceives in a publicly mandated insurance rather than the 'forensic lottery' of tort claims and an unregulated insurance market. As noted earlier, employers tend to believe that they carry the bulk of the cost of benefits and administration, and in fairness the employer remains the 'payer of first instance,' who must either absorb, or pass along to workers and customers, the cost of the system. The employer remains the necessary lynchpin in the system, and given the increasing tendency towards experience-rating programs and mandatory re-employment of workers, and recent moves towards employer-orchestrated 'labour market re-entry,' the employer is essentially being identified not only as a payer, but also as a primary provider of workers' compensation services.

3. Comparing Workers' Compensation and Tort

A first step in comparing and highlighting the difference between the two systems is to note the 'wrongs' they seek to address. In asking what 'wrongs' or social ills the systems seek to cure, it can be said that tort offers plaintiffs redress for a variety of damages; penalizes tortfeasors for negligent or hazardous conduct; and reinforces and refines the social consensus on appropriate conduct.

The workers' compensation system, by contrast, acts primarily to address the 'wrong' of injured parties having to take private responsibility for injuries sustained in environments where they spend most of their waking time, confront most of the hazards they are likely ever to face, and pursue more powerful economic and social actors for redress. The same system protects those employers from the potentially disastrous expense of tort claims lodged by numerous employees with clear claims of damage resulting from the employer's omissions or acts.

In tort, the action brought is 'public' insofar as it relies upon public administration of the courts to assert the claim, navigate the litigation process, and, where necessary, seek adjudication. The parties are addressing a private violation of a public standard (this is the key distinction from contract law, where the parties wrangle over the violation of privately negotiated standards of conduct between them alone). There is a strong public interest in the successful processing and resolution of tort claims, as the system is a mechanism whereby society reinforces and redefines the general consensus on norms of appropriate conduct. There is further public interest in the peaceful resolution, by court order or settlement, of these disputes, as the use of the law in this context displaces the need for 'private justice.'

Workers' compensation carries with it no sense of a 'duty of care' or, for that matter, any notion of a 'wrong' being committed or suffered. The WC regime focuses only on the matter of causation (was the injury caused by the injured person's employment) and compensation (to what, under the limits of the law, is the person entitled in respect of the injury).

In workers' compensation there are really no 'parties' at all, but rather workers and employers who have rights and responsibilities in respect of the workers' compensation legislation. The only 'party' in WC is the agency that receives, adjudicates, pays, and collects upon injury claims lodged by workers and reported through employers; that agency is usually called the Workers' Compensation Board, or some variation thereupon.

The administration of the WC system is a purely public responsibility, with purely public aims: to ensure that injured workers are compensated and rehabilitated under the terms of the law and applicable policy; to fund the system through insurance premiums mandatorily exacted from employers covered by the scheme; to enforce rules and apply penalties where stakeholders have responsibilities pertaining to the prevention, reporting, and management of injury claims and related issues.

Notwithstanding this 'public' agenda and administration, there are clearly 'private' effects upon both workers (who have some guarantee of insurance protection from destitution in the event of workplace injury) and employers (who have an ironclad guarantee of protection from liability in respect of those same injuries). Both actors pay a private price as well – the worker is restricted to the publicly determined schedule of benefits without a right to sue the employer, while the employer is bound to pay whatever premiums are demanded by the Board.

Nature of Damages and Forms of Compensation

Both tort matters and workers' compensation systems address the question of assessing damages, determining liability, and awarding compensation in respect of personal injury.

We categorize personal-injury awards in the following fashion: immediate post-injury income replacement; extended medical coverage; vocational rehabilitation and labour-market re-entry assistance; permanent-impairment loss-of-function awards; permanent-impairment loss-of-earnings awards; and other forms of damages.

Immediate Income Replacement

In the tort system, the party ultimately responsible for bearing the claim cost (presuming the defendant is found liable) will not be required to meet any costs immediately upon the claim, as redress is of course contingent upon a finding or admission of fault. As a result, the injured party falls initially upon her own resources, which in most instances means privately obtained disability insurance. Thus, the immediate availability of income-replacement coverage is absent from tort.

Further, while tort awards are perceived to be grander in scale than payments made by workers' compensation systems, the truth is that most claims are settled for an amount less than claimed, and that means a likely reduction of the income-replacement portion of any award. While WC systems pay high and almost-instant income, tort awards are commonly less than the actual loss and recipients must also sustain substantial tax and other deductions, when and if the award is paid.

Another factor reducing the real value of the immediate income-replacement element of tort is the fact of fees, not only those incurred in hiring counsel but also administrative fees required to register claims, file motions, and so forth. Thus, as a leading writer on Canadian personal-injury compensation recently observed (Cooper-Stevenson, 1996): '[I]n (workers' compensation) the amount recovered as income substitution will usually exceed what would be obtained in tort litigation, if one assesses the defacto compensation from that system, including settlement sums, deductions of legal fees and the availability of funds to satisfy judgments.'

Beyond the fact that tort does not appear to pay as well as workers' compensation in regard to income replacement, there is the fact that often tort does not pay *at all* – claims languish in the litigation system, are delayed or even withdrawn because of costs. In such instances, losses of income are absorbed first by the plaintiff and any other parties upon whom that plaintiff is dependent. Among those parties, it is worth noting, is the Treasury, for in Canada individuals with no other resort still have certain entitlements with respect to public support (be it, for instance, private disability employment insurance or the Canada Pension Plan). The measurement of these costs and losses is beyond the scope of this paper.

Extended Medical Coverage

Universal medical insurance in Canada has reduced the significance of 'medical aid' as a form of compensation today, in comparison with the first fifty years of WC in Canada. Nonetheless, most boards and commissions administering WC in Canada maintain provision for enhanced services to injured workers in the form of relationships with outside providers and in-house rehabilitation facilities.

This provision of enhanced medical coverage, in comparison with standard coverage under public health insurance, is controversial for what it implies about the injured worker population. The clear driver behind such programs is cost – boards are attempting to reduce benefit costs through rehabilitation efforts designed to maximize recovery and/or prove recovery. This is perceived to be necessary because of concerns over prolonged post-injury absence from work (believed to be longer in WC than in other areas of insurance).

The existence of such early-intervention programs itself underscores the impression that WC systems are more profitable forms of injury insurance than those managed by private insurers (cases that might ultimately surface in the tort regime). Further, enhanced medical coverage and rehabilitation assistance to the injured worker is a clear benefit advantage of the WC system: the worker gets more services, earlier, and at greater investment than patients outside the workers' compensation realm. Even if these investments were unnecessary and abandoned, that would imply that boards had greater control over costs, which in turn opens the possibility of other program advantages for the recipient and, at a minimum, reduces pressure on premium-payers.

Other forms of additional medical care (e.g., attendants, home care) are typically paid by both systems; for tort victims, this comes first through private insurance and then, once liability has been determined, those insurance costs are shifted to the responsible party's insurer.

In tort, again, there is no mechanism for charging the responsible party with the immediate costs of the medical care required by the plaintiff, who must fall upon her own insurance. A key difference from income replacement, however, is that in the realm of medical provision the WC system is a net payer *into* public health (most boards are billed for the costs of medical expenses afforded to injured workers) while in the tort regime, medical services are a net cost to the medicare plan.[4] Given the rigidity of Canadian publicly provided health care, there is little difference in the basic care afforded a patient regardless of forms of insurance, other resources, or reason for injury – save and except for the provision of specialty-care services.

In summary, the provision of medical care to injury victims under tort and workers' compensation in Canada is relatively equal, with certain small advantages being available to the WC recipient.

Vocational Rehabilitation and Labour-Market Re-entry

Whether they actually work or not, there is no disputing that workers' compensation driven and funded vocational rehabilitation (VR) and labour-market re-entry (LMR) provisions are a substantial investment in the injured party's long-term earnings ability that is basically absent from the tort system.

While private insurers will endeavour to test, and in some instances provide assistance in enhancing, employability, none has embarked upon the kind and degree of VR service-provision infrastructure witnessed in Canadian workers' compensation agencies. Further, the legal provision of new LMR rules (such as Ontario's re-employment provisions, or its newer obligations upon employers to re-hire or assist workers in seeking re-employment) offers greater benefits to the injured party under the WC regime.

The limitation on the value of this investment, noted at the outset of this section, is the question of whether these programs actually 'work' – that is, whether they achieve their putative end of rendering a worker employable or enhancing the earning capacity of that worker. Where they do not, of course, the cost will fall generally upon three parties: the worker him/herself, who typically absorbs some degree of wage loss over the course of the post-injury lifetime, (2) the WC system, which provides earnings-loss replacement benefits to workers up to retirement (or beyond in some cases), and (3) the Treasury and CPP fund, which are often called upon to shore up the minimum-income requirements of unemployable or unsuccessful graduates of the workers' compensation system.

The existence of these VR and LMR programs, like the medical services mentioned above, is a clear indication that the party responsible for paying in the WC system (the board) has incentives to try and mitigate wage-loss costs. It is the complete absence of such incentives in the tort regime that puts a break on the investment in the non-WC sphere. There, the ultimate payer is undetermined until such time as the respective insurers litigate or negotiate a resolution. The uncertainty as to 'who pays' shifts the cost of long-term earning loss onto one party – the injured person – who must bear greater personal responsibility and expense for the provision of services required to maintain or enhance earning ability. Even when the case is resolved in the plaintiff's favour, the delay in achieving that outcome precludes any 'early' efforts at VR or LMR.

Compensation for Permanent Functional Loss

Where the injured party suffers a permanent loss of function (an impairment) or other physical damage as a result of the accident, tort and WC grapple with the question of measuring that loss on a recognizable, plausible scale.

The issue at stake is assessing a dollar value for the loss of a person's enjoyment of his/her faculties, and the deleterious effects such loss entails upon that person's life and happiness. It can be said with confidence that there is absolutely no 'fair' or 'good' way to go about this unhappy task.

That said, the workers' compensation schemes have gone about it in a particularly odd and seemingly unfair way. Consider the different approaches taken by Ontario and British Columbia. Both provinces operated permanent-impairment assessment under a straight table of injuries. An impairment was given a percentage value of total functionality; that percentage value was applied to the statutory pension-calculation scheme (usually applying the degree of impairment to the worker's pre-injury monthly earnings – governed by the maximum and minimum compensation rates – and then paying 75 to 85 per cent of the result, every month for life, as a pension).

Putting aside questions on the viability of the 'meat chart' percentage values, this methodology is a peculiar mix of functional- and earnings-loss compensation. In fact, it uses earnings as a means of measuring the dollar award granted in respect of something that has, at the very best, a tenuous relationship to lost earnings. As a form of 'earnings-loss compensation' it is clearly neither rational nor efficient; as a form of functional-loss compensation, all that can be said for it is that it is well known, if not very well understood.

Both Ontario and British Columbia have recognized the problems inherent with this mixed system of calculating functional-loss awards. For Ontario, the solution was a complete bifurcation of impairment from earnings issues – hence its introduction in 1990 of the pure 'non-economic loss' (NEL) award that measures and compensates only physical and functional loss. Again, the process begins with a medical assessment and the establishment of a percentage value of loss (Ontario has abandoned its 'meat chart' for the more up-to-date and popular American Medical Association guidelines on disability).

Instead of an earnings benchmark, the NEL system draws a line at the maximum award payable to a worker in the case of a 100 per cent impairment, adjusting the maximum up or down in increments to reflect the worker's age (the younger the worker, the higher the maximum award to compensate for the greater likely duration of suffering).

British Columbia's answer to the problem of functional-impairment awards has been to partially abandon those awards. BC still measures and pays the functional pension, but where that pension would be less than the statutory provision for long-term loss of earning capacity, the pension is junked and the earnings loss award is paid instead.

In the realm of tort, fair compensation for a person's suffering a permanent functional loss is perhaps the most sensitive and difficult of tasks. The matters taken into account are the person's personal characteristics, age, gender, personal relationships, and activities, and the fashion in which the personal injury negatively affects any or all of these factors of life. The nature of the injury is a crucial element in making this determination. Trial awards use precedent, of course, as benchmarks both for the range of award appropriate in a case and where in the range the non-pecuniary damages should be placed. It is, frankly, more of an art than a science, and to that degree is far less predictable than the provision of permanent-impairment awards under the schedules employed in Ontario or British Columbia workers' compensation schemes.

Compensation for Permanent Loss of Earnings

This paper cannot describe, in adequate detail, the respective mechanics of assessing likely-future-earnings abilities or losses. It is sufficient to state that in both the Ontario and BC workers' compensation regimes, the boards are required to assess permanently impaired workers in terms of their likely ability to earn in future. The worker is 'deemed' able to command a wage consonant with his/her abilities and competitiveness in whatever field of endeavour is followed (of course, the deemed wage may be the actual wage that the injured worker is earning upon return to the labour market); this wage is compared with the pre-injury wage, which places a significant cap on the award. The wage-loss compensation decision reflects the gap between the pre-injury wage 'cap' and the current/future 'deemed' earnings.

In British Columbia this calculation is not meaningful in terms of benefits unless the prospective wage loss exceeds the calculated monthly permanent-impairment pension. In Ontario, prospective earnings form the basis for the worker's compensation up until retirement age.

In the tort regime, the process of projecting likely future earnings before, and after, injury is a remarkably complicated feat. Assessing the 'earnings stream' as if the injury had not occurred, the court begins with the base rate, rate of growth in income, positive and negative contingencies, proximity to retirement age, loss of pension income, and factors related to probability of survival as the plaintiff ages. The second, injury-related 'earnings stream' does this same extrapolation, based upon what the court now deems to be the worker's fitness and competitiveness in whatever alternative careers are left to him/her.

The court then measures the difference between the two 'streams' and, depending upon the defendant's degree of liability and the plaintiff's degree of contribution to the loss, awards damages for pecuniary loss.

4. A Comparison of Damage Awards in Selected Cases under the Two Systems

Tort and workers' compensation operate very differently, but for the plaintiff/claimant are similar in that they are expected to deliver an award of damages or compensation as redress for the losses sustained owing to the injury.

This paper cannot compare the relative generosity of the two systems on any comprehensive scale. Instead, it seeks to illustrate their attributes by examining awards made in instances of two specific types of injury: back injuries (primarily 'soft tissue' injury cases reducing mobility in the cervical, thoracic, lumbar, and/or sacral spine) and facial disfigurements.

The injuries selected are chosen because of their sharp differences. Back injuries are typically difficult to assess, rely heavily upon subjective reporting by claimants for evidence of impairment, and often significantly reduce the injured person's capacity to continue in pre-injury activity or employment. Facial disfigurements are very easy to objectively assess, do not require subjective pain reporting, and, in and of themselves, do not impair the worker's ability to function or work. It is hoped that these two forms of injury will illustrate divergent characteristics of the assessing system and the ways tort and WC award damages.

Back Injuries

In British Columbia, the WCB assesses permanent back impairments according to a scale laid out in the Rehabilitation and Claims Services Manual. The absolute maximum level of impairment, combining scales for the cervical, thoracic, and lumbosacral spines, is 51 per cent of total functionality. This means that in British Columbia, a worker with extremely serious loss of function throughout the spine can expect a pension of approximately 50 per cent of his/her pre-injury wages, reduced by one-quarter (BC pays 75 per cent of gross earnings as its compensation rate). For a thirty-five-year-old worker with pre-injury gross earnings of $4000 per month (a relatively high wage in Canada) this back-impairment award translates into a lifetime monthly pension of about $1500. Actuarial life expectancies suggest this person might live at least another thirty years, meaning that without inflation this serious back injury has earned an award of damages of about $540,000 current dollars.

That is not the whole story in British Columbia, of course, as provision exists to replace that award with a higher one if it can be found that the worker's likely future earning capacity will be reduced by an amount more than the value of the pension.

In Ontario, the new Workplace Safety and Insurance Board administers claims that fall under the old pension scheme, as well as the current NEL system described above. The pension system achieves results very like those described above in British Columbia. The replacement system, NEL and 'future economic loss' or 'loss of future earnings,' splits the calculation into two separate streams.

The NEL system uses the AMA guides to evaluate back claims, and few if any back cases under that scheme are rated at over 25 per cent impairment. When the system is applied to a formula where the maximum award ranges from $35,000 to $75,000 depending upon the claimant's age, it can be seen that even a high NEL award for back injuries will earn something in the range of $7500 to $20,000 as the total award in respect of functional loss. Obviously this constitutes a significant saving in comparison with the predecessor pension system, particularly when we remember that Ontario operated an extensive and expensive 'pension supplement' program alongside pensions, compensating workers for losses of earning capacity that exceeded those typically associated with a particular permanent impairment. (This program is still in effect for pensionable injuries arising before 1990.)

Where Ontario has incurred expense since 1990 is in the provision of future economic loss (FEL) awards, which lock in to age sixty-five a monthly payment in respect of lost earning capacity. Hinging these determinations to the success of VR programs, Ontario experienced substantially more cost than anticipated when it introduced FEL at the outset of the recession in the early 1990s. Recent changes (reductions in the rate of compensation from 90 to 85 per cent of net, recalculation of the earnings base, elimination of long-term funded job search, etc.) are designed to trim these awards, and to reduce the use of 'FEL supplements,' which top up benefits to the maximum amount during the worker's active rehabilitation program. A back injury is typically the worst, and most disabling, form of impairment in terms of future earning ability; at even a nominal FEL of about 10 per cent (and many exceed that greatly) the thirty-five-year-old average worker cited in earlier examples will receive about $130,000 in current dollars (for high wage-earners at or above the maximum compensation rate who are retrained for jobs just above minimum wage – not an uncommon result – the FEL cost could treble or quadruple).

A key point to make about both the BC and Ontario back-injury pension and NEL/FEL experience is that very few claimants actually receive the maximum awards. Typical back awards under pension schemes run in the 10 to 15 per cent impairment range, which on the earlier BC case example cited earlier would be valued at $100 thousand to $200 thousand over the average life of the pension. In Ontario, an NEL award of 5 to 10 per cent for a back is quite common, providing a lump-sum award of perhaps two to five thousand dollars for the 'average' claimant described above. By contrast with the BC pension and Ontario NEL/FEL programs, tort awards are almost always paid as lump sums (or are paid in 'structured settlements' designed to pay an annuity based upon the value of the lump sum). In a Goldsmith (1996) survey of damages paid in respect of non-pecuniary and pecuniary loss for injury cases primarily from British Columbia and Ontario in the period 1991 through 1997,

- of 97 spinal cases examined where non-pecuniary damages were allowed, 28 also included awards for losses of future earnings;
- of the 69 cases with non-pecuniary damages only, the average non-pecuniary damage award for spinal injuries was $72,600;
- of the 28 cases with both types of damages paid, the average non-pecuniary damage award for spinal injuries was $44,600;
- in those same 28 cases, the average loss-of-future-earnings award for the effects of spinal injuries was $118,000. The highest award was for $550,000, granted to a British Columbia registered nurse, who at age forty sustained lumbar spine injuries inducing 'paralyzing' pain that interfered with her sleep.

The source material for these statistics, a guide to personal-injury damage awards in Canada, is an admittedly unscientific, but relatively comprehensive annual survey of reported and unreported case law in the field. It must be emphasized, however, that these awards flow from trial decisions, which mean that they must be substantially discounted to allow for both delay in resolution and the cost of litigation. Further, it is also important to remember that out-of-court settlements of similar cases (which by anecdotal evidence far outnumber court decisions) will inevitably result in lower awards (and in lower costs).

Based on these numbers for the relative value of a back injury under the tort or workers' compensation systems, it is evident that the British Columbia workers' compensation pension scheme is more generous than either the courts, or the parties in settlement, under the tort regime.

Facial Disfigurement

Facial-disfigurement cases offer an example of a 'pure' non-economic loss, where the impairment has little functional impact and, usually, no significant effect on earnings. In British Columbia, a complex formula exists whereby a facial disfigurement is evaluated on five criteria and allocated 'points.' The higher the total number of points across the five criteria, the higher the range of award. Relatively minor, or 'class 1,' disfigurements earn awards of just under $5000 as a lump-sum payment. The most severe disfigurements, with possible impact on facial function, are grouped in 'class 4' and merit awards of anywhere from $25,000 to $45,000 in a one-time payment.

Ontario's pension scheme table for facial disfigurements assesses them as permanent partial disabilities, from about 2 per cent for relatively minor scarring to a maximum of 25 per cent for 'gross disfigurement.' Translated into a pension for the $4000 per month earner, this would amount to anywhere from $75 to $900 per month – but almost always in the range below 10 per cent, or about $300 per month. Even the minimal award of 2 per cent equals a total value of $27,000 in current dollars. Ontario's NEL awards for facial disfigurements are also quite small, not typically exceeding a 15 per cent impairment rating (about $2000 to $5000 depending on the worker's age).

Contrast this to the facial-disfigurement survey of twenty-one cases in the 1991–97 period, again primarily from the trial divisions of Ontario and BC courts. There, the highest award given for facial disfigurement was $50,000 for injuries requiring seventy-eight stitches and repeated plastic surgeries, and leaving residual pain and headaches. The average award in this class was $21,000 – and that includes the worst cases adjudicated. The comparison with the BC or Ontario pension schemes is striking, and again it would appear most advantageous to lodge one's claim in the workers' compensation realm as opposed to the tort system.

A Comment on Comparative Costs

The tort regime carries with it significant administration, as well as award-related, costs. According to a recent study of world tort costs, about 48 per cent of the total bill for tort claims is paid to parties in the form of damages; the remainder is paid to system participants and institutions charged with adjudicating or settling cases. By contrast, the BC board keeps its administrative costs generally under 15 per cent of total revenue, which suggests greater 'efficiency' in the workers' compensation system in terms of converting premiums into awards.

The costs of tort actions pose a real barrier to the achievement of justice by plaintiffs, and offer a welcome wall of defence and delay for the defendants. The other obvious advantage of the WC system for plaintiff/claimants is that awards for particular types of impairment and losses of earning appear to be greater in the WC scheme than under tort. Employers funding the WC system are protected from the hazard of extremely expensive litigation and atypical awards at the extremely high end of the tort damages spectrum, but it is difficult on the evidence seen here to argue that workers' compensation is more 'cost effective' for employers than would be a tort regime. The U.S. tort system is famously open, available to anyone who can sign a contingency agreement and rich with potential reward; there are few statutory limits in any state on the scope of non-pecuniary or exemplary (punitive) damages, and pecuniary damages (for loss of future income) are calculated in a refined, sophisticated environment born of a huge, complex litigation industry. The Canadian tort system, particularly in matters of personal injury, is notoriously tight-fisted – non-pecuniary losses are capped in accord with a series of Supreme Court rulings in the 1970s, lawyers are generally less free to offer their services on a contingent or percentage basis, and the whole 'litigation' culture is less aggressive and developed.

A variety of American litigants, jurists, and commentators have in recent years begun to test and challenge the principle that the workers' compensation system is the exclusive remedy for work-injury damages, particularly in that it so severely limits awards to workers.[5] The limitations on WC payments are particularly glaring in the United States, where benefit schedules are generally more restrictive in terms of amounts and durations than in Canada, in contrast to the almost notoriously generous American tort regime. This observation is important, not only in highlighting the sharp differential in awards under U.S. tort and WC, but also the differential in perceptions of the issue on either side of the border.

Our cautious take on the imperfect evidence is that the treatment of personal injuries in the Canadian courts (and by extension, in the vast unrecorded world of settlements out of court that use court rulings as a guide) is not strikingly more generous, even for those who ultimately receive an award, than is the fashion in which Canadian workers' compensation regimes treat similar cases.

5. Recent Judicial Comment

Canadian courts have not been much interested in opening the door to a return to employer liability, showing due deference to the legislatures. Some Canadian observers believe there is a risk to exclusivity if systems continue to retrench. In reality, there are few threats to the principle of exclusivity in the Canadian law – a worker's rights of action against his/her employer are effectively barred by legislation.[6] There have been two decisions of the Supreme Court of Canada (SCC) in recent years that have touched upon the matter of whether a worker may sue the employer in respect of a workplace injury, both upholding the principle of exclusivity.

The first is the 'Piercey' case, first adjudicated as a reference to the Newfoundland Court of Appeals,[7] the decision of which was upheld by the SCC.[8] Framed as a challenge to the alleged inequality of treatment afforded injured workers as opposed to persons injured away from work, the case tested the exclusivity principle in workers' compensation under section 15 of the Canadian Charter of Rights and Freedoms ('the Charter'). The Newfoundland appeal court upheld the bar on rights of action on the basis of a 'displacement test' – that WC benefits, in their global effect on the recipient, provided an effective replacement for tort remedies.

The Newfoundland appeals ruling underscores the basic principle of WC that a worker's rights of action are limited only against those specific parties enumerated in the exclusion (employers, their agents, and co-workers of the worker); second, it suggests that where the WC system fails to offer a reasonable substitute for tort damages, the courts may find that WC (in whole or in part) does not satisfy the equality provisions of the Charter. The Supreme Court of Canada upheld the Newfoundland appeals decision, albeit without reasons.

To some observers, the Newfoundland appeal theory of balancing benefits points to peril for the WC system if legislatures don't maintain and demonstrate equity between the results of WC and other remedies the worker might enjoy against the employer (Ison, 1997): '[I]f the range or level of benefits, as they operate in practice, deteriorate, the argument might be made that they are no longer comparable to workers' rights at common law; and that therefore the statutory bar violates the Charter. If that argument succeeds, employers would require employers' liability insurance as well as paying workers' compensation premiums.' To date, that argument has not been successfully advanced in the Canadian courts. In fact, a recent ruling of the Supreme Court of Canada casts doubt as to whether a form of 'balancing justice' is required to sustain workers' compensation schemes from constitutional equality challenges.

In *Beliveau St. Jacques v. Fédération des Employées et Employés de Services Publics Inc.* [1996] 2 SCR 345 ('Beliveau') the Supreme Court heard an appeal from the Quebec appeal court regarding a worker attempting to sue his employer in damages for harassment on the job. The worker had alleged harassment and sought exemplary (sometimes described as 'punitive') damages from the employer directly, on the basis that the Quebec workers' compensation statute did not capture such a claim.[9] In the absence of a statutory remedy, the worker argued, a civil one must exist.

Madame Justice L'Heureux-Dubé, dissenting from the majority, agreed with the plaintiff in distinguishing between damages in respect of personal-injury liability and those in respect of an 'exemplary remedy.' The latter, the justice maintained, was not captured by the Quebec statute either as a form of injury or a form of compensation, and therefore a workers' right of action in respect of same could not be barred.

The majority did not agree, enunciating a very inclusive principle of liability and damages under the Canadian law of worker's compensation. Workers' compensation, Mr Justice Gauthier wrote, is an exchange of a worker's civil rights of action for 'partial, fixed-sum compensation that did not necessarily correspond to the prejudice they had suffered.'[10] The legislation had abandoned fault, and in so doing had abandoned liability as well – the worker had absolutely no rights to sue the employer, or a co-worker, in respect of any damages sustained in connection to a work-related injury.

Beliveau appears to keep the lid tight on any expansion of worker rights of action without legislative change; further, Mr Justice Gauthier's pointed comments on the issue of WC benefits being inadequate to the case – but still adequate to the law – indicate that the Newfoundland theory of balancing benefits may pose little threat to the constitutionality of Canadian workers' compensation in the current high court.

Thus, we cannot soon expect a serious judicial test of exclusivity in Canadian workers' compensation law. Any expansion of a worker's right of action against those currently immunized falls upon the legislature to enact.

6. Reform: Bending but Not Breaking Exclusivity

The previous discussion points out these facts: Canadian exclusivity in workers' compensation is well respected and obeyed by both litigants and courts. Where remedies in and around exclusivity may exist, few parties seem to pursue them; when they do, the courts (at least one court, the Supreme Court in Beliveau) has resisted giving life to an employer's civil liabilities even at risk of straining the WC doctrine beyond logic.[11] If exclusivity were to be seriously challenged, or even slightly altered, it would inevitably fall upon the provincial legislatures to amend their laws to do so.

Why bother? What reasons would the legislature have for considering bending, if not breaking, exclusivity as it is practised? Why would anyone gain, and how would they gain, from expanding any areas of direct employer civil liability?

The answer lies in whether we perceive there to be evident, or latent, problems in the workers' compensation scheme. The absence of civil liability may overly shield the employer from the consequences of acts and omissions in the workplace. This immunity rewards inattention to workplace hazards. Some form of direct civil liability, even if limited in form or amount, might be a corrective to this fault of the collective liability system.

Intentional torts may be helpful in shaping a 'doorway to tort' from the current workers' compensation regime. The WC regime operates, clearly, to insure workers against the harm that befalls them at work, provided they suffer 'an injury by accident' or occupational disease. If that injury is not 'by accident,' but rather is a product of someone's direct and intentional tortious conduct, the intentional tort doctrine holds that the tortfeasor remains liable in the common law, whether she or he be the employer, its agent, or a co-worker of the injured party. This doctrine has been debated, and adopted, in a number of U.S. states.

While Canadian jurisdictions have hotly debated how to define 'by accident' (whether it means a specific traumatic event or an unintended result) there is no sign that boards or courts have much examined whether an injury not 'by accident' yet arising out of, and in the course of, employment could produce civil liability in the intentional tortfeasor. The Act is not of great assistance, for while the law generally penalizes a worker's benefit entitlement in cases of 'serious and willful misconduct,' that obviously refers only to the conduct of the injured party, and not to the serious and *wilful* acts of others (wilful being the key word in terms of tracing references to intention under the Act).

Intentional tort is a particularly worthwhile venue for the plaintiff, as more generous exemplary or punitive damages are often ordered in instances of heinous, wilful acts or omissions. In the United States, both employers[12] and co-workers[13] have been found civilly liable to injured workers for the harm flowing from their intentional acts or omissions in the workplace. While intentional torts are effectively outside the realm of exclusivity now, a legislature might consider specifically enacting provisions whereby the Act excludes intentional torts from the WC system – highlighting their availability to workers and their possibility to employers. This could be done with no substantial alteration to the existing system at all. We are not familiar with any Canadian jurisprudence on the question, although it is worth noting that the aforementioned Beliveau ruling does not suggest the courts are warm to the notion of expanding an injured worker's entitlements under any circumstances.

Another issue is the adequacy of benefits. As described earlier, the average benefit awards in certain types of cases deliver as much, or more, to the workers' compensation recipient as to the plaintiff successful in tort. Where this is not the case is in the 'high end' cases, where (a) a plaintiff's projected future earnings stream before injury greatly exceeds the pre-injury wage 'cap' placed on WC benefits, or (b) non-pecuniary damages for pain and suffering, such as in instances of multiple injuries with major disabling effect, do not compare, and (c) where egregious behaviour, particularly intentional behaviour by the tortfeasor, attracts exemplary or punitive damages.

These types of cases, where WC fails to compensate fully or properly, or fails to penalize in any recognizable fashion, could be opened to tort by explicitly removing certain forms of non-physical injury from the scope of exclusivity. For example, instances of harassment, emotional or mental harm, defamation, and so forth could be separated from the operation of the WC system. This would ensure that such cases were not squelched by Beliveau-type interpretations of workers' compensation statutes, would narrow the ground of compensable cases to matters in which the WC administrators have more expertise, and would highlight the availability of civil remedies to workers.

It would also be possible to import into WC the two-track system of benefits used in some auto-insurance regimes, where 'serious' and/or 'permanent' impairments may be subject to a basic payment under the WC regime, with additional damages available in the courts if the plaintiff can demonstrate (a) a threshold degree of impairment, (b) a degree of damage exceeding the WC scheduled benefit, and (c) some form of fault on the part of the employer, its agent, or the co-worker.

A further, and more radical step, would be to take areas of damage currently included in the realm of the WC system and push them out into tort. For example, workers' compensation might be confined strictly to pecuniary-loss evaluation and compensation, with the quantum of non-pecuniary and/or other forms of damages left to the courts. This approach would create room for the growth of 'high end' case benefits, create a new 'punitive' measure for culpable employers, and relieve the WC system of some cost. It should be noted, though, that other jurisdictions have achieved the cost-saving end in non-pecuniary loss compensation simply by cutting awards to a relatively small amount (e.g., Ontario's non-economic loss system).

The difficulty of removing non-pecuniary loss evaluation and compensation from the WC regime, however, is that the physical, functional, or emotional injury is the foundation for the pecuniary loss. It might make more sense to have the WC system compensate the non-pecuniary loss and to leave the plaintiff worker to seek economic loss compensation in the courts. The great advantage of having the court determine economic losses to workers would rest in the fact that many suffer losses of future income that the WC system does not recognize (i.e., anything exceeding the pre-injury rate of earnings); the gain for the system as a whole would be relief from performing tasks at which it isn't very good (predicting, preventing, and compensating wage loss). Such a move would create a serious incentive for employers to re-employ workers as well, in order to mitigate future long-term wage losses. It would cost employers considerably, however, if they were found liable for the worker's future loss of earnings, but that is something against which the employer would privately insure.

7. Conclusion

For many of those who have been injured at work, changes to North American workers' compensation systems have produced barriers to claims and have made awards less generous, inspiring unflattering comparisons with the tort regime abandoned by injured workers with the historic compromise of the early twentieth century. There is growing belief that an alternative system may be more generous to workers, and this view can only be buttressed by the conclusion that it is workers who are, after all, paying for the system.

On the other hand, a comparison of how the Canadian courts (in tort law) and workers' compensation boards (in the no-fault, scheduled-benefit system) treat similar injuries reveals that the workers' compensation system offers comparable awards, on average, to those won in tort. Recognizing that court orders resulting from tort claims represent a tiny fraction of personal-injury lawsuits, and that the majority are settled for less than the courts would award, it is fair to conclude that workers' compensation offers the Canadian worker not only the predictable, relatively 'automatic' awards promised in the 1900s, but also pays better than tort. Where this is demonstrably *not* true is in cases of extreme injury, where a plaintiff's severe impairment damages a more promising long-term earnings ability and warrants more significant non-pecuniary loss compensation. Those cases will always get better treatment in the more flexible and compassionate arena of the courts, but at a cost to the majority of plaintiffs, who do less well than under a no-fault regime.

In the torrent of debate and dissatisfaction with modern workers' compensation, what is remarkable is how the essential elements of the institution have remained unaltered over almost nine decades, a near-century in which almost every other economic, personal, social, and technological aspect of life has been profoundly altered. This is not an accident, as there is substantial reason to believe that the workers' compensation system continues to satisfy the three principal objectives envisioned by its founders – compensation for the injured worker, contained liability for the employer, and reduced social instability.

While employers may consider the cost of the WC program to out-weigh its benefits, the evidence strongly supports the conclusion that it is *workers* who pay for workers' compensation, primarily through wage reductions. The role of, and cost to, employers is essentially administrative.

Stating that workers are paying for the WC system might induce workers and those interested in their rights to conclude that they are the 'losers' in the workers' compensation environment. Service and benefits are bad enough, they may argue, but do we have to pay for it too? Those kinds of conclusions sway workers to view the tort regime more favourably, but in this paper evidence is presented to compare the treatment of certain kinds of injury under workers' compensation and tort in Canada. The results indicate that, regardless of whether workers pay for none, part, or all of their benefits, they're still collecting better awards under most WC systems than they would under tort.

Nonetheless, certain of the deficiencies of the WC system might be corrected through subtle, or more aggressive, action by legislatures to highlight or expand areas of employer liability to workers in respect of workplace events and injuries. Properly balanced, such a use of tort might greatly improve the environment for workplace safety, achieve justice in cases of intentional torts or egregious negligence, and possibly shift costs more fairly from the collective liability of covered employers onto individual actors responsible for harms. While Canadians have begun to query the ongoing feasibility and fairness of the WC system, exclusivity has seen few substantial challenges in the courts. It appears that only legislative action, either to expand a worker's rights of action, or to foreclose judicial 'loopholes,' will fundamentally alter the foundations of workers' compensation.

NOTES

Acknowledgment: Financial support for an earlier version of this paper (Law, 1998) from Royal Commission on Workers' Compensation in British Columbia (the Gill Commission) is gratefully acknowledged. The views expressed in this chapter are those of the authors and should not be attributed to the commission.

 1 Reference re validity of sections 32 and 34 of the Workers' Compensation Act, 1983, 44 DLR (4th) 501 (1988) Nfld. C.A.

2 Chronic pain or stress conditions have been explicitly removed from the range of compensable conditions in the statutes of Canadian jurisdictions such as Nova Scotia (the 1995 reforms) and Ontario (the 1998 reforms). There are also implicit barriers, such as practice limitations on back claims in Nova Scotia or the extremely narrow construction given to the concept of 'accommodation' in the Alberta modified work policy.

3 Section 120 of the new Ontario Workplace Safety and Insurance Act, for example, imposes a 30-day deadline for the appeal of decisions in respect of return-to-work issues. Another example is section 22 of the same act, which imposes a six-month time limitation on filing a compensation claim. If applied stringently, this provision will run contrary to the principle articulated in *Demnotigny et Komo Construction Que.* 1986 CALP Dossier no. 04-00006-8604 maintaining that delay in reporting was not necessarily prejudicial.

4 In 1991, the Ontario Workers' Compensation Board adopted a system whereby the Ontario public-health authority segregated workers' compensation-related medical charges and billed the board. For a thorough discussion of the detailed medical-aid provisions in workers' compensation schemes, see chapter 4 of Ison, 1989.

5 One method has been to argue a 'dual persona' or 'dual capacity' doctrine, wherein the employer is sued as an occupier, rather than as an employer. Another is to more aggressively pursue the manufacturers and providers of dangerous goods or substances that have played a role in the workers' condition, as was the case in the recent U.S. Supreme Court ruling in *Ingalls Shipbuilding, Inc. et al. v. Director, Office of Workers' Compensation Programs, Department of Labor, et al.*

6 The Supreme Court of Canada's conclusion that workers' compensation amounts to 'more or less a form of final exhaustion of remedies' for workplace injury claims still governs: *Bell Canada v. Quebec* (CSST) [1988] 1 SCR 749, at p. 851.

7 Reference re validity of sections 32 and 34 of the Workers' Compensation Act, 1983, 44 DLR (4th) 501 (1988) Nfld. C.A.

8 Reference re Workers' Compensation Act, 1983 (Nfld.), [1989] 1 SCR 922.

9 The statute in question is the Act respecting Industrial Accidents & Occupational Diseases ('AIAOD'), RSQ, C.A-3.001, s.438.

10 *Beliveau St. Jacques v. Fédération des Employées et Employés de Services Publics Inc.* 2 SCR 345 (1996).

11 The Beliveau decision rejected a civil-damages claim by a worker who alleged 'harassment' (a non-physical injury) on the grounds that it had occurred at work – effectively defining the tort as a form of 'personal

injury' under the Quebec statute (the Quebec CSST had adopted the same view).

If a worker claims damages in respect of harm owing to the employer's or a co-worker's conduct, where that conduct occurred in the course of employment but is not connected with a physical, functional, or psychological injury of any kind, it seems strange to see the cause of action barred by dint of the workers' compensation scheme. With the greatest respect to the court in Beliveau, rolling 'harassment' into the definition of 'injury' seems to stretch the workers' compensation scheme unduly. In this instance, the WC system operates to eliminate rights of action clearly not conceived by Meredith as requiring social insurance. Instead, the WC system inoculates the employer against most liability for its conduct, regardless of the nature of the conduct or the harm. This is particularly odd, when, as Madame Justice L'Heureux-Dubé wrote, the matter in question is conduct that normally would lead to exemplary damages.

The rule enunciated in Beliveau might be open to review and change, especially under a different provincial statute and perhaps with a more sympathetic plaintiff. Allegations of harassment, defamation, and discriminatory behaviour by the employer or co-workers towards a plaintiff should no more be barred by the WC exclusivity principle than should suits for wrongful dismissal.

12 *Johns-Manville v. Superior Ct*, 27 Col. 3d 465 (1980); *Blankenship v. Cincinnati-Milacron* (1981) 85 Ohio St. 2d 608, certiorari denied 459 US 857 (1982).
13 *Iverson v. Atlas Pacific*, 143 Col. App. 3d. 219 (1983).

REFERENCES

Cooper-Stevenson, Ken. 1966. *Personal Injury Damages in Canada*. Toronto: Carswell, 1996.
Goldsmith, Immanual. 1996. *Goldsmith's Damages for Personal Injury and Death in Canada*. Toronto: Carswell.
Humphries, C., D.B. Loewen, and S.A. McArthur. 1998. *Ontario Workers' Compensation*. Toronto: Carswell.
Ison, Terrence G. 1989. *Workers' Compensation Law in Canada*. Toronto: Butterworths.
– 1997. 'A Historical Perspective on Contemporary Challenges in Workers' Compensation.' *Osgoode Hall Law Journal* 34(4).
Jackson, Melissa M. 1995. 'Employer Liability under the Third Party Provision of the Washington Industrial Insurance Act: The Dual Capacity and Dual

Persona Doctrines in Evans v. Thompson.' *Seattle University Law Review* 19: 187.

Kendall Sage, Heidi. 1984. 'The Intentional Tort Exception to the Exclusive Remedy of Workers' Compensation.' *Labor Law Journal* 45(2): 67–78.

Koester, C. Elizabeth. 1997. 'The Workplace Safety and Insurance Act, 1997 – Understanding Key Changes to Employer's Responsibilities.' *Infonex*, December: 1.

Law, David K. 1998. 'Issues in Workers' Compensation versus Tort.' Report to the Royal Commission on Workers' Compensation in British Columbia. Vancouver.

Meredith, Sir William Ralph. 1913. *Final Report on Laws Relating to the Liability of Employers to Make Compensation to Their Employees for Injuries Received in the Course of Their Employment Which Are in Force in Other Countries.* Toronto: Queen's Printer.

Ross, Melissa. 1997. 'Ripples in Treacherous Waters.' *Wake Forest Law Review* 31(2): 513.

Thomason, Terry, Timothy P. Schmidle, and John F. Burton, Jr. Forthcoming. *Workers' Competition: An Analysis of Employers' Costs and Safegy Incentives under Alternative Insurance Arrangements.* Kalamazoo, Mich.: W.E. Upjohn Institute for Employment Research.